That Was the Wild East

Social History, Popular Culture, and Politics in Germany
Geoff Eley, Series Editor

That Was the Wild East: Film Culture, Unification and the "New" Germany,
Leonie Naughton

Languages of Labor and Gender: Female Factory Work in Germany,
1850–1914, Kathleen Canning

Anna Seghers: The Mythic Dimension, Helen Fehervary

Staging Philanthropy: Patriotic Women and the National Imagination in
Dynastic Germany, 1813–1916, Jean H. Quataert

Truth to Tell: German Women's Autobiographies and Turn-of-the-Century
Culture, Katharina Gerstenberger

The "Goldhagen Effect": History, Memory, Nazism—Facing the German
Past, Geoff Eley, editor

Shifting Memories: The Nazi Past in the New Germany, Klaus Neumann

Saxony in German History: Culture, Society, and Politics, 1830–1933,
James Retallack, editor

Little Tools of Knowledge: Historical Essays on Academic and Bureaucratic
Practices, Peter Becker and William Clark, editors

Public Spheres, Public Mores, and Democracy: Hamburg and Stockholm,
1870–1914, Madeleine Hurd

Making Security Social: Disability, Insurance, and the Birth of the Social
Entitlement State in Germany, Greg Eghigian

The German Problem Transformed: Institutions, Politics, and Foreign
Policy, 1945–1995, Thomas Banchoff

Building the East German Myth: Historical Mythology and Youth
Propaganda in the German Democratic Republic, 1945–1989,
Alan L. Nothnagle

Mobility and Modernity: Migration in Germany, 1820–1989,
Steve Hochstadt

Triumph of the Fatherland: German Unification and the Marginalization
of Women, Brigitte Young

Framed Visions: Popular Culture, Americanization, and the Contemporary
German and Austrian Imagination, Gerd Gemünden
The Imperialist Imagination: German Colonialism and Its Legacy,
Sara Friedrichsmeyer, Sara Lennox, and Susanne Zantop, editors

Contested City: Municipal Politics and the Rise of Nazism in Altona,
1917–1937, Anthony McElligott

(continued on last page)

That Was the Wild East

Film Culture, Unification, and
the "New" Germany

Leonie Naughton

Ann Arbor

The University of Michigan Press

Copyright © by the University of Michigan 2002
All rights reserved
Published in the United States of America by
The University of Michigan Press
Manufactured in the United States of America
⊗ Printed on acid-free paper

2005   2004   2003   2002   4   3   2   1

No part of this publication may be reproduced,
stored in a retrieval system, or transmitted in any form
or by any means, electronic, mechanical, or otherwise,
without the written permission of the publisher.

A CIP catalog record for this book is available from the British Library.

Library of Congress Cataloging-in-Publication Data

Naughton, Leonie.
    That was the wild East : film culture, unification,
and the "new" Germany / Leonie Naughton.
        p.   cm. — (Social history, popular culture, and politics in
Germany)
    Includes bibliographical references and index.
    ISBN 0-472-08888-2 (pbk. : alk. paper)
    1. Motion pictures—Germany (East)—History.   2. Motion picture
industry—Germany (East)—History.   I. Title.   II. Series.

PN1993.5.G3 N28   2002
791.43'0943'1—dc21   2001003726

In loving memory of my mother,
May Naughton

Contents

Preface   ix

Acknowledgments   xix

Part One

Introduction   3

Chapter 1. Barriers between East and West   12

Chapter 2. Film Production at DEFA Studios   23

Chapter 3. *DEFA wird abgewickelt* / Dealing with DEFA   45

Chapter 4. *DEFA—Das Ende für Alle* / The End for Everyone   60

Chapter 5. *Ost Fernsehen* / East Television   78

Part Two

Chapter 6. Unification Films   93

Chapter 7. Heimat Tradition and Revival   125

Chapter 8. Unification Comedies—*Rising to the Bait*
and *No More Mr. Nice Guy*   139

Chapter 9. The "Trabi Comedies," Part 1   165

Chapter 10. The "Trabi Comedies," Part 2   183

Chapter 11. Directions in East German Filmmaking
after DEFA   206

Conclusion: Unification *Siegergeschichten*   235

Bibliography   245

Index   263

Preface

In itself, absurdity is hardly a newcomer on the German political scene. For the better part of 30 years, unification has been an article not of faith but of cant. Nobody took it seriously, nobody believed in it, and in the West at least, there was hardly anyone who really wanted it.
—H. M. Enzensberger

After the Wall

Since its dismantling, the Berlin Wall has "turned into little more than a quaint historical footnote" (Philipsen 345). In the early 1990s when Berliners walked past the Reichstag and through the Brandenburg Gate, they occasionally tested their failing memories of the route "their" Wall once took. By the late 1990s, the scale and extent of real estate development around these landmarks and Potsdammer Platz all but obliterated signs that the city was ever severed. The monstrous construction of the Wall, which in eastern terms served as an "antifascist protection barrier," may have vanished, but not so the antagonism between many of the inhabitants of the "new" and established states of the Federal Republic: "as politics returned to 'normal,' most internalized prejudices and condescending attitudes resurfaced in an old form" (Philipsen 348). By the end of the decade, animosity between East and West Germans saw the emergence of a spate of derisive literature and publications dedicated to the verbal sport of *Ossi* (East German) bashing (Broder 158).

Now that the jubilation of the autumn of 1989 has well and truly subsided, ambivalence is one of German unification's unmistakable and distinguishing features. Public trepidation about unification intensified and diversified in the early 1990s: it emerged in various forms, which extended from the banal to the officially authorized. "Snap it up before someone snatches it away from you" was the defensive promotional slogan blazoned across a major chain of German department stores toward the end of 1992; evidently anxiety over the infusion of refugees and population shifts accompanying the disintegrating of eastern borders found its prosaic expression in advertising. Perhaps more insidiously, trepidation over unification extended to the coinage of hostile new words like *verosten,*[1] a pejorative term that refers to the "easternization" of West Germany and carries with it connotations of rotting and rusting. Soon after West Germans greeted their "poor brothers and sisters" from the east with open arms, those joyous days seemed like a mawkish, if not hallucinatory, episode in a family melodrama. Animosity between *Wessis* (West Germans) and *Ossis* was thinly veiled, and after unification it manifested itself in graffiti messages and T-shirts bearing the slogan "We want our Wall back and three metres higher." By the end of the 1990s 20 percent of West Germans and 14 percent of East Germans maintained this opinion (Broder 158).

Few in the east were in a position to share former chancellor Helmut Kohl's early vision of "blossoming landscapes" in unified Germany. He was quick to adopt the phrase Chancellor Willy Brandt used decades earlier to convey his feelings about German unification: "what belongs together grows together." In the euphoria that marked events late in 1989, many may have shared this belief. However admirable and optimistic this conviction may have been, it hardly counteracted widespread criticism of the escalating and seemingly never-ending costs of unification.

Throughout the 1990s, disquiet over unification surfaced in official and institutional discourses of the state, and it did so regularly. Shortly after the dissolution of the German Democratic Republic (GDR), medical metaphors replaced Kohl's horticultural allusions. The federal government's metaphors became more ambiguous: Germany was imaged as an ailing nation needing medical attention in the early 1990s when the government sought to promote the Solidarity Pact (*Der Solidarpakt*)—a tax initiative committed to the development and reconstruction of the eastern states. (The pledge was to support the eastern states financially by investing more heavily in them and buying goods there. It was estimated that the Solidarity Pact would involve the transfer of 57 billion DM to the new federal states by 1995.) The Solidarity Pact's remarkable slogan, "First a sour apple then a vitamin charge. . . . even if the Solidarity Pact tastes sour at first, it is exactly what our country needs," presents unification as something distasteful and disagreeable but necessary; as such it would have been unthinkable in Germany's first year of union. Perhaps even more

---

1. All translations from the German are my own.

unfortunate was the Solidarity Pact's use of the slogan "We are all in the same boat" (sinking?).

Concern over the well-being of unified Germany is undoubtedly profound: in 1993 only one out of three West Germans considered that unification had succeeded. By comparison, 58 percent of East Germans believed unification had been successful, and around the same percentage hoped that their financial situation improved (*Journal* 3). The integration of East and West Germans has faltered; lack of assimilation is perhaps most pronounced in Berlin, where, despite an acute accommodation shortage, in the early 1990s only 10 percent of easterners and 7 percent of westerners were willing to shift to the other half of the city. The situation among the city's youth was no more encouraging during this period: contact between teenagers from the east and west has remained consistently low since 1990, with only 10 percent regularly mixing together (Hartung 3). Doubt about life in unified Germany was further exacerbated by the prospect of European unification and drastic upheavals in neighboring eastern European states.

In 1989 and 1990, few anticipated that the path to unification would be as tortuous as it has proved to be, that its costs would be so excessive, that its casualties would be so numerous, and that grievances about unification would be endemic. In the first half of the 1990s, when every second deutsche mark of public money was being invested in the eastern states (where a quarter of Germany's population lives), suspicions were raised about the effectiveness of unification.

The exhilaration over unification was fleeting for the majority of Germans. In the media, sentimental television news reports about the first German-German heart transplant soon gave way to accounts of East Germans threatening employment prospects by undercutting minimum wage agreements set in the west. Disenchantment with unification grew—in the east because the adjustment it required was "more painful than expected," and in the west because it was not as painless as promised (Stares 2–3). Undoubtedly the extent of social and economic turbulence Germans faced as the eastern states were incorporated into the Federal Republic was almost as unexpected as the collapse of the GDR. A *Spiegel*/ZDF opinion poll conducted in early December 1989 revealed that 71 percent of East Germans "declared themselves in favour of sovereignty for the GDR, while only 27 percent declared themselves for reunification" (Brockmann 15). Even in the year of Currency Union (1990), unified Germany began to look like a bad address to have. No one, except the burgeoning neo-Nazi and radical right organizations, welcomed the side effects associated with unification—the reports and everyday reminders of mass unemployment,

the barrage of shameful Stasi (*Staatsicherheitsamt*/State Security) exposés
that further compromised socialism in the GDR, the deluge of reports dis-
closing the extent of corruption and brutality under the socialist dictatorship, the increase in political violence, the inflated crime rate, and the
intensification of xenophobia and racism.

In the early 1990s, media overexposure of events surrounding
unification was extreme enough to result in a profound and widespread
public aversion to references to this immediate chapter of German history.
Fear about reduced living standards in West Germany and resentment
over tax increases to offset the costs of unification escalated. Consequently, vast sections of the population in the "old" federal states were
loath to recall the former GDR and the events that contributed to its collapse. Acutely aware of the repercussions and objectives of unification and
the national imperative to rebuild the east, few wanted to hear any longer
of the millions of East Germans who categorize themselves as the losers of
unification. Disparities in living standards undoubtedly exacerbate antagonisms between east and west. Even by the mid-1990s, the wealth gap
between east and west remained dramatic: the "average household income
in the East is still only between 60–70 percent of western German levels"
and although West Germans constitute 71 percent of the total population,
they own 93 percent of the entire country's privately held assets (Welsh,
Pickel, and Rosenberg 117).

On the other hand, western apathy over disparities in wages and living conditions *dort drüben* (over there) was perhaps fostered by the emphasis the federal government repeatedly placed upon the sacrifices each individual would have to make for unification to be effective. In an official
statement, the former minister of finance, Theo Waigel, provided precisely
this emphasis when he stipulated:

> No one can evade the necessity to save . . . so that Germany can con-
> tinue to grow together, for the solidarity of people from Aachen to
> Frankfurt an der Oder. . . . Whoever needs help can depend upon the
> well-connected, solid net of social welfare. But everybody has to
> make sacrifices for it to be adequate for everyone. (*Journal* 8)

The upheavals faced by those in the east throughout the 1990s were
monumental: integration into the social order of the Federal Republic was
arduous. For the inhabitants of East Germany, "life planning seems to
have come adrift. Old orientations no longer exist and new ones have not
yet stabilized. Psychologists talk of 'critical life situations' which affect the
entire population of the new *Länder*" (*Chapters*).

For the great majority of East Germans, the security of knowing what to expect, of knowing how to behave, and oftentimes of just knowing how to get by, had simply vanished. . . . Simply stated, under the wreckage of the old regime lay most of the certainties of life that people had long taken for granted. (Philipsen 331–32)

In the haste of unification, ideals were abandoned and values that people had held for a lifetime were discredited, often at an alarming rate.

Speech and writing changed almost overnight. Whole areas of political jargon have been abandoned, while others, long forgotten, are suddenly being rediscovered and resettled. You hardly ever hear the word "Communist" any more, except in connection with the word "catastrophe." The concept "socialism" is only used with the hasty adjectival prefix "democratic," or else not at all. Mystifying variants include "socialist socialism" or "socialist Free enterprise." And what happened, by the way, to that previously common notion, the "anti-Communist"? That hoary insult seems on its way to becoming an honorific. (P. Schneider 67)

The wholesale discrediting of ideals left a massive vacuum in the old GDR, and a blanket of mistrust over political engagement enveloped a large part of its population. For many this led to embittered resignation. For some in the east, the collapse of the GDR entailed the dismissal and trivialization of decades filled with compromise and sacrifice. In her survey of East Germans in the "new" Germany, Catherine McArdle Kelleher observed:

Many see themselves as victims or those forced to sacrifice—first to the East German system because they were in the wrong place at the wrong time, then to a unification process and a free market that promised equity and prosperity but delivered neither. Unification has brought with it fewer jobs and higher prices, more expensive rents and fewer automatic social services, greater economic competition and fewer outlets for their goods. (32)

The Autumn Revolution

The history of unification emerged as the product of bewildering inversion. Idealism soon gave way to disenchantment during the first years of German unity. Socialist commitments were forsaken in a delirium of consumerism. Many of the spectacular incidents that precipitated the expulsion of the socialist government[2] from power riddled the history of unification with paradox and contradiction. Late in 1989 contradictions surrounding the sociopolitical upheavals in the GDR and the trajectory of unification were compounded: as Monika Maron has so perceptively reckoned, "a concept like revolution evidently seduces one into glorifying events and goals" ("Writers" 40). The revolutionary zeal that then drove East Germans to stage the largest demonstration in German history dissipated even more quickly than the dictatorship they opposed. Even though these people managed to overcome the "silent acquiescence that had characterised their lives for two generations" (Philipsen 339), the majority did so only briefly.

The strident demands for revision to socialism, which reverberated throughout the country in the last months of 1989, now appear more incongruous than ever. Then, a major objective seemed to be to salvage something of the decrepit GDR and the ideals upon which socialism rested: an impetus to transform the oppressive one-party dictatorship into a more humane and democratic state seemed to galvanize the newly emergent political opposition. Deliberation over "what kind of society they wanted to build" (Philipsen 346) was given precedence over unification, which was not an immediate concern. What was apparently at stake for those seeking reform in the east, as much as for sympathizers in the west, were the exalted ideals of the Left. Karl Heinz Bohrer maintained that to "combine the GDR with the Federal Republic would . . . mean to lose for all time a leftist utopian point of view" (73). Despite the vertiginous momentum of unification, oppositional political groups such as the New Forum and Democracy Now had other aspirations: members of each organization made reference to the roles they would play in "the reconstruction of . . . [their] society" (James and Stone 118). These were activists who shared "a lifelong dream, one for which generations of people had risked, and sometimes lost, their lives: the dream of an egalitarian society without oppression and without poverty (the idea of 'socialism')" (Philipsen 344).

Ultimately, such ideals had minimal impact upon the future of the GDR, nor did the proponents of such values play a significant role in shaping relations between the two Germanies. For political activists who were devoted to reforming the GDR according to socialist principles, unification brought the betrayal of their ideals. Friedrich Christian Delius points out that the "embarrassing thing for . . . intellectuals is that the economy and

---

2. To English speakers in the west, the GDR was regularly referred to as a communist regime. I use the label socialist because this is how the GDR government referred to itself, as the Sozialistiche Einheitspartei or the SED.

not ideas, dictate the future (even the German one)" (74). Much to the chagrin of many left-wing intellectuals in the east and west, it was in an unashamed frenzy that "The People" assumed their new role as consumers. Many observers were perplexed by their neighbors' transformation from "good revolutionary Leipzigers of the fall" to "bad commodity fetishists . . . of the spring" (Huyssen 113). As Günter de Bruyn observed, "in the forty years of poverty and silence people in the GDR learned a longing for wealth and conformity far better than they learned anticapitalism" (65). However idealistic the citizens of the GDR may have been when they spilled over the borders to the consumer paradise of the Federal Republic, it was pragmatism that eventually flourished. In a sense, these people did what they knew best when they encountered capitalism firsthand for the first time. As they were used to queuing for goods in short supply, they practiced "the lesson everyone learns under socialism: Buy it now if you can—tomorrow the shop windows will be empty" (P. Schneider ix).

Even before the demise of the GDR, utopian sentiments were being subordinated to more prosaic concerns, and this trend became more pronounced as the momentum of unification accelerated. As the Berlin Wall crumbled, the cleft between the broader population and newly established political groups from the Left was already widening: "unity in purpose within the East German opposition—and arguably within the East German population at large—disappeared the moment the common enemy, the one-party state was gone" (Philipsen 338). Reemergent parties, especially the CDU (Christian Democrats), bid extravagantly for the wavering allegiances of citizens in the eastern states. By early spring 1990 oppositional political parties were marginalized and rendered ineffectual, having failed to maintain the popular support they had gained during the Autumn Revolution of the year before. Even though 54 percent of East Germans surveyed in an opinion poll published on 6 February 1990 favored the newly formed Sozialdemokratische Partei (the SDP—the eastern variant of the Sozialdemokratische Partei Deutschlands), support dwindled for the party in the month that followed (*Fischer Chronik* 926). Neither they nor other politicians anticipated that the Christian Democrats would draw so much support from citizens of the GDR when they voted in the country's first free democratic election on 18 March 1990: the CDU won 48.12 percent of votes in its landslide victory over all other established and emergent parties. Consequently "revolutionaries in Leipzig, Dresden and Berlin . . . [were] swallowed up by the narrative whisper of the past tense" (Grass 67). The opposition's otherwise perplexing loss of favor has been succinctly explained as follows:

> The role of oppositional groups whose goal was a democratic socialism is overestimated, not in their moral power and organisational skills,

but rather in their representativeness, while the power emanating from the masses who were simply fleeing and demonstrating for the profane goal of a better life is underestimated. (Maron, "Writers" 40)

Dismantling the GDR

The "thoughtless haste" of unification will not help "what belongs together grow together." Instead, it will increase the distance that has been preserved for forty years: spoiled by wealth and punished by unemployment, the Germans here and the Germans there will be strangers to each other as never before. (Grass 71)

In matters of taste and culture the claim that we lived in a proletarian dictatorship was true. Suddenly that's all over, and it's a hard thing to bear. (Maron, "Zonophobia" 120)

In the east it was a largely bewildered population that hurtled down the tracks to unification, the velocity and direction being determined by the Federal Republic's Christian Democrats. Although apprehensive, those remaining in what was left of the GDR were not alone in miscalculating the severe socioeconomic consequences of unification. Unification meant that East Germans were obliged to familiarize themselves with a new social order, with the ruthlessness of a market economy and extraneous political structures. The newly federalized states were plagued by a massive economic crisis that extended beyond the early 1990s.

In terms of productivity and industry, the GDR may have been one of the most advanced countries in the eastern bloc, yet by West German standards, East Germany was a picture of indolence and decrepitude. This image is one that was magnified once the full extent of the economic ruin of the GDR was disclosed. Even though the GDR's levels of productivity were meager by western standards, after reunification those levels sank sensationally. By 1993, "free-market" competition had forced the shutdown of 70 percent of the ex-GDR's production capacity (Schares and Miller 22).

With the exception of its outstanding performance in environmental pollution (which was more than three times higher than in the Federal Republic), the Democratic Republic was a haven for mediocrity, inefficiency, and complacency (at least by Western standards). This was especially evident within the realm of industry, which was antiquated and commonly equipped with machinery that predated World War II. The GDR's "obsolete products had no chance on the world market" (*Journal*

4), and its industry could no longer rely on previously established trade relations with eastern bloc countries, themselves witnessing the deterioration of communism. GDR industry was doomed and was in no position to fulfill Western criteria of productivity and profit. After unification East Germany's failing productivity hit rock bottom: it was remarked toward the end of 1993 that the "current economic output of all five newly federated eastern states *combined* is equal to that of the Saarland" (P. Schneider 182) (Saarland is a tiny West German state with a population of 1.1 million people). The GDR was a country that had not seen the advent of the postindustrial age. West Germans commonly remarked about visiting the GDR before its reconstruction that the experience was like "turning back the clock."

For many East Germans, unification was a traumatic event that brought destitution and disenchantment. Economic rationalization, a procedure otherwise known as *Abwicklung* (winding up/winding down, wrapping-up or dealing with), resulted in the takeover or closure of the bulk of industry in the eastern states. The suspicion spread that "the Coke and Pepsi paradise of consumer capitalism" had gone a little flat (Rigby 25). Illusory expectations GDR citizens may have had of unification were short-lived. Resentment brewed as Germans in the eastern states feared they had been demoted to second-class citizens under unification. In short, "both sides felt vaguely cheated" (Enzensberger 85). West Germans worried

> about the cost of unity, about jobs, housing problems and interest rates. In the opinion polls, more than two-thirds complained about the excessive haste of unification.
>
> And such pedestrian sentiments were fully reciprocated by a growing part of opinion in East Germany. Citizens there . . . began to panic about the pitfalls of capitalism. They also resented the idea that the fruits of 40 years' labor had proved to be rotten. (Enzensberger 84)

Once the western annexation of the German Democratic Republic was complete, many left in the east may have felt "that rather than *coming home* to a shared Germany, they have been colonized yet again by a foreign power" (Rigby 26). As was acknowledged in a 1993 document released by the federal government's press and publicity service:

> The marks from forty years under a different system go deeper than many thought. Whoever travels through the new federal states at the moment senses that the psychological problems brought by the tran-

sition from socialism to the market economy still have not been surmounted. People find it difficult to cope with the radical existential
change. (Merkel 23)

Indeed, differences between the inhabitants of the two Germanies often
appear more pronounced than any similarities they may share. Even three
years after unification, for instance, around three-quarters of East Germans still considered that there were communication problems between
East and West Germans, and two-thirds were still conscious of having
lived under a different system (Hilmer and Müller-Hilmer, "Es wächst"
21). For several weeks toward the end of 1999 the *Tagesspiegel,* a popular
Berlin newspaper with a predominantly west Berlin readership, ran a series
of articles by East and West German authors addressing the theme "Why
we don't get on together" (Broder 158).

West Germans often criticize those from the ex-GDR for their supposed lack of initiative and regularly voice their doubts about the industriousness of their eastern neighbors. At the end of 1993, only one in five
West Germans expressed faith in East German diligence. By contrast 60
percent of East Germans believed in the diligence of their people (*Journal*
3). "[West] Germans argue that their new compatriots . . . cling to an entitlement mentality developed under 40 years of communism. In short, the
gaps between East and West Germany remain stubbornly intact" (Schares
and Miller 23).

Acknowledgments

Christoph Müller has been my gracious host, lively guide, and source of much merriment on numerous trips to Berlin.

Thanks to Eric Rentschler, Ralf Schenk, Karola Grammann, Jean-paul Goergen, the DEFA-Stiftung, and Hiltrud Schultz for the interest they have shown in my research and the support they have provided.

Staff at Progress Film Verleih GmbH, Berlin (in particular Frau Anita Wittkowsky) and Ice Storm International, Northampton, Massachusetts, have always been generous with their time, resources, and assistance. Katrin Schlösser at Ö Filmproduction, Unidoc, Expicturis, Peter Welz, and Jörg Foth kindly provided me with access to films. I am also grateful to Delphi Filmverleih, Berlin, and to Progress Film Verleih GmbH for the film stills they have provided. Further stills are reproduced, with permission, from *Apropros: Film 2000. Das Jahrbuch der DEFA-Stiftung.* Ed. Ralf Schenk/Erika Richter. Berlin: DEFA-Stiftung/Das Neue Berlin, 2000.

The Faculty of Arts, Monash University, Clayton, Australia, and the Goethe Institut in Berlin and Melbourne provided travel grants and awards to facilitate this research. Monique Phillips at the Goethe Institut, Melbourne, offered invaluable assistance. The Bundesarchiv/Filmarchiv, Berlin, the Stiftung Deutsche Kinemathek, and the epd Archiv, Frankfurt, were generous with their resources.

Gratitude is extended to William B. Routt, Conrad Hamann, Chris Worth, and David Hanan for their generosity of spirit, encouragement, and scholarly integrity. Special thanks to Liz Suhay at the University of Michigan Press, Belinda Yuille at HarperCollins, Ute Korallus, to my family, and to other friends.

Part One

Part One

Introduction

In the fall of 1999 I returned to Germany to conduct further research for this book and to meet up with friends living in Berlin. Ten years earlier I had been a resident of the city and witness to the euphoria that surrounded the fall of the Wall. I had returned many times since then, fascinated by the changes to the city: rapid property development was making parts of the city virtually unrecognizable, sometimes in the course of a few months.

I timed my last trip to the new German capital to coincide with the anniversary of unification, curious to see how the event would be celebrated and reported in the media. I wanted to gauge how unification would be reassessed and revisited a decade after the implosion of the GDR. My Berlin friends were perplexed that I would see fit to travel so far to be in their country on a national holiday honoring unification. German Day was something they were completely uninterested in commemorating. They remarked that only a foreigner would consider the anniversary of unification to be worthy of celebrating. Without exception, my friends proceeded to pack their bags for the long weekend and booked flights out of the country, to get as far away as possible from Germany and any reminders of unification. Even ten years after the fall of the Wall, the cynicism they showed about unification had scarcely diminished. They seemed equally bemused that I persevered with my research into the depiction of unification on film, noting that few Germans would consider embarking on such a dubious project. That was clear from the dearth of German writing on the subject.

West German film scholars and representatives of the local film industry I encountered in the early 1990s also seemed perplexed that a non-German displayed an avid interest in the impact of unification on local film culture; most spoke of East German film with derision if not disdain. For many, the DEFA studio complex, center of filmmaking in the GDR, could not be dismantled fast enough, and little of its heritage was seen as worthy of maintaining. Once again, it was suggested to me that only "foreigners" or East Germans would be concerned about the fate of eastern film culture in unified Germany. This assertion led to an imaginary point of identification with Ossis on my part, one that is evident at numerous points throughout this book.

An "eastern" orientation is most clearly evidenced in part 1, where I survey filmmaking practices and traditions at DEFA Studios. I also attend to the dismantling of the GDR's film industry and the Kulturpolitik of unification there. Whereas part 1 examines the impact of unification on film production and consumption in the east, part 2 concentrates on the varied representations of unification on film. Part 1 serves to guide the reader through general issues of unification and post-Wende politics and culture. It provides a sociopolitical and industrial context in which to situate the films discussed in part 2. Once I establish the context of production, I then direct my attention to specific texts: "unification films."

A major objective of this book is to examine the ways in which filmmakers in the new and old states of the Federal Republic have utilized film to dramatize, romanticize, and critique the major sociopolitical and cultural event of German history in the 1990s. Detailed consideration is given to the ways in which unification films from both halves of Germany prescribe cultural identity and highlight cultural difference and specificity. I explore the divergent and convergent impressions of unification fostered in films from the east and the west and the comic and tragic anxieties those films attribute to life in the "new" Germany.

The title *That Was the Wild East* signals an eastern proclivity that deserves some clarification. Until recently, in western European and English-speaking countries at least, the history of postwar German cinema has been overwhelmingly West German. Apart from Barton Byg's substantial essay "Generational Conflict and Historical Continuity in GDR Film" and Sigrun Leonhard's article "Testing the Borders: East German Film between Individualism and Social Commitment," very little on GDR film was published in English film monographs throughout the 1980s. That cinema rarely warrants a mention in other German film histories that appeared in English throughout the 1980s. GDR film was rarely acknowledged or considered worthy of attention in the West, and with the exception of a handful of "Germanists" in the United States and England, it was almost completely disregarded. Even in 1992, when the hefty and otherwise extensive anthology *Geschichte des Deutschen Films* was published, only one article (30 pages out of almost 600) was devoted to more than forty years of GDR film history, and that article was authored by a West German. GDR film had a long history of critical neglect in the old federal states, a matter I will discuss in chapter 4.

An eastern emphasis is further warranted, especially considering that it is really only in the last decade that DEFA films have become accessible to international audiences.[1] By contrast, the majority of English readers who have an interest in German film were familiar with the "New German" cinema by the 1970s. This cinema enjoyed considerable international exposure and, as Eric Rentschler reasoned, had many "American friends." There are already excellent histories examining the efflorescence and ultimate decline of the New German cinema: I do not wish to re-cover ground that is more than adequately charted. Others have covered the institutional history and cultural politics of the New German cinema in greater depth and detail than I could realistically expect to do here.

Considering the massive impact that unification had on the East German public sphere, an eastern focus is necessary in this context: mass entertainment and mass communications have been fully restructured and completely overhauled according to the long-standing West German model. Previously, the GDR was a country in which less than one in ten people had a telephone, where television was for the overwhelming majority black and white,[2] where there were no public photocopying facilities or computer technology. Since unification, this technologically backward region has been flooded with new media technology and forms of popular entertainment (cable and satellite television, pornography, video games, video and laser technology, cinema multiplexes, advertising, and electronic communication systems). These changes to the eastern media landscape are addressed in greater detail in chapters 2 to 4. The impact of unification on the public sphere in the west and western media was nowhere near as dramatic or consequential.

The infrastructure of the west and its political, legal, educational, and welfare systems have not been subject to such significant revision since unification. Although West Germans voiced their concern over possible reductions to their living standards in the new Germany, unification has hardly altered their life-styles, expectations, esteem, or psychological well-being. Their working lives, leisure time, communication technologies, and media remain much as they were when Germany was still divided. Yet, for those in the east it is very much western life-style, media, living standards, and commodities that now provide the norms against which existence is measured.

---

1. Ice Storm International now distributes a wide range of subtitled DEFA films on video throughout North America, and the DEFA library at the University of Massachusetts is well established. DEFA films are also distributed throughout Germany by Progress Film Verleih Gmbh, located in Berlin.

2. Gerhard Wettig notes that the GDR leadership selected the SECAM system rather than PAL so that West German programs could only be received in color by those in the GDR who had managed to locate a special adapter. Even though color television was introduced to the GDR in 1969, Wettig notes that the adapter for receiving color was not readily available at least until the 1980s (186).

For easterners, just about every aspect of life in unified Germany has necessitated some kind of adjustment or reorientation. Popular entertainment in the ex-GDR has changed almost beyond the point of recognition. With a population of 16 million people, the five new eastern *Länder* presented a lucrative area for the expansion of western-based commercial broadcasting services, including satellite, cable, and pay television. Devoid of the long-standing restrictions imposed on television advertising in Germany's west, throughout 1990 the GDR was especially alluring for advertisers from the west. Exhibitors also recognized the east as a territory where cinema chains could flourish. The east was quickly identified as a new terrain for distributors and for imported film. Immediate profits were also to be made by dumping second-release films that had long completed their cinema runs in the west. Previously, all aspects of the filmmaking and television industries had been nationalized and subject to decades of assiduous scrutiny by the SED Party. When the GDR's infrastructure imploded, the privatization of eastern media was engineered by interest groups from West Germany. Those engaged in the GDR's film industry were not familiar with the principles of the market economy nor with practices such as promotion, presales, and copyright. Economic viability was a foreign concept to all those in the GDR's film industry. It was the caretaker company, Treuhand,[3] that took over the GDR's film industry and deliberated over its fate in negotiation with representatives from government agencies in the west. Almost without exception, potential investors had bases in the old federal states, if not heavy capital investment further west. Similarly, the fate of television broadcasting in the ex-GDR, as detailed in chapter 5, was largely determined by the existing public networks in the old Federal Republic. Ost Fernsehen (East Television), as it was known, ceased broadcasting on 31 December 1992.

It is primarily within the domain of film and in the related arena of television programming and broadcasting that the ex-GDR's media landscape faced its greatest upheavals. Because the GDR was isolated from the west and its media was centralized and nationalized, it had not faced many of those upheavals that had previously afflicted film and television in the Federal Republic. The changes that reshaped the media landscape in the west over three decades since the 1960s were all implemented in the ex-GDR in a three-year period (decentralization, privatization, American domination of distribution and exhibition, the introduction of commercial broadcasting, the expansion of the video market, satellite and cable services, etc.). In effect, the GDR's media underwent more drastic revisions

---

3. Although Treuhand was set up more than half a year before unification by the East German government, after the expulsion of the SED, decision-making powers rested in West German hands.

during the period of unification than it had done when the Soviets occupied the eastern Zone of Germany at the end of World War II: at least then, the occupying forces maintained the existing centralized and vertically integrated structure of the film industry.

Crucial elements of the cultural identity of the former GDR were eroded with the remodeling of its media landscape. In particular, the restructuring of East Germany's film and television industries facilitated the naturalization of western perspectives on unification and on the east, issues that I address in chapter 1. When the old states of the Federal Republic took over these branches of eastern media and sought to privatize DEFA studios (Deutsche Film Aktien Gesellschaft), these moves precipitated the subordination of GDR culture as well as the end of DEFA film history. East Germans are justified to comment that, since unification and the western infiltration of the media market, they have not been allowed to speak with a unified voice. The public spheres and discursive spaces through which filmmakers represented the east diminished once the west capitalized on "renovating" this media market.

As was the case with most other branches of GDR industry, within the domain of culture and communications whatever was affiliated with the old regime of the GDR was disparaged, overhauled, or destroyed when the country faced unification. With varying degrees of severity, branches of GDR media were subject to all three responses when the eastern states were absorbed into the Federal Republic. The phenomenon of devaluing sociocultural aspects of life in the ex-GDR after unification forms the basis of chapter 1.

Probably the gravest upheaval in the eastern media landscape was the privatization of DEFA's production facilities. DEFA, which was one of Europe's largest film production complexes, was taken out of East German hands on 3 October 1990 when the Treuhand trustees assumed responsibility for the complex. The last films to carry the DEFA label were completed in 1992. Film production was wound down by the time the complex was sold to a French/British consortium on 25 August 1992. Unification has also meant that there has been no stable point of reference for East German film culture; the GDR's television broadcasting system, upon which DEFA studios were dependent, was disbanded, virtually erasing thirty-eight years of broadcasting history. The East German film community was gradually fragmented when access to production facilities was relinquished once the DEFA complex was privatized.

Before I examine the cultural politics of unification and its impact on filmmaking, it is first necessary to consider what DEFA once was. Because all filmmaking was nationalized and state-controlled in the ex-GDR, it is also vital that DEFA studios' vexed relationship to the ruling party, the SED (Sozialistische Einheits Partei), be considered. "Film Production at

DEFA Studios" (chap. 2) details cinema's contribution to the cultural heritage of the GDR. That chapter examines the characteristics and idiosyncrasies of East German films, the cultural policies that governed film production under the old regime, and approaches to film distribution,
exhibition, and import in the GDR. Crises relating to political censorship
of DEFA film are also outlined in chapter 2. The tribulations that
unification brought to East German filmmakers are also raised in that
chapter. Others have charted the history of DEFA in greater depth and
detail than one single chapter on the studios could possibly allow;[4] I provide this general overview as a courtesy to English-speaking readers who
may not have been exposed to much DEFA film and for whom the history
of postwar German cinema has, at least until recently, been almost exclusively West German.

The survey of film production in the GDR (chap. 2) is followed by an
examination of the western takeover of DEFA studios. In chapter 3,
"DEFA wird abgewickelt / Dealing with DEFA," I examine events leading
to the disbanding of DEFA. Chapter 4, *"DEFA—Das Ende für Alle /* The
End for Everyone," discusses the cultural implications of privatizing the
studios. Related issues concerning the impact of unification on the media
landscape of the newly federated states are considered there together with
the public and critical reception of the last DEFA films. Chapter 4 also
addresses industry-related issues surrounding the disbanding of East Television.

Whereas the disruptions unification brought to East Germany's film
industry form the focus of the first part of this study, part 2 focuses upon
a selection of films that were released in unified Germany during the
period 1990 through 1999. Chapter 6 attends to unification films. It looks
at the ways in which the DEFA story figures symbolically in a number of
films from the 1990s and the emergence of a specific unification genre, the
"Wall film." There and in the chapters that follow, I consider how the economic, industrial, and sociocultural consequences of unification, sketched
here and in the preface, are imaged in film. After some discussion of the
generic variety of films representing unification, in chapter 7 I identify
common sources of narrative conflict and resolution as well as the motifs
featured in this cycle, particularly in unification films funded and pro-

---

4. See the anthology *East German Cinema, 1946–1992,* ed. Sean Allan and John San-
ford (New York/Oxford: Berghahn, 1999), and the German publications *Das zweite Leben
der Filmstadt Babelsberg 1946–92,* ed. Ralf Schenk (Berlin: Film Museum Potsdam und Henschel Verlag, 1994) and *Babelsberg 1912 ein Film Studio 1992,* ed. Wolfgang Jacobsen (Berlin:
Stiftung Deutsche Kinemathek, 1992).

duced in the west. Chapters 9 and 10 also focus on western-backed productions made by filmmakers based in the west.

Ultimately, western perspectives of life in unified Germany prevail at the local box office. The close textual analyses of western-backed and -produced unification films discussed in chapters 8, 9, and 10 form part of the *Siegergeschichte* (victor's version of history) of German unification. What follows is based on the premise that "films can preserve memory and function as vehicles of History. They can also serve as a means of forgetting, a medium to stylize, distort or erase the past" (Rentschler, *Ministry of Illusion* 222). Western-produced and -funded unification films function as vehicles of history insofar as they present a romanticized view of East Germans' experiences of unification: easterners emerge as the beneficiaries of union with the west. They are presented with ample entrepreneurial opportunity and good fortune; they display a particular affinity with nature, gravitate toward preindustrial modes of production, and are often identified as "primitive" in that they embrace mysticism and champion residual forms of culture associated with the rural idyll. The ex-GDR is defined in narcissistic terms as the "before" to the Federal Republic's "after."

Eastern-backed and -produced films addressing unification (such as *Engelschen / Little Angel*, 1996, *Adamski*, 1993, *Abschied von Agnes / Farewell to Agnes*, 1993, *Bis zum Horizont und weiter / To the Horizon and Beyond*, 1999) rarely endorse these perspectives: they are more inclined to depict urban or suburban East Germans who fail to benefit from unification and are outcasts. Often they are mentally unstable, distraught, or forced to engage in criminal activity to survive in the new Germany. In eastern-backed unification films, Ossis are estranged from their local community and live isolated lives engaged in tedious forms of mass production or menial employment. Unification is associated with loss: of family, offspring, sanity, freedom, even lives. Some East Germans in these films spend their lives in exile. Even more remarkable, eastern unification films exclude West Germans, who are denied any significant narrative agency. These issues are addressed in detail in chapter 11, "Directions in East German Filmmaking after DEFA."

Chapters 9 and 10 concentrate on the most profitable and widely viewed unification films of the period, the "Trabi comedies." Close analyses of the textual operations of two of these distinctive unification comedies are presented. Apart from functioning as generic hybrids, these films are also viewed in relation to the specifically German tradition of Heimat (chap. 7). As a genre and concept, Heimat relates to origins, identity, cultural heritage, rural tradition, and customs. The concept of Heimat, much like Heimatfilme,

> celebrates the local, the mundane, the domestic; it refers to geograph-
> ical place of birth but also the peculiar landscape, dialect, customs,
> and traditions attached to that locality. As such, it has a strong emo-
> tional component, since it is invested with all of the sentimental con-
> tent of one's childhood. Encompassing both communal and personal
> identity, it denoted homeland, home, and hearth—with all of their
> myriad meanings and emotional associations. (Fehrenbach 150)

Particularly popular after the end of World War II and during the period
of reconstruction, the Heimatfilm has proven itself to be a resilient, even if
frequently maligned genre that "seemed to serve as social and psychic
balm" (Fehrenbach 151) in periods of uncertainty and upheaval. When
most favored by German audiences, Heimatfilme were as "powerful a
force in the popular imagination as the Western in America, the Samuri-
film in Japan, and the partisan epic in Yugoslavia" (Rentschler, *West German* 104).

The unification films I analyze that issue from the west share a concern for the recognition and preservation of Heimat. Almost invariably,
these films locate Heimat outside of the old borders of the Federal Republic. Long lost to those in the west, Heimat is rediscovered and reclaimed as
a type of haven in the east. Examining how western unification films draw
on and modify Heimat conventions means that I can view these early
1990s comedies as part of a broad generic legacy that is specifically German. With their antimodernist, utopian proclivities, their expressions of
longing for community harmony and togetherness, and their celebration
of rural charms and cultural heritage, a number of western-backed
unification films are seen as resurrecting and upholding the troubled heritage of Heimat. It seems fitting that various filmmakers and audiences
have gravitated toward one of Germany's oldest and most resilient of genres, granted the insecurities and apprehension that surrounded unification.
While national priorities and values were being hastily revised and many
Germans endeavored to adjust to another national identity, discovering
Heimat once again provided reassuring images of stability in a "sentimental sphere that offered 'respite from everyday social and political
conflicts'" (Confino, qtd. in Fehrenbach 150). Importantly, these films
evoked a part of local cultural heritage that predated the division of Germany. Occasionally the tradition of Heimat is satirized. Reclaiming the
east as Heimat emerges as a western vantage point, eschewed by filmmakers from the east who critically assess the consequences of unification.

Although eastern films from the early 1990s are less inclined to treat
unification as a comic matter, they nevertheless share at least one of the
unspoken convictions of the western unification films discussed in chapters

8, 9, and 10. No matter what their production histories or origins, the overwhelming majority of 1990s unification films refrain from positing enduring relations between inhabitants of the new and the old federal states. Ironically, even though these films address the consequences, challenges, and upheavals that unification has brought to the east, they tend to avoid any intimacies between East and West Germans. On the whole these films avoid any German-German relations, accepting that they simply do not exist. Love relations are insular in these films; East Germans have the option of coupling with other East Germans, or alternatively their dalliances are with foreigners.

In the following chapter I will consider issues that have contributed to the estrangement of East and West Germans before and after unification. I will turn to the fundamental disparities that distinguish East and West German perspectives on unification as well as the apprehension that has surrounded it. How these disparate views were presented in a series of television reports documenting and celebrating unification will also be discussed in chapter 1.

Barriers between East and West

Since their division, the Federal and Democratic Republics of Germany had presumably irreconcilable ideologies, disparate languages, histories, currencies, and cultures, and these differences were compounded over four decades. "Surveys show that many young West Germans perceived the GDR as considerably more foreign than Holland, Austria, Switzerland, or even Italy . . . the division of Germany . . . diluted identification with the GDR in favour of cultural empathy with other Western countries" (Markovits 214).

The estrangement between east and west predates the construction of the Wall: it was compounded and continues to be underscored by conflicting versions of shared historical events. When Germany was divided after the end of World War II, each nation-state formulated its own history and refuted its neighbor's version of the past. Conflict over history was especially pronounced in the two nations' disparate accounts of the history of Nazism and denazification (although it has never officially ceased in the FRG, denazification was "completed" on 26 February 1948 in the Soviet Zone of Occupation). Whereas GDR history glorified the German resistance to fascism, in the Federal Republic effectively organized opposition to Nazism was considered to be either nonexistent, a fiction, or an abysmal failure. For those in the west, the end of World War II brought defeat and surrender, but for those in what was to become the Soviet Zone, the end of the war brought liberation. Later, some in the GDR believed that the building of the Berlin Wall was justified as a defense against NATO threats. For their part, West Germans were more accustomed to viewing their eastern neighbors as prisoners, deprived of freedom of movement and expression.

For decades, the two Germanies subscribed to contesting and contradictory historical accounts of shared events: the history of fascism, Allied occupation after the war, the 1953 uprising in Berlin, the invasion of Czechoslovakia, the Vietnam War, and so on. One could also say that in the early 1990s east and west continued to adhere to divergent historical perspectives of past and recent events, and they did so despite reforms (legal, judicial, educational, constitutional, economic) that were instituted to ensure unity. Evidently, unification has not *resolved* the disparities that have characterized German conceptions of history. This disparity can be seen to extend to East and West German perspectives on unification. Some easterners see that unification has entailed a type of sociocultural subordination: "the (West German) 'other' continues to be experienced by many East Germans in a very real and immediate fashion as the boss at work, the superior in the office, the landlord at home, political leaders in Bonn and the new *Länder* capitals, and public opinion dominated by the West" (Welsh, Pickel, and Rosenberg 115).

Perspectives on Unification: Beneficiaries or Losers?

The most conspicuous and tangible advantages that unification brought to the eastern states involved a general improvement of the material conditions of existence (housing, electronics, motor vehicles, variety and supply of consumer goods) along with the overhauling and modernization of public facilities (the public transport system, roadwork, telecommunications, the health system, etc.). The introduction of a market economy to the ex-GDR also resulted in the import of western concepts like "lifestyle" and euphemisms for unemployment such as *Kurzarbeit Null* (short-term work—zero). The Federal Republic's "exports" extended beyond consumer durables. The Federal Republic brought with it not only its own divergent history of Germany when it "conquered" communism and the eastern states, but also its own perspective on contemporary events, most notably the former GDR's assimilation into the west.

By spring of 1990, the majority of East Germans realized that the introduction of the deutsche mark meant access to a greater variety of consumer goods they could not necessarily afford; suspicions that they had been "colonized" by a superior market force spread. Apprehension about unification and the western "victors" intensified as unemployment reached epidemic proportions in the east, and businesses and branches of industry were subject to wholesale closure. Even later in the decade many East and West Germans continued to view one another, and unification, with skepticism. And perhaps their suspicions were justified. Fears about the cost and efficacy of unification were endemic in Berlin and other Länder. In 1995, for instance, a poll conducted by the public opinion organization Emnid revealed that 43 percent of West Germans and 53 percent of East Germans believed that, since unification, things were worse than they expected. For many in the west the cost of unification is exorbitant and seemingly never-ending. East Germans, for their part, are disgruntled about their lives in the new Germany: unemployment is rampant in the eastern states, and an alarming 80 percent of the eastern population consider that they continue to be treated like second-class citizens (Dornberg). Even more disturbing, in terms of its GNP, East Germany is the most backward region per capita in the EU today (Dahn).

Hostility between Ossis and Wessis is barely masked in such a climate. By the middle of the decade, for instance, almost 70 percent of East Germans were of the opinion that the government was not doing enough for easterners (Dahn), a conviction that could only incite ridicule and disbelief in the west. In any case, many East Germans were dismayed by the experiences they have had as "poor brothers and sisters" to their western neighbors.

Inequities in living standards and the wealth gap between east and west (which is expected to take several more decades to diminish) continue to sour German-German relations. The majority of potentially lucrative eastern business and industry is long in western hands. Accordingly, it is understandable that East Germans fear they lack control over their collective future, especially when one acknowledges that the "proportion of east Germans in the elite of the country as a whole amounts, in the areas of economy and the military, to exactly 0 per cent, in the academic world to 7 per cent and in the area of justice to 3 per cent" (Dahn). Factors like these led many in the east to associate unification with loss, prompting the coinage of the popular psychological term *Verlust-Syndrom* (loss syndrome) to characterize a range of psychic ailments manifest in the east (Maaz, *Das gestürzte Volk* 34–44). The disintegration of communities and the invalidation of points of historical reference could be viewed as compounding this sense of loss among East Germans.

It may be the case that even those who were dissatisfied by the socialist regime and privately objected to its doctrine experienced unification in terms of loss and bewilderment, insofar as what they relinquished when they became citizens of the Federal Republic was a lifetime of "guaranteed social security, . . . welfare services, . . . shelter and safety" (Maaz, *Das gestürzte Volk* 37). Media analyst Peter Hoff explains that whether these people loved the country in which they lived or not, whatever benefits unification brought them, they still faced the loss of their familiar Heimat: "Even if these very people refused . . . to develop a 'national feeling' for their state . . . it was still the place where they were at home" ("Armenbegräbnis" 117).

The equation of unification with loss was scarcely shared by those entrenched in the old states of the Federal Republic. Such a perspective has not really been acknowledged in officially instituted discourses or

western-based chronicles on unification. Given the long-standing emphasis that western perspectives on the GDR placed upon privation, it was
unlikely that West Germans would consider the assimilation of the bank-
rupt eastern states to involve any form of meaningful sacrifice or loss on
the part of their eastern neighbors. For tens of millions in the old Federal
Republic, unification meant that a debilitated and indefensible regime had
been deposed by a population that sought assimilation into a land of
affluence, abundance, and opportunity. From a West German perspective,
unification could hardly be viewed in terms of the *misfortune* of those in
the former GDR: on the one hand because the east was *already* established
as the site of sacrifice and privation; on the other because unification
necessitated such a massive transfer of funds, merchandise, and expertise
from the west to the east—$600 billion (990 million DM) had been trans-
ferred to the east in various forms by 1995 (Welsh, Pickel, and Rosenberg
118–19). The unification account balance was still alarming later in the
decade. As was remarked in 1999, "The annual trade deficit in recent years
amounted to 220 billion marks annually. This gigantic sum means that in
the new states *every single day* 600 million marks are required that are not
covered by the proceeds of the local economy" (Dahn, emphasis added).
This "one-sided flow of resources, with no end in sight, continues to reinforce the impression of a zero-sum game between West and East, and from
the viewpoint of the West, is probably the single most important factor
that structures political conflicts along East-West lines" (Welsh, Pickel,
and Rosenberg 118).

In this sense, from a western viewpoint, those in the east were more
likely to be viewed as material beneficiaries than as psychological casualties of unification. This impression must have been strengthened when it
was reported that by the middle of 1991, "adding up the number of those
covered by short-term work, early retirement, training and job-creation
programs and unemployment benefits," more than 3 million people in the
east "drew their income from the federal labor office or the federal budget" (Kreille 74). By 1992, 3.6 million East German jobs out of 9.75 million
were lost. Of those still in the work force, almost one million were considered to be underemployed (Welsh, Pickel, and Rosenberg 115). Employment prospects for East Germans were still grim in 1994, with job losses in
industry and agriculture especially pronounced—employment in the agricultural sector dropped by almost 80 percent by that year (116). At the end
of the decade, real unemployment in the east stood at over 30 percent
(Dahn).

Considering the monumental expense of unification and the priority
and emphasis placed upon reconstructing the infrastructure in the eastern
states, it is perhaps understandable that those in the west disregarded the

negative aspects of eastern perspectives on unification. Peter Hoff notes that West German officials were not alert to the distinctions that differentiated their perspectives on unification from those in the east. He asserts that "all the claims the Chancellor and other conservative state functionaries" have made about unification have obscured "the different ways history was experienced in East and West Germany" ("Armenbegräbnis" 187). For those in the new federal states, life in unified Germany was affiliated with the unknown, with insecurity, and with a sense of inferiority, whereas it seems that for those in the west, unification was frequently associated with arriving at a destination and was accompanied by a sense of achievement and superiority. Media analysts Wilfred Korngiebel and Jürgen Link, as well as Hoff, note the emphasis the western media placed upon unification as a destination or as a point of arrival (Korngiebel and Link 68; Hoff, "Armenbegräbnis" 181). In his study of media perspectives and historical portraits of unification (presented in east and west television and videocassettes documenting the events of the "Year of German Unity," 1990), Hoff remarks:

> The "east-view," the point-of-view of eastern television journalists, is missing from the exalted view of their western colleagues. The perspective of the victors is denied those in the east. They seek grounds for their defeat. What for representatives of the "western" position provides reason for a sedate, panoramic-style magazine program, becomes a trip into the past for television people from the east. Whereas the "westerners" celebrate the realization of all of their political endeavors, the "easterners" begin a journey toward an unknown future. ("Armenbegräbnis" 181)

In other words, West German television programs presented unification as a celebration that marked the *arrival* of the eastern states in the new Germany, whereas East German television marked 1990 as a year of *departure* and a period of bidding farewell (Hoff, "Armenbegräbnis" 176). East German broadcasts depicted the "Year of Unification" as one in which East Germans ventured into unknown territories with alien customs.

Not only were there disparities in perspectives on unification in media reports, but also a disregard of eastern points of view. In eastern surveys of the events of 1990, "unification was problematized [rather than] . . . celebrated" (Hoff, "Armenbegräbnis" 176). Hoff notes that in contrast to those reports that came from the east, western observations of the events leading up to unification were neither critical nor especially analytical, and those reports and retrospectives obscured the contradictions and ambivalence expressed in eastern reportage:

The contradictions with which people in the five newly emergent federal states saw themselves confronted were not identified. The "mental wall" [*die Mauer in den Köpfen*] stands undisturbed. What was left out or was unnoticed in the [western] reports was the fact that the "new citizens of the Republic" were just as strange to the "old" ones as they were before, just as the "old" were strange to the "new." The representation of unification in the [western] media reports paralleled the behavior of many federal politicians, who more or less banished from their consciousness each and every contradiction [in] . . . the process of unification. These contradictions were suppressed until they could not be overlooked, having become the social and political reality of new Germany. ("Armenbegräbnis" 176)

A central factor contributing to the suppression of East German perspectives and points of view was the infiltration of West German collective symbols into the newly unified territories. Applying discourse theory, Korngiebel and Link appraise the popular imagery that circulated throughout Germany during the period that preceded and followed Monetary and Economic Union in 1990 (I will draw on their research in greater detail in chapters 9 and 10). The pair remark that, in the east, "the importation of money went hand in hand with the importation of symbols" (49). Consequently, the former GDR came to be understood as abnormal in relation to the Federal Republic: "the trend was to denormalize" what had been the GDR (51).

This process of denormalization entailed the redefinition of the ex-GDR in relation to the collective symbols the Federal Republic used to characterize itself. Korngiebel and Link observe that in its media, West Germany commonly symbolized itself as a house, an industrial vehicle, an athletic body, or balanced scales. Related imagery was also deployed to symbolize the ex-GDR after its collapse. Defined negatively in relation to the west, the ex-GDR was frequently represented by images of decay or chaos. The socialist state was symbolized medically, as a body in a state of collapse. Alternatively it was figured as a dilapidated house, an airplane crash, a crash landing, or a computer crashing (51). Like the perspectives the west provided on unification and the historical sensibility, priorities, and values it brought to the east, the collective symbols used to define the GDR after its collapse were foreign to the GDR. Evidently those in the east found those concepts difficult to grasp. Korngiebel and Link recall that even the GDR's *Ministerpräsident,* Lothar de Maizières, could not manage to "get straight" the use of these western collective symbols. They draw attention to his 1990 announcement: "Before the D-Mark comes, the social [welfare] net will have to be stretched out *over* the GDR" (37).

Clearly, German unification entailed more than the democratization of the ex-GDR. Western collective symbols and images have until now been granted predominance in the recording of one of Germany's most monumental chapters of history. On ARD (3 October 1990) a nationalistic mélange of images and sounds highlighted West German television's coverage of the official unification day celebrations. The West German report began with lap-dissolve images of the Federal Republic's flag together with the sound and image of the freedom bell (*Freiheitsglocke*) tolling, nighttime shots of the majestically illuminated Brandenburg Gate, culminating with the final rousing chorus of "Ode to Joy" from Beethoven's Ninth Symphony. These images and sounds, in particular the "Ode to Joy" (also highlighted at the start of the unification videocassette produced by West Berlin's public television station, SFB), have become synonymous with German unification—much more so than the sobering commentary that opened the East German report (by the GDR broadcasters Deutscher Fernsehfunk) on the "Year of German Unification": "On October the Third we are one people. The socialist experiment on German soil has finished." Not only have western images of unification overwhelmed eastern perspectives, the engineering of unification also resulted in the historic sensibility of the Democratic Republic being supplanted by that of the Federal Republic.

Devaluing GDR Cultural History: *Abschied von Gestern*

That the GDR vanished more quickly than anyone could have anticipated left many in the GDR in a type of limbo at the start of the 1990s: for some it seemed that the GDR and what it may have stood for was erased before they had a chance to come to terms with it and reassess it. Whatever the promise, or whatever East Germans anticipated in 1989, the ways in which the GDR past has been defensively warded off by some and marginalized and discredited by others form a vital part of the history of unification in Germany. East German values and ideals, together with the experiences and recollections of those who lived in the Democratic Republic, are part of a past that was by and large rejected by westerners in unified Germany, at least in the first half of the 1990s. When the borders between east and west were reopened in 1989, disparagement of most things eastern was widespread. Aspects of East German existence that for decades had been considered adequate, or even a source of national pride (housing, productivity levels, exports), were suddenly deemed substandard and became targets of ridicule. Life in the east came to be portrayed as second-rate in just about every way. The sense of shame generated by comparisons between east and west no doubt prompted many East Germans to further dissociate themselves from the GDR. Values and material relics from the old society became synonymous with inferiority, failure, or delusion when the borders within Germany were demolished. Just about everything affiliated with life in the "other" Germany, including its cuisine, its primary produce, and even the German shepherds bred in the east, was branded as inferior and potentially harmful (the dogs used as domestic pets, for example, were judged to be smaller, to have duller coats, and to be *bissiger*—more inclined to bite—than those bred in the west). Even aspects of the GDR's welfare system (legalized abortion, incentives for raising children such as lengthy periods of maternity leave, and the guaranteed provision of child care for working parents) were attacked as contributing to a fundamentally dysfunctional society. No matter what their value, a plethora of activities and aspects of GDR life, ranging from banal elements of schooling and family life to mass communications and culture, were denounced as contaminated by the ideology of a corrupt and nefarious dictatorship.

In the early 1990s at least, unification facilitated the erasure of whatever was associated with the GDR. All previously nationalized industries were privatized; monuments once erected to glorify the old regime were disassembled; generous welfare provisions that once protected the population of the GDR were decimated or eradicated; large parts of the population were dispersed; communism was "defeated," replaced by capitalism; in short, the infrastructure of the Federal Republic fully replaced that of the GDR.

In the latter half of the 1990s this tendency to desubstantiate the GDR's past underwent a novel inversion as a nostalgia for aspects of life under the old regime emerged in some eastern states. Books on design of quotidian goods in the GDR were published. A large second-hand warehouse selling every form of GDR memorabilia, from kitchen utensils to toys and records, prospered in Dresden. Entrepreneurs capitalized on the market for *Ostalgie* ([n]ostalgia for the east). The end of the decade also saw the emergence of a GDR revival in East German film. *Sonnenallee* (1999), a comedy about the escapades of a group of GDR teenagers, recaptures the idiosyncrasies and fads of eastern youth culture in the late 1970s. This film, together with another Ostalgie feature, *Helden wie wir* (*Heroes Like Us,* 1999), was given widespread promotion in the national press at the end of the decade. *Der Spiegel* included feature articles on these films and interviews with those associated with the productions. In the first six months of its release *Sonnenallee* became the biggest East German box-office hit of the decade. With more than 2 million viewers, by January 2000, it was the nineteenth top grossing film screened in Germany over a five-year period. Its budget of almost 8 million DM made it one of the most expensive and widely distributed eastern productions of the decade.[1]

The ex-GDR also found its graphic representation outside of film theaters: the socialist state was resurrected on the Internet. By the end of the decade, more than 300 East German websites were devoted to Ostalgie. Almost 10,000 visitors had accessed one GDR memorabilia webpage by mid-2000, with 3,000 visitors in a period of a little more than three months.[2] GDR nostalgia took varied manifestations on the web: Knobi's Ostalgie pages are devoted to supporting and promoting socialism; they include the constitution of the GDR, the GDR national anthem, and links providing information about Honecker, Trabis, businesses involved in Ostalgie-related trade, and private homepages celebrating the old GDR.[3] Other sites advertised forthcoming Ostalgie parties that revived distinctive features of life in the ex-GDR. Some included photographs of Ostalgie revelry. Adding to the social dimension of Ostalgie, various nightclubs and bars capitalized on a "GDR revival,"[4] with "old-time" sing-alongs. Erich Honecker look-alikes became a sought-after attraction at parties and various social events. In some nightclubs, staff dressed as party officials and border guards, while patrons were issued with replicas of GDR passports and the old GDR currency was revived for exchange and service. The novelty of nostalgia for the GDR did not, however, extend far into the west.

Throughout the 1990s there was little reason for West Germans to embrace elements of GDR history or uniquely eastern experiences as belonging to a unified Germany. Whereas the GDR distinguished itself from the west and legitimated the foundation of the socialist state in terms of resistance to fascism, in "the wake of unification, this foundation has been physically as well as ideologically obliterated." Consequently, a vital aspect of the "'historical memory' accepted by the population" of the former GDR has been nullified with the east's assimilation into the Federal Republic (Welsh, Pickel, and Rosenberg 127).

Whatever historical sensibility the Socialist Party doggedly strove to instill in the population of the GDR, that sensibility was discredited as "indoctrination" when Germany was unified. Many memories associated with life in the GDR were invalidated as mere delusions. For example, the GDR "revival" mentioned above caused a measure of alarm in the west: it

---

1. It opened with 107 copies. Over the New Year 247 prints were in circulation. <http://www.mediabiz.de/ciprod.afp?=cinebiz&Premium=N> (31 Jan. 2000).

2. <http:ddrnostalgie.de/> (31 Jan. 2000). Three thousand visitors accessed the site in a little over three months in 2000.

3. <http://home.t-online.de/home/ostalgie> (31 Jan. 2000).

4. The East Berlin *Ostalgie* bar, *Die Tagung,* opened in 1992. The bar has its own web page: <www.die-tagung.de> (31 Jan. 2000).

was feared that East Germans were romanticizing the past as preferable to the present, failing to recollect the oppressiveness, coercion, and brutality that were part of the old regime. When the CDU was still in power, the minister of finance, Theo Waigel, criticized East Germans for their selective memories. He provocatively suggested that one way to solve East German nostalgia for the past would be to make a video recording each year showing the improved living standards in the eastern states. Then the videos could be shown every five years to remind East Germans about their deprived pasts and to stop them from grumbling (qtd. in Zahlmann 73).

In the west a general disinterest in recovering GDR history prevailed throughout the 1990s, for this past was one that did not "belong" to the Federal Republic. With unification, many in the GDR "inherited" a history of which they had no direct experience and that they could not recognize as their own. In this sense "many East Germans feel that they are being offered assimilation into a western-defined 'German identity' rather than allowed an active role in creating a common founding mythology for the unified state" (Welsh, Pickel, and Rosenberg 133). Those in the new federal states did not necessarily acquiesce to "the political project of replacing the East German founding mythology with the West German variant" (127). For instance, in 1990 when attempts were made to rename streets in Berlin's east to rid the city of reminders of the old regime and its figureheads, many residents refused to cooperate with the changes, which were directed by western politicians. East Berliners objected when they realized that "part of their normal physical landscape and geographical orientation" was to be changed (131). They were offended by moves to rename streets that honored "members of the German and international labor movements, those who fought in the Spanish Civil War or the anti-fascist resistance, or others who were forced to emigrate, [were] persecuted, or murdered by the Nazi regime" (131). In short, East Germans resisted what they saw as an attempt by the political elite of the west to delegitimate eastern political history and heritage.[5]

Arguably, the act of historical recovery was obscured with unification when the gargantuan task of reconstructing and modernizing the east began. Reconstruction was given precedence over any widespread public *Auseinandersetzung* (analysis, evaluation, reassessment) of GDR history,

---

5. One of the most objectionable guidelines for evaluating existing street names involved the stipulation that "persons who fought after 1933 against the National Socialists in order to construct a communist dictatorship should not be honored" (de Soto, cited in Welsh, Pickel, and Rosenberg 130). Incidents like these, which took place in the months before unification was formalized, were telling indicators that the GDR was already situated as a subordinate culture whose distinctive features were misunderstood or ignored by the dominant culture of the old Federal Republic.

values, or ideals, at least throughout the first half of the 1990s. This process was actually taken up by filmmakers from the former GDR throughout the 1990s. Largely because of structural changes to the media landscape of the GDR, however, their critical engagement with and reassessment of the old regime had little resonance throughout the Federal Republic as a whole. Former GDR filmmakers' access to a viewing public changed dramatically with unification. Because of the problems they face in securing exhibition and distribution, low-budget East German films are difficult for local audiences to access. Relatively lavish West German comedies and Hollywood blockbusters have taken the place previously secured for GDR films.

However relevant or vital East German filmmakers' Auseinandersetzungen of the past may be, these impressions have little currency in the west or for western cinema audiences. The films, discussed in chapter 11, nevertheless provide traces of eastern "historical memory" and contend in the battle for cultural identity in unified Germany. Considering that "all [complex societies] periodically rewrite their dominant national mythology to reflect shifts of power, political expediency and taste [and] the past is a central battleground for the contestation of cultural identities" (Welsh, Pickel, and Rosenberg 123), in the context of unification, film functions as means of rewriting the past and redefining or consolidating cultural identity.

Of course film also performed a comparable function in the former GDR and was an important part of the socialist state's ideological arsenal. It was a medium through which the GDR could define itself, its objectives, imperatives, and ideals. It was also a medium through which the GDR could differentiate itself from the Federal Republic. In the next chapter I look at the cultural heritage of DEFA studios. For the remainder of part 1 of this book, I will concentrate on GDR film culture and the cultural politics of unification, moving to a consideration of the repercussions of the western takeover of the studios.

CHAPTER 2

Film Production at DEFA Studios

The end of GDR film history came after forty-six years of film production at the state-owned and -controlled DEFA studios. Landmarks of film history such as *Metropolis* (1926), *The Last Laugh* (1924), and *The Blue Angel* (1930) were made at the complex (when it went under the title of Ufa Studios). Hitchcock, Wilder, Lubitsch, Carné, and Garbo once worked at these studios.

From 1946 to 1989 more than 600 films for the cinema and 800 telefilms were produced at DEFA. Included among those productions were costume dramas and period films, biographies, industrial training films, children's films, fairy tales, animated films, love stories, workers' dramas, and antifascist films. The studios' films were shown at more than 450 international film festivals and in more than 60 countries. Even if the public did not always love these films, they were still a significant constituent of the cultural and political identity of the GDR. As Rolf Richter, one of the country's most respected film scholars, optimistically declared early in the 1980s:

> DEFA is something that belongs uniquely and eternally to the GDR; it is a treasure of cultural, political, and artistic experience that could never be stored in some kind of archive—it is alive in the heads and hearts of people. . . . [DEFA] films are influenced by the convictions and a sensibility of our country. Imagine: if DEFA films didn't exist, neither would . . . millions of artistic experiences. (qtd. in Freyermuth 11)

Some material in this chapter has been adapted from my article "Party Pooper: The Forbidden Films." *Film News* (September 1993): 11–12.

In accordance with communist cultural policy, in the GDR film was considered a medium through which audiences should be educated and enlightened. Party functionaries and members of the Central Committee placed great importance upon the medium, which was granted official status as one of the arts. The cultural prestige attributed to film was supposed to be in contradistinction to its function under capitalism, where it was assumed to have operated predominantly as popular entertainment made for profit and mass audiences. The socialist party, and those working at DEFA, accepted that film was a medium designed to edify. Although they were not always successful, they sought to produce films that struck a balance between pedagogy and entertainment. "Socialist cultural policy inhibited the production of films that *merely* [sought] . . . to entertain" (Byg, "Generational Conflict" 199, emphasis added). Filmmakers in the GDR had to embrace this objective and accept what was viewed as a political responsibility to contribute to the construction and advancement of a socialist society. Like members of GDR society generally, those who were employed to make films at DEFA sought compromise rather than conflict with the state.[1]

Considering the extent of state involvement in film production it is not surprising that "developments in GDR film art mostly ran parallel to the sociopolitical developments of the state" (Battenberg and Herdin 150). Filmmaking in the GDR was divided into four officially designated phases: the immediate postwar years (1945–49), identified as the "phase of radical antifascistic-democratic change"; then the "period of establishing foundations of socialism" (1950–61); the "period of comprehensive construction of socialism" (1961–70); and the last officially recognized phase, the "time of developing socialist society" (1971–) (Battenberg and Herdin 150).

Socialist realism was endorsed as the official aesthetic doctrine of the state and was often used as a "common standard against which . . . films [could be] criticized" (Feinstein 103). Even though socialist realism was an orthodox category, it was nevertheless an elastic concept that changed over four decades and could be "construed to varying effect" (Feinstein 79). In general terms it emphasized "exemplary characters . . . the inevitably positive course of socialism . . . and the political requirement of a single, positive view of socialist history" (Byg, "Two Approaches" 87). Frequently it resulted in didactic expressions of commitment to socialist ideals and attitudes. Throughout the 1960s and 1970s, for instance, many DEFA films promoted the objectives of the socialist state by placing

---

1. I am grateful to Erika Richter for drawing my attention to this point and for formulating it so succinctly.

emphasis upon the importance of industrial expansion, the development of new housing estates, and increased productivity. Many a narrative conflict was staged and resolved in factories or on construction sites:

> What united virtually all DEFA films set in the GDR was a complex set of filmic idioms—character types, dramatic locations, emplotment, etc.—used to define socialist reality. Inventing a character's biography or depicting such typical places of social interaction as the workplace or the classroom invariably involved making wider statements about the whole utopian project of socialism. (Feinstein 9–10)

Especially during the 1960s, the socialist realist directive saw DEFA propagate a cinema of redemption, which at times was blatantly pedagogic. The errant behavior and attitudes of film characters were reformed when they embraced socialism and party objectives. As Harry Blunk explains, "Regularly the schema that [DEFA] films followed consisted of four steps: a) aberrant behavior (mostly in the workplace) b) the appeal to (socialist) consciousness of those concerned c) insight/realization d) modification of behavior" (111). These films managed to fulfill their social responsibility by functioning partly as *Lebenshilfe* (guidance, life help), offering advice on coping with life's dilemmas and setbacks, especially for youth. The social concerns encompassed in DEFA films were relatively broad; the issues they addressed included courtship, parenthood, marital infidelity, housing, fatal illness, and relations in the workplace.

At least until the late 1970s, the GDR cinema's engagement with social problems was nevertheless of a paradoxical order. On the one hand, the socialist state "often attempted to solve problems without acknowledging that they exist[ed]" (Byg, "Generational Conflict" 202). On the other, problems tended to be acknowledged only when the state had already arrived at a solution for them. Throughout the 1950s and 1960s, it was rarely the case that films could address problems as personal, as exceptional conflicts of an individual for which there was no social remedy. Dramas of self-actualization, so common to Hollywood and the bourgeois European cinema, were spurned for many decades at DEFA, for, according to the state, subjective experience and individualism were products of capitalist ideology. "Ahistorical" perceptions of contemporary events were also discouraged in DEFA productions: expectations were that history had a single positive trajectory (Byg, "Two Approaches" 87) and that its outcome was shaped and determined by socialism.

The most celebrated of DEFA films are undoubtedly the studios' historical dramas, in particular the enduring subgenre of the antifascist film in which the fiction studios specialized. (The genre proliferated in various national cinemas throughout the eastern bloc.) Customarily these films glorified the resistance against fascism and presented Nazism as an evil, rectified by the Soviets when they "liberated" the defeated eastern zone of Germany. The durable subgenre, established at DEFA immediately after the end of World War II, lasted into the 1980s. Together with children's films and fairy tales, DEFA's antifascist films constituted an illustrious part of DEFA's tradition.[2]

Whatever the genre, any allusion to the grievances of GDR citizens had to be veiled in DEFA films, and especially in the aptly named *aufgepasste Gegenwartsspielfilme* (supervised fiction films dealing with the present). Indirect criticisms were, nevertheless, clearly discernible to local audiences, who were adept at deciphering metaphor and allegory and in interpreting insinuations of dialogue and nuances of demeanor. Problems "which were otherwise taboo, such as violence within the family, brutality, fraud as a result of shortages," together with social themes such as isolation and mistrust, were *intimated* through the medium of film (Hoff, "Continuity and Change" 21, emphasis added). The more abstruse those criticisms, the greater chance films had of avoiding the censorial attention of the Central Committee.

Ambivalence or pessimism about the present or the future was not generally tolerated in DEFA productions throughout the 1960s and into the 1970s. Erich Honecker made this clear in the 1965 Central Committee report:

> To those who . . . take pleasure in talking a lot about "absolute freedom" we would like to put the story straight: you are mistaken if you think that workers make sacrifices for the construction of the socialist order and that others need not be involved. You are mistaken if you think that the state pays and others have the right to preach negative, petit bourgeois skepticism as the sole religion. If we want to further increase productivity, and with it living standards (something in which all citizens of the GDR are interested) then we cannot disseminate nihilistic, hopeless, and morally disturbing philosophies in literature, film, [and] . . . theater.

Formal trends deemed debased and western were largely disregarded at DEFA, where greater emphasis was supposedly placed upon thematics, characterization, and styles of narration.

---

2. At least one such DEFA production, *Jakob der Lügner* (*Jacob the Liar,* 1975), attracted attention in Hollywood. In 1999 a Hollywood remake with Robin Williams in the lead role was released internationally.

The formal language [*Bildsprache*] of DEFA films was rather poor and the visual side of things was neglected, starting with the script. The ideology had to be correct, and one had to think about it beforehand, discuss and perhaps even laugh about what [the use of] striking images would lead to. There was discussion about formalism in the visual arts in the GDR; whatever our people couldn't understand immediately was western, decadent, and belonged to degenerate imperialism. One knew of the power of images, especially in film; the talk was [rather] of socialist topics and of German socialist film art. (Teschner 17–18)

To one of its most esteemed directors, Heiner Carow, DEFA was part of the GDR "idyll sheltered by power almost psychotically afraid of infection by the moral and psychic extremities of the west" (qtd. in Bohrer 75). Unlike the norm of commercial cinema in capitalist Germany, DEFA films were devoid of violence as spectacle, gratuitous sex, psychopaths, obscenity, brutal crime, sexually explicit scenes, and sensational action. The sexual objectification of women, a widespread practice in the media of capitalist countries, was not a salient feature of DEFA films, even if patriarchal attitudes flourished in that cinema.

Characteristics of DEFA Films

Even though socialist realism was favored by the state, it is not as if all feature production strictly adhered to that doctrine or aesthetic. "The doctrinaire concept of socialist realism . . . is an abstraction found more readily in the exhortations of Party functionaries than in cultural practice" (Byg, "Two Approaches" 87). Although the move was not especially welcomed by the state, a number of filmmakers gravitated more toward neorealism in their films and were clearly inspired by Italian proponents of the style. Such an aesthetic is evidenced in a series of "Berlin films" from the late 1950s that involved collaboration between Gerhard Klein and Wolfgang Kohlhaase (*Alarm im Zirkus* / *Alarm in the Circus,* 1954, *Berlin—Ecke Schönhauser* / *Berlin—Schönhauser Corner,* 1956, and *Eine Berliner Romanze* / *A Berlin Romance,* 1957). These filmmakers' commitment to "gritty, immediate production conditions" (Byg, "Two Approaches" 97) imbued their images of everyday life, on the street, in the workplace, amidst the family, with a documentary-style immediacy and veracity.

Neorealism's influence also extended into the 1960s, most notably in features that were either withheld from distribution or banned after the 11th Plenary of 1965 (*Berlin um die Ecke* / *Berlin around the Corner,* 1965/90, *Das Kanninchen bin Ich* / *I Am the Rabbit* 1965/90). Throughout the 1950s and 1960s, party officials were wary of this neorealist emphasis on the here and now, and what seemed to be unmediated images of life in the GDR. "A number of years would have to elapse before the state would be in a position fully to appreciate the political value of the type of 'authenticity'" that neorealism brought to some DEFA films. "East Germany 'in the raw' was still too tenuous a place, its 'everyday' too treacherous an ally" (Feinstein 117). In depicting random events in the everyday lives of unexceptional individuals, neorealist films failed to fulfill the Party's insistence upon exemplary socialist protagonists actively involved in historical developments.

Neorealism did not function exclusively as a counterbalance to the Party's commitment to socialist realism. Popular genres also flourished at the studios where a tradition of revue films, romantic comedies, historical adventures, and musicals was also established. Nevertheless, socialism still provided a stable backdrop to whatever degree of frivolity these films allowed. Work relations, industrial developments, and Party affiliations were details incorporated into if not highlighted in these films. For example, upsets in the workplace and state building initiatives are a feature of the late 1950s love story *Wo der Zug nicht lange hält* (*Where the Train Halts Briefly,* 1959). Apart from its romantic interest, the film foregrounds the concerns of a group of crane operators and the problems they encounter building a new Kulturhaus. Elsewhere, workers from the Baltic Sea shipyard enjoy leisure and holiday romance by the sea in the 1961 DEFA production *Ein Sommertag macht keine Liebe* (*A Summer Day Doesn't Bring Love*), whereas at least one DEFA musical integrated song and dance with a celebration of the GDR's achievements in industrial chemistry (*Sylvesterpunsch / New Year's Eve Punch,* 1960). Joshua Feinstein cites "rather extreme examples of the imaginative spirit that took hold at the DEFA in the early sixties." He refers to the DEFA genre of the "comic historical adventure . . . featuring busty women in tight corsets and sword-fighting cavaliers, whose prototype was the Gina Lollobrigida classic, *Fan Fan La Tulipe* (Jean-Jacques, 1952)" (163).

Among the most popular of DEFA action-adventure genres were the so-called *Indianerfilme* (Indian films), which were produced from the mid-1960s through the early 1980s. The most popular of the series, *Die Söhne der großen Bären* (*The Sons of Great Bear,* 1966), was watched by 10 million viewers. DEFA identified the series as Indian films to distinguish them from Hollywood and spaghetti westerns; rather than favoring the heroism of cowboys and pioneers, the DEFA variation glorified the courage and integrity of the Indians. Although these films included iconography and constellations of characters recognizable from American westerns, DEFA Indian films articulated "an outspoken critique of the colonialism and racism that fueled the westward expansion of the United States" (Gemünden).

However varied or tenuous DEFA films' relationship to socialist realism may have been, many displayed characteristics common to eastern European art cinema. The repeated use of devices such as direct address, intertitles, the inclusion of documentary-style footage, and lack of closure in DEFA dramas distinguished these films from commercial productions of the west. Such traits affiliated many DEFA productions with the cultural/commercial domain of art cinema.

Whatever similarities DEFA productions may have shared with art films from other eastern bloc countries, they were not ensured the same appeal to western audiences. For the larger part, the stylistic and structural traits of DEFA films were more than capable of bemusing western viewers. Abrupt shifts into highly stylized, sometimes surreal fantasy sequences were not uncommon in otherwise "realist" DEFA productions.

Western viewers were often perplexed by the absence of conventional Hollywood codes that marked the transition into a dream or fantasy sequence. For example, *Die Legende von Paul und Paula* (*The Legend of Paul and Paula,* 1973) devotes painstaking detail to the modest, sometimes tawdry events in the everyday lives of its protagonists. But it also attends to their daydreams: in one spectacular scene, the lovers Paul and Paula are shown in embrace in wedding dress. Surrounded by flowers and engrossed in one another, they float down a river on a raft, oblivious to the presence of acquaintances and disapproving observers.

For those accustomed to the pace and action of Hollywood films, DEFA productions may seem lethargic. As Sibylle Licht remarks, western viewers who first saw DEFA films in 1990 were astounded that there were hardly any sequences of rapid editing, and they found their "measured tempo" almost unbearable (107). Moreover, the caution with which potentially inflammatory contemporary issues were approached made DEFA films too abstruse for "popular" audiences. The metaphors many DEFA films used in allusion to events and culturally specific aspects of life in the GDR often made them inaccessible to broad international audiences.[3]

---

3. It would be hard to find work more heavily allegorical than Kipping's late DEFA film *Das Land hinter dem Regenbogen* (*The Country behind the Rainbow,* 1991). In that film Kipping concludes his personal reckoning with GDR history with the following images: a child paints a rainbow across a portrait of Stalin featured on a massive banner; a grandfather is crucified, wearing a crown of barbed wire rather than thorns, and he is wrapped in the Stalin banner; the dismembered head of Christ is suspended on a rod near a lake as an albino dances on the shores. Another late DEFA film, *Miraculi* (1992), includes perhaps even more perplexing conceits: for the greater part of the film Sebastian, the film's protagonist, wanders around the countryside dressed in a diver's wetsuit and snorkeling gear. His costume rouses neither comment nor curiosity.

Fig. 1.   *The Legend of Paul and Paula* (1972). Film still reproduced with permission of Progress Film Verleih.

State Restrictions on Film

The one-party state of the GDR did not tolerate films that could be expected to prompt public controversy, inflame social conflict, or highlight the contradictions that riddled the socialist dictatorship.[4] Consequently, approaches to characterization were heavily scrutinized by Party officials. In particular, skepticism was viewed as an insufferable petit bourgeois affliction that had no place in DEFA films nor any reason within the socialist schema. The Party also voiced objections about films that focused upon outsiders and dropouts who appeared to be alienated—for alienation was a condition endemic to capitalism, not socialism.

Films that had characters who suffered from an inability to declare political allegiances or to solve moral dilemmas, or that presented characters incapacitated by betrayal or a crisis of conscience, were either banned or subject to harsh criticism by state officials. This was the case with scenarios in *Dein unbekannter Bruder* (*Your Unknown Brother,* 1980), *Die Russen kommen* (*The Russians Are Coming,* 1968/87), *Jadup und Boel* (1980/81), and *Die neuen Leiden des jungen W* (*The New Sorrows of Young W,* 1978).

Party scrutiny of DEFA films led to the routine posing of a number of questions:

> The overall criteria were: did the film serve the steadfast friendship with the Soviet Union . . . ? What role did the Party, the SED play? How was the Party Secretary represented? Who should play him and was the actor who would play him in the Party? How were the powers of the state depicted—the *Volkspolizei,* the agencies of State Security? Was youth depicted optimistically enough? Were class enemies, adversaries, and sticks in the mud exposed? (Teschner 20)

The emphasis placed upon the ideological function of film and its social responsibility always outweighed formal concerns, but in addition, formal experimentation in film was never really welcomed by Party officials in the GDR. Whether during periods of relative leniency or stringent control, under the dictatorship the "social expectation placed upon film was high: the medium [was] supposed to offer a substitute for the lack of critical public discussion" (Hindermith 28). Among other esteemed art forms like literature and theater, in the GDR film assumed a special role:

---

4. Jürgen Bretschneider ridicules Party cultural policy and the predicament in which it placed its filmmakers with his parody of Party officials pontificating: "We didn't imagine openness and dialogue with spectators like that. And what The People of the GDR discuss, we decide" (302).

it "took over the function of informing citizens about the latest crucial events, which in the west are covered by a variety of papers and magazines" (Leonhard 52).

The Central Committee of the SED was censorial in other ways as well: it displayed extreme sensitivity to any allusion to betrayal or filmic depiction of moral dilemmas resulting from individuals informing on acquaintances.[5] One need not look far to understand the grounds for this sensitivity. It is generally accepted that the Stasi held files on more than six million individuals. The Stasi was undoubtedly one of the GDR's most astounding achievements. It

> relied on the cooperation of about a million informants over and above its permanent staff of 85,000 and the 109,000 "freelancers" it regularly employed. This means that among the approximately nine million employable East German citizens, one out of every ten was a stool pigeon. . . . almost every name in the country appears [in Stasi files] as either victim or perpetrator or both. (P. Schneider 114–15)

The Politbüro was also intolerant of filmic expression of "subjective views and values" along with "doubt about . . . authority" (Honecker), which were outlawed in the middle 1960s. Such expressions were never welcomed but were more frequent and, to a degree, begrudgingly tolerated during the last decade of DEFA's history: by that time, there was more room for negotiation over the restrictions the state sought to impose on subject matter. Consequently, and with greater frequency throughout the late 1970s and 1980s, this cinema featured artists or *slightly* eccentric or idiosyncratic characters, figures who sometimes lived on the fringes of society. Some films actually included figures who resisted integration into the communities of which they were supposedly part (in *Solo Sunny,* Sunny is denounced by her neighbors who report her upon trivial grounds to the police), which cannot have endeared the films to some members of the Party. Officially disapproved (Bretschneider 298) but ultimately tolerated, *The New Sorrows of Young W* addressed the issue of the outsider through its depiction of a teenage antihero: Edgar Wibeau is the film's omnipresent protagonist, a character who posthumously narrates and comments upon his life as a dropout, his aspirations, his artistic pretenses, and his own early death. The Party was critical of the film: Edgar, a long-haired, hip-talking, defiant teenager who loves rock music and is misun-

---

5. It was only after the Wende that films such as *Verfehlung* (*Missing,* 1992) and *Der Tangospieler* (*The Tango Player,* 1991) could critically address the GDR's extensive surveillance network and its impact upon everyday life.

derstood by employers and parents, was hardly the Party's idea of socialist youth. "Through the character of Edgar, youth could recognize the subjective state, the unspoken wishes, and the suppressed attitudes which characterize their own lives," and that recognition was something the SED did not wish to encourage (Bretschneider 298). The Party also disapproved of *Jadup and Boel* because the film shifts its vision to the fringes of socialist society. It weaves a mystery around a social outcast who, like Edgar Wibeau, prefers physical and social isolation to life in the community.

As a consequence of cinema's state-prescribed function, "to assist with the development of the socialist personality and the construction of the socialist State,'" the long-standing doctrine of the "positive hero" never really lost favor with the SED. *Berlin around the Corner, Jahrgang '45* (*Born in '45*, 1965/90), and *The Russians Are Coming* were among a string of films made in the 1960s and not shown publicly for more than twenty years. The Party did not approve of these features because, among other reasons, they did not comply with the "positive hero" edict. The restless discontent of characters who animated these films, listening to *beat-Musik* (in the case of the first two) and wearing jeans and leather jackets, were an affront to Party dignitaries (Heiner Carow's 1973 film *The Legend of Paul and Paula* is considered to be *the* film that made jeans-wearing acceptable in the GDR). And the images these films presented of youth dissatisfied with the opportunities the socialist regime provided were politically undesirable. *The Russians Are Coming*, like *Jadup and Boel*, was withheld from release because its view of history was "subjective," and the resistance to fascism was not glorified as prescribed by the state's cultural policy.

The banning of such films was described as a "bitter loss, of creative potential . . . of fantasy and of critical sharpness" (Richter). It was thought that the shelved films of the 1960s would have been popular with the public because they expressed an intense hope for change. Rolf Richter provides further insight into the importance of these films and why they were banned:

> Apart from profound disquiet, all of these films also display[ed] hope that this disquiet could be made public. It has to do with . . . a critique of leadership . . . with the incompetence and careerism of [Party] functionaries; methods of education were problematized. They looked into the dissatisfaction of young people, showed that democracy was lacking, spoke about the difficulties of being honest. Many things were being handled which until then, especially when they had to do with film, were taboo. Who would have dared earlier to depict a judge as a characterless person [as was presented in *I Am the Rabbit*]? Who

would have dared to speak about how dogmatism and bigotry could undermine the moral fiber of the society? (Richter)

The desire for reform and the expressions of frustration and conflict among socialist youth conveyed in *Berlin around the Corner, I Am the Rabbit,* and *Born in '45* were silenced by SED officials. Barton Byg explains that the move was actually a regressive one: "In banning the films, the party was actually reversing reform impulses it had earlier explicitly encouraged in its Youth Communiqué of 1963, which had expressed a desire to increase youth support for socialism" ("Generational Conflict" 201). Wolfgang Kohlhaase, scriptwriter of *Berlin around the Corner,* said of the 1960s political censorship: "It is not only that films weren't released: the motivation of people affected was also undermined. Resignation led to stagnation" (qtd. in Hindermith 39).

With reference to the circumspection that determined filmmaking in the GDR from the mid-1960s on, Sigrun Leonhard describes the variable relations between the state and its artists, acknowledging that although

> there have been times of great closeness between the State and its creative community . . . the brief periods . . . [during which] the government, [sought to] assure itself of the cooperation of the intellectual elite, were always followed by new restrictive measures, resulting in disorientation, discouragement and anger on the part of the victims of the respective clean-ups. (52)

When potentially controversial films were withheld from the public, the reputation of DEFA films suffered. Consequently, at the very start of the 1970s, local audiences did not seem to hold DEFA films in especially high esteem. Jürgen Bretschneider recalls that at this time the backhanded compliment "I'd even go to see a DEFA film with you" was bandied around (289). Early into the 1970s, however, the status of DEFA films appeared to improve. *The Legend of Paul and Paula, Die Schlüssel (The Key,* 1972), *Beethoven—Tage aus einem Leben (Beethoven—Days in a Life,* 1976), *Der nackte Mann auf dem Sportplatz (The Naked Man on the Sports Field,* 1974), and *Jakob the Liar* were among the 1970s features favored by critics, and once more they improved the reputation and credibility of DEFA films.[6] To Wolfgang Gersch these were the best years (347), but the DEFA films that were released from 1976 until the end of the decade were

---

6. See "DEFA ade," a survey of twenty-one film critics and historians from East and West Germany, detailing what they view to be the highpoints of DEFA film from 1946 to 1991 in *Film und Fernsehen* 2 (1992): 33–35.

cause for disappointment. Gersch described this period of GDR film history as one that saw the emergence of uninspired, ponderous, and clumsy DEFA productions (356).

No one really disputes that 1976, like 1965, marked a crisis point for cultural activity in the GDR.[7] It was then that the popular East German folksinger Wolf Biermann was expatriated while on tour in the Federal Republic. An "alarming exodus of artists and intellectuals" followed Biermann's expulsion (Leonhard 53), among them prominent filmmakers and some of East Germany's most famous actors who deserted the GDR for the west in protest. "Another wave of artists left for the West between 1979 and 1981, and when Konrad Wolf died in 1982, another period of cinematic doldrums began" (Byg, "Generational Conflict" 201).

State interference in the arts extended into the late 1980s with some local and imported films being banned, withheld, or withdrawn from circulation. Many a director's career had already been halted or ruined by the state. "So that he would take leave from the present, Heiner Carow was allowed many years in a studio to prepare the expensive [project] *Simplicissimus*" (Gersch 358). Gersch explains that it was not uncommon for the Party to obstruct the careers of filmmakers whose values and attitudes did not comply with Party doctrine:

> As coworkers for the Stasi, studio bosses were at the disposal of the surveillance apparatus. It [was a system that] worked with tricks and with pressure: [Stasi reports specified] 'With the objective of bringing the political and artistic activities of Mr. K under control again, he will be assigned to the sorts of film projects which have no chance of being realized in the foreseeable future.' (358)

After Ulrich Weiß completed *Your Unknown Brother* and *Olle Henry* (1982/83) and attracted unfavorable critical attention from the SED, he was no longer allowed to direct films. His next effort came to fruition only after the collapse of the GDR. The banning of Jürgen Böttcher's *Born in '45* was the last time that filmmaker was to direct a fiction film. Frank Beyer's filmmaking career was halted for eight years after the SED withheld *The Mark of Stones* to which they had taken offense; he was banished to a provincial theater.

Although filmmakers were part of the country's cultural elite, the varying intensity and severity of the state controls imposed on them was rationalized in at least two ways: on the one hand, film was a "public art,

---

7. The upheavals of 1976 devastated film production, but not in the long term as did Party intervention into film production, distribution, and exhibition in the mid-1960s.

and on the other it was expected that the medium had a special impact upon the shaping of political consciousness" (Hindermith 28). However oppressive state intervention became in the GDR, film clearly remained a medium that was prioritized by the state: its educational/propaganda function was given precedence over any economic concern with profitability.

Together with the state's regulation of film production, the nationalization of the film industry nullified the independence of filmmakers, but it also minimized some of the insecurities and hazards of an otherwise notoriously capricious industry: "It is difficult to make a film anywhere in the world, but nowhere else in the world other than at DEFA was it the rule that a director would never personally have to go into debt to shoot a film" (Foth, "Forever Young" 101).

Apart from financial independence, filmmakers were also granted a great degree of security: staff at DEFA were employed on a full-time rather than a contractual basis. Around forty directors and twenty authors were employed by the fiction film studios at Babelsberg. (Some directors were employed *not* to make films.) A further thirty screenwriters, thirty cameramen, and fifteen costume designers worked at the complex. At the Babelsberg fiction studios alone, more than two thousand people were employed. As exiled East German filmmaker Sibylle Schönemann remarked, "The supply of technical specialists at DEFA was something that an independent filmmaker working in the Federal Republic could only dream of" (72).

Approaches to Production at DEFA

Long-standing partnerships developed between various directors, cameramen, and screenwriters in the east, a phenomenon that was also common to New German cinema in the Federal Republic. Even though western *Autorenkino* often depended upon collaborative efforts and teamwork of figures such as Fassbinder and Ballhaus, Wenders and Müller, or Mikesch and Treut, New German cinema depended upon the institutionalization of the Autor, at least throughout the 1970s and early 1980s. The cooperative and collaborative system of film production that operated at DEFA was, however, more widespread and possibly of a more egalitarian order than in the west. The role of the director was undoubtedly prestigious in the GDR, but official recognition and creative acknowledgment was also given to various long-standing production groups such as Roter Kreis, Babelsberg, Johannisthal, and the Berlin Group. Teams such as these were responsible for initiating, developing, and executing a series of projects independent of other production groups.

The *Dramaturg* (there is no suitable English equivalent) was also a highly esteemed figure at DEFA, sometimes granted kudos and creative recognition comparable to the director's. The fiction studios employed twenty-seven full-time dramaturgs. They played an indispensable role as mediators between state officials, writers, and directors. Each year they sorted through around 200 proposals and treatments to determine which would be suitable for development. Their involvement in a project extended from writing rough treatments for scripts through taking a finished film to the ministry. They were key figures in the organizational hierarchy of the studios, functioning as "artistic consultant and ideological midwife" responsible for "rewriting much of the material" (Bathrick 37). Dramaturgs also accompanied films to premieres and festivals, introducing and discussing features in the director's absence. "Often the future of materials, people and films depended upon the dramaturg's talent to bring together the right people and to find the necessary arguments in opposition to studio heads" (Schönemann 79). Partnerships between directors, dramaturgs, and particular production groups regularly extended over decades. "As a rule, every director and every author had his/her own dramaturg, and each dramaturg had his/her directors and scriptwriters. Often directors themselves became dramaturgs" (79).

Under the DEFA system a director made on average one film every three years. Something like an apprenticeship system operated at the studios, which engaged students from the Film Hochschule. Graduates worked as assistants to directors and cameramen and were titled *Nachwuchs* (the new or the young generation). After a qualifying period, Nachwuchs were usually permitted the opportunity to make three "debut" films, after which they could be considered for "promotion" to director, although the allocation of the title was by no means automatic. Titles had to be earned. "The estimate was that for debuts I–III it would take about ten years. Before then you didn't feel like a properly valued DEFA director" (Foth, qtd. in Bretschneider 313). Some Nachwuchs were obliged to complete five debut films before they were appointed as DEFA directors. Others were never allocated the title at all. The apprenticeship system operating at DEFA studios (modeled on the Soviet system) meant that the Nachwuchs were not especially "young," the term commonly applying to those born after the end of World War II: "the predominance of established directors left very little room for young directors in the GDR. Because of the structure of internship and (for men) military service before film school, directors who endured the long process of becoming qualified rarely were able to produce their first feature films before age forty" (Byg, "Generational Conflict" 199). Yet even for the last generation of filmmakers who worked at DEFA there were benefits that may have compensated for the restrictions they faced. As one of the last generation of Nachwuchs to emerge from DEFA, Jörg Foth explains: "the GDR was neither a cul-de-sac nor the end of the line. . . . The belief that change and improvement are brought about led most of us to stay" (qtd. in Bretschneider 311).

The hurdles filmmakers faced in East and West Germany differed from one another much as the structure of each country's film industry did. For filmmakers in the east "most of the author's time and strength was spent trying to accommodate an idea, an exposé at DEFA. Every idea was examined from the perspective of ideology and subject to the political experiences of the day" (Hindermith 39). "Dependency upon the state was complete for filmmakers because they couldn't work without state sup-port; they would have neither technical nor financial means at their dis-posal and there was only this one studio [DEFA] in which fiction films could be produced" (Schönemann 79). It took on average two years for a proposal to be developed and approval granted for a project to go into production (79), and the "more institutions a film brought under critical scrutiny the more committees had to approve the project at every level" (Byg, "Generational Conflict" 199–200).

The Ministry of Education, headed by Erich Honecker's wife, Mar-got, was actively engaged in scrutinizing DEFA films. Information regard-ing the shelving of disapproved films and scripts was withheld from the public, which was generally unaware of the existence of such instances of censorship. Cooperation and compromise became vital skills for filmmak-ers who, when addressing what they saw to be the objectives and short-comings of socialism, quickly learned "the question and the answer could never come together" (Kohlhaase, qtd. in Byg, "Generational Conflict" 210). "Everyone knew from the outset what was feasible and what wasn't, which themes and material were illusory, and where you would have to accept cuts to details to get the whole [film] through. One's manner was cautious; defensive tactics weren't specific to the production of film but rather they were entirely the social norm" (Bretschneider 310).

The circumspection of everyday life, then, was further institutional-ized at DEFA even in periods of leniency, such as the relative liberalism in cultural policy signaled by Honecker's rise to power in 1974. As former GDR actor Armin Mueller-Stahl recalls, "For many years at DEFA . . . we had the feeling that no move was better than a wrong one" ("Aus Gesprächen" 61). Across the decades the relationship between the state and its artists fluctuated; as in other arenas, those whose reputation was established and whose loyalty to the Party was beyond reproach were occasionally treated more leniently than their colleagues. For instance, when it was rumored that Carow's *The Legend of Paul and Paula* was to be banned, the future of Konrad Wolf's *Solo Sunny* also seemed uncertain.

However, Wolf's reputation protected this unorthodox film from being shelved.

Although rigid, cultural policy in the GDR was not without its inconsistencies. Periods in which the government sought "to assure itself of the cooperation of the intellectual elite . . . were always followed by new restrictive measures resulting in disorientation, discouragement and anger on the part of the victims of the respective clean-ups" (Leonhard 52).

Filmmakers were perpetually wary of the state deploying new restrictive measures, and they tailored their films accordingly: "Even when one worked on developing material, one did so 'with scissors in mind.' The fear that a film wouldn't be produced because of its special content brought most authors and screenwriters to 'self-censorship.' Otherwise no one would have worked: you either made compromises or you never made another film" (Schönemann 80). "While a greater willingness to accept a variety of themes and artistic expression existed, taboos continued to operate. The vast grey areas made it only more difficult for artists to orient themselves and may account for the vagueness and tentativeness that characterises so many GDR films" (Leonhard 53).

It would seem that the GDR cinema's efflorescence was complete by the early 1980s. Bretschneider explains that this was a time when the comment "I'd even go to see a DEFA film with you" changed from being a backhanded compliment to "not such a bad idea" (302). Apart from *Solo Sunny,* it was then that films such as *Sabine Wulff* (1978), *Sieben Sommersprossen* (*Seven Freckles,* 1978), *Bis daß der Tod euch scheidet* (*Until Death Do Us Part,* 1979) and *Die Verlobte* (*The Betrothed,* 1980) found favor with audiences and critics alike. In the early 1980s, productions such as *Das Fahrad* (*The Bicycle,* 1982), *Bürgschaft für ein Jahr* (*Surety for a Year,* 1981) and *Märkische Forschungen* (*Mark Brandenburg Research,* 1982) further strengthened the reputation of DEFA films. East German film critic Bettina Hindermith sees the start of the 1980s as a period in which "not only were new material and milieus brought before the camera," but films such as *The Betrothed* and *Your Unknown Brother* exhibited an altered style of dramatization and new modes of narration (32–33).

The 1983 release of controversial features like *Insel der Schwäne* (*Island of the Swans*) and *Ollé Henry,* begrudgingly tolerated by the SED, reminded cinema audiences of the medium's potential for social critique. Byg recalls: "At the end of the 1970s and the beginning of the 1980s there again seemed to be a chance for DEFA to regain its artistic momentum and its credibility with its audience. Numerous provocative, contemporary films generated unprecedented public interest and discussion of their social implications" ("Generational Conflict" 201). The positive public resonance surrounding DEFA films continued through the early 1980s. In 1983–84 films such as Frank Beyer's *Der Aufenthalt* (*The Sojourn*), Helmut Dzuiba's *Erscheinen Pflicht* (*Semblance of Duty*), and Horst Seemann's *Ärztinnen* (*The Doctor,* a box-office hit that was viewed by 1.2 million spectators in the first seven months of its release) were praised for their topicality and relevance (Hindermith 32–33).

Bärbel Dalichow, Wolfgang Gersch, and Jürgen Bretschneider are among the film historians who have viewed the mid- and late 1980s as a period of decline at DEFA. Gersch refers to these years as a period of stagnation (361). Bretschneider, former editor of the East German journal *Film und Fernsehen,* recalled that in this period one became once again aware of

> circumstances becoming difficult [for filmmakers], of small and depressing compromises; [there were] slow and tenacious struggles over this sentence or that image. Studio bosses imposed pressures to get [films] through the cultural and political order as effectively as possible [whereas] filmmakers sought to escape pressures and restrictions. Artists did not take blows below the belt without complaining. . . . But no one was allowed to incite open polemic[s]. The outrage of those affected [by Party intervention, censorship, or restrictions] was released into a vacuum. (303)

To Gersch, DEFA films made in the latter half of the 1980s failed to accept the last challenge that faced them: the chance to describe a socialist alternative and to push ahead for the disbanding of a political system that was in ruins (357). Dalichow provides a different inflection on film culture during the Wende when she cautions that the relations between power, politics, and culture in the GDR were not as simple as may have been suggested by the press.

> It wasn't as if there was the evil *Staatssicherheitsdienst* and the doctrinaire government on one side and the maltreated people on the other, who after an upheaval adjusted to the brief feeling of liberation. Most of the population of the GDR and most artists longed for a socialism that finally kept promises of justice and diverse possibilities in life. They sought to see these promises honored, not through aggressive demands, but rather by cautiously referring to inadequacies and other such painful subject[s]. All the artists who did this did not risk their existence, but they did risk their access to state controlled means of production. The history of DEFA is also the history of struggle, taboos, and boundaries. There were times of restrictions and times to

breathe a sigh of relief. The 1980s were characterized as a period in which a fire smouldered and was repeatedly extinguished. Open flames were never anywhere to be seen. [On the other hand] in DEFA films of the 1980s there was no uncritical glorification of existing circumstances. ("Die jüngste Regiegeneration" 73)

Film Distribution, Exhibition, and Importation in the GDR

Given the extent of state control over film culture in the GDR, the range of films distributed and exhibited in the country was surprisingly diverse. Until 1990 film distribution was entirely under the control of the state-run company Progress, which then automatically handled all DEFA productions. The purchase of imported film was state controlled. Still, a relatively broad range of national cinemas was distributed with a lot coming from the eastern bloc. Throughout the 1970s, some Hollywood films, along with films from West Germany and Western Europe, found their way into GDR cinemas, usually several years after their original domestic release. Widespread debate surrounded the distribution of American blockbusters such as *Towering Inferno* (1974). Even though socialist cultural policy prohibited the production of films whose sole aim was to entertain, such products came to be viewed "by intellectuals and politicians alike as an unavoidable vice"; it ultimately "seemed practical to import . . . [such products] from the United States and other countries" (Byg, "Generational Conflict" 199).

From the middle of the 1980s there was a further liberalization in the distribution of imported American and western European films. This the SED did "in accordance with the motto 'bread and play'" (Gersch 360). Foreign films were also distributed without as much delay between their West and East German release. In the 1980s the distribution gates were opened wide for western films. "A lot was possible . . . from *Excalibur* to *All That Jazz* and *Out of Africa*—as long as 'real existing socialism' was left in peace" (Gersch 360). Still the bias of GDR import policy was political. Even as late as 1987, "two-thirds of all films distributed [in the GDR] came from socialist countries" (Kersten, "Von der Berlinale"). Not all films that came from eastern bloc countries met with the approval of the SED. Throughout the 1980s, for instance, "General Director of DEFA, Hans-Dieter Mäde, member of the SED Central Committee, obstructed the spread of radical films from Poland and Hungary as well as Gorbachev's Glasnost and Perestroika" (Gersch 358).

Although some DEFA films were extremely popular with GDR audiences in the 1980s (notably *Solo Sunny* and *Eine trage des anderen Last / Bearing Another's Burden*, 1988), audiences gravitated to imported western productions that had proved successful elsewhere, such as *Crocodile Dundee* (1986). Wolfgang Gersch maintains that "even before the fall of the Wall, the DEFA film wasn't competitive any more" (361). In 1986, the West German comedies "*Männer / Men* and *Otto* were box-office favorites and like *Star Trek* and *Heavenly Bodies—Aerobic Non-Stop* managed to break the barrier of one million GDR viewers" (Kersten, "Von Allen bis Zanussi"). *Platoon* (1986), *Moonstruck* (1987), *Dirty Dancing* (1987), and *Prince—Sign o' the Times* were among Hollywood films screened in the GDR in 1988, with *The Name of the Rose* (1986) and *E.T.* attracting mass audiences of 2.3 and 2.6 million viewers respectively (Kersten, "Von Allen bis Zanussi"). The tendency for profits to be concentrated on a handful of films was also a characteristic well established at the GDR box office in the 1980s. The popularity of imported films in the GDR prompted one West German commentator to remark "amusement is the predominant import from the Federal Republic"; despite the broader diversity of films offered, "audiences prefer western imports, a matter that is hardly recognized" (Kersten, "Von Allen bis Zanussi").

Cinema attendance may have been a great deal higher in the GDR than in the Federal Republic. East German writers surveying their film history before and after the collapse of the Democratic Republic usually estimate 1980s attendances to be in the range of 70 to 80 million a year. If one were to believe official figures provided by the old regime, cinema attendances in the GDR were six times higher before the Wende—after which they dropped to 12 million. This is a very surprising change. Although Dieter Wiedemann notes that the manipulation of attendance figures to statistically justify particular DEFA productions was more or less tolerated in the GDR ("Der DEFA-Spielfilm" 74), other East German media analysts and film historians scarcely mention the practice, even with the benefit of hindsight.

As far as the film industry is concerned, unification resulted in more than declining attendances in the east. It resulted in a major restructuring of all aspects of film production, distribution, and exhibition. But although all of the GDR's media awaited privatization in 1990, no one in the filmmaking community in the east anticipated that unification would have such grave consequences for their film industry (see chapters 3 and 4).

DEFA Filmmakers after the Fall of the Wall

At the start of the 1990s the film community was no more prepared for unification and its consequences than the rest of the population of the GDR. There was a lack of solidarity among filmmakers in the east; most displayed naïveté and a general bewilderment about the future of their film culture. Granted the extent of social upheaval that those in the east faced at that time and the extensive reorientation that unification demanded of them, it was perhaps less than surprising that there was no immediate solution to, or unanimous decision about, how (or if) East Germans could salvage and reform their film branch. As Knut Hickethier observed discussing the future of screen culture in the east: "There weren't any completed plans with other structures [stored away] in cupboard drawers. It was first expected that these other structures would emerge from a broader consensus, coming from GDR citizens themselves" ("Das Zerschlagen" 74).

When the Wall came down, the orientation of GDR cinema, which sought to assist in "the construction of the socialist personality and the building of socialist society," lost its relevance. The ideals that this cinema rationalized and promoted were by and large disowned. Michael Gwisdek, one of the GDR's most famous actors, noted, "We still wanted to shoot films about Stalinism and reckon with our own past. Naturally, no one wants to see that in the cinema any more, and no one wants to finance it any more" (qtd. in "Ein Filmland" 6).

Even though some DEFA filmmakers worked within the framework of popular genres, few had experience in producing sensational action-packed cinema that depended heavily on special effects: "pure entertainment" was a notion beyond contempt and dismissed by the socialist state as a by-product of capitalist degeneracy. The cultural specificity of much GDR cinema also limited its appeal and made it largely unintelligible for international "art cinema" audiences. As Wilhelm Roth has observed of the last generation of filmmakers from the former GDR, they "all have difficulties with the Federal Republic and real, existing capitalism, even if they can finally shoot what they couldn't shoot for a long time" ("Die letzte Generation" 10). Former DEFA filmmakers who specialized in the production of *heitere Filme* (upbeat films), a tradition that extends back as far as 1950s musicals, have not managed to prosper since unification.

The situation for documentary filmmakers has also altered considerably. Under the old regime they performed a vital role, informing the public of critical social developments—concerns and trends considered unsuitable for exposure on local television. After the collapse of the GDR, this function is largely fulfilled by the press, current affairs programs, and television news, previously "the mouthpiece of state propaganda" under the SED (Leonhard 54). Moreover, the sociopolitical reality of inhabitants of the GDR changed beyond recognition: the public these filmmakers previously sought, whom they generally found and with whom they communicated (E. Schmidt 92) dissipated in the early 1990s.

Those who were involved in film production in the former GDR have, with unification, reluctantly shifted from a position of dependency upon one state to dependency upon another, and the exchange has worked distinctly to their disadvantage. Never having had to give serious consideration to raising budgets and securing distribution, the access these people now have to state film subsidies is limited. Previously part of a cultural elite, filmmakers from the east are baffled by the intricacies of the Federal Republic's subsidy labyrinth. Even the vocabulary of West German film production was so foreign to authors, producers, and directors from the east that workshops had to be organized to introduce them to this new language and unfamiliar terms like marketing, interest, and production loans (Hochmuth, "Tausend Topfe"). Not all have managed to adjust to the FRG's decentralized system. Advanced in age and placing utmost importance upon the ethics and art of filmmaking, many eastern filmmakers were horrified by the commercialism of western film production, a marketplace in which they too had to compete. In the early 1990s, the vicissitudes and ruthless competitiveness of the western market were alien to the vast majority of filmmakers from the ex-GDR. "Now we face economic censorship rather than ideological" is the lament of directors, writers, and technicians from the east. The director of the Potsdam Film Museum, Bärbel Dalichow, concurs: she recollects that before unification, film was an object scrutinized and censored by politicians and party officials, whereas filmmaking in the east is now a matter for accountants ("Die jüngste Regiegeneration" 72). Unification has swollen unemployment figures, and East Germans now constitute a high proportion of those excluded from the film industry and the subsidy stakes. In the domain of culture, East Germany has assumed the identity of unification's spurned stepchild. Chapters 3 and 4 address some of these consequences, in particular the dismantling of DEFA studios and their western takeover. There attention is directed toward the economic, industrial, and cultural consequences of the privatization of DEFA.

CHAPTER 3

DEFA wird abgewickelt /
Dealing with DEFA

Film production, like so many other branches of industry in the GDR, was doomed by the trajectory and consequences of unification. Yet in contrast to other branches that have been privatized, film is an area of East German industry that cannot be expected to return to its previous level of productivity. For more than forty years, filmmaking in the GDR was fully sponsored at every level (from script development and production to distribution and exhibition) by the SED. Shortly after the GDR collapsed, however, East German filmmakers lost the shelter of the DEFA organization. These were the only production facilities in the GDR and consisted of studios for *Spielfilme* (feature films), animation, and documentary production.

DEFA filmmakers must have been bewildered as they witnessed the disintegration of the GDR's film community. "Only just released from the patriarchal care" of the GDR state, the independence these filmmakers faced during unification brought with it insecurity and dismay (de Bruyn 62–63). With the future of the GDR itself uncertain, film production at the nationalized studios was only secured until the middle of 1990. Then came currency reform, from which point "DEFA had to reckon differently—in DM. This change meant a total shake-up of economic reckoning and working conditions" (Radevagen 195). Meeting with the Ministry of Culture shortly after currency reform, DEFA management was told that the studios could no longer expect to be subsidized as they had been in the past and that, at best, they had 9 million DM at their disposal (Dalichow, "Letzte Kapitel" 329). This sum could only pay for a fraction of employees' wages. Despair prevailed at the studios, and employees renamed DEFA *Das Ende für Alle* (the end for everyone).

Some material in this chapter has been adapted from my article "Dealing with DEFA: The Euro-Chainsaw Massacre." *Metro* 91 (1992): 34–37.

The east's film community now watched western entrepreneurs and property developers deliberating over the value of the former GDR's media landscape. In 1992, when DEFA's fate was being decided, Hans Günther Pflaum observed that its filmmakers and technicians were

> estranged from one another . . . having resigned themselves to the situation. Once financially protected [by the state], the economic pressures which have confronted them . . . have been too great for sustained, collective action. Western business people have conquered DEFA and filled the existing vacuum. The directors and studio heads of the old DEFA are no longer in the picture. They aren't asked about the future of the studios and they no longer have a public voice. . . . Spokespeople from the west are in control. ("Kampf")

As decrepit as many other state-run enterprises, DEFA studios followed the pattern of rationalization and privatization common to industry in the former GDR. On 17 June 1990 East Germany relinquished control of DEFA studios (for animation, documentary, and feature films), which, like other branches of GDR industry, were handed over to Treuhand. This trustee company supervised the privatization of the DEFA complex and the real estate that belonged to the studios.

Treuhand employed a total of 3 million workers and determined the fate of more than "9,000 companies, 20,000 retail outlets, 7,500 hotels and restaurants and several thousand libraries and other enterprises" (Kreille 78). Treuhand's name immediately evoked the dreaded consequences of unification in the former GDR—unemployment on a massive scale, West German seizure of valuable property and real estate, and the widespread closure of local industry. In retrospect, Treuhand's dealings strike one as remarkably exploitative of eastern business interests and potential, no matter how modest those ventures may have been. When business in the former GDR faced privatization, Treuhand appeared to favor western-based investors over easterners. In supervising the rationalization, liquidation, and privatization of eastern industry and business, Treuhand made "no attempt . . . to ensure that former GDR citizens would have opportunities to acquire ownership in or of . . . state [ex-GDR] enterprises. . . . More than 80 per cent of privatized enterprises were purchased by non-eastern Germans. Management buy-outs by eastern Germans was a privatization method adopted by the Treuhand only after a drying up of western German investment interest" (Welsh, Pickel, and Rosenberg 117). Businesses that ended up in East German hands, by contrast, were usually small to medium "with 50 or fewer employees, and many of them continuing to operate on the verge of bankruptcy" (118). Taking these factors and strategies into account, in retrospect it seems inevitable that DEFA would be subject to a western takeover.

Needless to say, Treuhand was an organization much maligned in the east:

> As an agency directing the transformation of the whole industrial sector, Treuhand is to some degree an inherently political institution. Not surprisingly, it is also the ideal scapegoat, drawing attacks from dissatisfied would-be investors, union leaders denouncing the "job-killers," politicians lamenting the lack of parliamentary control, and the municipalities waiting for the assignment of property. (Kreille 61)

Because much of GDR industry was deemed to be overstaffed and grossly inefficient, privatization resulted in the liquidation of major branches of eastern industry. During German reunification, eastern industry first had to face massive layoffs. Two-thirds of all previously existing positions in industry were lost—2.4 million jobs out of 3.2 million (Bittorf 49). DEFA, which had boasted the second largest studio complex in Europe, now faced *Abwicklung* (a curiously ambiguous term that encompasses the operations of winding-up and winding-down, wrapping-up or dealing with), and the process was savage. On 30 June 1990, 2,400 people were on the payroll at DEFA in Babelsberg. Apart from technicians, crew members, and bureaucrats, included among the staff were the musicians in the studio's symphony orchestra, firefighters, kindergarten teachers, archivists, carpenters, painters, and sculptors. Early summer of 1991 saw the sacking of around 1,400 workers at the feature film studios in Babelsberg. It has been suggested that the extent of the DEFA retrenchments and details surrounding the mass sacking during 1991 were deliberately concealed to avoid political and social upheaval (Hickethier, "Statt DEFA" 9). The rationalization of further sections of DEFA, such as the documentary studios, was even more drastic than in the feature sector. At the end of March 1991, 620 employees from DEFA's documentary studios were "regrettably" fired, leaving 80 staff (Baum and Kuhlbrodt). The number of casualties was destined to escalate: "by the end of 1992, 700 of the 3,500 former employees remained" (Freyermuth 51). By the late 1990s half that number of former DEFA employees still had work at the studios. Although various individuals (filmmakers, journalists, film critics, writers) objected to the mass sacking after the fact, there was no large-scale, consolidated resistance among the film community in the east when the retrenchments took place. Bärbel Dalichow recalls:

There were no strikes, no demonstrations, no alliances for action or emergency organizations; there were hardly any legal countermeasures taken by individual employees. . . . [The layoffs] were accepted as an inescapable fate. Each person died a solitary death. ("Letzte Kapitel" 330)

Considering that state subsidy of film in the old states of the Federal Republic alone had already reached 180 million DM a year by 1992, the federal government was in no position to underwrite DEFA. The burgeoning debt of unification prevented the federal government from providing what these days would appear to be the minimal sum of "150 million DM . . . to make the old DEFA a competitive operation" (Brenner 280). With cultural affairs being the economic responsibility of individual Länder, it was impossible for the regional government of the small state of Brandenburg (where the feature film studios were located) or neighboring Berlin to ensure that DEFA continued to operate as a center of film production in unified Germany. The collapse of the GDR state meant that on an annual basis DEFA "was short over 35 million of state support for feature film production . . . and a total of more than 40 million in production commissions for [East] German Television / *Deutsche Fernsehfunk* / DFF" (Wolf 16).

In contrast to all the existing states of West Germany at the time, Brandenburg had no secure infrastructure or funds to deal with issues related to local film culture, film subsidy, or state support of film production. With DEFA's fate uncertain and the studio's former and remaining staff dejected, various compensatory measures were initiated by the Ministry of the Interior, the Ministry of Culture, and film funding boards, such as those of Berlin and Hamburg. This transfusion of film funds to the new federal states sustained a range of small-scale productions in the short term. For example, October 1990 saw the Ministry of the Interior set aside 3.5 million DM for film projects from the east, a sum that would perhaps pay for the completion of two low-budget features. Negotiations with the minister of culture, Herbert Schirmer, resulted in the pledging of 18 million DM for film projects to be produced at DEFA (Dalichow, "Letzte Kapitel" 329). The Brandenburg film subsidy system was established late in 1991 ("Brandenburg geht"), and by 1993, the state of Brandenburg had a total of 8 million DM in film subsidy money at its disposal (Alexandrow 45). It was in August 1994, after three years of speculation and discussion, that a joint Berlin-Brandenburg Film Board was established. Some other eastern states have also established modest regional subsidy systems in the period since DEFA was privatized.

By economic necessity, the "salvation" of DEFA involved the interaction of European money, the "new media" (satellite and cable broad-casting, high-definition television, and pay television) and the token consideration of the regional state interests of Brandenburg and Berlin. Grossly inefficient and equipped with much outdated equipment, DEFA faced a major overhaul if it were ever to operate competitively with other film production centers in West Germany. Even in the west, production centers like Studio Hamburg and Bavaria Studios had long depended upon television productions and contracts for their survival; they could not survive on film production alone ("Der Will" 9).

When those from the west toured the shabby studios and deserted DEFA offices for the first time, they could not believe "that art was once made there, let alone that art could be produced there sometime again" (Brenner 282). Basic renovations like the provision of effective heating and the installation of a functioning telephone system faced potential buyers. Even with massive investments of capital and time, the studios would be unprofitable for years and unable to compete with modern, well-equipped production centers like those established in Bavaria, Hamburg, and Berlin. With those in the west conscious of the financial burdens that would plague the studios for the decade to come, serious consideration was given to turning Babelsberg into a theme and amusement park. It was thought that further revenue could be secured by selling off DEFA's attractively located property (bordered by woods, lakes, and villas with rail connections to Berlin) for the development of high-rise housing estates, hotels, apartments, and facilities for tourists. Whoever the buyer, redevelopment of the land on which the studios rested was more probable than the future of film production at the studio complex. Other equally immediate sources of profit included the rights to thousands of films and telefilms in the DEFA archives, perhaps a bargain for entrepreneurs involved with satellite broadcasting.

The Deal

Under the trusteeship of Treuhand, the studios were subject to bungled dealing and a measure of sordid bidding. At a press conference held in July 1991, flustered Treuhand executives admitted their ignorance of another DEFA studio in Kleinmachnow. It seems that the Treuhand bosses may have been so blinded by their vision of the feature film studios at Babelsberg that they were "astounded that DEFA consist[ed] of further studios" (Brenner 283).

Representatives of various interest groups in West Germany's film industry were gradually implicated in the deliberations over DEFA's future. Figureheads active in film production centers such as those of

North Rhine–Westfalia, Munich, and Berlin were accused of industrial sabotage. It was alleged that they were intent on seeing a potential competitor disqualified, if not eliminated, from the field of production. Volker Schlöndorff, who was involved in negotiation deals over the privatization of the studios, prompted further outrage among the East German film community with his public pronouncement that "DEFA stinks," along with the dismissive "I've had more interesting discussions with architects and engineers than with DEFA scriptwriters" ("Was stinkt").

Feelings seem to have been mixed about DEFA surfacing as a potential competitor in the burdened and heavily subsidized field of film production. As one eastern writer noted fatalistically in 1991, "Rohrbach, head of Bavaria Studios, said a couple of months ago that films can be shot anywhere—speaking plainly, that means DEFA is superfluous" (Dalichow, "Wettlauf" 21). The deliberation over DEFA's role in German film production was also the studio's minefield of federal Filmpolitik, which has as one of its central and long-standing issues of contention the struggle for the title of film capital of Germany. The imaginary position is one Berlin, Hamburg, and Munich have been bidding on for more than a decade (Köhler, "Filmmetropole" 10–13). In 1992 they were joined by a new rival, Cologne/North Rhine–Westphalia, which, with 50 million DM in film money at its disposal, emerged as the richest regional subsidy organization in Germany. DEFA's entry into the competition for the title was signaled in 1991, when the studio's name was provisionally changed to Filmstadt Babelsberg (Film City Babelsberg).

It took longer to deal with the Babelsberg studios and settle their fate than was expected. Escalating negotiations over the studios and procrastination on the part of Treuhand and interest groups protracted the sale of the complex. Throughout 1991 and 1992, Treuhand announced numerous deadlines for investors interested in buying DEFA.

The potential buyers included groups based in Paris, Munich, and Berlin. The French corporate power group Compagnie Générale des Eaux (CGE) first entered into discussions about DEFA with Treuhand in the autumn of 1991. The company registered interest in the complex in November 1991 (Blaney, "Franco-German Group Plans" 1). CGE is a hydraulic engineering company that,

> among other things, holds a monopoly over French water supply, engages in building houses and urban development, runs theme parks, deals in real estate, owns the Paris film studios, Boulogne-Billancourt and holds a 22.7 percent share in the pay television channel, Canal Plus. (Dalichow, "Letzte Kapitel" 347)

In 1992 the organization also owned the film and distribution company UGC.

Because of their financial might and a seductive, if quickly forgotten, portrait of DEFA as the vibrant film production center of Europe, a "bubbling fountain of gold" that would invite "the marriage of French life-style and the success of French film with German industriousness and German efficiency" (Dalichow, "Letzte Kapitel" 347), the French company was most favored by Treuhand. Even those who had reservations about the sale of DEFA saw some potential advantages in CGE being the new owners: it was considered that they had the necessary experience in film production and that they also had investment capital at their disposal (Pflaum, "Kampf"). CGE was preferred over the Munich-based interest of Hans-Joachim Bernt and his Berlin-based representative, Regina Ziegler.

At this time it was claimed that rival bids for DEFA were part of a conspiracy, behind which Bavarian studios and some Bavarian politicians supposedly stood. It was alleged that the Bavarian intention was to incapacitate DEFA and hence consolidate film and television production in Bavaria. Similar claims were made of the Film Büro in North Rhine–Westphalia; it was thought that this high-profile agency wanted to ensure the continuous use of local production facilities while strengthening relations with its production partner, the public television station WDR (West Deutsche Rundfunk).

Accusations that potential investors found DEFA attractive only because of its valuable real estate were frequent. Even Berlin's minister of finance made public his concern that the privatization of DEFA would be nothing more than a straight real estate deal (qtd. in Freyermuth 30). As early as 1990, the Frankfurt Chase Bank indicated that "essentially the most valuable feature of DEFA was its real estate" (Fleischmann, qtd. in Giesen, "Troja Babelsberg" 322), which was then worth at least 400 million DM.

A Euro-Solution

The German directors Peter Fleischmann and Volker Schlöndorff became key players in the negotiations over the sale. Schlöndorff acted as representative of CGE. His faith (and reputation) were placed in a vision of Babelsberg as "the European film metropolis of the future" ("Wunderbares Spielzeug" 145). Schlöndorff's colleague Peter Fleischmann, representative of FERA/Verband europäische Regisseure/the Association of European Directors, placed additional emphasis upon the European media market in his 1990 rationalization:

The renovation and maintenance of DEFA would be too much of a
burden for Germany to carry alone. . . . For Europe, however, it
could provide a chance to establish a trade center for ideas and for
new technology—it could result in a productive encounter between
different national film cultures, keeping in mind the hitherto unrecognized scale of a collective European market for European film.
("Wunderbares Spielzeug" 145)

With the implementation and consolidation of European Community
(EC) film funding policies and strategies, plus support for the establishment of a European film center and film school at Babelsberg, it was predicted that DEFA's future orientation would be decidedly international.
Schlöndorff was particularly enthused by the possibility of DEFA special-
izing in the production of middle-range European coproductions. He
claimed the studios could play a vital role in safeguarding the diversity of
European cultural identity, long threatened by the American dominance
of most national film industries. During the long squabbles surrounding
decisions over DEFA's fate, his enthusiasm for promoting European film
production at Babelsberg never waned.

For Schlöndorff and Fleischmann, the question "Do you want to
counter American cinema with a competitive alternative?" was the
same question as "Do you want CGE?" Who could say no? In any
case certainly not Treuhand and not Berlin and Brandenburg's politicians; there was no comparable offer for DEFA's purchase at hand.
(Dalichow, "DEFA" 8)

The Sale

It was initially expected that the DEFA deal would be wrapped up by the
end of 1991. Legal intervention in the arrangements between CGE and
Treuhand delayed the decision. Mediation by a legal representative of
GAT resulted in demands for the provision of letters of intent from the
Paris-based company, which further delayed the sale. Although the
French bidders basically accepted the sale arrangements, they could not
have been trusted about taking on the remaining DEFA employees, pledging investments, and handing out 130 million DM (Dalichow, "Letzte
Kapitel" 348). Suspicions had already been aired in 1991 that the privati-
zation of DEFA was being deliberately delayed by Treuhand until all the
studio personnel were laid off and studio capital was "reduced to little
more than a property holding company that could sell the studio site in
Potsdam for a profit" (Blaney, "Treuhand Set" 2).

DEFA was in the trusteeship of Treuhand for more than two years before the French consortium became the legal owners of the studios. The details of the sale were not easy to fathom. Hans Günther Pflaum reported that Treuhand's board of directors decided in favor of selling DEFA to CGE on 27 April 1992, noting that on managerial advice, the resolution was deferred until 19 May ("Kampf"). When the sale was not finalized in May, accountants circled 1 July as the day on which the sale of the Babelsberg studios would take place (Dalichow, "Letzte Kapitel" 351). Even though reports stated without doubt that CGE was to be the new owner of Babelsberg, it was the Compagnie Immobilière Phénix Deutschland (CIP)/Phoenix Real Estate Company (Germany), supposedly a 100 percent daughter-firm of CGE, which officially bought the complex. CIP Germany finally signed the contract of sale on 25 August 1992. The transaction was made legally binding months later, when on 10 December it was approved by the federal minister of finance. On the last day of the year, CIP handed over 130 million DM for the sale of the studios. The name DEFA was struck off the stock market register on 12 January 1994 (Dalichow, "Von den Mühen" 439).

At DEFA Babelsberg, CIP's declared intentions were to "develop the real estate, renovate the studios, invest in the infrastructure right down to hotels, and, naturally, invest in film production itself" (Schlöndorff, qtd. in Pflaum "Kampf"). The contract of sale stipulated that, apart from devoting themselves to film production at Babelsberg, the new owners would establish a modern and competitive European media center on the site. CIP brought the Bertelsmann organization in as its partner in production. The Bertelsmann group's investment in new media was extensive. It owned Ufa Film and Television and a major share of the commercial television station RTL Plus (Radio Tele Luxembourg), was involved in commercial broadcasting in France, and had substantial shares in European cable and pay television services. Bertelsmann also owned a press and publishing empire. The leadership of the Babelsberg studios was assumed by Pierre Couveinhes, a French steel industry developer, together with Volker Schlöndorff, artistic director of the studios.

The 130 million DM that CIP paid for the Babelsberg complex was well under the estimated 280 million DM value of its real estate (Freyermuth 17). The new owners were, however, obliged to meet further costs. One of the conditions of the sale was that CIP would invest a total of at least 410 million in the Babelsberg site up until 2002 (*Gemeinsame Presserklärung*). Included in that sum was a total three-year studio maintenance fee of 150 million DM. It was estimated that day-to-day running costs would necessitate the provision of 20 million DM, and 60 million DM was pledged to be spent in modernizing studio facilities, a figure thought to be far too low by many (Freyermuth 33). A sum of 10 million DM was to be devoted to the "Filmtour" and other public attractions (Freyermuth 17). West German media magnate Leo Kirch bought the documentary studios. In the mid-1970s it had been revealed that Kirch held a monopoly over supplying films for broadcast on German public television. Apart from the documentary studios, Kirch owned Taurus Film, Beta Film, Beta Technik, Unititel, and Taurus-Film-Video. Together with the Springer Company, he had a 75 percent controlling interest in the satellite station Sat 1, the station that in 1985 broke the public television monopoly in Germany. Kirch was at this time not only the largest film supplier in western Europe, but was heavily involved in pay television and video.

By the time the Babelsberg complex was sold, only 621 employees remained. The new owners were contractually obliged to provide the remaining staff with work until the end of 1994. "They were paid, but the majority had nothing to do: at the start of 1993, CIP contacted the government Employment Agency to register 200 employees without work" (Dalichow, "Letzte Kapitel" 330). Moves such as these suggest that CIP had lost sight of the objectives declared when the sale was finalized. Then, as had been announced in the joint Treuhand-CIP press statement, the company said that its aim was to enhance employment prospects at Babelsberg on a large scale and to introduce jobs on a staggered basis. Its objective was supposedly to ensure that at least 3,500 employees were working on the site by 2002. By 1997, only 350 former DEFA employees were engaged at the studios (Hickethier, "Babelsberg im Aufwind" 7).

Despite the contractual agreement to "build up a modern studio system capable of operating competitively under the conditions of a market economy while also cultivating necessary services that support production" (*Gemeinsame Presserklärung*), very little emerged from the studio in terms of production in the early 1990s. Although some filmmakers, like Helma Sanders-Brahms and Karin Howard, were willing to use the postproduction facilities in the east (synchronization labs and copy works still operated while the sale was being negotiated), producers were reluctant to bring funds and projects to Babelsberg for realization in the first few years of the decade.

Indeed, the actual fate of film production at Babelsberg studios looked even grimmer after the sale than before. Even though the studios operated well under capacity from 1990 through the end of 1992, a reasonably diverse range of DEFA productions were completed during this period, features ranging from children's productions to historical epics. Wende comedies from the last generation of DEFA Nachwuchs together with literary adaptations and love stories continued to emerge from the studios in the early 1990s. In the period from November 1989 until November 1993, around forty films carrying the DEFA signature were completed—films that were funded by the GDR government's final grants and subvention from the federal government. Yet in the period after the sale, Babelsberg studios were not especially attractive as far as big-budget international productions were concerned. An anonymous American producer assessed the appeal of Babelsberg in the following devastating terms:

> Why the hell should we shoot at Babelsberg? . . . Name me one reason. What have they got there that you can't find elsewhere and better? What can they offer us . . . [apart from] production in a strange, distant place . . . tax problems, the time difference and language difficulties . . . higher wages, less flexibility in the work force and expensive hotels. The local color might interest me if I was ever so crazy as to want to shoot a film about old Fritz or Hitler. (Anon., qtd. in Freyermuth 33)

CGE's earlier vision of Babelsberg as a thriving production center for European film did not exactly materialize in the first half of the 1990s. Although the new owners pledged to invest the modest sum of 60 million DM in film production over a three-year period, in 1993 and 1994 only eight films were shot at the studios, out of which seven were coproductions. Of the coproductions that in some way utilized the Babelsberg facilities in the first half of the 1990s, none enjoyed critical or box-office success or have been awarded major prizes at international festivals.[1] John Schlesinger's adaptation of . . . *Und der Himmel steht still* (*The Innocent*) was premiered in 1993 to be ignored by the German public and dismissed by German critics. *Französische Frau* (*The French Woman*) was released in 1995, and in the same year, Schlöndorff worked on *Der Unhold* (*The Fiend*), an international coproduction with Poland. Upon release, its attendance figures were modest if not disappointing (173,608 viewers; "Black Box Office" 1998, 6), especially for a film with a 26 million DM budget.

---

1. Babelsberg studios did receive their measure of publicity at the end of the 1990s with the release of *Sonnenallee* (1999), which involved considerable work for the props and scenery department. The production involved a 7,000-square-meter studio reconstruction of a fictitious East Berlin street, complete with Berlin Wall. Although the film was extensively promoted in the Berlin press and in national publications like *Der Spiegel,* it was not treated all that favorably by western critics, a number of whom were critical of the film's nostalgic treatment of the ex-GDR and its contribution to the much maligned late 1990s phenomenon of Ostalgie. "Studio Babelsberg Independents," late 1990s productions such as *Nacht Gestalten* (1999) and *Wege in die Nacht* (1999), have attracted much favorable critical attention, the first receiving an Oscar nomination for "Best Foreign Film," the second opening the 1999 directors' fortnight at Cannes.

After the announcement had been made that ten internationally financed films with budgets between 10 and 15 million dollars were to be produced at Babelsberg each year, funded by Babelsberg studios and Island World B.V. Amsterdam, nothing more was heard. During this time it seemed that there was more action at the Babelsberg amusement and theme park, the Diana Park, than in the studios themselves. In 1994, the Bertelsmann company announced plans to invest 150 million DM in the park (Dalichow, "Von den Mühen" 441), considerably more than anyone had invested in the modernization of the studios up until that time. And film production was not the only area of activity that was dramatically curtailed in the early 1990s as a result of moves to privatize DEFA. Television production also dropped dramatically then, with consequences I shall detail in chapter 5.

When all of these factors are taken together, a certain suspicion about CIP's plans for the studios did seem justified. Speculation about the impending bankruptcy of the Babelsberg studios continued at least until the end of 1996. After the sale, fears grew that the investors' interests in the complex extended little further than its real estate. Curiously, the emphasis upon real estate even emerged in the promotion of the Babelsberg Studio Tours. In the latter half of the 1990s, tourists were invited to the studios and their surroundings, famous for their "Stars, Stasi, and villas." With the studios and surrounding land covering an expanse of 460,000 square meters, it was calculated that in "the inner city of Potsdam in 1992, the price of land was valued at between 800 and 1,200 DM a square meter. In 1991, the price of land directly in the region of the film studios was already between 350 and 450 DM per square meter. CIP paid about 70 DM in 1992" (Dalichow, "DEFA" 10).

Indeed, faith in CIP's intentions wavered in 1993 through 1995, especially since "with every new presentation of plans for Babelsberg, the proportion of land designated for film and media shrinks" (Dalichow, "Letzte Kapitel" 351). As the discussion of building hotels, cinema complexes, warehouses, offices, and other types of development became more frequent, the actual expanse of DEFA real estate was, all of a sudden, mysteriously irrelevant (Dalichow, "DEFA" 9–10). By 1994, the new buyers stipulated that only one-third of the DEFA property would be maintained for production: the studios, workshops, and studio halls covered an expanse of about fifteen hectares; the rest of the real estate would be put to other uses. Accordingly, twenty hectares were earmarked for offices, the film school, and the film tour, and the remaining ten hectares were designated for the building of hotels and apartments (Freyermuth 31–32). In any case, the new buyers' commitments to the Babelsberg studios are only binding for ten years, after which time they have the option of disposing of the complex.

CGE divested itself of the majority of its shares in CIP Germany around the time of the sale, and this, reasonably, provided further grounds for doubt about the future of film production at DEFA's old studios. Despite the public assurances made in June 1992 that CIP Germany was 100 percent owned by CGE, it has been suggested that Treuhand secretly agreed to the sale of CIP to British and French property developers before CIP Germany signed the contract of sale (Dalichow, "Letzte Kapitel" 351; "Von den Mühen" 439). In her detailed chronicle of the sale of DEFA, Dalichow reported that CGE had sold off most of its shares in CIP, letting its portion of the company shrink to 35.8 percent. Of the shares it sold, 50 percent were bought by the British real estate company Chesterfield Property Group, whereas another 20 percent of CIP shares were bought by the Paris-based business Kilford Real Estate. Dalichow explains that CIP was only in a position to pay the 130 million DM to close the sale of the Babelsberg studios after it had sold the majority of its shares to the French and British property developers. Despite these transactions, the majority of reports surrounding the sale of the studios either list CGE as the new owners or refer to filial relations between CGE and CIP (Hickethier, "DEFA-Verkauf Versprechung" 46; Pflaum, "Kampf"; "Ein Filmland" 4; Jacobsen 558; Pascheck, qtd. in Freyermuth 30). CGE was favored by Treuhand from the start, supposedly because of its previous experience and involvement in film production in France, the one country in Europe with a healthy film industry. It seems, however, that CGE was never really committed to promoting film production at the studios. If CGE had thought that Babelsberg had potential as a lucrative film production center, which was what it suggested before the deal was finalized, it would not have sold the majority of its shares in CIP to real estate developers. Apparently, by the time of the sale the new owner's expertise was more in property development than in media and film production as had been presumed. The emphasis placed upon film production when DEFA was privatized may have been nothing more than a diversion.

In the second half of the 1990s, Studio Babelsberg's salvation has been in the new multimedia services it is now equipped to provide. The complex's digitized facilities for sound recording, postproduction, special effects, and animation are in greater demand than one could have anticipated around the time of the sale. Whereas previously, if a filmmaker like Wim Wenders wanted digitized processing on one of his films, he would have had to go to London, now he can take his project to Babelsberg:

since its refurbishing and modernization, its digitized technology is considered to be among the best in the world (Hickethier, "Babelsberg im Aufwind" 9).

In the late 1990s it is clear that the Babelsberg complex is more dependent on multimedia endeavors and television productions than on large-scale European or American coproductions. To date, the studios have not managed to establish themselves as "Europe's answer to Hollywood," as Volker Schlöndorff had hoped. The studios have ultimately benefited from the boom in production of local television series. At least since 1996, "the average viewing figures for German film and television series was higher than for . . . American films and series: broadcasters turned to strengthened local productions" (Hickethier, "Babelsberg im Aufwind" 7). The late 1990s saw the production of a number of soap operas at Babelsberg. For example, after the thousandth episode of the successful television series *Gute Zeiten, schlechte Zeiten,* viewed daily by 5 million spectators, the production was transferred to the Babelsberg complex.

Many production companies have been drawn to Babelsberg and the studio's immediate neighborhood. Knut Hickethier attributes the growth of the complex not so much to the support of eastern television broadcaster Ostdeutschen Rundfunk Brandenburg, "one of the smallest of broadcasters in Germany, which only occasionally manages to get its own productions into [the nationally transmitted, West German based] ARD program," but rather to the commercial, transnational broadcaster RTL, whose involvement in the studios has marked a turnaround at Babelsberg ("Babelsberg in Aufwind" 8). Since it was established in 1985, RTL Plus is renowned for its extremely high percentage of popular entertainment and its heavy programming of fiction films and telemovies. As I noted earlier, behind RTL Plus and its various branches is the Bertelsmann group. Bertelsmann, partner in production with CIP at Babelsberg, owns one of Germany's most powerful publishing ventures. Bertelsmann's handling of the "Doubleday-Deal" in late 1986 made it the largest media concern in the world at the time, with extensive film, television, and video-branch engagement throughout Germany and Europe.

Bertelsmann's own film production company, Ufa Film and Television Productions, has certainly patronized Babelsberg studio's new facilities and services. Software for broadcasting is without doubt in demand for commercial services like RTL Plus, RTL 1, RTL 2, Sat 1, Sat 2, and Sat 3. The great German media moguls Bertelsmann and Kirch are capitalizing on their involvement at Babelsberg studios, where they have vested interests, even if their commitment may be stronger to producing software for television than to bolstering film production. As partners in "new media" expansion and proliferation in the old states of the Federal

Republic, Bertelsmann and Kirch have substantial holdings in the massive West German Springer consortium. Taking these interests into consideration, it seems that Bertelsmann and Kirch's involvement at Babelsberg has little to do with a need to support local film culture or to nurture young filmmakers who emerge from the Konrad Wolf Film School, part of the studio complex. Bertelsmann has been more involved with cable television and transnational, commercial broadcasting, at least over the last decade and a half.

The affiliation of CIP, Bertelsmann, and Kirch puts Babelsberg studios in a whole other league, far distant from the DEFA days. It is now part of a European arena, in competition with other state-of-the-art multimedia service centers like North Rhine–Westfalia: DEFA heritage and tradition have little relevance to the broader Euro-vista that the new owners and investors at Babelsberg have sought to exploit and expand. As is the case elsewhere, "film" has become an advertisement for what backers have really invested in: "a television and video programme . . . a video game, a lunch-box, a theme park ride." (Bertelsmann has already invested more in the Diana theme park on the Babelsberg site than the owners originally paid for the studio complex and surrounding land.) Kirch, Bertelsmann, and company are aware that films shown in the cinema are mostly an advertisement for the more lucrative "back end" of the market—the "ancillary exploitation of the film on various forms of television and other media [such as DVD and high-definition television]—video rental and sales, pay and basic cable, broadcast television and satellite transmission" etc. (Schamus 94). Accordingly, in terms of potential profit, film is one of the least predictable media branches developed at Babelsberg. In contrast to the days of DEFA, it is only of peripheral relevance to the studios.

CHAPTER 4

DEFA—Das Ende für Alle /
The End for Everyone

Banished with the privatization of the studios, the cultural heritage of DEFA no longer had a place in the Babelsberg studio scenario. The Treuhand chief, Detlef Rohweder, recognized what was at stake for East German film culture when he claimed: "Now that we are taking away everything from those in the east, at least we should leave them DEFA, because it is there that the consciousness of East Germany finds its artistic expression" (qtd. in Freyermuth 16).

It is clear that in the realm of film, as in every area of business in unified Germany, in the early 1990s easterners "were welcomed as consumers," but they weren't necessarily "needed as producers" (Dalichow, "Wettlauf der Zwerge" 21). The European market vision optimistically promoted at Babelsberg was one with which DEFA filmmakers and technicians had little experience. The insulation and provincialism that characterized most GDR cinema was far removed from the international, glossy Euro-films Schlöndorff sought to promote. Bärbel Dalichow puts the blame squarely on Schlöndorff: "he talks continuously of the Americans, of English-language scripts, of gigantic ateliers, of international casts, of European thinking—but who knows how 'the' Europeans think or how they ought to think apart from him?" ("Von den Mühen" 437). Local filmmakers may have had reason to feel excluded from the studios that once provided them with their livelihood when the new manager was quoted as reasoning that "A studio as great as this is not meant for Brandenburg films. Not even for German . . . And thank God for that. Otherwise Europe or even half the world would be exposed to bad German film" (qtd. in Freyermuth 56).

DEFA's directors, authors, and technicians have, by and large, been defeated in the reunification of Germany. Once the studios were taken over, former employees of DEFA were obliged to compete with West Germans on West German terms and to adjust to the vicissitudes of a hostile market and a foreign funding system. Considering the advanced age of many DEFA filmmakers and that those who worked at the studios had been cut off from developments and trends in western filmmaking for decades, it remained to be seen how willing (or able) they would be to adapt to western conceptions of spectacle, narration, and genre.

A sense of helplessness prevailed among former DEFA directors as they grappled with the complexities and intricacies of the Federal Republic's funding network (to name a few adjustments they faced: they had to adapt to a decentralized production and subvention system; unused to raising budgets, they had to seek funding from a perplexingly diverse range of subsidy agencies, many of which have differing criteria for loans, awards, and bonuses; and they also had to familarize themselves with the tax concessions that quality ratings brought to filmmakers in the west while fathoming complicated copyright rulings and distribution deals). For many former DEFA filmmakers, unification resulted in a type of demotion from being part of a cultural elite to being unwelcome second-class citizens in a land with incomprehensible customs. East German author and scriptwriter Thomas Knauf commented on the sense of bewilderment that afflicted East German filmmakers immediately before the sale of DEFA: "The GDR cinema is being wrapped up: our past is being denied and with it our future. . . . Almost all projects from former GDR filmmakers are being rejected by film subsidy in Bonn. It is actually like this: in the west no one knows DEFA filmmakers, and those who were known, no one wants to hear about any more . . . but nowadays they carry on as if they can't remember us any more" (qtd. in "Ein Filmland" 5). The state-sponsored system in which East German filmmakers had to learn to operate is one that was not only alien to them, but one to which many consider they are not granted reasonable access. For some the Federal Republic's funding network is an enigma they fear they will never comprehend. As the well-known GDR director Heiner Carow attested: "I don't know the people on the [funding] committees. No one has breathed a word as to why my scripts have been rejected" (qtd. in Freyermuth 40). Jörg Foth, director of *Letztes aus der Da Daer* (*Last from the Da Daer,* 1990), talks of the disorientation and isolation many ex-DEFA directors have faced in unified Germany:

> Now all the eastern filmmakers are caught up with their solitary struggles. We are the guests within this system. It is not the film culture we grew up with. People at the Ministry of the Interior and the Film Subsidy Board would rather work with people they know. They used to be supportive, but not any more. (Personal interview, Berlin, 18 Oct. 1993)

Western committee members allocating subsidy money and quality ratings may be uncertain how to evaluate films from the east. Some decision-making committees

> comprised exclusively of members from the old federal states . . . [have] obvious difficulties understanding and interpreting the images, metaphors, emotions, meanings, and montage sequences [of eastern films]. Emotional states and relations are recorded differently over here and there [in the west]. The qualities of a film should not be underestimated just because they are other than what is expected. ("Wessis über Ossis" 42)

This lack of understanding and insight into the conventions of representation in the east and eastern vision may have resulted in East German film projects and productions being discriminated against by funding organizations and quality rating boards in the west. In 1992, the East German media journal *Film und Fernsehen* reported cases in which three outstanding late DEFA films were refused quality ratings by the FBW (the Filmbewertungstelle Wiesbaden/Film Evaluation Board in Wiesbaden: if a film is awarded a quality rating, it is exempt from otherwise compulsory entertainment tax levies). The critically acclaimed *Banale Tage* (*Banal Days,* 1991) was rejected by the Board because its portrait of the destruction of the GDR "wallowed in self-pity." Similarly, Thomas Heise's film *Eisenzeit* (*Iron Age,* 1992), a documentary about disillusionment and protest among a group of youths from Eisenhüttenstadt, the first "Socialist town" in the GDR, was criticized because "the film provokes sympathy rather than awakening understanding" of the plight of eastern youth. The third film, *Östliche Landschaft* (*Eastern Landscape,* 1992) was refused the quality rating of "valuable" or "especially valuable," because "the evaluation committee could not understand all of the symbols" used in this film, which also addressed the disintegration of the socialist state and depicted the GDR as the garbage dump of history ("Wessis über Ossis" 42–43).

Since unification, ex-DEFA filmmakers and Nachwuchs have been expected to make films that appeal to committees and audiences with a different Weltanschauung; a population that, for the larger part, has been "conspicuously uninterested in everything related to the GDR and what came from there along with what has been there" (Blunk 107). The general public in the west has displayed an aversion to or ignorance of the cultural traditions associated with DEFA studios. East German cinema was never something with which the broad population of the Federal Republic was familiar, and the situation is hardly one that unification has altered. Harry Blunk has explained:

Feature films from the German Democratic Republic were and are largely unknown in the "old" Federal Republic. There are several reasons for this: during the long years of the cold war these films weren't shown in the west at all, [after which] they were hardly screened at all in the Federal Republic. (In the 1970s and 1980s television stations took over and broadcast a considerable number, but as far as viewers were concerned, it wouldn't have always been clear that these productions were about the GDR.) (107)

With the exception of a few films like *The Legend of Paul and Paula, Solo Sunny,* or *Winter Ade,* known perhaps to film enthusiasts in the Federal Republic, DEFA films have been ignored by the West German public. Discussing the reception of *Solo Sunny* in West Germany, one historian writes: "Without doubt, in the FRG a film from the GDR is still more exotic than films from Canada or Australia: in addition the film would mostly be judged in terms of western commercial criteria which don't relate to the film, and because of this some of its qualities have to remain unrecognized" (Klunker 136).

Although fleeting interest was given to a package of shelved films shown at the Berlin Film Festival in 1990, eastern films have had little critical or public resonance in unified Germany. The screening of the shelved films, banned by the SED in 1965, was viewed as a highlight of the Berlinale that year, and excitement surrounded their "unshelving." Yet this event was prompted by more than West German curiosity about a film culture that was to them foreign. Apart from whatever genuine interest in film history these features generated, in the west they may have provided an opportunity to emphasize the repressiveness and intolerance of the GDR state. To viewers in the west who are unfamiliar with the cultural politics of the SED, it is not immediately apparent why the films were banned in the first place. Moreover, the screening of these 1960s films provided further opportunity to identify GDR film culture as thwarted and deficient, insofar as the shelved films could be cited as proof that in the GDR, film was not allowed to realize its full potential. As Thomas Elsaesser and Michael Wedel observe, had the shelved films "not existed, [they] would have to be invented by the West" (2). Although a handful of late DEFA films have been singled out for Federal Film Prizes—*Der Tangospieler* (*The Tango Player,* 1991), *Verreigelte Zeit* (*Locked Up Time,* 1990), and *The Country behind the Rainbow*—they have been ignored by the public, whereas the western press tends to have dismissed these films or subjected them to harsh criticism (Heinz Kersten, H. G. Pflaum, Wilhelm Roth, and Stephan Lux have, however, treated this cinema more kindly).

East German films with local directors, stars, crews, and funding did not fare well at the box office after unification and throughout the 1990s. To date only one East German film, *Sonnenallee* (discussed in chapter 1), has attracted mass audiences in unified Germany. The West German market could barely manage to accommodate the sixty to seventy local films produced each year, let alone more films from the ex-GDR. Prospects for German film attracting healthy attendance figures were poor in the Federal Republic, even before unification. In the late 1980s, West Germans attended the cinema less frequently than the British, French, Italians, and Spanish (Klingsporn, *Filmstatistisches Taschenbuch 1991* 52–53). In a good year, less than a handful of films from the Federal Republic generated substantial profits at the local box office. Because the works of filmmakers like Ulrike Ottinger, Werner Nekes, and Helma Sanders-Brahms have been generally better received in France than in Germany, these Autoren have focused on the export market rather than the domestic and have sometimes shot their films in French. The precarious situation for German film on the local market did not improve immediately after unification. By 1990 the American share of the German market had escalated to 85 percent (Koll, "Deutsche Kinofilm" 8), more than double the 1979 figure ("Jammer statt" 155). Throughout the 1980s and into the 1990s, whenever there has been a substantial decline in attendance figures, it was German films rather than American films that suffered (Neckermann 114). In bad years, the German share of the local market has slumped to 10 percent or slightly less. If West German films have had to strain to attract a paying audience in the old federal states, the situation for East German films in unified Germany has been considerably worse.

Germans tend to spurn their own films. In the first half of the 1990s, only a meager number of German films were major box-office successes attracting 3 million viewers or more out of a total population of 81 million. Included in this group of profitable films are the two comedies *Pappa ante Portas* (1990) and *Werner Beinhart* (1990), Helmut Dietl's farce about the forging of the Hitler diaries, *Schtonk!* (1992), and *Das Geisterhaus* (*House of Spirits,* 1993). Throughout the 1990s, the overwhelming majority of German box-office successes were West German productions or international coproductions. Phenomenally popular comedies like *Der bewegte Mann* (*A Most Desirable Man,* 1996), *Männerpension* (1996), and *Das Superweib* (*The Super-Wife,* 1996) are among the most profitable films of the decade. By Hollywood standards these are modest productions that drew in excess of 3 million spectators (*Super-Wife* was viewed by closer to 2.5 million viewers).

In 1997, three West German films were among the top ten box-office hits in the country (*Knockin' on Heaven's Door, Rossini oder die mörder-*

ische Frage, wer schläft mit wem / Rossini or the Deadly Question of Who Sleeps with Whom, and *Das kleine Arschlock / The Little Arse-Hole,* each of which attracted more than 3 million viewers). Box-office returns for West German films were cause for jubilation in 1996 and 1997: Sönke Wortmann's life-style comedy *A Most Desirable Man* exceeded all possible expectations when it drew more than 6 million viewers to local cinemas. In 1996 the German share of the local market increased to a healthy 18 percent, whereas in the first quarter of 1997, the figure was as much as 37 percent ("Die Stunde" 12).

The runaway box office success of a number of West German films— mostly life-style comedies—did not, however, appease many German critics. Rarely showing fondness for their own cinema, local critics continue to lament the "misery of the German film" as they have been doing for decades. Depending on whom you listen to, the state of German film in the late 1990s aroused either euphoria or discontent. "The euphoria is economic and the discontent is of a cultural nature; the proponents of both positions are as distant from one another as art and economics" (see Blen and Jung 18).

No features from directors who worked at DEFA in the 1980s and no films from DEFA Nachwuchs have enjoyed such box-office success as the West German features mentioned above.[1] The majority of late DEFA films released after the disintegration of the GDR appear to have attracted less than 25,000 spectators each, a figure that *Der Spiegel* categorized as constituting a *Totalflop* ("Jammer statt" 154). This means that even the most celebrated of the former GDR's directors, such as Heiner Carow, Frank Beyer, and Roland Gräf, failed to make profitable films after unification.

That so many DEFA films made in the late 1980s and early 1990s dealt with problems specific to the GDR precluded their appeal to audiences anywhere once the country was absorbed by the Federal Republic. These films were all the more obscure because when they commented on life in the GDR they did so abstrusely, and that life was in any case foreign to those in the capitalist west. For potential audiences in the old states of the Federal Republic, these films used a *Bildsprache* (pictorial language) that was largely indecipherable and referred to experiences, events, and ideals into which those in the west had little or no insight.

Films that sought to critically examine the characteristics and short-comings of GDR society and the reasons for its collapse were not especially popular with German cinema audiences in the first half of the 1990s.

---

1. Leander Haumann originated from the theater, and *Sonnenallee* was his directorial debut.

Many in the west saw that their taxes were paying for unification and found neither comfort nor amusement in films that even vaguely reminded them of this national commitment. On the other hand, unification dramas and documentaries were often ignored by the general public in the east, most of whom were tired of the DEFA tradition of the problem film and reminders of the failure of "Real Existing Socialism." When eastern filmmakers reflected upon unification itself, the perspectives they took were not always relevant or of interest to those in the west.

The Reception of Late DEFA Films

Late DEFA films, conceptualized during the Wende or at the start of the 1990s, faced major problems that they never managed to surmount. A number struggled to secure distribution. Whatever their merit or historical value, these films were box-office poison. "Without judging their artistic quality, one can establish that for 1990/1991 just about all the films from DEFA which managed to make it into the cinema after the Wende could-n't succeed anyway, let alone find a niche there" (Radevagen 198). Late DEFA features such as *Miraculi* waited two years before finding a distributor (after its premiere at the Berlinale in 1991), and once *Miraculi* found its way into the cinema, it only had a run of five days ("Bundesstart").

Even finely crafted productions directed by the GDR's most esteemed directors, such as Roland Gräf's *The Tango Player* (an adaptation of a Christoph Hein story), performed poorly at the German box office. *The Tango Player* is worth considering, on the basis of the adversity and ill fortune it faced alone. Its case provides some insight into the historic obstacles GDR films faced once Germany was unified. Although a great deal of faith was placed in the future of this production, like other late DEFA films, it was doomed by the context from which it emerged. *The Tango Player* could never have been completed under the old regime, but it lost much of its poignancy and resonance when released after the Wende. The last day of the film's shooting corresponded to the day in which the deutsche mark was introduced as the new currency of the GDR (Dalichow, "Letzte Kapitel" 332). Heinz Kersten notes that relative to other DEFA productions shot after the collapse of the GDR, *The Tango Player* was "the most successful of all DEFA productions of the year" ("Pessimismus").

The distributor for *The Tango Player,* Progress, was especially optimistic about the film, indicating that its prospects were favorable, with most regional film organizations having signaled interest in the film. The distributor's optimism was, however, short-lived. *Coming Out* (1989) and the previously banned *Spur der Steine* (*Mark of Stones*) had already been struck off the screening lists in eastern cinemas, a move that was thought to be a final blow for DEFA films (Junghänel). Further disappointment followed. Exhibitors in the east canceled their bookings of *The Tango Player* as "American films began their triumphant journey through East Germany" (Dalichow, "Von den Mühen" 332). *The Tango Player*'s commercial release coincided with Treuhand's privatization of cinemas in the east, and the film only attracted 7,228 viewers during the period January through April 1991 ("Begrenzte Freude"). By the time *The Tango Player* reached theaters, cinema owners had realized that they could make more money selling popcorn than from screening DEFA films ("Kino mit Popcorn").

Other late DEFA productions received even less critical attention in the western press, and public response was less favorable still. None of the late DEFA productions came close to breaking even at the box office. *Krücke,* an adaptation of Peter Härtling's novel set at the end of World War II, was only viewed by 642 spectators in the six months after its premiere in January 1993 ("Black Box" 12). The Wende comedy *Farssmann oder zu Fuß in die Sackgasse* (*Farssmann or by Foot to the Dead End,* 1991), the unification comedy *Der Brocken* (*Rising to the Bait,* 1992), and Heiner Carow's literary adaptation of Werner Heiduczek's German-German love story, *Verfehlung* (*Missing,* 1992), strained to attract a viewing public. *Cosimos Lexicon* (1992), another East German feature addressing the impact of unification in the east, attracted a meager total of 4,636 viewers ("Dick und Doof" 213).

These films were further disadvantaged when they were released, in that whether they struggled to find distribution or not, they usually appeared "hopelessly outmoded" by the time they reached the cinema (Radevagen 198). Thomas Til Radevagen comments on the context out of which these films emerged:

> With the change from one system to another . . . film projects that began before the Wende became wastepaper. A lot of the films produced after the Wende are introverted analyses of changed relations. [Those relations are] examined on a highly intellectual level—they aren't a big hit with the public or of public significance. (197)

For Bärbel Dalichow, the late DEFA films that sought to be topical were doomed: "Although alterations were made during the process of shooting, blueprints for films lost their relevance within a couple of weeks. In relation to this reality [the tumultuous lead-up to unification], film production moved more slowly than a dying dinosaur" ("Letzte Kapitel" 330). Even the most compelling and accomplished of these films, like *The Tango*

Player, Jana und Jan (Jana and Jan, 1992), and *Verlorene Landschaft (Lost Landscape,* 1992), remain relegated to the absolute margins of German film history, where they constitute an archive of "unknown German films" (Dalichow, "Letzte Kapitel" 333). No matter how astute critically acclaimed films such as *Banal Days* were in their depictions of the unrest and dissatisfaction that led to the Wende, by the time they were released, the events they referred to were distant, if not dim memories: "Like some other DEFA productions . . . [*Banal Days*] came too late to be able to find a broad public. It went completely under in German cinemas. The grotesque experiences of both youths [depicted in the film] may have been taken as a piece of subversion in the old GDR, but today they have an anachronistic effect" (*Fischer* 29–30).

Structural changes to the media landscape in the eastern states clearly worked to the disadvantage of local film. Unification resulted in the upheaval of the film market in the east; changing patterns of distribution, exhibition, and consumption of film in the former GDR made it virtually impossible for indigenous film to find a place or an audience in the new federal states. But there is more. Any film that was released in the early 1990s found itself in a marketplace in which another currency was circulating. The introduction of the deutsche mark to the former GDR meant that East Germans had to pay much more to attend the cinema. In 1990, when the price of cinema tickets more than tripled in the GDR, attendance fell by 40 percent (Wiedemann, "Wo bleiben die Kinobesucher?" 81; Böhmer). The cost of viewing films increased from 1.50 east marks to 6.50 deutsche marks—and even the higher price was a type of concession ticket for East Germans. These concessions were applied in the East and in West Berlin cinemas and were meant to compensate for the low wages East Germans earned at the time. (For those who lived in the old states of the Federal Republic, attending the cinema was more expensive, ranging between 8 and 11 DM.) Declining attendance figures in the east were attributed to Currency Union by at least one analyst (I. K. Wetzel). The privatization of cinemas, which occurred in the middle of 1991, was another major hurdle that DEFA films failed to negotiate, a matter I will discuss shortly.

Even before unification was legislated, East German directors could no longer rely upon compatriots to attend the screenings of their films. The audiences that once viewed their films continued to curtail their visits to the cinema so that by 1991 East Germans only made up around 11 percent of the total cinema viewing public in united Germany. Not only was the population in the west four times higher than in the former GDR, but West Germans attended the cinema twice as often as those in the east at this time.

Diminished eastern attendance in turn restricted access to East German film. The exhibition of East German film in GDR cinemas decreased within a period of months after the collapse of the Wall. Frank Junghänel reported that even by July 1990, DEFA films were a scarcity in local cinemas. He observed that the "Camera" screenings, which were a feature of six major cinemas across the GDR, were discontinued. "Camera" programs showcased eastern bloc films, silents, DEFA films, and samples of various national cinemas. Two weeks after Currency Union the *Ostsee Zeitung* reported that the Leipzig film theater, "Casino, the most profiled and committed film theater in the GDR, only plays its Camera program once a week. . . . Lovers of European art cinema [now] have to look for films of their taste with a magnifying glass. . . . Fans of GDR cinema are even harder hit."

Critical Reception

Of the West German critics who bothered to attend to late DEFA films or those made by East Germans in the early 1990s, extremely few did so with much tolerance or benevolence. Here again one may take *The Tango Player* as an example. Although the production showed promise of positive critical reception since it was a literary adaptation from a controversial novel that embodied the Wende zeitgeist, had been made by a top-ranking East German director, and starred one of the GDR's best actors, Michael Gwisdek, most western critics were either dismissive of the film or treated it especially harshly. In the western press, *The Tango Player* suffered the critical fate of most late DEFA films. As Bärbel Dalichow recalled, "no one in the west felt impressed [by the film]" ("Letzte Kapitel" 333). When it premiered at the Berlin Film Festival in 1991, *The Tango Player* was said to be "as honorable as it is harmless" by the *Berlinale Tip,* whereas the *Frankfurter Rundschau* described the film as "a rambling series of events, devoid of passion and reveling in self-pity" ("self-pitying" being the criticism the Film Evaluation Board made when it refused to award other East German films "Quality Ratings"). The *Tageszeitung* also viewed *The Tango Player* negatively and accused it of indulging in "deceptive nostalgia" (Dalichow, "Letzte Kapitel" 333). It took the sensibility of East German critic Fred Gehler to recognize that *The Tango Player* featured "an exemplary figure of German history" and invited comparison with Franz Biberkopf's epic, *Berlin Alexanderplatz* (Dalichow, "Letzte Kapitel" 333).

However, even less ambitious films that sought entertainment value through depictions of the dilemmas and experiences of East Germans during unification (the Trabi films*, Cosimos Lexicon, Farssmann or by Foot to the Dead End, Burning Life*) appeared to be beneath the contempt of many

West German critics. And West German critics were not alone in their disapproval of East German film. Once the GDR collapsed, some East German critics began to scrutinize local film in an especially ruthless fashion. Perhaps because they had previously been held accountable to the SED and were restricted from making candid criticisms of Party cultural policy and the films it fostered, some eastern writers were dismissive of DEFA films or treated them with ambivalence or a measure of disdain (see, for example, the writings of Thomas Knauf, Bärbel Dalichow, and Oksana Bulgakowa). Sibylle Licht explains that by 1990, East German journalists were among the harshest critics of this cinema. "East colleagues' treatment of DEFA productions of 1989 and 1990 was noticeably more radical. What was bad was bad, and flops were flops." Evaluating the critics' positions, she sides with them in concluding that "films from 1989 and 1990 appeared hopelessly outdated, even from another world" (107). Licht goes on to comment that "an unforeseen malice resonated in many of the West German critics' commentaries and reports about the decline of East German, state subsidized art, including film art. Whereas in the East German [commentaries] outrage and powerlessness dominated" (109).

DEFA Film in the 1990s

For those involved in filmmaking in the GDR, unification resulted in the demise of their film and television industries and ejection from the only studio system they had known. When the GDR collapsed, DEFA filmmakers were plunged into another moribund industry where market restrictions on locally produced and European films were already severe. By the start of the 1990s the import of European films diminished to the point of insignificance in the Federal Republic, whereas the market for German film had also shrunk. DEFA films were disadvantaged by their curious status as German *and* imports to the Federal Republic. East Germans faced adaptation to a market that barely accommodated its own film and in which imports of and distribution returns for everything other than American film was in steady decline. Whereas in the 1970s, French films had a 10 percent share of the German market, by the end of the 1980s that figure dropped on average to under 5 percent. The situation was worse for Italian film on the German market, which fell from a 13 percent share in the 1970s to under 1 percent in 1988 and 1989. Imports from all other countries (except Great Britain whose share of the German market fluctuated from year to year) had also been subject to drastic reductions (Neckermann 111), and the pattern is one that was consolidated, at least in the early 1990s (Klingsporn, *Filmstatistisches Taschenbuch 1992* 7). East German film had no established niche to occupy in the old states of the Federal Republic. Throughout the 1980s, films from Hong Kong were far more prevalent and profitable on the West German market than DEFA films. Even the importation of Australian films to the Federal Republic exceeded those coming from the Democratic Republic throughout that decade (Klingsporn, *Filmstatistisches Taschenbuch 1991* 37, 28). Moreover, despite the GDR's proximity to the Federal Republic and a shared language, throughout the 1970s and 1980s almost three times more Japanese films than East German films were distributed in the Federal Republic (Neckermann 110). In short, DEFA films had an even slimmer chance on the market in unified Germany than West German films.

It is no wonder that easterners floundered and were disoriented as they attempted to adjust to the Federal Republic's bewildering, decentered funding system. As I have suggested, former DEFA filmmakers were not always welcomed by those who were part of the film industry in the west and the infrastructure of the state that supported it. For their part, many filmmakers from the old federal states dreaded the arrival of disenfranchised, unemployed newcomers whom they suspected would threaten local employment and drain film subsidy funds that they themselves depended upon.

The Federal Republic's subsidy network, a system that Alexander Kluge once described as functioning like capitalism without money (filmmakers saw neither the money the state invested nor profits from their films), presented unimaginable obstacles for filmmakers from the east. Even though state intervention in film culture in the former GDR was often erratic, East German filmmakers were unprepared for the irregularity and uncertainty of the Federal Republic's marketplace. Unification brought with it total dependency upon a long-standing, state-sponsored film industry that rationalized its own existence arbitrarily, now in terms of artistic, now on its commercial merit. Neither of these criteria was commonly evoked in GDR cinema, and so unusual were they that features distinguished by their presence—*Die Mördere sind unter uns* (*Murderers among Us,* 1946), *Der Untertan* (*The Subservient,* 1951), *The Russians Are Coming, Mark of Stones, The Legend of Paul and Paula, Solo Sunny*)—were legends of GDR film history. Very few filmmakers accustomed to DEFA tradition seem to have been capable of making the adjustments of vision and principle necessary for survival in unified Germany. For them it was too late. "The future has been sold out" (Dalichow, "DEFA" 11).

Unification has not meant a new beginning for the majority of artists and filmmakers from the ex-GDR: for many of them the Wall *was* positively a protective barrier. Its dismantling restricted rather than enhanced the career prospects of most of the technicians and artists who worked at DEFA. Since the regime disintegrated, the futures of the GDR's most innovative and internationally esteemed filmmakers have been jeopardized. Unification has resulted in the discontinuation of many directors' careers, even those who, in their films, were critical of the old regime. Heiner Carow was one such figure. Despite his exceptional popularity in the former GDR, he was unable to make a film in unified Germany, and up until the time of his death in 1997, he saw his future restricted to the production of television series (Becker viii). However rich the history of DEFA may have been, it is of minimal consequence to the film culture of unified Germany. What in the east was glorified as the tradition and heritage of DEFA has been breezily dismissed as myth in the west (Freyermuth 60; Dalichow, "Von den Mühen" 436).

With the new federal states requiring an annual infusion of 180 billion DM in the early 1990s to ensure the subsistence of its population and the modernization of industry, buttressing eastern film production was not an immediate priority. And in any case, artists, authors, technicians, and directors from the former GDR lost the industrial framework within which they had operated. The television stations they used to work for were closed down, the film studios were sold, and they can no longer be assured of state patronage, for even the state film subsidy system that operates in the regions of Brandenburg and Berlin invests on average in one eastern film project for every seven supported from the west ("Erfolg" 8).

The process of unification is one that, in "erasing the history of the G.D.R. and the very idea of socialism" (Schöfer 205), has expedited the disintegration of its cultural tradition. "The collapse of the GDR has pushed its films into an abyss. DEFA films will only ever be shown in retrospectives. The significance those films once had will not be regained again" (Gersch 323). The GDR cinema was fraught with idiosyncrasies: uncannily, to examine its film culture is to contemplate the history of a country that no longer exists. The closure of this period of film history is absolute.

The Impact of Unification on Cultural Life and the Media Landscape in the Former GDR

> Once the initial euphoria over unification subsides, it will become painfully clear that not only did two states spring up on either side of the Wall, but two cultures as well, and two different ways of life. We can't yet say how much of each will disappear and how much will survive. For now, one thing is certain: . . . [Germany's] neighbours aren't the only ones who need to fear a unification that may wipe out every difference. (P. Schneider 41)

Now that the *Traum* (dream) of unification has for many turned into a *Trauma,* and the monuments of East German history have, like the state, been dismantled forever, the cultural heritage of the former GDR has been largely obliterated. East Germans' access to, involvement with, and generation of local culture was harshly curtailed under unification at least in the early 1990s. The closure of local cinemas, theaters, and concert halls disfigured the cultural landscape of the GDR. Even by the end of 1991, in Brandenburg it was evident that "if the Berlin Philharmonic wanted to give a free concert there wouldn't be an open-air arena [suitable]. The whole region is sold out. There is no longer an auditorium where people can congregate" (Weis).

The severity of changes to cultural life in the former GDR is evident if one recalls that under the old regime, theater, opera, film production, distribution, and exhibition, together with the costs of running cinemas and film clubs, were fully subsidized by the state. Subvention of the established arts and (what in the west are classified as) popular cultural forms was comprehensive in the old GDR. In contrast to the west, theater, opera, ballet, and film were accessible and inexpensive as far as the broad general public of the GDR was concerned. When that subvention diminished in the early 1990s, eastern incomes hardly permitted the exorbitant cost of these cultural experiences. "Variety in cultural life in the east is now something only those with money can afford. People who have a monthly income of less than 2,500 marks at their disposal feel excluded from cultural life" (Hilmer and Müller-Hilmer, "Es wächst zusammen" 20). By the latter half of 1993, around 50 percent of eastern households were in this low income bracket (Hilmer and Müller-Hilmer, "Die Stimmung" 17).

Easterners were understandably displeased over what they saw as the inhibition of their cultural lives in the early 1990s: two out of three East Germans surveyed in an opinion poll conducted around the third anniversary of reunification complained that their involvement with culture had deteriorated since Germany had united (Hilmer and Müller-Hilmer, "Die Stimmung" 20). Here "cultural life" is understood to encompass activities such as theater attendance, recitals, cabaret performances, concerts, involvement in film clubs, and going to the cinema or the opera.

Evidently cinema played a central role in that cultural life, with attendance being especially high: it is reported that East Germans attended the cinema around five times per year per head of population. Film was a cheap form of entertainment with the price of a cinema ticket "varying from between 1.20 and 1.80 marks (mostly 1.50 marks) . . . about half the cost of a pack of cigarettes" (Lacher-Remy 26). Children were catered to by a wealth of films from East German and eastern bloc countries, which they could view for a nominal cost of 25 pfennig. The accessibility of film was further enhanced by the existence of cinemas in sparsely populated, provincial regions; 53 percent percent of cinemas operated in towns with populations of 20,000 or less (Klingsporn, *Filmstatistisches Taschenbuch 1991* 15).

The sustained popularity of film was in part a consequence of the limited range of leisure time activities available in the GDR. As a *Mangelgesellschaft* (a society of shortage[s]) without a developed entertainment industry, the GDR had little to offer youths that were seeking distraction and amusement. There were no video games or amusement parlors housing electronic entertainment, pool halls were a rarity, and color television and video recorders were extravagances socialism did not indulge. Attending the cinema was an activity GDR youth preferred over watching television, playing sports or reading, and together with "meeting up with friends" was recorded as the most favored pastime in an early 1980s study by media analysts Lothar Bisky and Dieter Wiedemann (23).

The changes that unification brought to the media landscape of the old GDR were as swift as they were drastic. By 1992, cinema attendance in the east plummeted to 12 million, a spectacular decline if attendance in the GDR had ever been as high as 70 to 80 million. Privatization and the "rationalization" of exhibition meant that hundreds of cinemas in the GDR were closed because they were unprofitable after Monetary and Economic Union. Whereas in 1988 more than 800 cinemas were registered in the Democratic Republic, two years later almost 300 cinemas had closed down, and by October 1991, only 336 remained (Klingsporn, "Zur Lage" 794–805).

Before the Wende, residents of Thüringen, like many other East Germans, may have taken for granted the cinemas that operated in small towns across their state. Before unification 120 cinemas were registered in the region, but by 1993 there were only 45 (Weber 8). In Thüringen and the other four eastern Länder, local access to film was jeopardized not only by wholesale closure of provincial cinemas but also by the disbanding of hundreds of film clubs. Film clubs had been a vital part of film culture in the former GDR. Just about all middle-size towns had such clubs, which were a popular attraction not only in high schools, sports halls, universities, and "cultural houses," but also in business organizations throughout the country. Apart from its 120 functioning cinemas, Thüringen had, for example, between 50 and 80 established film clubs before unification (Weber 8). Most film clubs had no option other than to disband after the fall of the Wall. When films were distributed by the state-owned company, Progress, hundreds of film clubs throughout the GDR were relieved of the financial burden of film hire in that they were charged a nominal fee for the prints they screened—about 35 DM (Weber 9). In his 1991 survey of the Kinoszene in the new federal states, Joachim Kürten reports that whereas every effort was once made to ensure that even remote areas of the GDR had access to film, since the Wende, provincial cinemas were neglected and faced extinction (11).

Communal cinemas and film theaters located in the provinces had little hope of survival once the east's media landscape was remodeled. Repertoire cinemas (known as "Off-Kinos") in both the east and the west also faced extinction. In 1993, for instance, Frankfurt's only communal cinema was threatened with closure. As Johannes Klingsporn observed of Germany's dwindling art-house cinemas:

> Repertoire cinemas and art-house cinemas have been more heavily affected by changing social values than the rest of the film industry: the target groups for these cinemas, socially committed sorts of people [*sozial engagierte Typen*], are regarded as relics of the 1960s and 1970s [whereas] the hedonist represents today's life-style. . . . The programming styles of repertoire cinemas have [in the meantime] been partly copied by television. ("Zur Lage" 802)

Those exhibitors in the east who were committed to sustaining support for art cinema or for East German, central European, or non-American film were arguably the hardest and most swiftly hit within the first year of unification. In the short term, pornography proved to be highly profitable in East German cinemas and was accordingly favored by local exhibitors.

When the borders between East and West Germany were opened and the GDR's cinemas faced privatization, most of the country's cinemas did not meet western standards. They were considered antiquated, ill-equipped, uncomfortable, and run-down. The legendary and massive Babylon theater, for instance, suffered from inadequate heating: the projectionist was also responsible for stoking the coal furnace that was the cinema's sole source of heat. Further operation was hampered for some time after the cinema's ceiling collapsed. Only around one-quarter of GDR theaters were reported to be in good general condition when moves for privatization were under way (Hennings 4). Predictably, the cinemas in small and isolated towns were the first to close.

In contrast to West Germany, the vast majority of cinemas in the ex-GDR were in towns with relatively small populations. In his annual report issued at the end of 1991 (commissioned by the Spitzenorganisation der Filmwirtschaft), Klingsporn argued it was precisely these cinemas that had least chance of survival: cinemas in towns with populations of less than 50,000 people. More than two-thirds of the GDR's cinemas were in this category ("Zur Lage" 797–98).

Moreover, in relation to the west, where multiscreen cinemas and cinema complexes had proved to be more profitable, the former GDR had an extremely high proportion of single-screen cinemas, some 90 percent. In proportional terms this was three times the ratio of single-screen film theaters operating in Germany's west (Klingsporn, "Zur Lage" 796). The chances of East German cinemas surviving were further reduced by their seating capacities, which were much larger than those in the west. In 1991, "only 16 percent of cinemas in the west had a housing capacity of more than 300 seats, whereas in East Germany the figure remained at 40 percent" (Klingsporn, "Zur Lage" 796). Escalating real estate prices, along with increased rental costs, prompted the closure of yet more cinemas in the eastern provinces, whereas cinema multiplexes in and around the more heavily populated city centers mushroomed.

For audiences used to viewing films of diverse national origins, variety in film supply is another facet of eastern film culture that has been restricted since unification. East German films are relegated to the German film festival circuit, the fate of a whole range of unification comedies like *Adamski* (1993) and *Wer Zweimal lügt* (*Whoever Lies Twice,* 1993) and documentaries such as *Stau—jetzt geht's los*[2] (1992). Films like these rarely gain theatrical release in the east or west.

Reduction in diversity of film screenings was accompanied by a predictable level of concentration of ownership of cinemas throughout the east. Joachim Kürten remarked on the situation in the new federal states in 1991: "The great majority of large cinemas in city centers have been taken over by West German cinema chains. Only now and then does one come across a centrally located, solitary film theater leased to a cinema manager from the former GDR" (11). "Developers have their central company bases in the old federal states and as a rule there is no competition in the regions in which they buy cinemas" (Hennings 6).

The university town of Ilmenau can be cited as an example of the fate of cinemas in many middle-size East German towns. Previously, the town had two cinemas and around twenty films were shown each month. At one point in 1993 it was noted, "Now one single film (*Home Alone in New York*) . . . has been playing for four weeks in the remaining cinema" (Weber 10). One of the most immediate consequences of unification involved the flooding of East German cinemas with Hollywood films and recent releases from West Germany. This access to imported film was something that East Germans apparently welcomed, at least in the short

---

2. I know of no adequate translation for this title.

term. Millions turned their backs on East German and eastern bloc features in favor of western genre cinema throughout 1989 and 1990. With access to Hollywood films previously determined and limited by the Central Committee of the Communist Party, audiences were finally provided with greater opportunity to view withheld by-products of "western decadence and depravity." In ignoring East German films conceived at DEFA studios during the period of the Wende, the "new" citizens of the Federal Republic gravitated more toward imported commercial films that filled their remaining cinemas. They saw the sorts of blockbusters and imported films that were being viewed by mass audiences everywhere else in western Europe. East German audiences were attracted to films made with dollars and deutsche marks rather than those sponsored by GDR money, the currency that the population of the east scrapped in anticipation of unification. Radevagen recalls that East Germans had "access to all new films from the west by fall 1989 or by July 1990 at the latest." They were able to view films that they heard through watching West German television—films that they had previously been denied access to or that were long delayed in their local release "because of currency issues or on ideological grounds" (198).

Discussing changes in viewing patterns in the east, Radevagen emphasizes that during the Wende and in the time up until unification, East Germans were overwhelmed by a desire to "catch up" (195, 198). Catching up with western life-styles, standards, and attitudes was something East Germans could do more swiftly in the cinema than in their daily lives. DEFA films were hardly part of this process and may have been viewed, at least in the short term, as representative of what easterners were expected to leave behind: that is, relics of what was becoming a bygone and denigrated age. Relatively modest in budget and special effects, DEFA films had little chance of competing with Hollywood extravaganzas. DEFA films became the outsiders in a market where, for decades, they had been guaranteed a privileged place.

CHAPTER 5

Ost Fernsehen / East Television

Not only was East Germany's film industry demolished and its film culture overwhelmed, television broadcasting in the newly unified states was completely restructured in the early 1990s. The changes to "East German broadcasting turned out to be one of the most contentious of the many upheavals that the five new states were to experience in the year or so following unification" (Sandford 204).

It would be reasonable to suppose that if the East German broadcasting services, DFF (Deutscher Fernsehfunk), had continued to operate in unified Germany, the broadcasters would have provided employment for DEFA filmmakers, crews, and technicians and have ensured that the industry in the east was kept afloat through the production of telefilms. DFF could have provided a receptive environment for showcasing eastern films, together with a network for local filmmakers. It may have been able to provide production assistance to eastern filmmakers, investing in locally produced films like public broadcasters do in West Germany. Had DFF survived, it should have made East German filmmakers' futures more secure, not only by encouraging and promoting DEFA-oriented talent, but also by advancing common ideas about the purposes of screen production and what sort of programming East Germans would have wanted.

But those in the east had little control over how broadcasting would be organized once the ex-GDR became part of the new Germany. As with the film industry, revision to the broadcasting system in unified Germany was "almost exclusively one-sided": the changes to the eastern media were drastic, whereas in the west "things carried on in their own way" (Sandford 199). Moreover, the restructuring of East Television was orchestrated predominantly by West Germans; in fact, advisers to the Broadcasting Commissioner, Rudolf Mühlfenzl, were exclusively West German (Sandford 204).

The restructuring of East Television had further, disastrous repercussions for film production in the east, expediting the disintegration of the local film industry. As was the case with other studio complexes in Germany, throughout the 1980s DEFA studio's most important client was local television. "Normally DEFA produced about thirty films for television each year," whereas the studios produced between fifteen and twenty features per year for the cinema (Dalichow, "Wettlauf" 20). After the collapse of the GDR, contracts for the production of telefilms and television series became more important for the studio's survival than ever. Yet, after Currency Union, the future of Deutscher Fernsehfunk was even more uncertain than that of DEFA. With DFF concerned about its own prospects of survival, contracts between the East German broadcasters and DEFA were dissolved in 1991. This provided cause for complaint, because although the public broadcasters extracted 16 million DM in television fees from East German viewers, they were unwilling to invest in production in the east ("Die Vision"). For their part DFF "wanted to keep their own studios, those for television dramas . . . and for children's television, and their own staff for as long as possible" (Radevagen 197). Matters were exacerbated in the early 1990s by the refusal of potential West German clients, such as the public broadcasters ZDF, to supply DEFA with contracts.

Although audiences in the GDR were critical of the use the Party made of the electronic media, and public cynicism about many DFF programs was widespread, East Television still provided an important cultural reference point and Weltanschauung for East Germans. A comparable situation may be cited in Australia, where television viewers are critical of commercial services and state-supported public channels such as SBS and the ABC, even though they acknowledge that they still provide important and divergent cultural reference points. Many DFF programs attended to East German value systems, life experiences, and predicaments—preoccupations that were evidently of little consequence or meaning to broadcasters and audiences in the Federal Republic. Without wishing to become involved in deliberation over the aesthetic merit or quality of domestic television in the former GDR, I maintain that the restructuring East Television was subject to during unification entailed the erasure of a further component of GDR screen culture—after all, "quality" is not really a determining issue in discussion of West German television culture. Programs on West German television like *Man O Man, Tutti Frutti,* and *Flitterabend* have been ridiculed by many viewers, but no one would seriously contend that public and private stations should be disbanded because of these programs—or that they are superior to everything East Television produced.

Even though hope may have surrounded the democratization and reform of East Television, and those in the industry may have considered that unification brought with it a much welcomed opportunity to revise the principles and ethics of eastern broadcasting, reforms such as these did not take place. Any aspiration to fortify the integrity of East Television proved as futile as the ambition to secure East German access to and control over DEFA studios. Part of the motivation for disbanding DFF was to eradicate the origins and heinous effects of communism, but in eradicating East Television, cultural values representative of the east were also dismissed before East Germans had a chance to reassess their worth and relevance.

East Television: The Window in the Wall

Although GDR society was detached from the Federal Republic and its citizens were prohibited access to the west, East Germans still had a window through which they could observe their capitalist neighbors. West German television provided East Germans with a vantage point; it extended their vision beyond the Wall to the Federal Republic and to countries even more foreign and distant. Discussing viewing patterns in the GDR and television's role as an intermediary between the two Germanies, Helmut Hanke observed that West German television "was the only open window on the world, a window that, even during the cold war, was opened each evening in the living rooms of GDR citizens, letting in the messages of another richer, freer world, regions of longing to which the island of dreams referred" (Hanke 10).

Not only did East Germans eagerly turn to western television, they tended to watch more television than their neighbors in the Federal Republic (Hanke 13). Since the 1960s, about 80 percent of the GDR had been capable of receiving West German television. In the late 1980s, in particular 1989, current affairs and news reports presented by West Germany's public television stations provided insight into events in eastern bloc countries where communist regimes were disintegrating. Western television also provided information relating to the Soviet policies of glasnost and perestroika, policies that the Central Committee of the SED would not acknowledge. In the late 1980s, East Television's reluctance to address events that emerged as a result of growing political discontent in the GDR also prompted viewers to watch western television. If they relied solely upon the eastern media, they would be ignorant of the extent of Wende agitation throughout the GDR. In 1989, for instance, GDR citizens turned to western television for confirmation of the rumored mass exodus of East Germans fleeing to the Federal Republic. Moreover, during the period of the Wende, West German television continued to provide sympathetic insight into the sociopolitical upheavals that spread throughout the GDR. The western stations, rather than DFF, initially carried reports about demonstrations in the GDR and the peaceful, weekly Leipzig gatherings. DFF not only ignored such events, it even reported that the hundreds of thousands of GDR citizens who deserted the GDR as refugees in 1989 had in fact been expelled by the SED.

The information programs, the entertainment programs, and the "infotainment" series that were beamed from the Federal Republic to the GDR were generally already more popular than locally transmitted television. Clearly, the popularity of western television was a source of irritation to the ruling party of the Democratic Republic. The Politbüro actively sought to dissuade GDR citizens from watching West German television throughout the 1960s, but it did so without any success. In periods of revision of DFF (one in 1972, another eleven years later), the Party begrudgingly recognized western television's ability to attract eastern viewers. Gerhard Wettig recalls the repercussions of the first period of reform when the SED conceded that west television was appealing to East Germans:

> Early in 1973, a secret public opinion survey, conducted by an institute of the SED central committee apparatus, finally made clear that official efforts to discourage people from watching [West German broadcasts] had utterly failed. Seventy per cent of the population generally preferred to switch on to West German programs. . . . On 28th May, 1973, SED Secretary General Erich Honecker publicly announced that everybody in the GDR was free to listen and watch whatever they wanted. (211)

Throughout the 1970s and 1980s DFF 1 and DFF 2 continued with attempts to counteract what the Party saw to be ideologically offensive material disseminated by the Federal Republic's electronic media. News and current affairs shows broadcast by DFF, like Schwarzer Kanal, often responded directly to items and reports transmitted from the west, emphatically contradicting if not refuting the validity of the western information. DFF also presented regular reports condemning capitalism and western life-styles, counteracting images of western materialism and luxury with censorial accounts of rampant crime, corruption, violence, and unemployment in nonsocialist countries.

As part of their competition with West German television, East German broadcasters scheduled more imported, popular entertainment throughout the 1980s, in particular after 1983, the second major year of reform to DFF. In this period, "GDR television looked much more like western television, at least in prime time" (Hanke 10). Dieter Wiedemann notes that, whereas in 1980, 31 percent of films shown on GDR television came from non-socialist countries, by 1988 that figure had risen to 56 percent ("Wo bleiben" 89).

In an effort to boost viewings, DFF implemented programming strategies used by West German stations, especially in the latter half of the 1980s. A sense of democratic interactivity was, for example, promoted by DFF when it adopted the principle of *Film Auswahl* (Pick a film), a practice established in the west whereby television viewers were provided with a trio of films, any one of which was potential viewing material for a designated prime-time slot. Viewers were encouraged to "select" the film they wished to view (notifying the relevant station of their preference), and the feature most favored by viewers was broadcast. DFF used other strategies in an attempt to draw viewers back to watching East Television. The two East German stations sought, for instance, to undermine the impact of news and current affairs shows from the Federal Republic by presenting popular western films and television series in the same time slots.

DFF also sought to improve declining youth audiences late in the 1980s by expanding and updating what was already a considerable number of programs directed at teenage audiences. DFF began to utilize music video clips in those programs, just like the popular life-style/pop culture programs shown on the commercial stations in the west. On 1 September 1989, for instance, in a successful attempt to entice GDR youth to watch locally produced television, DFF 2 introduced a new youth magazine program called *ELF 99*. This two-hour-long series was in part modeled on MTV-style shows featured on Federal Republic's commercial stations Sat 1 and RTL Plus. *ELF 99* included rock, pop, video clips, film previews, and information about politics and sports (Stiehler 114–32). The program took its rather precious title from the post code for Adlershof.

While East Germans regularly gravitated to programs transmitted from the west, citizens in the Federal Republic did not display a reciprocal interest in GDR television. Or, as Gerhard Wettig concisely remarks, viewing patterns were asymmetrical (215). Media analyst Helmut Hanke elaborates:

> Without doubt, the GDR citizen was informed about and oriented toward the FRG through television in a different way than the FRG citizen was informed about the East. In the east, the majority had a lively interest in the Federal Republic. But in the Federal Republic there was only ever a minority that looked at . . . GDR [television] . . . because East Television only reached the border zones of the GDR it was therefore the exception. Right up until the last months [of 1989] the GDR remained a foreign land for the population of the Federal Republic, whereas most in the GDR regularly looked to the west and set their hopes on the FRG. (13–14)

With the majority of the population watching West German television on a regular basis, television came to be viewed as a central means of binding the German nation together, even though the country was divided by the politics of separation, the Wall, and travel bans (Hanke 14).

However frequently GDR citizens viewed television shows transmitted from the Federal Republic, East Germans were not totally dismissive of, or disinterested in, East Television. It was not "minority" television, like various community access stations elsewhere. Apparently the attitude that much of the GDR public had toward local television was ambivalent. As has been affirmed, even though a high percentage of GDR "citizens could receive West German television, it should not be assumed that they always preferred these channels from the outset. . . . This was a people who learned to live with different sources of information. . . . By and large, East German viewers who could receive all the channels tended to use them for the purpose of comparison" (Hoff, "'Continuity and Change'" 22–23).

However distrustful East Germans may have been of the media in general and Party manipulation of televised information and news reportage in particular, there were still programs on DFF 1 and 2 that were of considerable interest to local viewers. A number of locally produced drama and light entertainment programs seem to have been popular with Eastern German audiences, despite Party intervention in programming and content. "The many letters received by television critics in the newspapers, and others sent to GDR television, reveal that there was a great interest in domestic affairs in the GDR and in critical discussion by the East German media" (Hoff, "'Continuity and Change'" 22). British scholars Geoffrey Nowell-Smith and Tania Wollen have also emphasized the interest GDR citizens had in some locally produced television programs: "Quite a few of these programs were in fact surprisingly popular, both in terms of ratings and of appreciation—though it is only the introduction of western-style market research that has enabled this fact to be ascertained" (5).

Although accurate and reliable ratings figures are scarce, a variety of sources attest to the solid followings of various programs such as *Prisma* (a political magazine that the public favored because of its investigative journalism), the criminal series *Polizeiruf 110*, the entertainment show *Ein Kessel Buntes*, and even the news report *Aktuelle Kamera* (see Hoff "'Continuity and Change'"; Hanke; Stiehler; Bleicher; Hickethier, "Das Zerschlagen"). As part of a discussion of viewing patterns in the ex-GDR, Peter Hoff explains:

> Entertainment series were able to maintain this relatively high level of popularity at a time when the political side of television broadcasting (news bulletins, current affairs, etc.) was already being rejected by the

public. Series dealing with everyday issues achieved very high viewing figures and were keenly discussed by viewers despite poor artistic quality. . . . Drama programs thus acted as a partial substitute for genuine television journalism, and offered answers—through an artistic medium—which biased current affairs programs were unable to provide. . . At this stage [before the Wende], East Germans had no real expectation that social problems would be covered by current affairs programs. . . . East German television was identified by viewers almost exclusively with its fiction and entertainment programs. ("'Continuity and Change'" 21)

With unification, western-based broadcasting has expanded. Unification resulted in the proliferation of commercial and public services throughout the eastern states and the development of cable, satellite and pay television. DFF 1 and 2 have been disbanded. The old states still have the national public networks of ARD and ZDF. East Germans now have greater opportunity to watch more western television more often.

DFF wird abgewickelt / Dealing with East Television

Granted East German television's relation to the discredited state, some would consider it inevitable that an organization like the DFF would be decimated once Germany was unified. The East Television networks did, after all, play a vital role in disseminating state propaganda under the old regime. Whereas DEFA could minimize the role its films often played as vehicles of party ideology—emphasis could be and was placed upon the history of the studios and their relation to UFA and German expressionism—there was little that could deflect the reproaches directed toward GDR television after the Wende (Hickethier, "Das Zerschlagen" 88). Indeed, as has already been acknowledged about DFF reportage, television viewers in the GDR generally distrusted current affairs and news programs. These viewers were conscious of the degree of state control over television, which extended to all aspects of programming, documentation, and entertainment, and were fully aware that DFF current affairs programs distorted, withheld, and falsified information on a regular basis.

Consciousness of the extent of Party intervention in eastern broadcasting made the prospect of SED-free East Television all the more exciting for those intent on media reform in the GDR. Many in the east welcomed the overhaul that faced East German television and were optimistic about a democratic restructuring of the medium. John Sandford comments that

GDR television transformed itself more rapidly than the other media when SED control collapsed in the autumn of 1989. Direct party interference in program content faded away almost as soon as Erich Honecker resigned in mid-October, and programmers and presenters quickly began to explore the limits of their new freedom. The following weeks turned out to be an interlude of undreamt-of liberation for the broadcasters. (202–3)

Whatever the degree of optimism that surrounded the democratization of East Television, few in the east were pleased about the sort of restructuring that did take place. Hickethier explains:

For those who dreamed of a great renewal [of the GDR's broadcasting system] the process of reorganization has produced much anger, bitterness, resignation, and resistance. Instead of transformation many saw only annihilation [*Zerschlagung*]. Instead of cooperation they saw the taking over of territory and the complete removal, not only of the existing structures, but also of staff. ("Das Zerschlagen" 71)

Media spokespersons in the east and west tended to favor different models for the future of broadcasting in the new Germany. The prospect of a dual broadcasting system operating in unified Germany was favored by many in the GDR media and the Media Ministry ("Medienpolitischer Überblick"), but this model was dismissed by public broadcasters in the west as early as 1990. In that year (when East Television was still broadcasting), Paragraph 36 of the Unification Treaty stipulated that GDR television no longer existed. A dual broadcasting system was never seriously considered, despite public surveys conducted in the east after the Wende that revealed that between 80 and 90 percent of East Germans wanted to retain their own television and radio (Hoff, "'Continuity and Change'" 22). Public opinion played little role in determining the fate of DFF: "political decisions sealed DFF's fate" (Goodwin 50).

Suggestions that DFF operate as a third public broadcasting network in unified Germany, next to the western networks ARD and ZDF, were rejected by media representatives and politicians from the old federal states. They favored the rapid integration, *"Anschluß,"* of the East German broadcasting services into the existing West German networks, rather than supporting transformation of the existing structure or a process of gradual transition (Hickethier, "Das Zerschlagen" 80). Western broadcasters were of the opinion that options in the east were limited: they "saw the alternatives of integration under western conditions or the end of program operations, or as *Die Zeit* summed up the situation in 1990, 'Integration or bankruptcy: there is nothing else'" (Hickethier, "Das Zerschlagen" 81).

Easterners involved in the industry objected to the western presumption that there was no option other than to dismantle East Television and incorporate it in existing western networks.

> The argument goes that [in the] future Germany could not afford three public broadcasters. But why should it be that Germany as a whole could afford less television than both of its parts? And if this were to be the case, how come no one thought about letting ARD and ZDF [West Germany's first and second public networks] disappear?
> . . .
> It's the same scenario with the media as with the whole of industry: television programs should be consumed all the time east of the Elbe—production will take place in the west (with the exception of purely local programs). (Ehrich 47–48)

Unification resulted in the complete restructuring of the east's centralized broadcasting system. The first move took place in December 1990 when DFF 1 and DFF 2 were amalgamated, and the DFF 1 frequency was given to the West German public broadcaster ARD. Alfred Roesler-Kleint, DFF editor-in-chief for policy, recalls that the east public disapproved of the reduction of eastern services: "Previously people were critical of DFF because of the old GDR association. But when we announced that there was going to be only one channel there were a lot of complaints. It is like a [married] couple. It is only when the wife leaves the husband that the husband knows what she meant to him" (qtd. in Goodwin 50). Originally, 7,500 staff were employed by DFF: mass firing left 4,700 employees by the end of March 1991, and more were fired in autumn of the same year. The staffing level had been reduced to "barely a third of that in GDR times. Many Germans in the East saw the whole operation as one of the most blatant examples of arrogant Western colonialism" (Sandford 204).

In the following year, what remained of DFF was dismantled. East Television would no longer be broadcast over all of the ex-GDR. From 1992, broadcasting in the east was to be regionalized. Eastern states were to have a share of the Third Channel, the public broadcaster that operated alongside of ARD and ZDF. The east was divided into regions with various states being absorbed by broadcasters established in the west. East Berlin was allocated to Sender Freies Berlin/SFB; the region of Mecklenburg-Vorpommern was incorporated into North German Broadcasting/Norddeutscher Rundfunk/NDR, whereas the state of Brandenburg was supposed to be absorbed by the West Berlin broadcasters SFB. The East German states of Sachsen, Sachsen-Anhalt, and Thüringen were grouped together to form Middle German Broadcasting/Mitteldeutscher Rundfunk/MDR, whereas the state of Brandenburg asserted its independence and resisted moves for incorporation within any West German station. Brandenburg established its own regional station, ORB/Ostdeutscher Rundfunk Brandenburg. ORB and MDR are the sole eastern television broadcasters operating in the five new federal states.

Reforms to East Television resulted in readjusting eastern broadcasting to fit the West German public broadcasting system. Before east broadcasting was restructured, those in the east had three nationwide channels, DFF 1, DFF2, and the Third (eastern) Channel (previously inactive during the Honecker regime). After 1992, when East Television was dismantled and decentralized, broadcasting in the east was restricted to two avenues—a fixed time slot five days a week on ARD and shared access to the Third Channel. (Previously, the Third Channel served the cities and provinces of the west. It continues to operate regionally, has been expanded to incorporate the east and has varied programming from state to state to accommodate regional interests and emphasis.)

This restructuring of the broadcasting system in the former GDR could not help but result in a sharp drop in eastern content and eastern-based production. Programming for Third Channel audiences in eastern regions is not predominantly eastern. Eastern reports and shows are interspersed with repeat programs from ARD and contributions from regional broadcasters located elsewhere in Germany. Similarly, ORB is not exclusively eastern and is regularly taken over by the western broadcaster 1 Plus.

Whereas West German television may once have been "a window on the world" that East Germans could open at will, with unification, constrictions to east broadcasting gave the window metaphor another application. When the West German public broadcaster ARD took over DFF 1 and 2, it was the western services that then provided a constricted aperture through which the east could be viewed. Since 1992, eastern producers have been provided with a regional window for their own shows and reports on ARD, and that window usually opens on the east between the hours of 5:25 and 7:58 P.M. Monday to Friday. (Mitteldeutscher Rundfunk and ORB utilize a similar system of regional windows, seeking to maintain a degree of eastern interest and appeal within the wider western network system.) Apart from taking over DFF 1's and DFF 2's frequencies, ARD and ZDF were allowed to continue to broadcast western programs on the same frequencies with which they reached GDR households before unification. Regret over the demise of East German screen culture may have been most pronounced in the new states when the Broadcasting

Commissioner responsible for restructuring broadcasting in the east refused Third East Television permission to continue broadcasting after the end of 1991. Easterners complained about the loss of the popular newly established Third East Channel that they "had come to regard as uniquely their own" (Sandford 204).

Since unification, East Germans have repeatedly remarked that the "integration" of their networks into the existing West German broadcasting system has resulted in the dominance of West German visions of the east (Bleicher 131). "After the Wende, the public networks only took over those programs which fitted the basic, West German, journalistic model . . . and even then those programs were treated with skepticism by colleagues from the west" (129). Evidently, the western takeover of DFF was anything but subtle. Joan Bleicher recalls how, at the turn of the decade, West German television began broadcasting from locations in the east and the GDR television studios located in Adlershof.

> Countless live switch-overs [to the east] and the transmission of entire [western] programs [from the east] were characterized by a sense of conquest. West German moderators had advanced into the territory of the former "enemy" and captured the center of "evil" propaganda, extolling the western model of democracy. Journalists from the west used what had been previously inaccessible to them for a long time; they utilized the premises and production centers of their East German colleagues, but not their television productions.
>
> After the opening of the Wall . . . [West German] programs which switched over to Adlershof or were transmitted from Adlershof were the order of the day. Journalists who were from Adlershof seldom managed to get a word in. In their hometown of East Berlin, East Germans were turned into the guests of West German television; next to the predominance [*Übermacht*] of their western interlocutors, they were humiliated. . . . Instead of being allowed to speak for themselves, the comments of [eastern] guests were often actually interpretively elaborated, introduced from an unformulated west perspective and in relation to western horizon[s]. (127–28)

The dismantling of the former GDR's centralized networks has, in effect, allowed for the expansion and extension of West German programs. As was predicted, in the early 1990s the eastern population ended up "simply receiving, officially, the programs they unofficially received already" (Nowell-Smith and Wollen 5). The contribution of the eastern Länder to broadcasting in united Germany has been relatively small.

Whatever merits and shortcomings East Television had, they were not thoroughly assessed before Germany was unified. As with other aspects of GDR culture, people had more urgent problems that needed to be solved other than how television would "change and adapt to the new Germany" (Hoffmeyer 40). Insofar as a reevaluation of DFF took place at all, for many in the east, it took place much too late. As Hickethier so poignantly remarks when he discusses the demise of the GDR's television broadcasting system: "one only began to properly learn about it when it was no longer allowed to exist" ("Das Zerschlagen" 88). No matter what ambivalence the population of the GDR felt about its television programs, without doubt these people lost part of their cultural identity when DFF ceased broadcasting. "A large part of the population recognized that through the DFF they felt they were being directly addressed and saw that its programs were made by people of the same background, the same origins, the same lease of life, and with the same fate that they had themselves" ("Das Zerschlagen" 89).

DFF 1 and DFF 2 broadcast for the last time on 31 December 1991. Those in the east relinquished one main avenue through which they could define themselves, represent their experiences, and examine their own history when the region's own television broadcasting system was dismantled. As easterners have often commented, the disbanding of DFF and the decentralization of television broadcasting have denied East Germans the opportunity of speaking with a resonant, collective voice in unified Germany. West German public broadcasters are now the hosts who may regulate the conditions of their eastern guests' accommodation. Inequities in east and west programming and broadcasting extended to the latter half of the 1990s. An analysis of news content on nationwide television (December 1997–May 1998) revealed that of 1,300 broadcast hours, only 65 were devoted to events in the new Länder (Dornberg). Eastern filmmakers and producers faced other obstacles: when they sought commissions they found themselves going cap in hand to the large, public broadcasters, which, with the exception of ORB and MDR, are located in the old states of the Federal Republic. For a number of recently established East German production companies,

> the experience with television over the last few years had been very bitter. There are fewer culturally aware people in the field of television than is generally believed. The process of standardization has reached an extreme level. Most television programming managers see what we bring to them not as something that might enrich or broaden the medium. . . . [Rather] they undertake everything that can be . . . stan-

dardized with what they see on other stations and in neighboring programs. A devastating tendency to [regulate to the point of] monotony
rules. (Tschirner, qtd. in "Aufgeben oder weitermachen?" 35).

Once East Television was dismantled, and the country's film production
facilities were taken out of East German hands, the depletion of GDR
screen culture was assured.

Part Two

CHAPTER 6

Unification Films

Retelling the DEFA Story through Film

Having discussed the Abwicklung of DEFA and of DFF, it is worth recalling here that in the first years of unification the GDR's media suffered a similar fate to GDR industry in general. Considering this similarity, it is perhaps understandable that when some filmmakers depicted the unification of the former GDR and the FRG in their films, their stories echoed, even if inadvertently, the sorts of tribulations that DEFA faced in the early 1990s. Unification films, in particular dramas and comedies that address the reconstruction of the east and the adjustments that unification necessitated, display a marked preoccupation with issues related to privatization, the acquisition and loss of property, inheritance, and disputes over rightful ownership of real estate. Eastern audiences were no doubt personally familiar with these tribulations: millions had firsthand experiences of the adverse consequences of economic rationalization, even if they were not aware of the details surrounding DEFA's demise.

When DEFA faced privatization, suspicions that the cultural heritage of the east would be jeopardized by the sale of the studios spread among the east's film community. A number of unification films seek to reassess the value of eastern cultural heritage in relation to the changes demanded by unification and strategies for reconstruction, modernization, and development (*Das war der wilde Osten / That Was the Wild East*, 1992, *Rising to the Bait, Miraculi*, 1992, *Last from the Da Daer*).

The protracted negotiations surrounding the sale of DEFA raised very real concerns about the motivation of potential buyers. Similarly, profits derived from unification and the western takeover of the east are issues that are regularly featured in films about German unification, in particular in unification comedies. The motivation of characters that come to the east to invest is normally cast in a dubious light in such films.

A number of these films contrast the cozy, humane forms of cottage industry production of the former GDR with internationally financed or West German big business. They regularly present big business as ruthless, capricious, and detrimental to local customs and culture, a perspective shared by many who opposed the international takeover of DEFA (*That Was the Wild East, Apfelbäume / Apple Trees,* 1992, *Rising to the Bait*).

As an organization operating with outmoded equipment and staffed by employees who valued their craft over any concern about productivity, profit, or commercial viability, DEFA could be viewed as a model for East German–style production. Wherever eastern production and business are presented in unification films they are usually characterized in terms relevant to DEFA: parochial in focus, quaintly obsolescent, inefficient, staffed by craftspeople, and threatened by the exigencies of bewildering market forces. Whenever eastern characters in unification films venture into production they regularly do so with an integrity and a sense of community that capitalists from the west are shown to lack. Similarly, those who worked at DEFA accepted the social responsibility that the state attributed to filmmaking, and they were committed to socialist ideals and the construction of the socialist society (*Apple Trees, That Was the Wild East, Solinger Rudi,* 1990, *Rising to the Bait*).

In addressing the might of western capital, the majority of unification films display concern over pillaging and swindling in the new federal states. Criminality (in particular, theft) emerges as a vital narrative catalyst in many of these films (*Go Trabi Go,* 1990, *Wir können auch anders / No More Mr. Nice Guy,* 1993, *Burning Life,* 1994, *Ostkreuz,* 1990,[1] *Miraculi,* and *Adamski*). Comedies and parables such as these present theft as one of the earliest lessons to be learned when East German characters undergo initiation into private enterprise: pilfering is figured as a natural component of capitalism and a by-product of unification. In *Adamski,* for example, when the central character is employed as a store detective, he investigates a professional shoplifter and uncovers a bribe system instigated by other shop detectives who accuse innocent shoppers of stealing department store goods.

In some instances it is not just that East Germans are the targets of thieves. Now and then, theft becomes a defiant, anticapitalist impulse that characters resort to so that they can survive in reunified Germany. Katja steals food and a gown in *To the Horizon and Beyond.* A drug addict who survives through prostitution steals a wad of money from one of her unsuspecting clients, a naive farmer who visits Berlin and the city lights, in *Night*

---

1. Films that are named after locations like the towns Ostkreuz and Herzsprung, or even fictional streets like Sonnenallee, keep their original titles throughout.

Fig. 2. *Adamski* **(1993). Film still reproduced with permission of Progress Film Verleih.**

Spirits. Theft also emerges as a vital activity in *Burning Life.* In that film Lisa and Anna are turned briefly into folk heroes as they travel throughout the eastern provinces robbing banks and giving booty to the deserving. The whole narrative of *Miraculi* is set into action when Sebastian steals cigarettes from a kiosk. Elfie sees no other way to prosper than to engage in petty-criminal activity in *Ostkreuz* (1991).

In attending to burgeoning criminality and lawlessness in the east, a number of unification films present the old states of the GDR as either a frontier or a wilderness. A couple of unification films even vie for the generic classification of "easterns." *No More Mr. Nice Guy* is complete with highway robbers, a sheriff, an undertaker, and a posse that hunts down lawbreakers who ride off across the plains on horseback. Derek Lewis notes that the "(western) view of the eastern federal states as *der wilde Osten* ('the wild east')" was popular in the early 1990s, and, in all its ambiguity, the designation "the wild east" "not only pinpointed the economic depression and increased criminality in the east, it also evoked images of a land of opportunity for swashbuckling entrepreneurs" ("German Language" 308). The last impression was certainly one that Volker Schlöndorff cultivated when he was seeking investors to ensure the privatization of DEFA. As I noted in chapter 5, a spirit of conquest also prevailed when western television crews started to broadcast from the east after unification.

Most strikingly, fiction films that address the division and unification of Germany usually entail consideration of the cultural differences that distinguish East and West Germans, with unification comedies, particularly western-backed productions, asserting the moral superiority and integrity of eastern culture and ways of life over those of the west. These films render East and West Germans in brazen stereotypical terms. In early 1990s films West Germans can be identified by accessories such as leather jackets, blue jeans, sunglasses, fashion-conscious reading glasses, trench coats, expensive suits, and luxury automobiles, along with their car and cellular phones. Virtuous characters in unification comedies and dramas from the west are normally apolitical, naive East Germans. Almost without exception, characters working in bureaucracies and figures with political ambitions, allegiances, or histories of political engagement are presented as sinister: if they are not western they are often seen as having links with the west.

Apple Trees, an eastern-based drama directed by the West Berlin filmmaker Helma Sanders-Brahms, probably provides the strongest and most direct link between its own diegetic world and the events that sealed DEFA's fate after unification. The narrative closure of *Apple Trees* coincides with details surrounding the privatization of the studios and the end of DEFA. Indeed, the comparison in this instance may have been intentional on the filmmaker's part. Sanders-Brahms spoke out about salvaging DEFA. She was one of the few western filmmakers who publicly praised DEFA films and DEFA tradition at the start of the 1990s; she made her visits to DEFA public when she was photographed there, and she used DEFA postproduction facilities for *Apple Trees.* In 1991, she stressed the importance of East Germans telling their own stories and documenting their own histories in an article in *Film und Fernsehen* (24).

Apple Trees, scripted as well as directed by Sanders-Brahms, tells the story of an East German couple, Lene and Heinz, who work on a farming collective where they tend an apple orchard. The collective is located to the south of Berlin—as are the Babelsberg studios. Lene and Heinz live in a modest drab apartment near the director of the collective, Sienke, a greedy and overbearing man who resides in a more spacious and well-appointed villa. When the GDR collapses, and efforts to privatize industry, property, and business are under way, it is rumored that an amusement park will be built on the site of the orchard—as was the case with Babelsberg.

Despite Lene and Heinz's objections, Sienke decides to sell the orchard for property development after unification. Having already abandoned his Heimat for the west, Sienke rationalizes his sale of the villa that was once his family home: "It will be renovated or torn down," the same, limited options that faced the studio complex at Babelsberg. At the end of the film, Sienke justifies the sale of the orchard in terms directly relevant to the privatization of DEFA: "I don't want to have anything to do with things here any more. *I have sold everything to a real estate agent. The income from your apples . . . is very little compared to the land's value.* The sooner you realize that the better" (emphasis added). Lene responds, "What about the people? They have no jobs." Sienke responds with a gesture of indifference—he simply shrugs his shoulders. The liquidation of the farming collective, the destruction of the orchard at the end of *Apple Trees,* and the discarding of its produce (substandard by EU requirements and unprofitable by western standards) make the correlation with DEFA explicit. Just as unification resulted in a season's harvest being dumped at the end of *Apple Trees,* so too were thousands of copies of DEFA films disposed of in the early 1990s. Throughout *Apple Trees,* the orchard is used as a synecdoche for the GDR; at the same time it is an equally fitting emblem for DEFA studios and the fate of DEFA films after unification.

Two other unification films allude to issues surrounding film culture and the fate of DEFA in unified Germany, even if they do so less directly than *Apple Trees: Go Trabi Go* and its sequel, *That Was the Wild East* or *Go Trabi Go II. Go Trabi Go,* a comedy I will discuss in detail in chapter 9, follows an East German family, the Struutzes, on holiday. No longer restricted by borders, the East Germans set out on their first journey to the west in their Trabant. Their destination is not the old states of the Federal Republic, but rather Italy. The East Germans embrace Italian culture instinctively, in preference to that of their affluent "relatives." The Struutzes' travels are guided by Goethe's *Italianische Reise (Italian Journey),* suggesting a cosmopolitan disposition rather than any particular nationalistic proclivity. Goethe's guidebook provides ample opportunity for displaying the tourist sights of the Italian countryside, coastline, and capital.

Go Trabi Go allows the East Germans to experience firsthand spectacles and monuments recognizable from tourist brochures, and Papa Struutz becomes our guide, just in case we cannot identify all of the landmarks.

Go Trabi Go identifies the Struutzes as Europeans: they mingle with Italians rather than getting to know their "neighbors" in West Germany. In this "Trabi comedy," the Struutzes are presented as likable characters who share the good humor of the Italians they encounter. Even despite language barriers the Struutzes seem to have a greater rapport with those from the south than with any West Germans. The language of the Struutzes' West German relatives, whose preoccupation is with sales tax and computer technology, is more foreign to the East Germans than Italian is. The Struutzes have a particular affinity with Italian cultural tradition in that they can appreciate the same things about Italy as Goethe did. Following Goethe's travel diary, the family's journey allows for the promotion of southern Europe as a spectacle. Although a humble figure, Papa Struutz is not simply a parochial East German. As a European, he is sensitive to the beauty and history of a country other than his own: he exclaims at one point that he is in Arcadia.

Focusing upon Europe as spectacle, *Go Trabi Go* advances a type of "Euro-vision" similar to that promoted at DEFA in the early 1990s. At that time it was anticipated that the studios would become a European production center that could foster and produce "Euro-films." It was very much an international rather than a provincial East German flavor that was advanced at the Babelsberg complex, and that this film manages to exemplify.

The "Wall film"

With the GDR disintegrating and DEFA's fate uncertain, filmmakers in the east and some in the west (many in Berlin) could not resist addressing the turbulence that surrounded them with unification. In the early 1990s, the emergence of a wave of documentaries addressing these aspects of history prompted those in the German film industry to identify the advent of a new genre referred to as "Wall films." These films were singled out because they dealt with issues of the division and/or reunification of Germany, although only some dealt specifically with the Berlin Wall. Essentially, the label applied to documentary films: documentaries addressing the division and unification of Germany were more immediate, more numerous, and usually produced more swiftly than unification comedies and dramas, some of which took three years or more to be completed. Hoards of local filmmakers experimented with variants of the Wall film. The genre was in full force in 1991 when it swamped Germany's film festival circuit. Wall films were especially conspicuous at the Berlin and Leipzig film festivals that year. Among the Wall films screened at the Berlinale in 1991 were *Ich war ein glücklicher Mensch* (*I Was a Happy Person*), *Letztes Jahr Titanic* (*The Last Year of the Titanic*), *Berlin Bahnhof Friedrichstraße 1990, Lindenhotel, Im Glanze dieses Glückes* (*In the Splendour of This Happiness*), *Berlin—Prenzlauer Berg, Ein schmales Stück Deutschland* (*A Little Piece of Germany*), and *DDR—Ohne Titel* (*GDR—Without [a] Title*). The genre was also a feature of documentary programs at the Berlin Festival in the year that followed. Then *Rostige Bilder* (*Rusty Pictures*), *Der schwarze Kasten* (*The Black Box*), *Brüder und Schwestern* (*Brothers and Sisters*), *Eisenzeit* (*Iron Age*), and *Kein Abschied nur Fort* (*Not Farewell—Just a Parting*) were screened.

Wall films were also featured in prominent East German film festivals early in the 1990s. In 1991, *Östliche Landschaft* (*Eastern Landscape*), *In einem schönen Wiesengrunde* (*In a Beautiful Meadow*), *Zwei Brüder, zwei Welten* (*Two Brothers, Two Worlds*), *Deutschland, Deutschland* (*Germany, Germany*), *Jetzt fahr'n wir übern See* (*Now We Will Travel Overseas*), and *Kinder, Kader, Kommandeure* (*Children, Cadres, Commanders*) were among the selections screened at the Leipzig Documentary and Animation Film Festival. These films addressed life in the east or the social problems East Germans faced as they adjusted to the political and economic order brought with unification. The profile of the Wall film was gradually raised: "In 1990 two documentary films recording the process of unification even achieved cinema release; in 1991 the number was fifteen and in 1992 twelve" (Hughes and Brady 279).

The status of the Wall film was further enhanced by the Goethe Institut during this period. The cultural agency provided official recognition of the genre, just as it had done when it organized retrospectives of the work of Fassbinder and other Autoren, or when the Institut distributed packages of German feminist films and documentary series throughout the 1980s. The Institut gave the Wall films international exposure. It packaged more than twenty-four hours worth of films drawn from the genre together, ready for presentation anywhere in the world.

A startlingly diverse range of filmmakers documented the historic events that galvanized Germany around the turn of the decade. Jürgen Böttcher, DEFA documentary filmmaker and director of the banned film *Jahrgang 45* (*Born in 1945,* 1965/1990), simply titled his chronicle *Die Mauer* (*The Wall,* 1990). In his commentary-free film, Böttcher captures events surrounding the dismantling of the Wall as well as the public spectacles of unification. Early in the film, he records a pastime favored in Berlin in 1990: locals and tourists are shown chipping away at the Wall to dislodge souvenirs of its graffitied surface. Other groups of tourists are shown as they take photographs of one another standing before the barrier.

Böttcher's film displays a cool detachment from the most jubilant displays that marked unification. He captures the spectacular public celebrations that saw East and West Germans (and others) united on New Year's Eve 1990, euphoric witnesses to firework displays at the Reichstag. When the camera is positioned outside the crowds of celebrators, however, the event vaguely resembles a blitzkrieg, with the fireworks simulating the sound of missiles being launched and bombs dropping. Elsewhere the director provides a skewed perspective on a massive rock concert by Pink Floyd held in front of the Wall. The jubilation and impatience of the concert crowd is juxtaposed with the banal activity of tradesmen. A panoramic view shows the concert crowd as it appears to spread to the horizon. Standing on the rooftop in the foreground of the shot are two chimney sweeps who are clothed in the distinctive uniforms of their ancient guild. The chimney sweeps are only momentarily distracted by the monumental scene in the distance; it does not disrupt the everyday routine of their trade.

By contrast, the documentary *I Was a Happy Person* presents a more personalized account of the GDR's demise. It focuses upon the recollections of Tilbert Eckertz, a state official and patriot of the GDR, beginning immediately after he has picked up his Stasi files. Archival footage accompanies the old man's recollections, particularly of the 1950s. Eckertz reflects upon his commitment to the SED and repeatedly asserts that he was "absolutely satisfied" with the socialist state: he insists that although the dictatorship was on the verge of collapse "for me they weren't forty lost years." His devotion to the old regime becomes all the more disturbing when it is revealed that he was imprisoned for four months in 1953, when he was falsely accused of espionage. With a faith in the Party that is almost religious, he manages to rationalize his imprisonment, viewing it as a type of penitence through which he could be accepted again by the Party. Although betrayed by the state, Eckertz remained loyal to it, a matter that resulted in conflict with and estrangement from his own children. Eckertz emerges from this somber documentary as an idealist with an unshakable faith in the ideals of a defunct system disclosed as corrupt.

Other Wall films deal with the adversity and disillusionment of easterners during unification. *Not Farewell—Just a Parting* chronicles the movements of an East German family who left the East and all they had behind when they headed to the Federal Republic before the Wall collapsed. The family reveals its aspirations and impressions of life in the west throughout the documentary. *Not Farewell—Just a Parting* records not only aspects of the family's life as refugees and the disappointments they faced in the west, but their ultimate decision to return to the ex-GDR after the Wende. This Wall film closes with the family returning to take up residence in the shabby apartment and neighborhood they had previously abandoned.

Part of the longest researched documentary project from the east, *Wittstock! Wittstock!* (1997) chronicles the lives of three women who worked together in a textile factory in the former GDR. Spanning a period of twenty-two years, the documentary includes excerpts from other earlier documentaries in the series. *Wittstock! Wittstock!* traces the working and family lives of Renate, Elsbeth, and Edith through 1996, providing startling insight into their youthful aspirations in the GDR as much as the impact unification had upon their lives and their families. One of the many things that is remarkable about the film is the resilience the women display despite the adversities of unification. One of the women is chronically unemployed; another, the former manager of the textiles factory, can only secure menial work as a chamber maid; the third is perpetually undertaking retraining courses to prepare her for nonexistent jobs.

For some filmmakers the genre of the Wall film provided the chance to delve into their own personal histories of persecution, coercion, and terror under the old regime (*Locked Up Time, The Black Box*). In *Black Box* individuals who were interrogated by the Stasi tell of methods deployed to intimidate and humiliate those held captive. Victims track down Stasi interrogators and confront them with their deeds. On one visit to the Stasi archive, tracking shots show aisle after aisle of stored reports: the magnitude of the collection is truly overwhelming.

Filmmakers living in Berlin could hardly ignore the collapse of the Wall and the mass influx of East Germans that followed. In the words of one representative of the Berlin film community, "Questions were asked if you *didn't* address this topic." Even Ulrike Ottinger, an uncompromising Berlin director famous for flamboyant experimentation with cinematic spectacle, fetishism, and narcissism (*Bildnis einer Trinkerin / One-Way Ticket, Johanna d'Arc of Mongolia*) contributed to the Wall film genre when she made a three-hour-long epic, *Countdown,* documenting Germany's last ten days before Currency Union.[2]

---

2. The genre of the Wall film also attracted directors living outside of Germany. Marcel Ophüls was among a barrage of filmmakers who brought international crews to Germany in an attempt to interpret events that precipitated unification. In *Novembertage* (*November Days,* 1990) Ophüls interviews a series of SED Party dignitaries, representatives from GDR reform movements, officials from the Stasi, and "little people." One year after the collapse of the Berlin Wall, he asks them about their recollection of events surrounding the Wende and their expectations and perceptions of life in unified Germany.

Unification Fiction Films

Just as unification was a topic many documentary filmmakers felt compelled to address in the early 1990s, many fiction filmmakers were also
alert to the dramatic or even the comic potential of unification as a topic
for their films. It seems that some, like Peter Timm and Wolfgang Büld,
thought that unification was an entertaining and amusing enough topic to
attract large audiences and box-office profits, and they were right. Others,
like East German directors Roland Oehme and Peter Kahane, may have
also shared this faith, but they did not manage to successfully exploit
unification as a subject with comic appeal for mass audiences, in the early
1990s at least. By the end of the decade, however, Kahane's production *To
the Horizon and Beyond* managed to draw relatively healthy attendance
figures, though still not enough to generate substantial profits.

Fiction films of the 1990s that address unification or life in divided
Germany are as diverse as the Wall documentaries. Filmmakers who used
the Wende or unification as a subject in their films during this period drew
on just about every existing genre imaginable. For a number of directors,
melodrama was the appropriate genre within which to frame stories surrounding the division of both halves of Germany and the subsequent
merger of the Federal and Democratic Republics. Many thought
unification an appropriate backdrop for romantic comedy. Some could
only treat the historic developments of 1989 and 1990 as a farce. A couple
of filmmakers turned to subgenre variations of the musical and the horror
film; in at least one instance the Wende and unification provided inspiration for a musical cabaret. *To the Horizon and Beyond,* with its pop songs
and rock 'n' roll classics, is a unification film one can sing along to. At least
one filmmaker reverted to splatter to depict Germany during and after
unification. In what follows, I will provide a brief survey of examples of
unification films drawn from some of the categories listed here.

Tragedies, Love Stories, and Romantic Comedies

When some of Germany's best-known women directors turned to the subject of the division and unification of Germany, they interwove historic
events among tragic love stories. Helke Misselwitz worked within this
framework when she made her first fiction film, *Herzsprung* (1992). Misselwitz set the film in a small northeastern village called Herzsprung, just
after unification. *Herzsprung* addresses controversial issues of radical right
violence, xenophobia, and racism in unified Germany as it charts the love
affair between a beautiful young village woman, Johanna, and the enig-
matic African-German man who enters her life.

Helma Sanders-Brahms also located *Apple Trees*—which I have already discussed in relation to its symbolic articulation of the fate of DEFA—in the provinces of the GDR. Sanders-Brahms traces the effects that Party politics, surveillance, and oppression had upon love, marriage, and family life in the GDR. She tells an unrelenting and bitter tale of stagnation and betrayal both within a marriage and within a country—events that lead to the collapse of both. Her protagonists seem destined to live a life of despair in the GDR: Lene is a passive conformist to the state and a supporter of its objectives. Whereas she subscribes to the general ideals of socialism, her husband, Heinz, becomes increasingly critical of the Party, its doctrine and corruption. Once Heinz is imprisoned for his hostile attitudes to the state, he and Lene become entangled in an intricate and devastating web of deceit and betrayal. Adultery and treachery lead husband and wife to inform on one another to the Stasi, leaving their lives in ruins.

Sanders-Brahms's portrait of the collapse of the GDR and the fate of individuals living in the east during unification is almost unbearably bleak and caustic. The film conveys in painstaking detail the tawdriness and drabness of aspects of daily life. Stifling domestic interiors and austere public spaces influence the demeanor, outlook, and expectations of characters. Garish synthetic drapes and unsightly furnishings are the only details that provide contrast to the oppressive and dingy domestic interiors of the film. Public spaces are lit in ugly fluorescent light, which illuminates the ashen complexions of ordinary East Germans as much as the delusions promoted by the Party.

Margarethe von Trotta's portrait of divided Germany, *Das Vesprechen* (*The Promise,* 1995), presents a more conventionally melodramatic view of life in the socialist state. Her German-German love story, which spans a period of almost thirty years, tells the tale of a couple physically separated by politics, history, and the Wall as they live their lives in each half of Berlin.

Romantic comedy provided an appealing generic framework within which numerous filmmakers depicted unification. Rudolf Thome's delightful comedy of manners, *Liebe auf den ersten Blick* (*Love at First Sight,* 1991), is set in the suburbs of Berlin after unification. It follows the blossoming love affair between an unemployed East German archaeologist and single father, Zenon Bloch, and a West German futurologist and single mother, Elsa Süßeisen. Other German-German love stories set during the period of unification include the romantic comedies *So schnell es geht nach Istanbul* (*As Quick as Possible to Istanbul,* 1990) and *Adamski,* which charts the romantic entanglement of characters who first encounter one another in an East Berlin department store.

Heiner Carow's *Verfehlung* (*Missing,* 1992) is set in part during the period of the Wende. The film revolves around Elisabeth, a middle-aged East German woman who falls in love with Jacob, a West German dock-worker. The pair conduct a clandestine affair when Jacob visits the East, but after he and Elisabeth announce their engagement on New Year's Eve in 1988, Jacob is arrested and expelled from the GDR. When the borders to the west are opened the next year, Elisabeth is in prison. The fall of the Wall provides no consolation either for Elisabeth or for her son, Holger. After his involvement in a Wende reform movement Holger also finds himself incarcerated, not in prison like his mother but as a patient in a psychiatric hospital.

Other tragic unification romances of the early 1990s focus upon the relations between homeless East German youth—juvenile delinquents abandoned or mistreated by their parents. The late DEFA production *Jana and Jan* is one such poignant drama set in a juvenile detention center during the time of the Wende. This film tells the story of two teenagers who fall in love while incarcerated. *Ostkreuz* and *Weltmeister* (*World Champion,* 1993) present equally grim portraits of neglected youngsters facing the upheavals of unification in the east.

Splatter

Known for the stylistic excess of his films, West German filmmaker Christoph Schlingensief turned to the horror subgenre of splatter to critique unification when he made *Das deutsche Kettensägenmassaker—die erste Stunde der Wiedervereinigung* (*The German Chainsaw Massacre—The First Hours of Unification,* 1990). Promotion for the film declared that in 1989 hundreds of thousands of East Germans left the GDR for the west. "Four percent never arrived. They came seeking unification: they ended up mincemeat."

In this film the homage is clearly to *The Texas Chainsaw Massacre* (1974), which Lew Brighton views as "the *Gone With the Wind* of meat movies" (qtd. in Clover 22). Schlingensief recycles familiar props like the pickup truck and stylistics (handheld camera, raucous sound effects) from the original film. In Schlingensief's version, the incestuous, murderous family is West German while their unsuspecting victims come from the east. Such a scenario presents plenty of opportunity to satirize stereotypes of Ossis and Wessis. West Germans are deranged, exploitative, and perverse in this film. Alfred keeps the corpse of his dead father in the family parlor and impersonates him like Norman Bates in *Psycho* (1960). However, Alfred and his family are industrious. They run various businesses, which include the Café Porsche where Johnny performs gruesome cabaret numbers involving mutilation and dismemberment (he cuts off his hand and draws a peace sign with his own blood)—and, in one instance, his rendition of the tune "Big Spender." They also own a hotel (like Norman Bates) and a small goods business through which they indulge their cannibalistic instincts. East Germans are savagely murdered to provide the vital ingredients for sausage production. They are conspicuous targets when they travel to the western border in their Trabis, swilling Coca-Cola and chanting "We are the People, yeah, yeah, yeah." Evidently there is no shortage of supply or demand for the foodstuffs Alfred and his family manufacture. In this film West Germans are presented as barbaric and the process of unification as depending on the victimization, brutalization, and bloody sacrifice of unsuspecting East Germans.

Musical Cabaret

East Berlin *Nachwuchsregisseur* (new generation director) Jörg Foth turned to musical cabaret-revue when he directed *Last from the Da Daer,* a film that charts the journey of two East German clowns through the ruins of the GDR. This film, which was one of the last to be subsidized with money from the GDR, draws on the absurdist humor of the Dada movement and the German tradition of political cabaret that flourished in Berlin in the 1920s and 1930s. It includes some of the sketches Meh and Weh (cabaret artists Steffen Mensching and Hans-Eckardt Wenzel) developed in their stage presentations *Neues aus der Da Daer / New from the Da Daer* (1982/83) and *Last from the Da Daer* (1989/91).

Foth explains that he extracted material for the film from "the documents and reality" of the GDR, which are "as real as Don Quixote's windmills and from our fears and dreams which are as unreal as our daily headlines" (Letter 3). The film begins with a segment titled "Breakfast in Sing Sing" that sees the clowns being released from the jail in which they have been living. The cult actor who starred in so many of Fassbinder's films, Irm Hermann, is their prison guard. Foth explains: "They are imprisoned as we were in the GDR. Born in sorrow. From here they go to work and lose their way in life and country" (Letter 3). The clowns visit various industrial and rural locations in the provinces of the GDR and its capital: a slaughterhouse; the cement works; an underground railway station in East Berlin; a garbage dump on the edge of Berlin. Christoph Heim is the truck's driver who presents a savagely critical soliloquy on the demise of the GDR in this scene. Later in the film, the clowns venture to the Brocken, where the pagan ritual of Walpurgis Night is celebrated each year. Surreal locations such as these provide backdrops for their skits and cabaret numbers, which satirize the bureaucratization of life in the GDR, the oppressiveness of the state, official state celebrations, the failure of the October revolution, and the drive for unification and the deutsche mark.

At the end of their journey, Meh and Weh find themselves in a leafy East Berlin graveyard, squabbling with one another about which day of the week "the revolution" can be staged. Tuesday is ruled out as one of them has a dental appointment that day. They cannot agree upon a suitable timetable. The sight and sound of a couple of German shepherds draw the clowns' attention. The dogs are stationed on apartment block balconies decorated with the flags of the Federal Republic. The spectacle signals the imminence of unification and the nationalistic fervor that surrounded it. Meh and Weh add to the madness of the scene as they drop to their hands and knees. On all fours they mimic the dogs and bark back at them. Irm Hermann surveys the final scene, standing in the graveyard. The film ends with a shot of a gravestone bearing the inscription *Auf Wiedersehen,* a poignant closure that also marks the closure of GDR history. "It is a bitter-sad farewell, a requiem, and not the sort of film you should see if you are living in Bielefeld and the roof is caving in around your head" (Meier).

Last from the Da Daer was the very first film in GDR history that was made at DEFA that the old communist distributors, Progress, refused to handle. Foth's film distinguishes itself from many other unification films through its episodic structure, its eccentricity and artifice, its black humor and biting satire. What it shares with many other unification films, however, is its East German focus. The film's clowns do not display any interest in experiencing the indulgences and attractions of the other half of Germany.

All Quiet on the Western Front

Despite the apparent diversity of genres that unification films draw upon, there is a remarkable continuity of various images and ideas in these films. The common thematics, sources of narrative conflict, and resolution these films share will occupy me for the rest of this chapter. These films are consistent in their depiction of familial relations and approaches to characterization. Western-backed productions tend to use the same sorts of strategies to idealize the East.

The overwhelming majority of fiction films (and documentaries) addressing unification are set in the east. Apart from their eastern setting, these films regularly involve the movement of protagonists further eastward. Unification comedies such as *No More Mr. Nice Guy* and *That Was the Wild East* exemplify this trend, with the former relocating protagonists "somewhere on the Don River" surrounded by Russian peasants and the latter having one of its characters head off "beyond the Urals." Rather than embracing unification, some characters in films such as these appear to be dubious about its repercussions and flee from its influences. This tendency is pronounced in *Apple Trees*. In that film, East Germans turn their backs on the wider world and the impact of unification. Their vision and interests become more parochial. Finally granted the freedom to travel, some characters in unification films resolve to stay put. In western-backed and -produced films, characters emphatically declare their preference for living rustic lives divorced from the west and its influences. In the last scene of *Apple Trees,* for instance, we observe Lene and Heinz as they board a ferry that takes them to their newly inherited, isolated property.

The geographical emphasis that the majority of 1990s unification films place on the east seems logical when one acknowledges that the genre seeks means through which unification can be turned into a spectacle. Early in the decade unification's impact was hardly discernible in the west whereas in the east it necessitated widespread adjustment and change. This was made perfectly clear by what happened to the media in unified Germany where upheavals were "almost exclusively one sided" (Sandford 199) and restricted to the east. With the exception of massive-scale development in Berlin's center, referred to in the 1990s as the largest construction site in Europe, the west has remained visually much as it was; the east presents far greater potential for presenting unification as a spectacle. Usually when filmmakers from the west depict the east in unification films it is in terms of rustic, rural images that evoke old-fashionedness and a bygone era. East German filmmakers hardly ever embrace pastoral imagery or use it to characterize the east during or after unification. The filmic depiction of the east as a paradise abounding in rural charms is a western vantage point, an issue I will discuss in detail in chapter 7.

Sometimes western filmmakers portray the ex-GDR as a type of Eden *and* as an industrialized, heavily polluted region. *Apple Trees* promotes this dual impression with scenes of polluted, industrial wastelands replaced by idyllic springtime scenes of orchards in full bloom. Many western productions succeed in turning unification into a spectacle by adopting this kind of rural focus and by addressing issues related to heritage that manifest themselves primarily through the family and secondarily through the act of inheritance.

Disrupted Families

Just as unification films display a particular geographical proclivity, familial relations in these features follow a particular pattern. Unification films habitually focus upon broken families and present diegetic worlds in which the nuclear family is either absent or imperiled. This emphasis is equally evident in eastern and western productions. In *Burning Life,* protagonists Lisa and Anna come from families that are not only "incomplete," but in some way maladjusted. Lisa comes from a one-parent family: her mother left home long ago. Lisa's father, a former town mayor, was involved in shady development deals. Because of his clandestine transactions and greed, the family home and neighborhood face immediate demolition at the start of the film (the area is to become the largest golf course in Europe). Lisa discovers the body of her father hanging from the rafters of the family home: guilt and dishonor have led him to commit suicide. Lisa leaves the desolate community just as it is about to be leveled. Her companion throughout this road movie, Anna, is also part of a troubled family and broken home. It is established that she has no parents, only a brother. At the start of the film, Anna is already separated from her young child and husband, who is identified as a wife beater. When Anna attempts to visit her son and give him a teddy bear, her husband cannot control his fury and savagely attacks her. Lisa and Anna live their lives in exile.

Lost Landscape presents life in the east as revolving around a single family unit, but that unit is so brittle it can only survive in total isolation from external forces and influences. Similarly, there is only one nuclear family in *Apple Trees:* Lene, her child, and her husband, Heinz. No mention is made of Heinz's relatives, and we only hear of Lene's parents in the first scene of the film when they verbally abuse one another and argue about separation. Although Lene has one child, a son, we are unsure if Heinz fathered the boy. Life in the neighborhood is no more gratifying or harmonious: Sienke's marriage is not only loveless but also childless. In the course of *Apple Trees,* adultery and mistrust shatter Lene's fragile nuclear family.

The configuration of families in *Little Angel* is even more disastrous. Ramona's desperately lonely life changes when she falls in love and becomes pregnant. Any prospect of personal fulfillment through establishing a nuclear family evades Ramona when her baby is stillborn. Stable nuclear families do not seem to belong in her immediate community either. Living in a tenement block in Ostkreuz, Ramona repeatedly observes the drunken domestic arguments of her neighbors who violently abuse one another and neglect their children.

A number of unification films, such as *Herzsprung, Ostkreuz, Burning Life, Missing,* and *Love at First Sight,* feature fragmented families headed by single parents. In *Ostkreuz,* Elfie's mother faces financial hardship as she struggles to find decent accommodation for herself and her daughter. When Elfie runs away from her mother part of the way into the film, the

Fig. 3.   *Jana and Jan* (1991). Reproduced with permission of Progress Film Verleih.

youngster initially visits her only other remaining relative, her grandfather. By the end of the film, Elfie teams up with a *Kellerkind,* a child who lives in deserted cellars having been abandoned by his parents when they headed West, and the pair of waifs is left to scavenge among the ruins of the east.

Similarly, Jan, the young East German juvenile delinquent held in a detention center in *Jana and Jan,* is parentless. Early in the film the youth is asked to provide a photograph of himself. The only one he has is crumpled and old, torn from a newspaper report announcing that his parents have abandoned him, presumably to travel to the west. Although *Jana and Jan* portrays the community of a detention center populated with misfits, malcontents, and reprobates, interestingly enough, the film does present an opportunity for a nuclear family to be reestablished. When Jana becomes pregnant by Jan, the pair determines to keep the baby and to become a family, something that both of them appear to have missed out on in childhood. Jana and Jan manage to escape from the detention center after the barriers between both halves of Germany have collapsed. The pair heads west. It is only after they arrive at the border that Jana goes into labor. The film closes with the teenagers sheltered in an abandoned border station. Director, Helmut Dziuba, explains that "in the final scene the child is born and Jana . . . waits for its cry. The child remains still" ("Nahe der Katastrophe"). However ambiguous the closing scene may be, the film still presents the *possibility* for the restoration of the nuclear family, even if its structure is precarious and its foundation involves gravitation to the west. In this limited sense, *Jana and Jan* could perhaps be called optimistic.

Many unification films, some more frivolous than *Ostkreuz* and *Jana and Jan,* display little more than the remnants of a family. Often these films feature characters who only have one aged, distant relative or one surviving grandparent. At the start of *Go Trabi Go,* Rita speculates about the surprise Udo will bring with him from Leipzig and wonders whether it will be grandfather's new car. It isn't. In the sequel, *That Was the Wild East,* it is clear that Udo has no living relatives apart from his immediate family. Similarly, in *Apple Trees* Lene appears to have no siblings and no contact with either of her estranged parents: her relationship with her grandmother is presented as more significant and formative, but we are told at the end of the film that the older woman has died. And in *To the Horizon and Beyond,* Henning has just one remaining relative, his aged mother. Jan's father is only featured as a corpse in *Das Leben ist eine Baustelle* (*Life Is a Construction Site,* 1996),[3] and his sister is separated from the father of her child.

Unification brings more rifts and tragic losses to *Herzsprung*'s fractured and extended family: Johanna's husband commits suicide in despair over his desolate existence in unified Germany, leaving his young widow, herself a mother, to fend alone with her widowed father. "In *Herzsprung* people die as senselessly as they lived" (Renke): Johanna ends up losing her own life as a result of the (misdirected) racial hatred of a group of neo-Nazis.

Von Trotta's unification love story *The Promise* also sees a family forcibly divided, this time by the Berlin Wall. Sophie, a young East German woman, is separated from her true love, Konrad, when their plan to escape to the west is thwarted: she manages to flee, whereas one moment's hesitation on Konrad's part makes his escape impossible. After Sophie escapes, she is briefly reunited with Konrad in Prague just before the city is invaded by Soviet troops. Later Sophie has a child by Konrad, but the lovers live their separate lives in a partitioned city. The film closes in 1989 with a freeze-frame image of Sophie as she recognizes Konrad among a crowd at a Wall checkpoint.

There are no conspicuous German families at all in the unification comedy *Adamski.* A Turkish family is briefly present in one scene, falsely accused of shoplifting. Adamski himself and Lili (the professional shoplifter whom he falls in love with) don't appear to have any relatives.

---

3. The film is also distributed as *Life Is All You Get.*

The absence of the parental generation, the inclusion of single parents, and/or a sole aging relative (either a grandparent, grandmother, aunt, or uncle) is a marked structural characteristic of films that assess life in the new federal states, whether the productions issue from the east or west. The absence or fragmentation of the family in many of the unification films mentioned above may be related to the collapse of the GDR state and the discrediting of its authorities. The removal of figureheads of the state during the Wende may translate into an absent generation in unification films. It may also be related to a tendency of former citizens of the GDR to dissociate themselves from the defunct structures and way of life supported by the deposed regime. The degeneration of family life in so many unification films could, moreover, suggest that it is only when unification has become a social and economic reality (rather than something legislated and implemented by the state) that family life can be upheld.

What many early 1990s films set in the east intimate is that neither the sociopolitical climate of the GDR nor that of the first years of unification has proven capable of sustaining the family or allowing it to prosper. The long-established division of Germany has led to the east being repeatedly pictured as an incomplete and fragmented family, lacking in harmony. In various unification films, being part of the social fabric of life in the former GDR has tainted the family. Constrictions the state imposed on its citizens somehow rupture the family in these films (*Apple Trees, Ostkreuz, Burning Life, Missing, Little Angel, The Promise*). The state is presented as an intrusive force, distorting relations and prompting duplicity in the most intimate and seemingly innocent of familial relations.

The intrusiveness of the state and the internalization of its values is conveyed effectively in *The Promise*. When Konrad's daughter receives a gift of a stuffed panda from her half brother, Sebastion, who lives in West Berlin, Konrad faces a dilemma. He realizes that his daughter will never have the chance to see a panda in real life, as they were only a highlight of the zoo in the western half of the city, not the east. In one poignant scene, Konrad seeks to protect his daughter from disappointment over perceived disparities between life in the east and west. One night, while she sleeps, Konrad paints the face of his daughter's toy panda in an attempt to obliterate not only her memory of pandas, but also any awareness of deprivation associated with life in the GDR. Although his actions are motivated by compassion, they are also in complicity with the state, which never allowed any hint that GDR citizens suffered from shortages or privation.

Apart from the constraints and impositions of the state under the old regime, family life may also be threatened by the upheavals and challenges brought with unification. Demands to adjust to a fundamentally foreign socioeconomic order and power structure are so great in these films that these exigencies fragment the family (*That Was the Wild East, The German Chainsaw Massacre, Ostkreuz, Burning Life, Rising to the Bait, Herzsprung, World Master*).

The absence of the parental generation in so many unification films is made all the more conspicuous through the genre's preference for childlike protagonists. *No More Mr. Nice Guy*'s Kipp displays the sort of naïveté and innocence that key figures often show in unification films. Like Udo in *Go Trabi Go*, Kipp is a simple and trusting figure. He displays the sort of meekness common to male protagonists in unification films. In *No More Mr. Nice Guy*, even after Kipp and his brother, Most, have been kidnapped by Viktor, a deserter from the Red Army, Kipp still displays a childlike sense of fairness. As the three men drive through the countryside in the dead of night, Kipp sits wedged between Most and Viktor, holding two recently purchased ice creams. Although Viktor has commandeered Most's truck and holds the brothers at (machine) gunpoint, Kipp innocently insists that the ice cream be fairly shared with the kidnapper. When Viktor impatiently throws the ice cream he is offered out the truck window, Kipp protectively guards his own ice cream. Evidently the prospect of it being confiscated causes him greater alarm than being held hostage.

Kipp displays a wide-eyed wonderment at the world. His innocent fantasy is to "go to the beach. Go fishing. Take your shoes off . . . the whole family and go barefoot." The illiterate brothers and the baby-faced Russian soldier, who is only too happy to play dumb in a number of scenes, blunder their way from one adventure to another throughout the film. East German protagonists in unification comedies such as *Adamski* and *Go Trabi Go* display comparable levels of simplicity and ineffectualness. They are largely impressionable figures who rely upon chance and whom fortune favors, often because of their innocence, their naïveté, or their virtue.

German-German Relations

The comedies and dramas I have referred to in this chapter seek to assess the impact of unification upon individuals and the community, often in critical terms. Most unification films go further than suggesting that German-German relations are strained or difficult to sustain since unification. These films assume that German-German relations do not exist. A kind of cultural apartheid is sustained in most unification films so that often the only enduring relations presented are between East Germans or between East Germans and non-Germans who are identified as foreign. This segregation of East and West Germans is presented as a completely natural and acceptable occurrence in the diegetic worlds of these films. They usually

Fig. 4. *No More Mr. Nice Guy* **(1993). Film still reproduced with permission of Delphi Filmverleih.**

eschew German-Germany relations. This is perhaps the unification film's greatest, albeit inadvertent irony. *Love at First Sight* is a notable exception to this tendency of the genre. Thome's film appears to be the sole early 1990s unification comedy that can establish an untroubled German-German heterosexual couple. More characteristic of unification comedy is *Adamski,* which includes a romantic triangle composed exclusively of East Berliners.

Some films represent German-German relations obliquely. Set in spring of 1990 before Currency Union, *As Fast as Possible to Istanbul* depicts a budding romance between Klara, a young East Berlin woman, and Niyazi, an enterprising Turkish youth living in West Berlin. Keen to maximize his savings so that he may return to Istanbul, Niyazi sets out to acquire cheap accommodation in the eastern half of the city. He quickly realizes that his plan could be expedited through a romantic dalliance with an East German girl. On his way to the east where he is about to be introduced to Klara, he rationalizes his plan in voice-over:

> It's like this: for one deutsche mark you get a lot of east marks. So one should live here [in the east] and go to work in the other Berlin to earn

more money. Of course it's forbidden and you can't have your own apartment in the east; but only millionaires can afford a clean conscience after all. All you need is a girl with a room [in east Berlin] and you'll be a rich man.

After spending the night together with Klara in her modest apartment, Niyazi endears himself to her by his display of currency and disclosure of a lottery-ticket scheme. He justifies his weekly expenditure of 4 DM on the lottery to Klara: "Prospects of becoming rich are very slim but if I don't gamble, the chances of becoming rich are even worse. You can never be rich enough. And for me, hope is worth four marks." Here the relationship between Niyazi and Klara is possible because both are identified as outsiders (Klara explains that she feels like a beggar when she travels to West Berlin and Niyazi longs to return to his homeland).

Like in several other unification films, love relations in *The Promise* are varied, but German-German relations are not among the variations displayed. In that film Sophie's first love is Konrad, yet, even when she escapes to West Berlin, she couples with a French man rather than taking a West German as a partner. In *Ostkreuz,* the young East German Elfie teams up with a Polish petty thief, Darius, whereas the young protagonists in *World Master* are an East German girl and the son of a Red Army soldier destined to return to the Soviet Union. There are no West Germans featured in *Apple Trees, Jana and Jan,* or the late 1989 feature *Coming Out,* making love relations exclusively eastern in these films. Similarly, the most significant bonds between characters are established between East Germans in *Burning Life.* In *Herzsprung,* Johanna embarks upon an affair with a black foreigner whose name and origins remain a mystery whereas in Misselwitz's more recent melodrama, *Little Angel,* the East German woman, Ramona, falls in love with a Polish man.

One unification film set in the inner city of Berlin, *Life Is a Construction Site (Das Leben ist eine Baustelle,* Wolfgang Becker, 1997), goes further than other unification features discussed above. In Becker's film, promoted as a story about "love in the Kohl era," the West German male protagonist, Jan, has numerous sexual dalliances, at least one of which is with an East German woman. But that sexual encounter is brief and unsatisfactory, and it ultimately leads to disaster. When Jan leaves the apartment of the East Berliner—having been unable to perform to either his or her satisfaction—he stumbles onto a scene of street anarchy. A riot has broken out in the Berlin Mitte, and riot police and looters are in combat. Jan literally stumbles out of the East Berliner's bed into a full-scale riot, attracting the attention of the police and a 1,000 DM fine. Jan's sexual "transgression" is temporally linked to the anarchy and violence on the street and seems to precipitate his arrest and punishment in the ensuing scene. Later still Jan suspects that he is HIV positive—the result of an earlier casual sexual encounter. Even if only inadvertently, or as a result of displacement, the casual sex that Jan and the easterner are shown to engage in preempts all the calamity, social unrest, and anguish that follow. *Life Is a Building Site* suggests that cross-cultural German-German liaisons are pernicious.

In two other unification films, sexual relations between East and West Germans also bring disaster. Heiner Carow's drama *Missing* presents an impossible love affair between an East German woman, Elisabeth, and a West German man, Jacob. The relationship is obstructed by Elisabeth's imprisonment. German-German relations in *The German Chainsaw Massacre* prove to be lethal. Although the film does allow for the East German, Klara, to engage sexually with the West Germans, Hank and Brigitte, Klara ends up killing West Germans in self-defense.

Magic, Superstition, and Fairy Tales

Like many other unification comedies and dramas, *Rising to the Bait* vaguely identifies East Germans with superstitious and mystical elements. Unification films commonly align East Germans with folklore, magic, fairy tales, pagan rituals, and Fortuna. Folklore and mythology even inform the story of *Herzsprung,* which is based on a mythical tale explaining how the village featured in the film was given its name. In that film, a male protagonist evidences belief in a quasi-animistic spirituality, likening himself to the wind. One haunting scene has that figure charming a group of children who follow him across the countryside, mesmerized by the music he plays, just like in the story of the Pied Piper.

In *Apple Trees,* Lene and her grandmother are also linked to magic and superstition. An early scene in the film sees the grandmother pass on a set of doll's eyes to Lene to protect her from evil spirits. Lene later passes on the talisman to her own son. *Burning Life* also includes elements of mysticism and magic that are associated with the survival of the East German protagonists, Anna and Lisa. In one scene they consult their horoscopes before they attempt a bank robbery. Earlier in the film they cross paths with a vagabond East German magician and medicine man who travels around the provinces in an antiquated painted van, evocative of a circus wagon. He performs feats for his curious public, like drawing skewers through his hands, miraculously without any pain or injury. He also sells magic potions and mystical charms to his audience. Toward the end of the film, when Anna and Lisa's car temporarily breaks down, and they seem doomed to be captured by the police, the magician gives the women

Figs. 5 and 6. *Burning Life* **(1994). Film stills reproduced with permission of DEFA-Stiftung.**

a talisman. As he hands them an American Indian arrowhead, he explains that it is supposed to bring good luck, then proceeds to talk of the mystical powers of the charms he peddles. He confides in Lisa that there was a time when he "really did bring magical stones and holy water from the *jungle*" [emphasis added], at least until he realized that faith in mystical power was more important than charms. "Faith can move mountains," he claims. Apparently the "magic" arrowhead assures Lisa and Anna protection from evil, facilitating their escape from the police who have falsely identified the pair as dangerous terrorists. In the final scene of the film Anna and Lisa become airborne. They talk of flying to Africa in the police helicopter they have stolen—most certainly a fanciful, if not magical closure. Presumably Africa appeals to the women because they view it as a country with cultural and mystical links to the ex-GDR. What may be suggested here is that both cultures depend upon faith in magic and the favor of the gods.

In *Burning Life* and *Rising to the Bait* a type of spiritualism and mystical power alien to West Germans characterizes East German protagonists. Those powers allow characters like Ada, Udo, Anna, and Lisa to contend with unification, its demands and tribulations, but they also make their accomplishments all the more miraculous.

Inheritance

Inheritance is the chief means through which bad fortune is reversed in this cycle of films. It provides the necessary element of coincidence, allowing for the innocence of East German protagonists to be favorably contrasted to the machinations and deliberate deceptiveness of big business and entrepreneurs from the west. Inheritance of the family estate is one means through which concerns regarding the preservation or erosion of heritage in unified Germany can be made concrete. Emphasis on inheritance is largely a preoccupation in unification films produced in the west. Such films highlight unification as a territorial issue dependent upon fate.

The prevalence of the inheritance motif is also common to postwar Heimat films produced in the Federal Republic. In his analysis of Heimatfilme from 1947 through 1960, Willi Höfig observes that inheritance is one of the genre's central themes, noting that its treatment is constant whether the overall tone of the film is humorous or serious (347). There are certain conventions that determine characters' attitudes to the properties and estates they inherit, and these conventions extend to the cycle of western unification films discussed here and in greater detail in chapters 8 to 10. Höfig observes that heirs in the Heimat film are not free to wheel and deal with the property they inherit: it is more important that they learn to display a particular positive attitude to their inheritance. Heirs must accept the conditions of the inheritance and resist any innovations, which could jeopardize the unity and coherence of what is bequeathed. They must behave responsibly in relation to their inheritance, meaning they must strive to preserve continuity and integrity and protect their inheritance, property, or estate against profiteers and exploitation. The heir must conform to the norms and values of Heimat, if necessary through the restoration of the old order (348).

Unification films, in particular those produced in the west, retrace these narrative trajectories and revitalize such Heimat conventions. Hence, in *Rising to the Bait* Ada resists suggestions that she renovate her country cottage. Although she advertises her homestead for sale in the newspaper, she has no intention of parting with her property: she simply uses it as a lure to attract wealthy West Germans to the east to save the livelihood of her community. Udo Struutz struggles to secure ownership of the garden gnome business his uncle bequeaths him in *That Was the Wild East*. He must protect his country estate from avaricious capitalists and property developers from the west.

Wrangling over the rightful ownership of property is source of narrative conflict in western-backed unification films as much as in the Heimat genre (Höfig 350). Unification films frequently present East Germans dealing with threats of eviction posed by unscrupulous West German businessmen, developers, or relatives. *Rising to the Bait, Lost Landscape, No More Mr. Nice Guy, Gruß Gott, Genosse* (*God Bless, Comrade,* 1993), and *Cosimas Lexicon* all deal with issues surrounding residence, property, and/or inheritance. As with the Heimat genre, "characters are depicted in a pejorative manner if they show a dishonorable attitude to the hero. Their main mistake is that their motivation is egotistical. Their second mistake is that they are incapable of recognizing the special bond between the hero and the inherited property" (Höfig 350). These characters are invariably shamed, ridiculed, or ostracized because they threaten the ordered world of Heimat or they are oblivious to its charms. Such is the fate of Zwirner the West German antagonist in *Rising to the Bait*. He is obliged to return defeated to the western mainland at the end of the film, after scheming to cheat Ada, an East German widow, out of her estate. Although Zwirner initially enlist Ada's nephew Karl to assist in an inheritance scam, Karl eventually learns and accepts Heimat values; he prioritizes family and community over profit and relinquishes his claims on Ada's estate. Heimat remains unscathed.

The little-known East German production *Cosimas Lexicon* also establishes antagonism between profiteers and heirs. Cosima is a principled young writer who opposes the development of the run-down East Berlin apartment block in which she and her neighbors live. They face eviction if the developers get their way. Cosima discovers that the rightful owner of the building is a homeless derelict who sleeps on park benches in West Berlin. When the derelict is located, he is turned into an upstanding citizen who can rightfully claim the property. The developer's proposals are invalidated, and the tenants' home is saved. Fortune favors the well-intentioned proletariat (not to mention the Lumpenproletariat) in this film, and virtue triumphs over the greed of big business. *No More Mr. Nice Guy, That Was the Wild East, Apple Trees,* and *Rising to the Bait* all rely on these kinds of reversals of fortune that, in some way or other, are all related to a basic inheritance plot. These plot devices accommodate essentially passive protagonists who bow to the dictates of fate, like their counterparts in earlier Heimatfilme. Conflict is resolved in favor of those who value Heimat, rural heritage, and custom.

The focus upon property and inheritance in these films serves various functions. On the one hand, the inheritance motif is a means through which nostalgic sentiments, sometimes directly related to the old GDR, can be expressed. This avenue is used in *Apple Trees.* Lene's recollections of visiting her grandmother on her farm appear to be the happiest memories she has of her own childhood, and when she herself inherits the farm, nostalgia for those idyllic times resurfaces. In *No More Mr. Nice Guy,* Kipp and Most's dream inheritance harks back even further to a feudal age of lords, manors, and serfs.

On the other hand, the inheritance motif allows for the effects of unification to be made tangible and provides opportunity for the introduction or resolution of narrative conflict. Importantly, this emphasis allows for deliberation over otherwise abstract and amorphous issues related to heritage. It also allows for the integration of issues related to fate and to commerce. Heritage is redefined in unification films where it takes the material forms of property and productivity. Ultimately this means that eastern cultural heritage is interpreted according to the priorities and values of the market economy.

Private property becomes a vital element in unification films allowing for distinctions to be drawn between the foundations of socialism and capitalism. Private property is capitalism's Urform. In mythical terms it allows capitalism to be positioned as socialism's opposite. (The relationship is mythical insofar as the socialist state did not abolish inheritance or private property completely.) These plot devices—inheritance and wrangling over rightful ownership of property—also allow for further distinctions to be drawn between East and West Germans, particularly in western productions. Usually it is only East Germans who have a heritage—they inherit property—whereas all that West Germans normally have is capital—they attempt to acquire property by making devious takeover bids.

It is through focusing on private property in the form of criminality, theft, and inheritance that unification is represented as spectacle in this cycle of films. Theft, inheritance, and sudden reversals of fortune are vital elements in unification comedies. They allow for virtue and integrity to be rewarded by good fortune, providing the genre with its all-important happy ending. Wild contingencies such as these, when complemented by windfalls and caprice, enable unification to be treated as a comic matter—and capitalism to assert itself as spectacle in much the same way that the west has asserted itself in unified Germany.

Reception

Less than a handful of all the films I have referred to throughout this chapter have enjoyed at best modest box-office returns (although, as I have noted, German films rarely do, and it is even rarer for documentaries, like the Wall films, to attract substantial audiences). One film from all those I listed in this chapter did, however, attract an audience of more than a million cinema viewers; the unashamedly commercial, comic travelogue *Go Trabi Go*. Only two other unification films enjoyed healthy box-office returns. They were Detlef Buck's comedy *No More Mr. Nice Guy*, a low-budget 2.8 million DM production, and *Go Trabi Go*'s sequel, which is closely analyzed in chapter 10. Each of these films attracted around 500,000 viewers.

Few West German critics, and even fewer English writers, have seen fit to address unification films, and those who have done so tend to display annoyance over this cycle of films. For example, in their survey of "German Film after the *Wende*," the English critics Helen Hughes and Martin

Brady are especially critical of Sanders-Brahms's *Apple Trees*. They openly object to what they see as the film's critical treatment of the west, ignoring the film's sometimes scathing treatment of East Germans and its damning portrait of corruption and deceit under the old regime. Remarkably, Hughes and Brady overlook a crucial scene in the film where Heinz delivers a diatribe against the Party (repeated in voice-over at the end of the film). He accuses the Party of failing to fulfill the ideals of socialism, promoting instead "arse kissing, lies, and hypocrisy." Rather, Hughes and Brady suggest that *Apple Trees* commends life in the ex-GDR. Moreover, even though there are no West German characters in the film, and Lene repeats that her long-standing dream is to venture to the west, Hughes and Brady write:

> Paradoxically the film appears to be more a criticism of the cold and calculating West than an attempt to come to terms with GDR history. As in many other films the one-dimensional representation of the evils of Western capitalism tends to project an image of life in the former GDR that is uncomfortably similar to the clichés of community life propagated by the GDR government itself. The distortion is compounded by the implication that life in the East was more natural, less polluted and altogether more healthy than in the West. In addition the portrayal of GDR citizens as simple, almost mindless provincials caused considerable offence in the east. (286)

Holand-Moritz is another critic who has contributed to the denigration of the genre of the unification comedy. She did so with utmost economy when she titled her review of *Farssman or by Foot to the Dead-End*, "Whether East or West—German Flops are the Best" (Schenk, *Zweite Leben* 530). Even esteemed media analysts, who otherwise treat GDR screen culture with sympathy, found their patience tested by eastern Wall films.

> Somehow or other the positions taken in these films are all similar. You sense a curious tension between waiting for something new and better and a general attachment to what has been experienced up until now, a holding on to what is known and what one feels at home with.
>   When you have seen one documentary film about the new relations [brought about by unification], you quickly get the impression you have seen them all. The endless sequence of images of the misery of the former GDR, the faded society, the unrelenting grayness of the [country's] landscape, [it all goes to] show it isn't enough simply to fix

the camera [in front of this]. . . . This panoramic tour of the GDR's misery is tiring after a while and all of the confessions made [by individuals in these films] remain superficial. (Hickethier, "Neue deutsche Filme auf der Berlinale" 6)

A number of West German critics who were willing to acknowledge DEFA films were contemptuous of them as well. Surveying all the German films released in 1991, one critic remarked that most of them would not be worth seeing again: "At least in this field unification is real: in east and west the same sentimental films, laden with dismay and concern are being made, films which are fully subsidized and are ruinous at the box office" (Neumann, "Im jahr der naiven Helden" 55).

Unification films suffered doubly in that they could be criticized if they failed at the box office, whereas if they were commercially oriented, as unification comedies were inclined to be, they usually weren't considered worthy of critical attention at all. Margret Köhler is one of the extremely rare West German critics who has seen fit to acknowledge the existence of unification comedies. Nevertheless, she barely contains her outrage in surveying the genre:

It cannot be denied that German unification is an irreversible fact. But must a "unified folk" live with German unification films? That [situation is one that] has to be energetically disputed. The unification films that up until now have come to the cinema are health hazards; they almost constitute bodily harm or the neurological equivalent, brain damage. Whoever hoped the Trabi films were a one-time slipup was mistaken. . . .

In comparison to these works, which assume a spectator with an intelligence quotient bordering on idiocy, the often-ridiculed soap operas like *Denver* and *Dallas* are an intellectual challenge ("Opas Kino lebt!" 10–11).

Escapism and Festive Freedom

Above all, Köhler objects to the infantile, formulaic, and escapist nature of these films, and she is probably justified to do so. It is true that unification comedies such as *Cosimas Lexicon, Rising to the Bait,* and the Trabi films are frivolous and escapist, if not downright inane. But they are often so in interesting and resourceful ways. For example, *No More Mr. Nice Guy* closes with a scene that is escapist in the most literal sense. Having been pursued as outlaws for the major part of the film, *No More Mr.*

Nice Guy finally sees Kipp, Most, Viktor, and their enthusiastic hostage Nadine flee from the law, to find safety and acceptance in Viktor's village, by a quiet riverside.

The ending of *Burning Life* also indulges an escapist impulse. In this East German road-trip comedy, Anna and Lisa enjoy their status as folk heroes (at least for the major part of the film). Characters ask for their autographs, and in one scene a man sports a T-shirt decorated with an image of the pair brandishing guns during a holdup. The first half of the film sees the women repeatedly identified as the most popular robbers in Germany's postwar history. In bar scenes, locals cheer when they see news reports of Lisa and Anna's escapades on the television. Toward the end of the film, when the police hunt intensifies, it looks as if Anna and Lisa will be forced to drive over a cliff to their death as in *Thelma and Louise* (1991). This pair manages, however, to outwit the law. They steal a police helicopter and fly away to freedom, leaving the police stranded and humiliated.

Whatever criticisms or qualms these films may have about unification, movies like *Rising to the Bait, No More Mr. Nice Guy,* and the Trabi comedies are infused with a carnival spirit. They are cast in what William Paul has called a "festive mode." Although these films can accommodate contradictory, ambivalent voices, "they never lose . . . [their] air of celebration" (80). In the first Trabi film, for instance, Udo experiences a sense of freedom when he creates the popular "Trabi Peep Show," complete with a circus-style banner that helps to draw in crowds of spectators. A similar spirit of celebration prevails in the sequel when the family returns to East Germany, delighted at the prospect of their Festa Italiana. Kipp and Most also have their moments of exhilaration and euphoric liberation in *No More Mr. Nice Guy* when Kipp frees a truckload of pigs, saving them from the slaughter. Another occurs as the brothers emerge from a country bar where a wake is being held. Most departs in delight. His pockets bulge with the money he has won playing poker machines, and his glee sounds as if it has even infected the mourners, whom the brothers leave in an audible state of drunken revelry. Someone has died, but the impression finally conveyed is of relief rather than sorrow.

A comparable air and vibrant energy are conveyed in the title *Burning Life* as well as in a number of scenes early in the film. On various occasions, witnesses to Lisa and Anna's bank robberies are invited to sing in chorus, and during one such holdup, Anna delights the bank's customers when she launches into a calypso song and dance routine. All those present enter into the spirit of Anna's bank cabaret as they sway their arms in unison to the rhythm of her song, while she performs to the security camera.

These films revel in and celebrate communality wherever they can find it, "much as any festive art does" (Paul 71). Because of, not in spite of, their escapism, frivolity, and flights of fancy, unification comedies (like the gross-out comedies William Paul discusses) are still based on all-too-common social experiences and fears of such things as unemployment, homelessness, corruption, criminality, exploitation, estrangement, and isolation. These films are driven by the pursuit of festive freedom, an aspiration that is often presented as being at odds with the demands and challenges unification poses for the east. Although not investing as much in images of excess, unification comedies have a lot in common with the gross-out comedies and horror films Paul analyzes, films that are "most fully focused on the relation of the individual to the community. If every community necessarily operates as a constraint on the individual, the oppositional quality in these works is centered on questioning those constraints" (75). Unification comedies loudly question issues related to avarice, corruption, and deception in the new Germany. As Paul says (of more extreme forms of Hollywood genres), films like these are capacious enough to "move in several different directions at once" (80) and to tolerate large measures of ambivalence and contradiction, allowing for the exposure of utopian vision (79) and cynicism, sometimes within the same film. Accordingly, "these apparently frivolous works" can "speak in the voice of festive freedom": "some truths are more available to their mode of address" (75) than in other more "serious," more respected generic forms.

In comedies such as *That Was the Wild East, Burning Life, No More Mr. Nice Guy,* and *Rising to the Bait,* unification doesn't necessarily bring with it liberation, but rather is presented as a force capable of tempering "festive freedom." Unification does not necessarily result in the *immediate* consolidation of communities in these films, making complete detached parts of the country. The most immediate impact registered with unification is rather the division and fragmentation of the community. In part, what these films nevertheless clearly highlight is a yearning for community harmony and for Heimat. Heimat becomes the linchpin that most clearly distinguishes eastern and western depictions of life in unified Germany in this cycle of films. The struggle to preserve Heimat and to celebrate it are central to the western-funded productions like *Rising to the Bait,* the Trabi films, and *No More Mr. Nice Guy.* The concept of Heimat and the film genre have virtually no currency in eastern productions like *Little Angel, To the Horizon and Beyond, Nikolaikirche,* and others discussed in chapter 11. The reclaiming of the east as Heimat is a western initiative and perspective to which eastern filmmakers addressing unification do not subscribe. This discrepancy underscores the films discussed in each of the following chapters. Having examined the points of narrative and thematic convergence that link the broad cycle of eastern and western unification films, I now turn to Heimat as the salient feature that distinguishes eastern and western visions of the new federal states. In chapter 7 I consider the heritage of Heimat in the old states of the Federal Republic, and in chapters 8 to 10, I continue with an examination of the revival of the concept and genre in western-backed unification films.

CHAPTER 7

Heimat Tradition and Revival

Heimat Heritage in Western-Backed and -Produced Unification Films

Heimat was a handy concept and genre springboard for some 1990s western productions that sought to capture events, impressions, and experiences associated with German unification. Western unification films like *Rising to the Bait* and *That Was the Wild East* revive Heimat as a central cultural construct through which aspects of life in the new Germany could be sketched and grasped. Evoking the Heimat heritage provides opportunity for sentimental and often reassuring reflection on national identity in these films, an activity that may otherwise have been cause for bewilderment and dismay, especially, as I have suggested, for those in the east. The generic revival of Heimat in the 1990s features from the west may have provided Germans with the sort of stable cultural identity that otherwise eluded many of them as they confronted the disarray brought by unification. These films posit Heimat as a concept of national relevance: even though various unification comedies delight in emphasizing the sorts of cultural differences that distinguish Ossis and Wessis, Heimat is a concept that could be evoked in an effort to transcend those differences. The rediscovery of Heimat allows for the delineation of a common heritage, shared priorities, and values with which Germans in the old and new states could identify. It provides the opportunity to consolidate a national imaginary, "inviting audiences to imagine some form of collective unity or identity" (Walsh 6), while promoting a sense of common recognition of ideals and virtues.

Heide Fehrenbach's observation, that 1950s Heimatfilme provided "a vision of the future in which Germans could regain both their prosperity and their pride," a guarantee of "personal and national redemption, forgiveness and forgetfulness" (163), takes on a broader historical relevance in this context. Some 1990s unification films seem to provide a similar

125

vision for citizens from the former GDR as Heimat films did for West Germans during the period of occupation and reconstruction. As in the 1950s, some early 1990s unification comedies offer "consolation, compassion, and the prospect of reconciliation and inclusion" (Fehrenbach 163) for characters and, by extension, audiences. When Heimatfilme were at their peak in the Federal Republic, they provided audiences with a "promise of what prosperity should mean, long before it was a reality for the broad public" (Oehrle 84). Similarly, the display of sumptuous banquets, shopping sprees, international travel, and western fashions in the most widely viewed of unification films, the Trabi comedies, could possibly have enhanced these films' appeal to East German audiences anticipating prosperity through unification.

At a diegetic level at least, prosperity, pride, and contentment in Heimat are certainly what the protagonists of *That Was the Wild East, Apple Trees, No More Mr. Nice Guy,* and *Rising to the Bait* recover in the course of each film. Such optimistic scenarios may have provided welcome relief for East German audiences: honoring Heimat appears to be the key to good fortune and opportunity in these films. For their compatriots in the west, on the other hand, unification films may provide a consolation of a slightly different order. From a western perspective, the vision of the east regularly promoted in these films is nostalgic and narcissistic: the ex-GDR is viewed as a fledgling version of the Federal Republic—not so much as a former ideological and political adversary, but in terms of the west's mythical vision of its own past—simple, rustic, pristine. The utopian yearnings of the Heimat film, with its romanticized recollections of a lost and bygone past (Trimborn 29), resurface in various unification films of the 1990s. The east is transformed into a region that shares yearnings and myths of origin similar to the west's: that is, it is represented in part as an eco-paradise, a long-lost Heimat where community and harmony can be restored and secured. Like the Heimat film, numerous western unification films of the 1990s present fantasies of social integration, opportunity, and prosperity rather than evidence of the suspicion, hostility, and resentment provoked by unification. Mass unemployment, destitution, environmental pollution, xenophobia, escalating right-wing violence, alienation, and despair have little place in the idealized portraits of the east circulated in early 1990s unification films from the west. These films invest in the construction of a national imaginary through emphasizing the mythical plenitude and social cohesion that the concept of Heimat supposedly affords, ignoring the disparity and discord that have characterized German-German relations in the 1990s.

Similarly, Heimat films also presented a blinkered vision that ignored the upheavals and affliction that millions of Germans faced when the country was defeated in World War II. "After the war between 10 and 14 million people fled from the east" rather than returning to where they had lived during peacetime. Included among the hordes of displaced people

> were many who had been evacuated during the war, many who sought their families, many who were bombed out. It is estimated that at this time around a third to a half of the German population was on the move. In the face of this more or less enforced mobility, it is no wonder that finding a Heimat became a collective wish—a Heimat complete with concepts like security, clarity . . . harmony; a Heimat that could exist as a filmic ideal. (Oehrle 81)

In contrast to the *Trümmerfilme* (films shot among the ruins of the war) made by DEFA filmmakers immediately after the studios were founded, the Heimat film did not deal with the social reality of postwar existence and survival—"wherever possible all problems related to the political reality of postwar existence were excluded from the diffuse, distant . . . and transfigured life sphere of the Heimat film." Everything that was upsetting or disturbing about the past and postwar existence could be ignored (Trimborn 30).

Western unification films adopt a similar approach to history and politics. They display historical and political myopia by avoiding reference to invidious aspects of life in the ex-GDR. Fehrenbach's observations about the Heimat genre in the 1950s are again applicable to many films central to this study:

> While stressing the interplay between past and present, *Heimatfilme* are nonetheless riddled with gaps, ellipses, and silences. They emphasize history and tradition but only in its vaguest form; they contain few specific references to the more recent national past, yet such references are not completely absent. *Heimatfilme* never mention politics and are stone silent on national socialism, yet allusions to the war do appear (albeit in the most oblique form) in a couple of the most popular films. (153)

Similarly, western unification films are populated with apolitical protagonists, and references to Party ideals, accomplishments, and disgraces scarcely warrant mentioning. Credible representatives of the state or card-carrying communist enthusiasts do not feature in these films.

Western unification films also share the utopian impulses of the Heimat prototype. Jürgen Trimborn argues that Heimat was not a politically motivated, territorially determined, or revisionist concept as much as a utopian formulation (32). Heimat films of the postwar period reflected what Germans would have liked to have, not what they actually had (33). And the genre provided Germans with a positive and productive feeling for Heimat and a Heimat consciousness that was otherwise lacking (32). "What was not achievable in reality could be realized through the generic construct of *Heimat* and could be experienced, however briefly, by cinema audiences" (Trimborn 30). When audiences saw Heimat films in the cinema they were presented with a utopia worth striving for (Trimborn 14). Having experienced the fragmentation of communities, the loss of livelihood, the introduction of a new economic and political order, and the disbanding of the infrastructure of the old regime, eastern audiences may have derived a comparable measure of assurance from scenes of existential security and community harmony celebrated in various unification films. Like the Heimat film, unification films "emerged and peaked at a specific historical moment—during a period of political and economic uncertainty and emotional and social upheaval" (Fehrenbach 164). Moreover, neither Heimatfilme nor western unification films depict the relics of the previous political regime—the fascist dictatorship in the case of the Heimat film or the communist dictatorship in the case of the 1990s variant. Each film cycle adopts a comparable vantage point by depicting monuments and architecture that predate World War II.

Rather than being reminded of the wretched and depressing fields of debris and mountains of ruins that cluttered postwar German cities, 1950s audiences sought refuge in the Heimat film's vision of mountains, forests, and fields of heather: in reality the untouched Heimat glorified by the film genre no longer existed when the Heimat film reached its peak in the Federal Republic (Trimborn 16). Even when reconstruction was under way, the preindustrial, rural idyll showcased in the genre was difficult to reconcile with developments in agriculture: "fields and farms looked different than most Heimat films suggested. . . . the vocations of farming and forestry were struck by radical technical rationalization." The tractor and the chainsaw replaced the horse and axe (Konz 93).

Following *Heimat* conventions, western unification films that reclaim the east as *Heimat* refrain from depicting any widespread form of mechanization, mass production, or industrialization. The satellite towns and bleak high-rise housing estates, sprawling factories, ugly power plants, and mining sites that scarred the landscape of the former GDR are hardly ever granted the predominance they once had in the east in these films. Cobblestone streets, quaint cottages, and thatched roofs are more prevalent than high-density housing in western depictions of the east. The preference is to depict the east as a region that abounds in natural beauty and picturesque country scenery unscathed by the exigencies of the industrial age. Any impression that life or labor in the new federal states may involve alienation, isolation, or loss of purpose is assiduously avoided.

Just as Heimatfilme of the 1950s were a form of escapism in which "the everyday banal dreams that one dreamed at that time were fabricated" (Oehrle 81), unification films issuing from the west also display strong escapist tendencies. Udo Struutz becomes a millionaire in *That Was the Wild East;* in *Go Trabi Go* he and his family find themselves in Arcadia; Ada Fenske and her community celebrate their newfound riches in *Rising to the Bait;* Most and Kipp escape from police pursuit and are integrated into a scene of bucolic abundance at the end of *No More Mr. Nice Guy.* Characters in these films seek sanctuary in the country where they can avoid any form of modernization, in much the same way as Heimatfilme entailed "escapist projections away from existing industrial and city landscapes" (Oehrle 86). In the 1990s cycle of films, it is only when characters experience the countryside and embrace rural traditions that harmony can prevail: families are reconstituted, couples are united, and community solidarity is celebrated. Arthur Maria Rabenhalt's[1] account of late 1950s zeitgeist, as embodied in Heimatfilme of the period, rationalizes the escapism of the Heimat film. His observations are also of relevance to the films I discuss in chapters 8 to 10. "The escapism of today—especially in Germany—is particularly complicated. It's not just an escape from the present, but an escape in two directions. One flees from the unmastered past and also from the future that one cannot yet cope with" (qtd. in Oehrle 81).

Western-backed and -produced unification films revitalize other sentiments and conventions related to the Heimat film. They clearly revive the old town-country antagonisms and constellations of characters common to the Heimat prototype identified by Jürgen Trimborn, Willi Höfig, and Wolfgang Oehrle. In the late 1940s and 1950s "a town-country opposition was evident in the Heimat film as much as in postwar reality. The countryside [and its] untouched natural landscape become equated with Heimat, whereas one is confronted with history and destruction in the city, along with continual problems of supply of foodstuffs and heating material" (Oehrle 82). Unification films like *That Was the Wild East* and *No More Mr. Nice Guy* revert to such oppositions. In the first film, Dresden is presented as a city that is host to a trio of dim-witted, neo-Nazi vandals; attention is devoted to various landmarks restored to their original condition after the bombing of the city during World War II. After experiencing city life, the family is splintered, and it is in Dresden that the emblem of

---

1. Rabenalt directed seven Heimatfilme himself.

East German-ness, the Trabant, is disfigured. Although there is no short-age of food in the Dresden of *That Was the Wild East,* the protagonists of *No More Mr. Nice Guy* have to resort to stealing food to survive in the new Germany. It is only in the final scene when the film's vagabonds find con-tentment and acceptance in a rural community that they experience the abundance of the land. A clearer opposition between city and countryside is established in *Rising to the Bait,* which contrasts the natural beauty of an East German island with the slums of urban West Berlin.

Both *Rising to the Bait* and *That Was the Wild East* recycle the char-acter constellations of the West German Heimat film from the period of reconstruction. City dwellers are defined negatively in relation to those who value rural customs and life-style and are sensitive to the appeal of nature. Urban figures like the West Germans Zwirner and Kühn threaten to despoil the countryside in these films: they cannot appreciate or recog-nize the charms of Heimat like rural dwellers can. In *That Was the Wild East* Kühn schemes to build an autobahn over Landwitz, a pristine and historic village that neighbors on a national park. In this film, the Ameri-can millionaire Bill Buck is more overt in his development plans for the east, which involve the construction of futuristic skyscrapers and golf courses. Here the familiar antagonisms between development, progress, and industry, on the one hand, and tradition, rural custom, and heritage, on the other, resurface as in earlier Heimatfilme. As in the genre during the 1950s, progress is represented negatively as "something with the funda-mental potential to threaten or ruin the ordered world of Heimat" (Trim-born 52).

Following established conventions of characterization of the Heimat film, virtuous figures in western unification films display an affinity with the land and an aversion to the city. Ada, the protagonist of *Rising to the Bait,* has neither reason nor inclination to see the city lights of the west. When Lene seeks to visit her lover in West Berlin in *Apple Trees,* she is rebuffed in callous indifference. Country bumpkin brothers Kipp and Most can only find contentment and acceptance in an agrarian community in *No More Mr. Nice Guy.* The naïveté of protagonists like Kipp and Most or Udo in the Trabi comedies may be comic, but these rural dwellers are nevertheless presented more positively than those from the city: sympathy is reserved for the rural dweller or farmer as in Heimat films (Höfig 313). Treasuring Heimat becomes an index of virtue in these films.

Before attending in further detail to various unification films and ana-lyzing them as "ideological, discursive practices in . . . specific historical moments" (Walsh 6), it seems appropriate to recall the emergence of the Heimat film and particularly its place in German film history. Then the ideological and cultural implications of its restoration become disturbingly clear.

The Origins and Consolidation of the Heimat Genre

"*Heimat:* that is the harmonious sphere of love of the father state and mother nature as they sit together under the linden tree, pleased that all is, and remains, as it always was" ("Geh über" 253). Recognized as an enduring and authentically German film genre, Heimat has literary and theatrical origins that date back to the nineteenth century.[2] "Rural landscape and peasant life serve as the raw material for the idealized images in the emerging *Heimat*-literature, a body of writing glorifying the simplicity and stability of the countryside" (Rentschler, *West German Film* 105). In this literature, Heimat "is synonymous with naturalness, simplicity, morality, vitality, but also . . . with social cohesion, solidarity, and harmony" (Dierick 158). The rural tradition of the *Volksschauspiel* (folk or peasant theater), popular in southern Germany and Austria in the last quarter of the nineteenth century, was also an important source and stylistic influence for Heimatfilme (Rentschler, *West German Film* 105).

In part the Heimat genre is related to the *Bergfilme* (mountain films) of the 1920s and 1930s. "Other branches that make up the 'family tree' of the Heimat film include village tales, nature poetry, historical novels, and peasant novels of the nineteenth century." They in turn are the more or less "legitimate offspring" of the German Romantics' conception of Heimat, which was simultaneously utopian and retrogressive (Kaschuba 9).

The very first film to bear the title *Heimat* (although not the first example of the genre) was Carl Froelich's 1939 award-winning feature of that name, which starred Zarah Leander. Heimatfilme celebrated the residual culture and traditions of a bygone era. These films embraced the innocence and wholesome simplicity they associated with rural life and sought reassurance in the domestic, the familiar, and the parochial. Following the theatrical tradition of the Volksschauspiel, protagonists in Heimat films "bowed to the dictates of an omnipotent Fate" (Rentschler, *West German Film* 106).

Heimat sensibility exploited the eternal over the transient, tradition over change, and the rural myth over modernization and urbanization. Accordingly, Heimat was a notion deployed by the Nazis as part of their

---

2. This material on Heimat draws in part on my article "*Heimat:* Backs to the Past." *Film News* 15.6 (1985): 13–14.

ideological arsenal, and the film genre flourished under their rule. Heimat was something sacrosanct, and following the nationalistic and imperialistic ethos of Nazism, it was something to fight for. Heimat functioned as an expression of the political movement's reactionary protest against modernization (industrialization and social progress). It embodied Nazism's "romantic yearning for a mythical past, in which heroic and racially pure Germans lived together without class bitterness or exploitation" (Nicholls 68).

The genre, which "never wanted to be the embodiment of 'great cinema,' but rather craft work and family film entertainment" (Kaschuba 11), provided distraction for German audiences during the Third Reich, and later during the period of reconstruction. As I noted earlier, Heimat films also flourished throughout much of the "Economic Miracle" in the west. The genre endured after the Third Reich and avoided the attention of the Allied censors in the western zones of occupation possibly because it was redolent of what Höfig calls "trivial literature" (29–35): Heimat films dealt with the "world of tradition," not history or political history (Kaschuba), and were therefore presumed to be apolitical. In any case, postwar Heimat films were not viewed to be ideologically offensive when they were released insofar as they did not refer to the Third Reich but "to a completely untainted time before 1933" (Kaschuba 11). Accordingly, Heimat "came to embody the political and social community that could be salvaged from the Nazi ruins" (Appelgate, qtd. in Fehrenbach 151).

Nevertheless continuity between Heimat films of the 1940s and 1950s was pronounced. In postwar examples of the genre "various nuances had to be eliminated, like anti-Semitic tendencies and attacks against western powers. But otherwise everything else was preserved [in] *Heimat* films and melodramas: anti-communism; the admiration of authoritarian character traits and systems; love of the German *Wehrmacht;* . . . the German psyche" (Kochenrath, qtd. in Wilzcek 77). Many filmmakers who specialized in the Heimat film during the Third Reich continued to work in the genre after the war. "Hans Deppe's career as a director, from which we have twenty-four Heimat films to thank him for, came to an end with the Adenauer era. . . . With almost seventy films [to his name] in twenty-six years, he hardly had time for a great deal of reflection" (G. Schmidt 73).

During the golden age of West German film, which was actually a time when more local films were produced than the German market could accommodate, producers' financial risks were minimalized by virtue of a system of government-guaranteed credits. "In the period from 1953–1956 state subsidy for film production [in the Federal Republic] was 100% of the budget and this in turn led to the overproduction of poor quality films of dubious artistic merit" (Wilzcek 78). Marketable genres like Heimat films, thrillers, and Karl May westerns prevailed (78), whereas representatives of the film industry, the church, and the FSK (Committee for the Voluntary Censorship of the German Film Industry) favored "light genres" like these (77). The popularity of Heimatfilme, such as *Schwarzwaldmädel* (*Black Forest Girl,* 1950) and *Grün ist die Heide* (*Green Is the Heather,* 1951) no doubt contributed to the proliferation and formulaic nature of the genre later in the 1950s. *Green Is the Heather* was seen by over 19 million people between 1951 and 1959 (Oehrle 88).

By the late 1950s "there was hardly a production company [in the Federal Republic] that did not shoot a Heimat film. Berolina and its successor Kurt Ulrich Film Pty. Ltd. were most strongly involved in the Heimat business, [producing] 15 and 19 films respectively" (Wilzcek 79). The West German production companies Peter Ostermayr Film, H.D. Film, König Film, Carlton-Film and Rex film were responsible for the production of another 55 Heimat features (a number of which were coproductions) (Höfig 454). In the Federal Republic during the 1950s "the overall proportion of Heimat films on the market was 25 percent, that is 300 out of 1,206 features" (Wilzcek 79).

However much they were ridiculed or discredited after the Economic Miracle, Heimat films had great public resonance in the west throughout the 1950s. Even as late as 1961 this was the most popular genre favored by West German audiences in the 45- to 65-year-old age group (Höfig 452). Hans Günther Pflaum has remarked on the durability of Heimatfilme, which "seemed to be the only genre that had survived the Nazi era, the post-war years, and the Economic Miracle. Ludwig Ganghofer's novel, *Schloss Hubertus* has, for instance, been made into a film no fewer than three times, adapted to the tastes of 1934, 1954 and 1973, and each time it was a success" (qtd. in Elsaesser, *New German* 141). The popularity of the genre meant that many Heimat films made during the Third Reich were remade during the period of reconstruction: between 1947 and 1960, thirty-two earlier Heimat films were released as remakes. The themes remained the same over twenty years, "even when it didn't entail the second or third rehashing of old material" (G. Schmidt 74). Interest in the genre, Heide Fehrenbach notes, nevertheless began to decline (along with cinema attendance) in 1956, after which Heimatfilme seemed to be "little more than advertisements for domestic tourist destinations" (164).

However popular Heimatfilme may have been during the Economic Miracle, they contributed to the appalling international status of West German film during this period. Then, general consensus was that this national cinema was among the worst in the world. "Complaints about the quality of domestic films escalated and the Heimatfilm became emblematic of all that was wrong" with them (Fehrenbach 148). This situation prompted the spread of the common belief throughout the Federal Republic that "life is too short to watch German film," and this impression prevailed until at least the mid-1960s.

In the late 1960s and early 1970s, some filmmakers of the New German cinema directed their critical attention to the genre and the ideals and mythology that it had come to represent. They exploded stereotypes that had grown out of the genre and deconstructed "false images of the past while fashioning new ones addressed to the present" (Rentschler, *West German Film* 104). Reinhard Hauf, Peter Fleischmann, Uwe Brander, Rainer Werner Fassbinder, and Volker Schlöndorff were among those who reworked the genre, often satirically, as they ridiculed the idyllic scenes and sentimentality common to the original genre. Whereas the "chief features of the old *Heimat* film were an Alpine setting, and usually a plot in which a poacher, in love with the daughter of the richest farmer, becomes the defender of the peasantry" (Elsaesser, *New German* 141), the "new" (or anti-) Heimatfilme manipulated this formula, often to brutally funny ends. In new Heimat films from the period, such as *Die plötzlicher Reichtum der armen Leute von Kombach* (*The Sudden Wealth of the Poor People of Kombach,* 1970), and *Jagdszenen aus Niederbayern* (*Hunting Scenes from Lower Bavaria,* 1968), German country folk are presented as dim-witted, bigoted, and hypocritical. As in Fassbinder's *Katzelmacher* (1969), which is located in the suburbs of Munich rather than rural Bavaria, characters are presented as narrow-minded and xenophobic, driven to persecute and brutalize a stranger (Georg, "the Greek from Greece") who disrupts their insular lives. Edgar Reitz recalls that in the early 1970s, New German directors parodied the genre enough to make the countryside a bad address to have (qtd. in Pawlikowski 5–6), at least among fellow intellectuals and filmmakers.

Perhaps the biggest single Heimat revival since the 1950s was Edgar Reitz's own fifteen and a half hour long teleseries film of the same name. He worked on the series from 1981 through 1984 and ended up with an epic that spanned a period of more than sixty years. Although it was shown first in cinemas and was screened internationally, it was viewed by about 10 million Germans in biweekly episodes when it went to air. In the Federal Republic, the series was popular enough to prompt the spread of a Heimatkult and a new wave of nationalism together with nostalgia for a past that was largely denazified and whitewashed.

Heimat was also a concept favored and exploited by the Federal Republic's politicians in the early 1980s as they prepared their election campaigns. Heimat was included in the party slogans of the Christian Democrats who claimed "security and identification of Heimat." It was also used by the SPD who promoted themselves as "the Social Democrats, whose identity is clearly carved out, along with their Heimat." Even the KBD (Kommunistische Bund Westdeutschlands) drew on Heimat when, to the embarrassment of the conservatives, they formulated their election slogan "Hier sich wehren, heißt die Heimat ehren" (loosely translated as "Those who defend themselves here, honor Heimat").

Chancellor Helmut Kohl raised his Heimat consciousness in the mid-1980s and further promoted the term when he publicly asked himself:

> What is Heimat? *Heimat* is a German word that defies translation in any other language.[3] Heimat is the place or country where one is born and where one grows up. To it belongs the commitment of values and eternal ways of living. Heimat stems from the word home, from house and farm, from heritage and possessions. Heimat answers the question, "Who am I? Where did I come from? How did I become what I am? ("Geh über" 255)

The chancellor's appropriation of the term reminds us of its emotional resonance, its political potency, its capacity to reinforce the national imaginary, and its falsity. To varying degrees, western unification films also invest in this process and promote a yearning for and awareness of Heimat.

The films I turn to in the next three chapters draw in various ways on the Heimat tradition. Many unification films from the west adopt a Weltanschauung that can be traced back to the Heimat genre of the 1950s. In particular they utilize the Heimat film's faculty for romanticizing life on the road and musical vagabonds. These films

> held out a fantasy of the future. They showed . . . worlds unencumbered by material want, in which the begging of the musical vagabonds is politely and generously answered with free food, beer, and social acceptance. In this case, mendicancy is romanticized as a life-style choice, and the freedom of the road becomes a metaphor for self-realization in the developing democracy of plenty. (Fehrenbach 163).

Go Trabi Go, That Was the Wild East, and *No More Mr. Nice Guy* are among the unification comedies that focus on characters who either are homeless or delight in their adventures on the road. Often they display

---

3. It was public knowledge and a source of embarrassment to many Germans that Kohl was a monolingual chancellor.

their glee about wandering by breaking into song, as one character frequently does in *That Was the Wild East.* Similarly, another character is
turned briefly into a musical vagabond in *Go Trabi Go,* and the protagonists of *No More Mr. Nice Guy* are itinerant for the duration of the film,
until they stumble into a harmonious world of festivity, music, and plenty.

These unification comedies are linked in terms of their generic heritage and their production backgrounds. They are all films from directors
living and working in the west, and for the greater part they are backed by
western finances, production companies, and television stations. East German collaboration extends to casting and, in the case of *Rising to the Bait,*
to the script. Essentially these features draw on a film genre that, in the
postwar period at least, is West German. These films come from the west
even though they are located in the ex-GDR: they address changes and
challenges unification has brought, but they do so within a genre framework that has a special place in the film history of the Federal Republic,
not the GDR. In this way, a West German film genre is used to depict,
define, and examine the East.

The Heimat genre was not favored at DEFA because it was ideologically offensive to the SED and socialist imperatives and values. When the
Heimat film was at its peak in the Federal Republic, the Democratic
Republic prioritized the modernization and reform of agriculture. Production was collectivized with a vengeance in the period between 1952 and
1960 and led to state violence. Collectivization "meant a radical integration of rural life into the centralized system of government and into met-
ropolitan lifestyle" (Bathrick 33). This type of integration and modernization of the agricultural sector hardly coincided with the Heimat idyll.
DEFA films were more inclined to support the objectives of the *Aufbau-
jahre,* the construction years (for example, the construction of housing
estates and high-rise complexes that would provide basic, affordable
accommodation in city centers). As I remarked in discussing established
DEFA genres in chapter 2, when East German directors turned to the
past, they usually sought to glorify the antifascist foundations of the GDR
and to resurrect the history of the resistance. By contrast, Heimatfilme
from the FRG sought to obscure any recollections of Nazism. The Heimat
film's depoliticized past and the lack of political allegiance and historical
insight of its protagonist never found acceptance with the Socialist Party
in the GDR. The historical indeterminacy of the West German Heimat
film could not be reconciled with GDR cultural policy. Although some
critics may be justified in suggesting that Heimat sensibility is evident in
DEFA films, not named as such but rather bearing the more clearly politi-
cized label of "Socialistic Fatherland," most are convinced that the concept and characteristics of the genre had little significance in films pro-

duced at DEFA. On the rare occasion that exceptional DEFA productions such as *Der geteilte Himmel* (*The Divided Sky,* 1964) or *Einmal ist keinmal* (*Once Is Never Once,* 1954) are mentioned under the Heimat rubric, such films are described as falling "back on 'compromised' cinematic formulas" (Elsaesser and Wedel 5).

Historians who have analyzed Heimat films, such as Jürgen Trimborn, view the Heimat genre as an exclusively West German phenomenon. In his examination of eighty Heimatfilme from the period 1947 through 1960, Willi Höfig treats the Heimatfilm as a popular form of entertainment exclusive to the west, indicative to some of the "restorative tendency of the Federal Republic of the 1950s" (71). Indeed the term Heimat and DEFA film are hardly ever mentioned in the same sentence. When they are, it is usually to dissociate one term from the other. Annette Battenberg and colleagues explain:

> Love of Heimat, Heimatfilme, being banished from Heimat, and local history were concepts that were on everyone's lips in the Federal Republic during the 1950s. Not so in the GDR. Morphologies with Heimat were viewed with suspicion there: it was assumed that the bourgeois ideology of Heimat served to disguise class struggle above all else, insofar as it sought to propagate an illusory form of community while disguising all the alienation that existed in capitalist society. One kept one's distance because of terrible associations with the national socialists' perversion of the bourgeois love of Heimat through their Blood-and-Earth ideology. A Heimat film boom, like the one experienced in the Federal Republic, could not therefore have occurred in the GDR. . . . Officially the genre of the Heimat film did not and does not exist in the GDR. (149)

What is at issue here is not so much whether Heimat surfaced in a different guise in DEFA films, or under a different name. It is rather the reappropriation of the genre within a 1990s context and its relevance to 1990s unification films that concern me here. A disparity emerges when one compares eastern and western features that seek to evaluate what the GDR was or what it has become since unification. The concept of Heimat and the conventions of the genre are not embraced in eastern-backed, -directed, and -produced unification films. Throughout the 1990s this cultural construct was dismissed as irrelevant to East German depictions of life in the new Germany (as I will elaborate in chapter 11). Reclaiming the former GDR as Heimat is a cultural and ideological phenomenon limited to western unification films. These divergent views are symptomatic of irreconcilable east and west perspectives on German unification.

Once again Heimat is resurrected in western features to provide a society in ruins facing a complete political reorientation with reassuring images of harmony and integration. A genre whose Weltanschauung was anathema to the sociopolitical values and priorities of the ex-GDR has been recycled to shape impressions of what life in the east has become and what the East has to offer. A western framework is imposed on the east to define it in western terms. At a popular cultural level, this could be viewed as a further disconcerting instance of the colonization of the east.

CHAPTER 8

Unification Comedies:
Rising to the Bait and
No More Mr. Nice Guy

Rising to the Bait is an east-west coproduction that displays many traits that characterize western-backed unification films. It presents the east as a preindustrial paradise; it highlights the virtue and resilience of East Germans; it presents unification as a threat to community solidarity. Together with *That Was the Wild East,* the films *Rising to the Bait* and *No More Mr. Nice Guy* recycle what Höfig refers to as the "central theme" of the Heimat genre (347)—inheritance. *No More Mr. Nice Guy* and *That Was the Wild East* are further associated through their mutual concentration on itinerant protagonists, a focus that strengthens the correlation between these features and the Heimat genre. In the postwar prototype it seems as if the "vagabonds [depicted] have freely chosen their own fate and could change it at any time" (Oehrle 82). In 1950s Heimatfilme the life-styles of those on the move are highly romanticized (Oehrle 82), and this accent is also evident in both 1990s comedies. As I elaborate in chapter 10, the majority of East German characters who populate western unification films embrace the ideals of Heimat: they seek consolidation of the family and integration into a harmonious rural community. Initially, this is something that evades them. Unification films regularly depict East Germany as a region in which the nuclear family is threatened with extinction.

Rising to the Bait and *No More Mr. Nice Guy* command attention here because they espouse Heimat sentiments through common approaches to narrative closure. In each film, closure entails a festival celebrating the establishment or augmentation of a community. Closure also involves the constitution of a surrogate family in both films. *Rising to the Bait* and *No More Mr. Nice Guy* end with idealistic scenes of conciliation: not only is community harmony inaugurated at the end of these films, but importantly protagonists find acceptance, a sense of belonging, and social integration. These forms of conciliation echo the narrative imperatives of the Heimat genre. As is typical of unification films from the west, the communities that are nurtured and celebrated are agrarian and geographically isolated from the old Federal Republic. In this sense, *Rising to the Bait* and *No More Mr. Nice Guy* both provide utopian solutions to problems that life in the new Germany may pose. Integration into a harmonious community is only achieved in these two unification comedies when the east and west are segregated. Unity and community are only assured through isolating easterners from unification and its consequences. Both films effect a seclusion from unification: in *Rising to the Bait* this is achieved by literally depicting the ex-GDR as an island separated from the mainland of unified Germany. *No More Mr. Nice Guy* takes a more extreme position. In that comedy, Kipp, Most, and companions have to leave unified Germany altogether before they can find an integrated, harmonious community to accommodate them. For them Heimat can only be experienced outside of Germany.

Another issue that leads me to group these films together relates to the strategies they deploy to avoid German-German relations. *Rising to the Bait* suggests that only relations among East Germans are natural and destined to endure. The film goes to great lengths to redefine the heritage of characters to avoid any possibility of east-west miscegenation. *No More Mr. Nice Guy* utilizes a similar strategy, even though its inferences about the lineage and the cultural affinities of its protagonists are more subtle and circuitous. Not only does *Rising to the Bait* refrain from acknowledging any German-German relations, it suggests that family relations and love relations are soured in the west, if they exist there at all. The impression that German-German relations are improbable is also fostered in *No More Mr. Nice Guy.*

Rising to the Bait

Even though it characterizes interactions between East and West Germans in competitive, potentially exploitative terms, *Rising to the Bait* is one of the most optimistic unification comedies to emerge from the 1990s. The film displays considerable faith in East Germans and the prospects their lives were presumed to hold when the GDR was incorporated into the Federal Republic. *Rising to the Bait* focuses upon easterners adjusting to the market economy and reckoning with the power of West German capital. However, in this film the initiative, integrity, and community sensibility of the East Germans allow them to make the transition profitably and with ease. Accordingly it comes as no surprise that many reviewers evaluating the film were alert to its fairy-tale qualities ("Ein 'deutsch-deutsches Märchen'").

Rising to the Bait recognizes some of the tribulations that unification has brought to those in the east (unemployment, closure of local businesses, redundancy): it's just that in this film all obstacles are proficiently surmounted. Dealing with bureaucracy or the coercive agencies of the state do not present major problems in this film as they do in *Burning Life, Miraculi, No More Mr. Nice Guy, Apple Trees,* and *The Promise.* Equally remarkable, once *Rising to the Bait*'s East Germans familiarize themselves with the rules of the market economy, they manage to beat the West Germans at their own game.

Obstinately idealistic, *Rising to the Bait* has been held responsible for the introduction of an unusual type of character, the *Besser-Ossi* or superior easterner (Kruttschnitt, "Oer Osten"; Köhler, "Opas Kino" 11). In this way it inverts the unification comedy stereotypes that commonly introduce West German characters as well-informed, manipulative, and domineering and East Germans as gullible and childlike (as are the protagonists in *Adamski, Go Trabi Go, Stein,* and *Miraculi*).

The Production

In production and preproduction, *Rising to the Bait* sought to maintain a representative balance of east and west involvement. Its director was the West German actor/director Vadim Glowna, but the film's script was authored by Knut Boeser, former writer for the *Schauspielbühne* (the East Berlin State Theater), and the film's cameraman, Hans Ritschel, also came from the east. The role of the protagonist is filled by a famous East German actor, Elsa Grube-Deister, whereas a West German actor, Rolf Zacher, plays her antagonist (Zacher, who is regularly cast as a gangster, usually provides Robert de Niro with his voice when films he stars in are dubbed for German audiences).

For their part, the East Germans who were involved in the production of *Rising to the Bait* were generally enthusiastic about the film, its sentiments, and its depiction of former GDR citizens. The director explained that the film was designed to make East Germans courageous. It appealed to East Germans "not to sink into self-pity and to lose self-respect in the face of corrupt bureaucratic mentality and everything that smells of authority" (qtd. in Römer). The scriptwriter promoted the film by saying that its lesson was to show that "East Germans can only protect themselves from their western neighbors when they take matters in their own hands." The film's star, Elsa Grube-Deister, observed that *Rising to the Bait* deserved to be distinguished from other films addressing the fate of

East Germany after unification because it focused on courageous and brave "little people": it refrained from depicting everything in the east as being dull and faded ("Berlinale—Abschluß").

Many eastern critics also valued aspects of *Rising to the Bait.* Numerous reviews of the film in the local press of Thüringia, Magdeburg, Leipzig, Potsdam, and East Berlin saw fit to praise the film. In the case of the *Märkische Allgemeine, Rising to the Bait* was favorably distinguished from other unification films, a "positive exception to these films which, on the whole, weren't much good" ("Wen ein Wessi"). East Berlin's *Junge Welt* handled the film more critically, remarking that the filmmaker was naive and out of touch with the grave economic reality facing those in the east ("Dein Lebens-Budget"). In any case when the film was premiered at the Berlin film festival in 1992, it could be seen to provide relief from the seemingly interminable scenes of eastern misery that West German critics objected to in surveying German contributions to the Berlinale in the previous year (Hickethier, "Neue deutsche Filme" 5–7).

Rising to the Bait is reported to have done well at the box office, "above all in the east" ("Haie"). Helen Hughes and Martin Brady refer to the film as one of the "most successful reunification comedies" (287), although they offer no hard evidence that it profited at the box office. Progress, distributor of DEFA films in the GDR and postunification, picked up the film. Expecting that it would do well at the box office, Progress released forty prints of the film, at a time when 70 percent of all German films released had to make do with ten prints or fewer. In the first six months of its commercial release, *Rising to the Bait* was only seen by 11,301 viewers ("Black Box Office" 1992, 6).

Events surrounding the production of *Rising to the Bait* seem to confirm the director's observation that the film's story is "a German-German fairy tale" (Glowna, qtd. in Tok). The reality surrounding the film was harsh indeed. The real-life production brought disaster to some of the crew who normally worked for East German television. With the eastern broadcasting services undergoing rationalization, "quite a few received their layoff notices" while they were shooting the film (Tok). The film was shot on Rügen, an island off the coast of Mecklenburg-Vorpommern. The inhabitants of Rügen, in contrast to the determined and resourceful easterners featured in the film, were less fortunate in defending the natural assets of their island. Even as he was promoting his film, Glowna was outraged that a local initiative to preserve the spectacular rugged chalk coastline of the island featured in the film had failed. To his dismay, the coastline, one of the island's most distinctive features, was about to be taken over by the West German shipyards, Meyer, and "shaved clean" (Tok).

The East as Preindustrial Paradise

Whatever ecological damage Rügen may have faced, the island provided an ideal location through which the east could be pictured as some sort of preindustrial paradise in *Rising to the Bait*. The film focuses on the island's isolated rural community and the simple lives of its inhabitants. Like *That Was the Wild East, Rising to the Bait* takes as its location a pristine area of the former GDR where there are hardly any signs of industrialization, mechanization, or modern technology. Even though the film is set in the fall of 1991, *Rising to the Bait*'s world is one where there are no television sets, video recorders, computer games, or forms of mass communication, and only villainous characters—those who lack integrity and insight—use telephones.

Rising to the Bait presents a village community where manual labor prevails and subsistence skills like spinning wool, fishing, herding sheep, and tending geese flourish. Like other western-produced unification comedies, this film presents East Germany as a harmonious eco-paradise complete with unspoiled natural beauty. When westerners arrive on the island by helicopter the film takes full advantage of the opportunity to display aerial views of Rügen's spectacular white cliffs and foreshore. For their part, the jaded, world-weary West Germans who are drawn to the east are clearly invigorated by their encounter with wholesome and unpretentious easterners.

A single brief comparison between life on Rügen and existence in the west makes the ex-GDR look all the more idyllic in this film. In contrast to the well-preserved thatch-roofed and quaint half-timbered cottages of the east, West Berlin is imaged as ugly and decrepit. Wrecked car bodies and refuse litter the neighborhood we see, and idle youths lounge around outside slum tenements, lazing around on discarded furniture. The first image we have of life in the west is of a couple engaged in a violent domestic argument. Graffiti decorate the stairwell of the partly demolished apartment block. The interior and exterior of the slum look like industrial wastelands, making the contrast to the rural idyll of Rügen even more striking. Western civilization is represented in terms of images of decay and ruin. No wonder those who live there are eager to seek whatever refuge and beauty the East may have to offer.

At the very center of the *Rising to the Bait* is Ada Fenske, an elderly East German pensioner who lives in a modest cottage overlooking the foreshores of Rügen. In contrast to the neglect and decay of the west, Ada's estate is the picture of old-world charm. The interior of her cottage is adorned with lace, baubles, wicker, and embroidery. The flowers in her window boxes are in full bloom; a gaggle of geese scurry around the house, and an overall impression of robust wholesomeness is conveyed by the nearby ocean as well as by the bundles of clean white linen Ada hangs out to dry in the bright sunshine at the start of the film.

Although the film is set after unification, it seems that Widow Fenske has not taken advantage of the right to travel, and there is little to suggest that she has been to the mainland, let alone anywhere else in the world. Her only ambition is a global one—to see a massive mountain, like Mont Blanc or Mount Everest. She displays no discernible interest in the other half of Germany. After all, she doesn't really need for West Germans to come to her. When she is visited by a number of western businessmen, Ada realizes that her home and the property that surrounds it are not only valuable, but much sought after by different interest groups. Appreciative of the unspoiled locale, a wealthy, benevolent West German, Herr Naujock, offers to buy Ada's cottage. Unbeknownst to Ada, German army intelligence also has an interest in her property, which adjoins a Soviet military installation. The German Bundeswehr and military intelligence launch a scheme to secure possession of this strategically located stretch of coastline. Their objective seems to be to occupy this terrain when the Soviet troops leave the area, and to facilitate their aims they send West German undercover agent Albert Zwirner to Rügen.

Zwirner uses a variety of devious means in his attempt to force the widow to sell her estate. His coercive strategies include forgery, bribery, falsification of documents, and threats of arson. He uses blackmail to embroil the local mayor, Herr Solter, in his scheme. Zwirner threatens to make public some documents he has falsified that identify Solter as a former Stasi agent. He also threatens to disclose information about the mayor's love child, Karl Funke, born secretly to Ada's sister, Elfriede. Zwirner succeeds in locating Karl (who was orphaned as a young child) in West Berlin. He enlists the unprincipled young man, an impoverished would-be artist and layabout, in his scheme by persuading him to claim an inheritance that by law would be his mother's: half of Ada's estate.

Meanwhile, Ada sets about establishing further business contacts with wealthy West Germans who wish to buy her home. In an attempt to attract them to the island, Ada places bogus notices in western newspapers advertising the homestead's sale. At the same time she organizes local traders, craftspeople, and pensioners in an effort to promote the natural produce of their island. Jams are preserved, fruit juices are bottled, and country scenes and seascapes are painted by a local artist. Ada, meanwhile, ventures into cottage industry, providing neighbors with wool (from the west) that they knit into cardigans. Later she capitalizes on the natural produce of Rügen and decides to use homegrown, hand-spun wool from the local sheep.

When a troop of West German buyers arrive on the island anticipating the sale of Ada's property—the bait referred to in the film title—she strikes business deals with them to sell the goods the locals have made. Rügen's collapsing economy is suddenly buoyant, and locals who were threatened by unemployment find work once again. Local trade flourishes—and the east manages to retain "the best" of its culture. The resident artist resolves to sell some of his paintings to the mainland and keep some on the island for an exhibition. The shepherd's flock is saved, and Ada manages to encourage the local fisherman (who somehow or other has been "fired") to set up a fish shop on the island.

Family ties among estranged relatives are also reestablished, and several generations reconcile their differences. After Ada meets Karl, the relative she never knew she had, the pair develops a special rapport. Karl undergoes a character transformation. He falls in love with the village sweetheart, Ada's tenant Swetlana. Eventually he denounces Zwirner and the scheme to force Ada to sell her home. When Karl's true identity is finally revealed, any possibility of familial or sexual relations between East and West Germans is ruled out. Karl metamorphoses from being "half-Wessi" to "100 percent" eastern when Mayor Solter accepts his role as Karl's father. Karl's western heritage is negated, and to the glee of all present he is identified as a "genuine Rügen boy." Ada doesn't have to spare any thought about the assimilation of a West German into her family. The revelation is followed by the public announcement that Swetlana and Karl intend to marry. The prospect of a "mixed" marriage is conveniently eliminated. Mayor Solter gives the pair his blessing.

In the end, Ada triumphs over all of her antagonists, which include the (West) German army, (West) German intelligence, (east) local council, the remnants of the SED, and (West) German business and industry. For reasons that are not very clear, the army loses interest in Ada's property. Most of the western capitalists and property developers who have been lured to Rügen have undergone life-enhancing experiences, also a narrative outcome common to Heimatfilme that show city dwellers rejuvenated by brief country sojourns (Trimborn 40). At the close of the film merriment prevails, with locals and visitors united on Ada's property, jubilant in their anticipation of Rügen's prosperous future. Zwirner is emphatically excluded from the final community extravaganza, which includes fireworks, a brass band, dancing, and a banquet.

As the embodiment of virtue and resilience, Ada is responsible for saving the idyllic island and its population from financial ruin and colonization by West Germans. She is the narrative agent who sees that greed, deceit, and corruption are banished from the community. Ada is described by Margret Köhler as a character who remembers her Brecht, acting like a cross between Mother Courage and Robin Hood ("Opas Kino" 11), thus allying her with the socially conscious bank robbers Anna and Lisa in *Burning Life* and the impressionable shop detective/"department store Robin Hood" in *Adamski* (Koll, *"Adamski"* 28).

With its convulsions of plot, hysterical instrumental musical score (for which one of the director's relatives is responsible), complicated characterization, and inversion of allegiances, *Rising to the Bait* might have been more effective if it had been serialized and presented episodically as a midday soap opera. The film includes romantic interest, commonplace and unengaging puzzles over individual identity, long-lost relatives, along with the usual soap issues of heritage, paternity, and kinship. Other more specifically German links may be drawn, especially considering that these elements and motifs are heavily represented in Heimat films. In his extensive 1973 analysis Willi Höfig provides statistical accounts of recurrent motifs and incidences such as the rediscovery of illegitimate children, the identification of fathers of unknown children, returning home (321, 423), betrothal (299), and the imperative of preserving Heimat in the form of family property (337, 347–51).

Rising to the Bait's approach to characterization may seem as intricate as many soap operas, but here again an affinity is established with traditions of characterization common to the West German Heimat film of the postwar period. A degree of confusion, if not structural imbalance, seems to be generated throughout the film when it presents protagonists who are without a past, while minor characters are burdened with dark and intricate personal histories. For instance, Ada Fenske is represented as a simple, decent figure whose past is so uneventful it is scarcely mentioned. All we know about her is that she dreams vaguely about travel, is widowed, and her husband was in the navy. By contrast, secondary characters have pasts so complicated they are difficult to fathom. This constellation of characters and their complicated or nonexistent pasts harks back to the Heimat film. There, characters who embrace family, home, and hearth are insulated from the adversities of history: "they are . . . without a past" (Höfig 360). As widow, sister, and surrogate mother, Ada is a proponent of the family, a structure that is attributed recuperative power here as in the Heimat tradition. In Heimatfilme, family is not narrowly defined, "but its bonds are so strong that all those that live within a family or new people who enter into [a family structure] leave behind them all earlier ties" and associations with the past (Höfig 360). Following this pattern, once Karl-Funke, the former West Berlin malingerer, becomes part of

Ada's surrogate family and announces his plans to marry Swetlana at the end of *Rising to the Bait,* he has a newfound integrity and motivation to realize his artistic potential. Swetlana can also put her troubled past behind her[1] once she assertively announces her desire to marry and accepts her place in the surrogate family that Ada heads. Eventually both Swetlana and Karl-Funke embrace family and heritage, the central values championed in Heimat films (Höfig 360): their impending marriage both makes them legitimate heirs to Ada's estate and announces the establishment of another family unit.

Moreover, *Rising to the Bait* displays the morally schematic universe common to soap opera melodrama as much as to the Heimat film. The honorable inhabitants of *Rising to the Bait*'s contented community are in tune with their environment and their society. Virtuous East Germans are involved in trading primary produce (sheep, fish, flowers, fruit, wool) or processing it. Disdainful, or dim-witted characters, on the other hand, are bureaucrats who are involved with the bank, army, or local council. They are either obstructive, like the loan officer in the bank, or corrupt, like Fiedler and the West German villain, Zwirner. Within the Heimat schema, no reprieve is possible for these characters: they do not respect the sanctity of the family or of Heimat. The bank officer literally devalues Ada's estate, and the others instigate or are implicated in scams to disrupt the legal ownership and heritage of her property. The West German businessman, Herr Naujock, is distinguished from these miscreants in that even though he is an acquisitive capitalist, he is sensitive to the rustic charms of both Ada's homestead and eastern ways of life, and, importantly, he is a family man cherished by his children who accompany him on holiday.

In accordance with the East German characters who populate western-backed unification comedies and dramas made in the 1990s, all characters but one in this film have no specific political allegiance. They are uninvolved with party politics in unified Germany. *Rising to the Bait* makes a special distinction between the majority of its apolitical characters and the one individual identified as contemptible because of his politically active past. This is also the only card-carrying former communist in the film's community: the repugnant clerk, Erich Fiedler. He is ridiculed by the film for his pedantry and bureaucratic servility. Things are made worse for him when his history of Stasi service is revealed, and he is identified as the former Party secretary.

Fiedler is the embodiment of the old regime. This is established partly

---

1. Her parents deserted her, she is dejected by a trip to the west, and her relationship with her stepfather is fraught with conflict.

Fig. 7.   *Rising to the Bait* (1992). Film still reproduced with permission of DEFA-Stiftung.

by his demeanor, but also by details of his office. The old insignia of the GDR is jammed into one corner of his dark work space. A high-angle shot of the room reveals an official portrait of Walter Ulbricht secreted above eye level: Fiedler hangs on to relics of a dishonored past. The presence of the partially concealed official portrait suggests not only that Fiedler's allegiances remain with the SED but that he favored the division of Germany (Ulbricht had the Wall fortified). By contrast, Fiedler's boss, Mayor Solter, appears to welcome unification, for he has replaced the ubiquitous portrait of Erich Honecker (that normally graced the walls of East German public offices) with a picture of Richard Weizsäcker, elected the Federal Republic's minister president in 1989.

Apart from the relics of the past stored in Fiedler's room, his affiliation with the SED is also signaled by the Christian name that he shares with Honecker. The atmosphere of Fiedler's office further consolidates the links with the old regime. His Büro is overcrowded with filing cabinets containing detailed files about the residents of Rügen, and he is pedantic in handling and administering the documents. His pettiness leads him to attend to insignificant details and surely is intended to be read as symptomatic of the inefficient, rigid bureaucracy of the old regime. In one scene, for instance, he refuses to stamp paperwork registering the return of a file because he has not completed his Kaffeepause, which he times by the minute. He is a weak, dishonest figure who displays a predilection to blackmail and exploitation. It is implied that he brutalizes women. He sneaks around in the dark at night literally trying to bury incriminating evidence about his past. He also owns a pistol, which suggests that he may have darker secrets he wishes to hide. He is selfish, opportunistic, and largely indifferent to any injustice he may see around him. His previous commitment to the Party is equated with cowardice, corruption, and avarice. Political activity is turned into something sinister and relegated to the past.

The West German profiteer, Raschke, is indirectly linked to Fiedler, for neither of them supports unification. Raschke is one of the most consistently odious figures in the film. He treats East Germans with condescension and disdain. He remarks that "Somehow they [East Germans] are not the same as us [West Germans]" and suggests that East Germans are still "in hibernation." His objection to unification is evidenced by his complaints about its cost and his cynicism about East German initiative.

Apart from ridiculing Fiedler, *Rising to the Bait* is circumspect in its reflection on life under communism. It refrains from making overt criticisms about the old GDR and is generally dismissive of critical allusions to life under the old regime. It rebuffs any suggestion that East Germans themselves may have been responsible for what happened to them in the GDR. "We were always forced [to do things]," Ada recalls of life under communism. In another scene Ada responds indignantly to the offensive Herr Raschke: the old woman challenges the West German by asserting that he would have done no differently from any East German had he lived under the old regime. In the same scene, when Raschke complains about having to pay unification taxes, Ada silences him, declaring that the expense is not excessive considering that West Germans have been better off than those in the east for forty years. It is implied that the taxes are justified as a form of compensation for the hardships undergone by GDR citizens.

Rising to the Bait manages to favorably rationalize other aspects of life in the former GDR. The severance of the GDR's ties with the western world together with withdrawal of traveling rights are excused in one scene when an urbane West German, the benevolent Herr Naujock, explains to Ada that international travel is simply not "worth it." Sedentariness and provincialism are presented not only as admirable East German traits, but as marks of wisdom. The weary West German renounces his globe-trotting: "It's not worth it. You are either ripped off or killed by terrorists. Go see a movie. Much nicer than reality. Ever been to New York? Don't go. They rob you. Nothing but trouble. Just like Thailand. Ever been to Thailand? Forget about it. Singapore. Malaysia. Hawaii. You are ripped off and cheated everywhere. Stay here. It's nice here."

Ada heeds his advice. By the end of the film she recognizes that with some compromise, she can fulfill her wish to see a mountain. When the local pastor suggests to Ada that her newly found prosperity will allow her to visit Mont Blanc or Mount Everest, Ada responds that, with her business activities, she is too busy to travel far, and in any case she has a better idea. She suggests that an excursion be organized the following weekend to visit the Brocken in Harz, and that all of her coworkers join in the tour (the Brocken is the highest part of a mountain range on the mainland and gives the film its German title). Ada's decision to visit the German mountain in preference to other more majestic mountains is an indication of her patriotism. Her choice marks an acceptance of what Germany has to offer. It also represents an acceptance of unification because the mountain is located right on the border that used to separate Germany: half of the mountain was in the GDR and the other half belonged to the Federal Republic. Ada's imminent trip becomes a symbolic journey in recognition of unification, but it is still a form of compromise because the region she intends to visit is not completely western.

Ada's intention to visit the mountain may be associated with a German cultural tradition dating back to the 1920s, namely, the German genre of the mountain movie, which in turn is viewed as an antecedent of the Heimat film. Before she turned to directing films herself, Leni Riefenstahl became a film star in a series of mountain films directed by the geologist Arnold Fanck. Riefenstahl displayed considerable athletic skills and expertise as a skier and rock climber in Fanck's films. To Susan Sontag and Siegfried Kracauer, the mountaineering films in which Riefenstahl starred and that she later directed were part of the fascist vision she perfected. Sontag argues that in these movies, "mountain climbing was a visually irresistible metaphor of unlimited aspiration toward the high mystical goal, both beautiful and terrifying, which was later to become concrete in Führerworship" (33). To Kracauer, the heroism of Fanck's mountain films "was rooted in a mentality kindred to the Nazi spirit. . . . The idolatry of glaciers and rocks was symptomatic of an anti-rationalism on which the Nazis could capitalise" (Kracauer 110, 112).

Apart from these unfortunate cultural associations, the Brocken is of special significance among mountains in that many Germans attribute a mystical value to it. The "specter of Brocken" refers to the awesome shadows the mountain casts late in the day on low-lying clouds and mountains. At the beginning of the film, Ada makes a cryptic allusion to the mountain's mystique when she points to the sky and singles out a formation of shadows and cloud, stipulating that she would like to view a mountain of such grandeur. The mystique of the Brocken relates to the festival of the witches, Walpurgis Night, celebrated on 30 April each year. Walpurgis Night rituals continued into modern times with a night of festivities including a witches' fire dance and fireworks. Following the division of Germany, however, only East Germans were allowed to celebrate Walpurgis Night. West Germans were not allowed to visit the Brocken, observe, or take part in the rituals—because the part of the mountain that was in the west was flanked by a military installation, and the whole area was out of bounds to civilians. When Ada notifies the pastor she will visit the Brocken, she is invoking a ritualistic celebration practiced exclusively by East Germans at least for the last few generations. Perhaps there is even a suggestion that her financial success has been due to witchcraft. Her journey may be motivated by a quasi-spiritual or superstitious impulse to guard the good fortune of the east, affirming the power of ancient mysticism and rituals over western religion and wanderlust. The Brocken pilgrimage Ada envisions for herself and her coven of cottage industry employees is sanctioned by Rügen's pastor, so that the excursion assumes a stronger mystical dimension, perhaps a kind of charismatic Christianity. Indeed, if the economic survival and expansion of the east were actually dependent upon a bunch of geriatrics knitting jumpers and preserving jams it would be truly an "economic miracle."

"Economic Miracle Number Two"

Even though *Rising to the Bait* does not really invite any sustained reflection upon life under the socialist regime, the film does manage to engage critically with a number of issues historically specific to East Germany in the early years of unification. For instance, *Rising to the Bait* enthusiastically favors an eastern-led "small is better" recovery, but at the same time it displays an acute sensitivity about the cost of welfare provisions for the east. Whereas the film is keen to portray virtuous Ostlers who embrace every opportunity to prosper, it also damns complacent East Germans willing to accept welfare. In a number of scenes, criticism is directed at sedentary East Germans who lack enterprise. Ada's personal endeavor, her independence and self-sufficiency, on the other hand, are presented as exemplary. Her vocation is to provide locals with alternatives to welfare payments. She saves the local shepherd from joining the queues of the unemployed by rescuing his sheep, which, although bred for their wool, are at one point in the film destined for the slaughterhouse. She negotiates a deal for the local painter with Herr Raschke, who supplies "art work" to furniture warehouses on the mainland. At one point, Raschke agrees to pay 800 DM for some of the local artist's paintings—

roughly the early 1990s equivalent of one month's welfare payment. Eight hundred marks is also the figure Ada cites whenever she estimates what can be earned knitting jumpers. Ada's business acumen leads her to save the local fisherman, the shepherd, the artist, and the florist from depending upon handouts from the west. Only unlikable characters are willing recipients of welfare in this film.

The film articulates a series of forthright discourses assessing economic union in the former GDR and the west's colonization of the eastern states. Probably more explicitly than any other unification comedy from the early 1990s, *Rising to the Bait* displays a wholehearted faith in the official *Aufschwung Ost* (upward turn east) program—an early 1990s initiative to boost production in the eastern states and to encourage investment there. Aufschwung rhetoric is blatantly manifest in the final scene of the film where community harmony and solidarity are literally applauded by residents and visitors to Rügen. The concluding scene provides opportunity for East and West Germans to extol visions of eastern prosperity. One of Ada's western business associates, Herr Naujock, promotes Aufschwung tactics to a fellow West German, amazed by his own realization that "they [East Germans] are Germans too!" Naujock utilizes the medical metaphors commonly deployed to promote the Aufschwung in offering the opinion that the East just needs "a strong injection of capital and it will be all right." In this scene the nasty Raschke provides a cynical voice that questions the likelihood of an Aufschwung in the east. Even after having been reprimanded by Ada when he complained about unification taxes early in the film, he is still pessimistic about East Germans' prospects and potential. He is not convinced by Herr Naujock's predictions about "Economic Miracle number two" for the east. He still has serious misgivings when faced with Ada's initiative to save the community, and he displays the same preoccupations at the beginning of the film as at the end when he mutters, "The cost of all this [unification] worries me. It could ruin us [West Germans] financially."

At the close of the film Ada addresses all the East and West Germans who have gathered on the island to join in the festivities and, implicitly, the viewing audience as well. Bunting, balloons, and colored lights enhance the festive spirit of a scene of abundance: drinks circulate among the guests, plenty of food is on the barbecue, and even though the guests already look sated, and a number are drunk, an animal is being roasted on a spit. Amid the merriment, Ada's guests insist that she make a speech. Ada reluctantly complies, bringing cheer to all gathered when she refers to them as belonging to "one big company," the capitalist obverse of the "one big union" of the GDR. Her speech marks a point of ideological excess involving a peculiar fusion of materialist impulses and humanist sentiments. The jubilant country folk are receptive to Ada's commemoration of the community's emergent affluence. She impresses upon them the need for investing their "profits": "Without investment, there is no future, and believe me, we will all become rich. Rich in assets, I hope. Rich in feelings and rich in happiness. It is up to us."

The recovery of the east has been initiated, tradition is preserved, Ada's estate is secured, and an extended family is finally reconstituted on East German soil: Ada has behaved like a true Heimat hero. A fete brings harmony to the community, lovers announce their betrothal at the party, and a brass band adds to the festivities, replicating the formula that brings so many Heimatfilme to closure (Höfig 294–95). Swetlana embraces her stepparent, Trude Fiedler, and calls her "Mother." Mayor Solter identifies himself as Karl's true father. Ada completes the configuration of the extended family in her role as surrogate grandmother. A family of three generations has been identified and reconciled. Ada and her community have effectively resisted the attempts of West Germans to colonize their island, and community togetherness and harmony prevail, at least for a night.

For Swetlana and Karl it is only in the east that they can be part of an integrated community and a family while escaping the poverty and distress that this film associates with the west. Ada's sovereignty is also assured by the close of the film when she realizes that even her wanderlust can be gratified without leaving the east. Her imminent pilgrimage to the mystical mountain, the Brocken, likens Rügen's economic miracle to a spiritual wonder.

Rising to the Bait presents incredible solutions to socioeconomic problems that plagued the eastern states in the early 1990s. In the year in which the film was released, Germany was on the verge of "the worst recession of the postwar period" ("Volle Fahrt voraus!" 5). In the following year, unemployment among East German women "reached a staggering 65 percent" (Koch 146), something that makes Ada's scheme to employ women as part of her cottage industry timely, if not credible. By 1994, more than 500 billion DM were invested in the new Länder. In real terms, relative to population, this figure is three times as much as was invested in West Germany at the start of the Economic Miracle after the deutsche mark was introduced ("Wir sind ein Volk" 17). *Rising to the Bait* displays awareness of these issues insofar as a concerted effort is made to fend them off: the film dismisses any criticisms about the costs of unification. Instead it portrays resourceful East Germans leading the recovery of the new federal states and disregards the east's virtually complete dependence upon the west for survival at the time.

It is only the film's antagonists who seem to realize that the resolutions to conflicts presented throughout the film are senseless. Raschke persists with his suggestion that unification is leading to disaster for the duration of the film. Similarly, the final encounter between Zwirner and the widow prompts the West German to query the feasibility of Ada's scheme to bring prosperity to the east. He asks incredulously, "Do you really think you can save the GDR by preserving jam, squeezing fruit juice, and knitting jumpers?" She rebuffs his comment with the declaration that "the GDR doesn't exist any longer."

Like other western-produced and -funded unification films such as *Apple Trees, No More Mr. Nice Guy,* and *That Was the Wild East, Rising to the Bait* presents a fanciful solution to various problems it attributes to unification (unemployment, fragmented families and communities, corruption, exploitation). Perpetuating the Heimat film tradition, all obstacles are surmounted, differences are resolved, and community spirit and prosperity prevail.

Rising to the Bait can also be seen to present a miniature reenactment of the spontaneous and official festivities that celebrated the opening of the Wall. Ada's version is complete with fireworks, champagne, crowd jubilation, and speeches. The scene evokes historic spectacles of late 1989, but with a difference: here it is not East Germans swarming to the west, excited about what it might have to offer them. West Germans become the visitors drawn to the east in this scenario. The final image of *Rising to the Bait* displays a crowd of East Germans and their remaining western guests united, ecstatic over the prospects that the East holds. Roles are clearly redefined with East Germans assuming the role of producers while West Germans have no alternative other than to become the consumers. The film rewrites the outcome of unification so that East Germans are the beneficiaries and the victors who triumph over capitalists from the west. Even though West Germany resorts to sending in its army to the old GDR, the army is defeated and withdraws from the east (the army/police force is also beaten in *No More Mr. Nice Guy* and *Burning Life*). This unification comedy ends not with the east being colonized by the west, but with western powers vacating the east. The aerial shot of the increasingly distant crowd that closes the film provides another dimension to Ada's unification celebration. What is celebrated here is not so much the fusion of east and west, but the westerners' retreat from the ex-GDR. Ada and guests are ecstatic as they wave the helicopter and what we can only presume are West German officials good-bye. We are left with the point of view from the helicopter. The departure of the westerners is the high point of the community celebration. The only West Germans that remain are those that accept the conditions of transactions East Germans stipulate. Any others, like Zwirner, are banished. What is ultimately championed is the sovereignty of the east rather than its assimilation into or integration with the west.

Ultimately, *Rising to the Bait* identifies the east as Heimat, where family, community, and a sense of belonging can be consolidated. The west does not present these possibilities in this film. Nor does it in *No More Mr. Nice Guy*. That film goes further still in suggesting that family and community have no place in East Germany either.

No More Mr. Nice Guy

No More Mr. Nice Guy may be distinguished from most other early 1990s unification films in that it has proven to be a considerable box-office success. By the middle of 1994, the film had been viewed by 652,837 spectators ("Black Box Office" 12). It was the second feature-length film made by the young West German director Detlef Buck. His earlier comedy, *Karniggels* (*Little Rabbits,* 1991/92), which has as its protagonist a young trainee-policeman who investigates a series of cow murders in the northwestern provinces of Germany, was also a box-office success. Like *Go Trabi Go,* the films *Little Rabbits* and *No More Mr. Nice Guy* have also been commercially released on video. Made for a modest budget of 2.8 million DM, *No More Mr. Nice Guy* was distributed with sixty copies in circulation, a relatively high number of prints for a small-budget local film. Not only was *No More Mr. Nice Guy* popular with German audiences, it even received "official" approval from the Ministry of the Interior, which saw fit to award the film five gold and one silver Federal Film Prizes in 1993. To date no other unification comedy has been granted as much official acknowledgment in the form of state awards.

No More Mr. Nice Guy traces the journey of two hillbilly brothers as they meander through the provinces of East Germany. Kipp has been let out of some kind of special-care home in a rural region in the west, close to the old border. His corpulent brother, Most, also seems to have rural roots; he dresses like a farmer and drives an ancient diesel-powered pickup truck. Together the pair resemble Laurel and Hardy or, as they are known to German audiences, Dick und Doof (Fat and Stupid). Most and Kipp set off in the pickup truck to travel to Schwerin to claim the property they have inherited from their recently deceased grandmother.

Both brothers are illiterate. Most rationalizes his illiteracy, acknowledging that, although he did attend school, he has forgotten all he was taught. (The director of the film has commented, "You can only shoot a road movie in Germany with people who can't read. The others understand the signs and they are where they want to be within six hours" [Arnold, "Wir können" 40].) Because neither of the brothers can decipher maps and road signs, their journey through Mecklenburg-Vorpommern becomes haphazard, and of course they lose their way. With the innocence and insistence of two children in a fairy tale, Kipp and Most nevertheless persevere with their journey to Grandma's house.

When night falls and Most tries to repair his pickup at a gas station, the brothers and their vehicle are hijacked by a young deserter from the Red Army, Viktor. The soldier speaks no German, and the brothers know no Russian. Initially Viktor directs the brothers' journey east. Presumably he is motivated by homesickness. He holds them at gunpoint at first, but gradually tensions between the kidnapper and his hostages ease, and a sense of comradeship develops between the men. Most finally lets Viktor behind the wheel of the truck to drive, and in one such scene the brothers join in a friendly sing-along with him. They know neither the words nor the song, which is probably just as well, because Viktor sings a Russian folksong, "N'Putz / Große Fahrt," which was popular with Red Army soldiers when they fought against Germany in World War II. The tune becomes the signature music of the film.

As the bizarre trio continue their journey throughout the east, they are threatened by a band of thuggish highway robbers. Kipp, Most, and their Russian accomplice outwit the bandits and force them to drive their Mercedes into a lake. Two of the thugs cannot swim, and, unbeknownst to Viktor and the brothers, they end up drowning by accident. Subsequently, Kipp, Most, and Victor are mistakenly identified as part of a gangsters' ring responsible for cold-blooded murder. They only realize they are wanted men much later. After an encounter with a Turkish con man who sells Most an exorbitantly priced rowboat, the brothers are left destitute with only a handful of worthless east marks. Most tries to remedy the situation by bartering for food at a fast-food kiosk but is rebuffed by a supercilious East German proprietor.

Kipp in the meantime is drawn to a nearby truckload of pigs that he sets free. The animals mill around the kiosk, and chaos prevails, allowing Most to spontaneously steal the cash from the kiosk till. Kipp rescues a piglet from the convoy, and Most reluctantly allows his brother to take it with them. Once again solvent, the brothers and Viktor proceed on their way to Schwerin to claim the estate they have inherited. Simultaneously the police instigate their search for the three men who are held responsible for murdering the highway robbers.

After another windfall that comes from playing poker machines, the trio finally arrives at what they think is their new estate. They survey the country manor house and its grounds, but are informed of their mistake by the rightful owner, a rude and condescending West German woman. A proper lady of the manor, she appears to have just returned

Fig. 8. *No More Mr. Nice Guy* (1993). Film still reproduced with permission of Delphi Filmverleih.

from horse riding as she still carries a riding crop. She inspects the will the brothers carry with them and curtly informs them that they have inherited a simple farmer's cottage—which ends up being a decrepit shell of a hut up the road.

The trio then visits a bar to call a real estate agent interested in their hut. In the bar they are distracted by the television news. They learn from the broadcast that they are sought after by the law and are referred to as armed and extremely dangerous killers. As Kipp later stutters, "We are m-murderers. We just didn't know it." The neo-Nazi bar patrons (one of whom is played by director Detlef Buck) recognize the trio and flee the bar in fear. Viktor takes the East German barmaid, Nadine, as hostage. A lascivious exchange of glances between herself and Viktor reveals that she welcomes the newfound adventure.

The group escapes, with hostage, after which Kipp steals a new Mercedes from a condescending West German used-car salesman. After crashing the car, the brothers confiscate a pair of horses from a couple riding in the country. The fugitives and Nadine continue their journey on horseback. Meanwhile, the police escalate their search for the outlaws, and the army is called in on the pursuit.

Fig. 9.   *No More Mr. Nice Guy* (1993). Film still reproduced with permission of Delphi Filmverleih.

Nadine and Viktor become romantically attached. The police search reaches a fevered pitch with helicopters and squadrons of police tracking down the group, who make it to the seaside. Nadine succeeds in distracting the police, enabling the trio to steal a boat and escape by sea. Kipp resolves that they "drop Viktor off" in Russia and then proceed to other "lovely countries . . . Denmark, Scandinavia, Romania."

The final scene is introduced by the intertitle "a few days later on the quiet River Don." Viktor and Nadine have been reunited in Viktor's native village. Russian peasants gather around Kipp and Most, exhilarated and in a festive spirit. Most pours beer for his new neighbors, and all engage in the fete. Much to their amusement, Kipp attempts to explain to the Russians the benefits of purchasing goods through mail order catalogs. He lectures them on pig farming. Not one of them understands a word.

The fete that closes *No More Mr. Nice Guy* serves a comparable narrative function to that of the celebrations at the end of *Rising to the Bait* and also can be related back to conventions of the Heimat genre. Höfig notes that the vast majority of Heimat films he examines involve similar kinds of fetes or community celebrations (294–95). Trimborn also refers to community festivities, in particular the *Trachtenfest* (party with national costume), as an obligatory component of the genre (129). *No More Mr. Nice Guy* also includes a slight modification of the betrothal motif that Höfig identifies as vital to the closing festivities in numerous Heimatfilme (299): in the final scene, Nadine emerges from the interior of Viktor's cottage, and Viktor lifts her up after she steps over the threshold, suggesting their future partnership as husband and wife. The ultimate bringing together of one or more pairs, heralded throughout the film, which takes place during the festivities, signals the happy ending in the Heimat film (Trimborn 129), as is also the case here.

No More Mr. Nice Guy draws on the conventions of the Heimat genre in other, even more remarkable ways, particularly with its recycling of the inheritance motif. Analyzing Heimatfilme, Höfig identifies a narrative trajectory duplicated in uncanny detail in *That Was the Wild East:* "It is not uncommon for Heimat film heroes to inherit a neglected and dilapidated estate"; either that "or their rosy ideas about the . . . inheritance are in crass contrast to the real state of affairs. . . . There are many instances that involve the hero's overvaluation of the estate" (349). *No More Mr. Nice Guy* exploits the comic potential of this particular Heimat scenario when it shows Most and Kipp surveying the grounds and interior of the mansion they mistakenly think they have inherited. That estate is then contrasted with the burned-out shack they are actually bequeathed. A scavenger rummages through the ruins of the cottage salvaging scrap metal, apparently all that is left of value.

Stereotypes and Inversions

No More Mr. Nice Guy was considered to have greater satiric potential than other unification comedies because of the casual way in which it draws upon clichéd impressions of East and West Germans and stereotypes of the western genre, throwing these ingredients together and mixing them vigorously (Lux, "*Wir können auch anders*" 28). As I mentioned in chapter 6, the film recycles the iconography of the western: prairie scenes, sitting around the campfire at evening, escaping from the sheriff and a posse on horseback. The film also draws on the conventions of early slapstick comedy. Although Most is cheated into buying a rowboat that he must ultimately relinquish, he insists on retaining its paddles. Later he uses the wooden paddles in harmless self-defense just as they were originally used in slapstick comedy routines (Neale and Krutnik 20–21).

No More Mr. Nice Guy draws from a number of genres (the road movie, comedy, thriller, Heimat film). It quotes various spaghetti westerns, in particular Sergio Leone's *Once Upon a Time in the West* (1968). The comic swatting of the buzzing fly in the first scene is taken from that western, and in various scenes (when the men are about to be held up by the robbers and when they enter the bar at the end of the film) Buck copies the way Leone composes shots, places characters, and has them move into frame to occupy different planes of space. The film presents East Germany as a wild west landscape, a vision that Harald Martenstein observed was not uncommon in the first years after unification. The East is depicted as a region relatively free of stifling social restrictions; a place that still may provide adventure but also has its dangers ("Narrenjagd"). Buck's "eastern" plays around with everything that the western takes seriously: highway robbers, grouchy sheriffs, and an apparently willing hostage. With Buck no one is in the role elsewhere prescribed for them. The murderers are peaceful, the hostage is sovereign, the band of skinheads is as scared as their German shepherd. Things are turned upside down in Buck's world (Bylow 56).

Kipp and Most are naive and harmless figures who metamorphose into gun-slinging outlaws, gangsters, and cowboys. Kidnapper and hostages befriend one another, and a pair of endearingly dim-witted brothers triumph despite their limited intelligence. In one way or other, Viktor and the brothers ultimately manage to defeat just about all the mean and patronizing characters they encounter. They steal a Mercedes from a hostile, uncooperative used car salesman after he tells them to "get stuffed." Most steals the receipts from the fast-food proprietor who calls the men lazy and accuses them of taking advantage of others' generosity. They drive over the motorbike of a real estate agent interested in their property. Elsewhere, the trio emerges unscathed from an encounter with a group of West German thugs who threaten them with violence and try to rob them. They manage to effectively intimidate their aggressors. Most even seems to get some kind of revenge for being taken hostage by Viktor at the start of the film. That scene sees him suffer the humiliation of being bound and gagged. Viktor instructs Most to remove his shoes, then Viktor stuffs Most's mouth with his socks to muffle his captive's cries. Most later binds and gags a pair of equestrians in a similar fashion. He too stuffs socks into the mouth of his female captive. Perhaps this scene acts as a displaced fulfillment of Most's desire to humiliate the lady of the manor (also identified as a horse rider) for her dismissive treatment of the brothers. They also manage to outwit the West German police chief and avoid the full force of the law and troops of German soldiers. By the end of the film, Most and Kipp have managed to mete out revenge for the indignities they have suffered on their journey, occasionally with assistance from their accomplices, Viktor and Nadine.

Honorary East Germans

No More Mr. Nice Guy also involves an inversion of east-west stereotypes normally promoted in unification comedies. At the start of the film, Kipp and Most are identified as coming from West Germany. We see them drive past a border observation tower at one point, after which Kipp asks his brother whether they are now in the east. The brothers are already deep in the east when they first encounter Viktor, and Kipp observes, "That's Russian that you're speaking, isn't it? We are not from here either."

Despite being identified as westerners, it is possible to argue that Most and Kipp are actually surrogate East Germans.[2] Non-German viewers are inclined to identify them as eastern because of their clothing and demeanor. The characters are the embodiment of stereotypes normally applied to Ossis. In redefining the brothers as East Germans, the film can effect the sort of segregation that I discussed earlier in this chapter and in chapter 6: it can avoid consolidating any German-German relations. If Kipp and Most are surrogate East Germans, it rationalizes their movement further east with Viktor, because the brothers show their preference for what East Germans are familiar with: Soviet influences. They eschew the westernized GDR with its fast-food kiosks, gas stations, twenty-four-hour convenience stores, thugs, and con men. Moreover, Kipp and Most's designation as honorary East Germans is supported by their lineage. They have no parents and the only relative they appear to have known is their grandmother who was an East German. For us, they only truly begin their lives in the east. The brothers also display the naïveté and innocence normally attributed to East Germans in western unification films. They are backward, old-fashioned, and unsophisticated. Their clothes are ill fitting and unflattering. Most wears braces to keep his trousers suspended well above his bulging midriff and sports a checked shirt and narrow-brimmed hat. Both Kipp and Most are affiliated with farming. Kipp has been released from a shelter where he was responsible for tending pigs (as he remarks, "feeding them, hygiene, everything"), a form of farming widespread throughout the east. Kipp also has an interest in and a special fondness for horses—in particular East Prussian horses, which he appears to value over all other breeds. In most western unification films, it is normally East Germans who are the rural dwellers whereas the West Germans are urban. Kipp and Most do not behave like capitalists from the west either. They have no business sense or understanding of the workings of capital, contracts, or deal making. They are gullible in their business dealings.

---

2. Most is played by the Dresden actor Horst Krause, whereas Joachim Król plays the role of Kipp. Król's surname is Polish, suggesting an eastern affiliation.

Kipp is unaware of the different values of East and West currencies and does not realize he has been cheated by a callous gas station attendant in one scene. Most carries away his winnings from the poker machines in coin, commenting "Real money is really heavy."

The brothers are ignorant about any form of communication technology. Neither knows how to use a telephone or how a radio works or how to drive a car with power steering. They are more comfortable on horseback than in a new Mercedes. They encounter poker machines for the very first time in the middle of their adult lives.

The brothers are impressed by outmoded industrial merchandise. Most's proudest possession is his ancient truck that repeatedly breaks down and is outpaced by everything else on the road. He is pleased to announce to his brother that the vehicle has four gears, one of them for reverse, and boasts about the speed the vehicle can travel when driven "forward." His brother seems genuinely impressed by this information and asks which gear are they presently traveling in. Later in the film, Kipp seems to share his brother's pride in the vehicle, when he shows off in front of a couple of middle-aged East German women, gauchely announcing, "We are motorized." Kipp is also fascinated by Viktor's ancient machine gun. Moreover, the brothers display an ignorance of the ways of the world along with the parochialism commonly associated with East Germans in western unification films. Kipp has a curiosity about social rituals, but he doesn't appear to have much understanding of them. Oblivious to the lady of the manor's disdainful acknowledgment of her new neighbors, Kipp welcomes the prospect of having a new neighbor with genuine enthusiasm, commenting, "That's nice too. We can have nice parties here [together]. New Year, Carnival, Father's Day. There are so many lovely festivals to celebrate." Unsettled by the lady of the manor's expression of disbelief, Kipp consoles her with, "We don't want to lose ourselves in euphoria."

Kipp and Most have no experience of international travel. Most hands over his entire life savings for a small rowboat, inspired by his brother's fantasy about visiting distant lands. Kipp daydreams about traveling overseas in a sailboat. Viktor has equally unrealistic ambitions to travel: when he and Nadine sit momentarily by the seashore, Viktor suggests through gesture and in Russian that they go to Africa together. Later, Kipp's ignorance of geography and distance are confirmed when he rationalizes that he and his brother can travel by boat and drop Viktor "off [in Russia] and then we'll see."

The Family, Community, and German-German Relations

There are no surviving families in the unified Germany depicted in *No More Mr. Nice Guy*. The closest thing resembling one is at the wake in the country tavern that the men visit halfway through the film. Perhaps the association of the sole German family in the film with a funeral suggests that the structure is dying out. The association is strengthened by Kipp who carries with him a wreath for his own grandmother's grave when he and Most set off on their journey. The emphasis is underscored by the conspicuous presence of the funeral director in several scenes. He is the first "private" undertaker in Brandenburg, and his business is evidently thriving.

Not only is the family extinct in the new Germany represented in the film, the country itself provides no real sense of community. The only experience of community Kipp seems to have had is in a home for social outcasts. When he is identified on the television news report as a wanted man, he is shown in a group photo with other toothless, cross-eyed, and demented-looking men of various ages. Kipp and Most are unwelcome just about everywhere they go in East Germany and are dismissed by just about everyone they meet, whether East or West Germans. All encounters are hostile, dishonest, or exploitative. West Germans are invariably snide and patronizing. The engineer that Kipp encounters at the start of the film, for instance, presumes he is an imbecile and makes fun of his future plans by asking whether he intends to become lord mayor or not. The East German women whom the men briefly encounter end up viewing Kipp with a degree of suspicion and swiftly reject his friendly advances. The brothers establish no meaningful relations with anyone other than Viktor. The Russian and the East German woman, Nadine, on the other hand, establish an immediate rapport.

It is only when the German fugitives reach Viktor's village on the Don River that they experience community harmony and family life. The Germans are welcomed by the Russian peasants in Viktor's village, and Most and Viktor help them prepare for a fete. The Russians laugh and joke as they cluster around Kipp, who, despite language barriers, is only too happy to chat with the locals. He and Most are at ease with their new neighbors, who display none of the reserve of the lady of the manor near their East German property. Nadine looks especially contented as she stands in the doorway of Viktor's cottage and draws heavily on a cigarette. Viktor joins her and embraces her. The gesture of smoking and the image of a domesticated woman is one that contrasts with previous scenes set in East Germany. There the women are isolated in their houses as they watch events outside with apprehension. In one such scene, an old woman who is fearful of Most, Kipp, and company retreats inside her house dragging with her a cat on a leash. In Viktor's village old women are not fearful and isolated, but happy to be part of the rural community.

Viktor's village is presented as lively and associated with fecundity. Viktor and a few neighbors examine homegrown vegetables collected in a wicker basket at the start of the scene. When Kipp lectures the villagers on farming and primary produce he refers to fishing for carp and the impression he promotes is one of plenitude. He says the fish are so abundant one can pull them out of the river by hand. (Although he does not specify that he is talking about Viktor's village, the association is there, already marked by the intertitle that identifies the village's riverside location.) As distinct from Germany, where families are dying out, in the Russian village we see hordes of children and relatives of various ages delighting in one another's company outdoors. The emphasis upon family togetherness is enhanced when Viktor's mother arrives by bus and is reunited with her son. Viktor in turn introduces her to Nadine. For the first time in the film, the brothers are part of the merrymaking. This is something Kipp has yearned for all along. He welcomed the prospect of festivities in talking with the lady of the manor, and when Most tells him he has stolen money from the fast-food kiosk, Kipp suggests they spend the money on "a lovely party."

It is only when the brothers and Nadine are out of Germany that we actually witness three generations of families side by side. Children and grandmotherly figures are a conspicuous part of Viktor's community. One prominent shot in the final scene is a medium close-up of a toothless old woman watching events and cackling with raucous laughter. She is especially amused by the scene that sees the Germans accepted as part of the community. She completes the picture and compensates for the conspicuous absence of the brothers' own grandmother throughout the film. (They never make it to her grave.) At the same time, like the virtuous East Germans in *Rising to the Bait,* Kipp, Most, and Nadine have distanced themselves from unified Germany. In deserting their homeland, the brothers need not establish or sustain any German-German relations. Uncannily, part of Kipp's final lecture to the Russians is about mixed breeding in farming. He warns his audience about the undesirable consequences of cross-breeding pigs.

CHAPTER 9

The "Trabi Comedies," Part 1

Go Trabi Go demands attention here because it is one of the earliest West German productions to depict the adventures of an East German family during the period of the Wende. It places good-humored emphasis upon the markers of cultural difference that distinguish East Germans from their western neighbors, such as their accents, dialect, clothing, and motor vehicles.

Go Trabi Go bears a number of traits common to unification comedies, as well as others that distinguish it from the cycle of early 1990s unification films. Its focus differs slightly from comedies like *Adamski, Rising to the Bait, Whoever Lies Twice,* and *No More Mr. Nice Guy,* which are concerned with the socioeconomic consequences of unification in the east. It is precisely this territory that this comic road movie avoids, distancing itself as far from East Germany and unification as a Trabant can possibly travel. And it does this by giving geographical and cultural preference to Italy, moving its protagonists swiftly away from the Federal Republic and its newly incorporated states. At first, then, *Go Trabi Go* seems divorced from the films I have just addressed because it does not deal directly with the repercussions and contradictions of unification.

Go Trabi Go nevertheless indulges in the sort of revelry evidenced in unification comedies like *Rise to the Bait* and *No More Mr. Nice Guy.* The first Trabi comedy functions as a celebration of various novelties East Germans were able to experience immediately after the Wende, in particular the freedom to travel to distant lands, consumer opportunities, and access to a variety of commodities. In this sense, it can be compared to the road movie *No More Mr. Nice Guy,* which, to Hans Günther Pflaum, is about "poor swine who discover a sense of freedom" ("Im Osten") at a literal and metaphoric level. For the protagonists in each of these films, that freedom is attained outside of Germany. They have to leave their homeland before they find Arcadia.

Go Trabi Go's levity and innocence is largely dependent upon what the film manages to avoid. Even though it is set during the period when the borders between the GDR and the FRG disintegrated, *Go Trabi Go* clearly displays a reluctance to develop relations between East and West Germans like in the unification films I addressed in chapter 8. Apart from a fleeting visit to supercilious relatives in Bavaria and an occasional encounter with a hostile West German salesperson, the East German family in this film does not engage, interact, or socialize with *any* West Germans. Again, German-German relations are inconsequential.

The Production Formula

Go Trabi Go is one of those German films that everyone in Germany seems to have heard of yet no one will admit to having seen. Directed by Peter Timm (who was expelled from the German Democratic Republic in 1973), this feature managed to avoid the harsh criticism the German press normally saves for local films: its critical dismissal was complete. *Go Trabi Go* didn't even warrant the usual outrage about the inferiority of local film, nor did it inflame indignation about imprudent allocation of state subsidy money. That this film caused neither widespread critical offense nor alarm over the degeneration of German film culture is in itself remarkable. Even *Go Trabi Go*'s nomination for a Federal Film Prize was dismissed as foolish and inconsequential (Koll, "Ruhe" 9).

Critical indifference aside, *Go Trabi Go* was one of the most financially successful German films of the early 1990s. This flagrantly commercial feature received financial support from a number of branches of state film subsidy, with the FFA (Film Subsidy Board/Filmförderungsanstalt) providing an 800,000 DM "loan" for the production in June 1990 ("FFA Fördert" 42). Bavarian Film Subsidy, Bavarian Broadcasting, and South German Broadcasting (BR and SDR, both public television stations) also invested in the film. *Go Trabi Go* was a box-office hit, attracting 1.5 million viewers. In the first six months of 1991, it was listed as the second most successful German film at the local box office. *Go Trabi Go* outgrossed Schroeter's award-winning *Malina* and Schlöndorff's *Homo Faber / Voyager* during the same period (Blaney, "Screen Box Office" 12). Most other German films screened the same year and in the years to follow "were relatively successful if they drew between 100,000 and 150,000 spectators, something only a few really managed to do" (Koll, "Ruhe" 9). This was the first unification comedy to have had a wide cinema release in Germany and to enjoy international exposure, at least on television.

Go Trabi Go was made during a period when comedy was among the most lucrative of German genres, as was the case later in the decade: *Ich und Er / Me and Him* (Doris Dörrie's 1988 film about a man with a talking penis), *Ödipussi / Oedipussy* (1988), and *Otto—Der Ausserfriesische / Otto the Outer Friesian* (1989) were all highly profitable. Following the formula established by the much-loved Loriot and Otto series, *Go Trabi Go* also has a television celebrity playing the role of the protagonist, in this case the cabaret star and talk-show host from Dresden, Wolfgang Stumph.

In conception, even if not in tone, *Go Trabi Go* parallels three other profitable West German comedies, *Man spricht Deutsch* (*German Spoken [Here]*, 1988), *Manta-Manta* (1991), and *Manta—der Film* (1991) (Peter Timm directed *Manta—der Film* the year after he made *Go Trabi Go,* and after directing *Manta-Manta,* Wolfgang Büld was codirector of the unification comedy *That Was the Wild East,* the first Trabi sequel).[1] Both the Manta films and the Trabi films follow a somewhat similar formula. They focus on German automobiles and the attitudes and behavior displayed by the owners of these vehicles. Both models of cars carry with them particular cultural connotations and are generally considered representative of certain socioeconomic groups. The Trabi was a state-issued automobile that was exclusive to the GDR. Trabis are notoriously slow; they break down regularly and contributed substantially to the pollution of the environment. The vehicles run on two-stroke engines and have plastic bodies. With the unification of Germany, the Trabant took up the symbolic function of representing the "backwardness" of the GDR (Korngiebel and Link 48), just as Mercedes and BMWs are viewed as symbols of West German efficiency and affluence. Whereas the Trabant evokes the unproductiveness, inefficiency, and obsolescence of GDR industry, the successful export of the BMW and the Mercedes reminds one of Germany's economic strength on the world market.

The Manta, although a West German vehicle, carries with it none of the connotations of status of the BMW and the Mercedes. The Manta appealed to a group in another economic bracket: it was favored by car enthusiasts who valued speed but could not afford to buy more expensive models. The Manta was a car associated with West Germany's lower-middle and working classes—it was a *Raser-Auto* (a car for speed enthusiasts), often decorated with G-T stripes, chrome ornamentation, and details evocative of racing cars.

In the years before unification, Mantas and their owners were the butt of ridicule and condescension, and provided inspiration for a barrage of jokes that circulated widely throughout West Germany. Later, the Trabi assumed this comic function. And, just as the Manta jokes inspired a series of films, the pattern extended to the production of the Trabi comedies that

---

1. *Trabi Goes to Hollywood* followed. Because that sequel focuses neither upon Germany nor upon the experiences of East Germans during unification I have omitted it from this study.

Fig. 10. *Go Trabi Go* (1990). **Film still reproduced with permission of DEFA-Stiftung.**

used German unification for their social and historic backdrop. *Go Trabi Go* utilizes the Trabant as the most conspicuous, immediately recognizable index of difference between East and West Germans, in a comparable fashion to the Manta films, which used that motor vehicle as an index of cultural difference between the West German bourgeoisie and its lower-middle and working classes. (The Manta films followed a formula that included a series of car races between Mantas and more expensive and prestigious automobiles.)

While the Manta films and the Trabi films utilize the automobile as a prop through which cultural difference and social standing can be articulated, *Go Trabi Go* also shares similarities with *German Spoken Here,* a film that focuses primarily on the family holiday and secondarily on the family car. *German Spoken Here* is possibly the most socially adept comedy of the group, insofar as it is more rigorous in scrutinizing and parodying what is typically German than the other films mentioned. In contrast to *Go Trabi Go,* which was neglected by German critics, critical response to *German Spoken Here* was extensive and varied. It was a success at the local box office where, immediately before the Wende, it attracted more viewers than *Wall Street* (1987) and *Rambo III* (1988). *Go Trabi Go*'s aspiration was to attract comparable returns by recycling the basic *German Spoken Here* scenario. Both films depict a German family on holiday in Italy, although the family in *German Spoken Here* is West German rather than East German. *German Spoken Here* distinguishes itself from the Trabi comedy by its unrelentingly savage treatment of a grossly bourgeois Bavarian couple, Erwin and Irmgard Löffler, who come from a provincial town "near Dachow." The film is devoid of the picture-postcard images of the Italian landscape and tourist attractions highlighted throughout *Go Trabi Go*. With a level of verisimilitude that is discomforting and immediately recognizable, *German Spoken Here* locates the Löfflers on holiday on a polluted Italian beach overcrowded with German tourists who have brought with them all the comforts of home. The couple listens avidly to traffic reports from Bavarian radio that add to the perpetual cacophony of the holiday. Like the other German tourists that surround them, the Löfflers are neurotic and xenophobic: fearful of theft, they keep their station wagon under constant surveillance "because you can never trust Italians."

Ödipussi, another tremendously popular comedy released at the same time as *German Spoken Here,* also draws some of its comic potential from situating a parochial German on the Italian Riviera. *Ödipussi*'s popularity depended heavily upon the casting of Loriot, the nationally recognizable celebrity, in the film's leading role (he also directed the film). A Bavaria Studios production, *Ödipussi* was the most profitable German film of 1988. In terms of its production history and story formula, *Go Trabi Go* involved the revival of what had already proved to be financially successful on the local market.

Both *Go Trabi Go* and its sequel, *That Was the Wild East,* were produced by the head of Bavaria Studios, Günther Rohrbach, who was not only one of Germany's most successful producers but also one of the most influential figures in federal film politics. "Rohrbach alone" decided what actually went on at Bavaria at the time, maintains an anonymous close colleague of the former studio boss (qtd. in Freyermuth 54). "When he speaks, the industry sits up and takes notice" ("Mehr Geld" 1).

Divested of any artistic pretense or aspiration, the commercial success of *Go Trabi Go* depends upon a production configuration lacked by the majority of other unification films, in particular eastern productions like those discussed in chapter 11: *Go Trabi Go* was produced by one of the most powerful and successful figures in the West German film industry; it worked within the framework of the most salable and profitable of film genres; its director's orientation was unashamedly commercial; and, importantly, it was not distributed by a small-scale distribution company circulating strictly limited copies of low-budget independent films. It was taken up by Neue Constantin, a company that has distributed many of Germany's most successful big-budget productions (and *Manta—the*

Film). At the level of funding, production, direction distribution, and narrative formula, *Go Trabi Go* is a West German feature.

Go West Trabi

Go Trabi Go revolves around the Struutzes, a family of provincial and unexceptional East Germans, and their Trabant, "George." The film opens as the family leaves the polluted and industrialized town of Bitterfeld to travel to Italy. On their way south, the Struutzes pass through Bavaria where they briefly visit some fatuous West German relatives. It would seem that the film can't get the Struutzes to Italy fast enough. A chance encounter with a truck driver prompts him to *transport* Udo and Rita Struutz, their teenage daughter Jacqueline, and their Trabi across Europe in his massive truck. This hastens what would otherwise be a slow, protracted journey. Once in Italy, the Struutzes experience the life-style of the west and the indulgences of consumerism. The family and "George" also become the targets of petty theft.

In contrast to its own sequel and other more recent unification comedies and satires, *Go Trabi Go* refrains from making caustic or critical comments about unified Germany and the assimilation of *Ostlers* (East Germans) into the Federal Republic. To one of the film's scriptwriters, Reinhard Kloos, the film's Italian emphasis makes it "more of a story about north-south yearning . . . than an east-west scenario" (Kloos, qtd. in Umard 40). The world of *Go Trabi Go* is one of goodwill, integrity, naïveté, and innocence—a carefree *elsewhere*. Because it divorces itself from Germany and takes a holiday from history, *Go Trabi Go*'s characters can afford to be frivolous and amiable. A similar strategy of designating and specifying German attitudes, traits, and attributes by distancing characters far away from Germany is deployed by Percy Adlon in *Bagdad Cafe* (*Out of Rosenheim*, 1988) and by Müller in *German Spoken Here. Go Trabi Go*'s likable, carefree figures are in contrast to most of the other characters populating other unification features made since 1989. In other more recent unification dramas protagonists have a greater range of negative traits: they are dishonest and in breach of the law (*Whoever Lies Twice, Adamski, Ostkreuz, Jana und Jan*), traitorous, deceptive, and/or deluded (*Apple Trees, Quiet Country*), and generally ineffectual (*As Quickly as Possible to Istanbul, Stein, No More Mr. Nice Guy, Quiet Country*).

In *Go Trabi Go* disparagement is rather directed toward the Struutzes' Bavarian relatives. They are satirical targets and without doubt the most grotesque figures in the film. The encounter with these West Germans further highlights the Struutzes' good humor and congeniality. By contrast, the western relatives are the embodiment of bourgeois self-indulgence, small-mindedness, and mediocrity. Their inhospitable treatment of their eastern relatives sees them desperately conceal the rich confectionaries they normally devour, as they begrudgingly ration staple foods for their guests. The West Germans are an amalgam of ugly opposites. They personify the disparate traits of excess and parsimony, of the slovenly and the fastidious. Rita's sister patronizingly asks what she can offer her guests, and one expects her display of food to be especially flamboyant. To the dismay of the Struutzes, they are simply offered a handful of crisps and a couple of pieces of unripe fruit.

Food is also the means through which Rita's brother-in-law is turned into a comic target. He is as disgusting in his obesity as in his gluttony: although in appearance and culinary habit he is a figure of excess and abandon, his behavior is also marked by fastidiousness; he is compelled to vacuum away crumbs around the plates of his guests as they eat, obsessive behavior accepted as the norm by his own immediate family. Alphons, the Struutzes' nephew, is an even more boorish figure than his father. As a young commodity fetishist, the West German teenager is totally obsessed with his personal computer to the exclusion of all else, except the anatomy of his cousin. He, like the other members of his family, is egotistical and conceited, and is condescending to his eastern relatives.

A general lack of communication between the East and West Germans is emphasized by differences in gesture and language. Rita's sister giggles inanely and inappropriately throughout the encounter with her relatives. The Bavarians exchange expressions of bewilderment when Udo recites from Goethe. Jacqueline is totally uninterested in her cousin's explanation of computer programs, and Udo cannot share his brother-in-law's preoccupation with various levels of sales tax. The lack of affinity between the East and West Germans makes the inclusion of the unification-inspired pop song "White Doves Have Crossed the Borders" even more ironic, as its lyrics proclaim: "A new age has been born / No more prejudice, no more envy / Let's take the chance to come together / Whatever is in the way belongs to yesterday."

Go Trabi Go nevertheless captures the celebratory mood that preceded the harsh social and economic reality of the first year of unification. Whereas other unification comedies and dramas (*Rising to the Bait, Quiet Country, Herzsprung, Apple Trees, Ostkreuz, Life Is a Construction Site*) take as their central themes unemployment, avarice, criminality, and xenophobia, *Go Trabi Go* either ignores or displaces these spiraling side effects of unification. So, for example, even though escalating criminality was a fear and a social reality in united Germany at that time, in *Go Trabi Go* crime only takes place outside of Germany, presumably perpetrated by Italians. Even more fanciful is the representation of the Struutz family's initiation into the world of capitalism and consumerism.

Throughout the course of *Go Trabi Go,* capitalism is presented as synonymous with prosperity and wealth. The film equates capital and the prosperity of the west with neither labor nor productivity but almost exclusively with consumerism or spectacle. Presumably unemployed and with only modest means at their disposal, the Struutzes specialize in acquiring money by chance. Rita and her daughter, Jacqueline, find a wallet bulging with money in the street that allows them to go on a shopping spree. Elsewhere, when Jacqueline spontaneously bursts into song (and another language—she sings in English), she is observed by Italian bystanders who mistake her for a busker and pay her a small fortune for her performance. Earlier in the film, Udo is transformed into ringmaster when he stages a "Trabi Peep Show" and collects hundreds of DM repair money for his automobile. The Struutzes generate funds to sponsor their European sojourn spontaneously and without effort. Theirs is not a deliberate, predetermined design to capitalize: their entrepreneurial skills are instinctive rather than calculated.

The Struutzes are virtuous characters: in their earliest encounters with consumerism they are neither acquisitive nor covetous: goods are simply bestowed upon them like prizes in a television show. Reminiscent of game-show spectacle, *Go Trabi Go* takes the Struutzes to locations flaunted in tourist brochures: providence awards them shopping sprees, a banquet, and luxury hotel accommodations. It is the working of chance, rather than effort or initiative, that results in the family being showered with money. Indeed, the film's portrayal of capitalism seems informed by the ethos of a program like *Glücksrad,* a popular German television variant of *Wheel of Fortune. Go Trabi Go* presents the acquisition of wealth as a game of chance, and this film says that East Germans need not be the losers in such a game, as they are in *Ostkreuz, Apple Trees, Quiet Country, Herzsprung, To the Horizon and Beyond,* and *Little Angel.*

One of the most striking things about *Go Trabi Go* is its consistent level of mediocrity: considering that the film functions as a fantasy that aligns prosperity and capitalism, the Struutzes' moments of splendor are curiously insipid. Rita's and Jacqueline's greatest moment of merriment and indulgence appears to be when they stay overnight in an opulent hotel in Rome. There they delight in the luxury of room service and are thrilled by the extravagance of a champagne dinner, apparently considered all the more lavish because they consume it in bed. When Rita has the opportunity to purchase clothes from Italian designers, she emerges from an exclusive boutique in a gaudy, unflattering costume that makes her appear more gauche than before. We are not afforded the excesses of a *Pretty Woman*–style fashion parade: despite the family windfall, Rita only has the opportunity to buy a bathing suit and one really ugly dress. Jacqueline's purchases are even more modest. The Struutzes' initiation into capitalism does not allow for especially lavish or tasteful spectacle, apart from the tourist sights of Rome.

Go Trabi Go's ambitious and erratic sequel *That Was the Wild East,* or as it is otherwise known, *Go Trabi Go II,* actually manages to address some of contentious issues that its predecessor ignored. *That Was the Wild East* finds the Struutzes at the end of their Italian holiday, returning to Bitterfeld to face the consequences of unification. The incongruity between the two films is of critical interest: each film is irreconcilable with the other. Whereas *Go Trabi Go* is consistent in its idealism and optimism, *That Was the Wild East* oscillates between mawkishness and cynicism—its general incoherence is further exacerbated by a continual assault of preposterous and barely integrated events. Whereas the first film is about celebrating newfound freedom and the second is about reconstruction, both films precisely mirror shifting social and cultural attitudes.

Within the framework of comedy, *That Was the Wild East* provides a survey of the antagonisms and prejudices that have blemished German unification as much as the cultural differences that distinguished Ossis and Wessis. These differences elude *Go Trabi Go,* which identifies the Struutzes as Europeans rather than as Germans or as trainee capitalists adjusting to the new sociopolitical order of the Federal Republic. The latter is a role the Struutzes are left to assume in *That Was the Wild East.*

That Was the Wild East was released after the euphoria over unification had well and truly subsided. Even though only two weeks of story time are designated as lapsing between *Go Trabi Go* and its sequel, it is astounding that the second Trabi comedy presents unification in such acrimonious terms. The value of these films rests in their portrait of the changing face of German-German relations: *That Was the Wild East* articulates sentiments and attitudes that, although common in the early 1990s, were not usually articulated so openly or publicly.

With a wide range of characters and a plot that is not immediately intelligible, *That Was the Wild East* is even more capricious than *Go Trabi Go.* In *That Was the Wild East,* when the Struutzes return to Bitterfeld after their short holiday in Italy they are startled by the changes to their hometown. The family drives through the desolate streets where businesses (including the local cinema) and homes have been abandoned. Unification is signaled by a newspaper slammed onto the Trabi windshield, the headline a record of the historic declaration "Wir sind ein Volk" (We are one folk [people]). The family belatedly realizes that plans for the "development" of Bitterfeld include the installation of a golf course (golf was never widely played nor was it a popular game in the GDR): they are astonished when they return to their deserted neighborhood. They are just in time to witness the demolition of their home, which is destroyed to facilitate development (promoted by Buck, an American multimillionaire).

In a moment of narrative fortuity, Rita finds a letter among the smoldering ruins of the family home: the Struutzes are summoned to Dresden by Dr. Schlimmelpfennig, where he informs the family they have inherited a property from their great-uncle who emigrated to Australia when Udo was a child. Udo and Rita learn that they now have the right to claim a business known as Red Cap, situated in "Landwitz" on the outskirts of Dresden. In Landwitz Udo discovers that Red Cap is a garden gnome factory located on potentially valuable real estate. Like other businesses and industries, Red Cap faces privatization. In order to secure his claim on the company, Udo Struutz must formulate a financial proposal, detailing how he will salvage the business while finding financial backing of 1 million DM. Herr Kühn, an unscrupulous West German developer who assumes the position of mayor of Landwitz, plays the role of Udo's adversary. Mayor Kühn has clandestine plans for the town dependent upon his acquisition of the Red Cap estate: his scheme is to modernize the region and introduce an autobahn. The West German also attempts to seduce Udo's wife and to bribe her into collaborating with him in his development scam.

Udo is separated from the family Trabant and the family in an early scene. The car disappears for most of the film after it is pushed over a bridge in Dresden by a group of neo-Nazis. Jacqueline decides to remain in Dresden to investigate the city's nightlife after she meets up with Diana, an old girlfriend who now works as an erotic dancer. Rita spends most of her time in the company of Mayor Kühn. Udo befriends Charlie, a benevolent yet opportunistic West German, who seeks his fortune by trying to sell banana-flavored condoms, bearing the patriotic colors of the German flag, to the locals in Dresden. Charlie attempts to assist Udo in his business dealings and drives him around in his bright red American convertible. The pair establishes a special rapport.

When Udo visits a casino to gamble with the one mark he has left to his name, he succeeds in winning a large sum of money. He then travels to New York with sample garden gnomes in an effort to locate funds to save Red Cap. There he actually encounters the millionaire developer, Buck, face to face. Buck smashes one of the gnomes and experiences a wonderful sense of exhilaration. He spontaneously orders a million dollars worth of gnomes from Udo, in order to benefit from their therapeutic powers. Udo returns to Dresden to save the Red Cap enterprise and its employees. He is reunited with his wife, daughter, and automobile (the Trabant has been recovered and restored to original condition). The family drives away from Landwitz, off into the sunset, destination unspecified, and Charlie leaves the region to travel further east because "that is where the future is."

Although both *Go Trabi Go* and *That Was the Wild East* start out with the same central characters in the same location, the upheavals attributed to unification could hardly be more grimly imaged than they are in the second Trabi film. When the family returns to their hometown at the start of *That Was the Wild East* suspicion is immediately aroused that Bitterfeld has undergone a sinister change. Images of eastern squalor greet the Struutzes. Shells of Trabants lie abandoned in the streets. Winds whistle through decrepit buildings and the town's desolate business center. Without warning, explosives are detonated, leveling the Struutzes' family home to rubble. Bitterfeld has disintegrated beyond recognition. This former GDR town is reintroduced as a region that has been contaminated or decimated by unification.

The Struutzes are conveniently dissociated from such negative developments because they were elsewhere when unification took effect. When they return to Bitterfeld, their car is decorated with the *Italian* flag, rather than the West German flag that was bandied by so many East Germans during the period of the Wende, currency reform, and election. The Struutzes' first priority in returning to Germany is not to celebrate unification, but rather to indulge in a Festa Italiana. They are seemingly oblivious to the historic events that have taken place and are startled when the newspaper with the headline "We are one folk" is aggressively slammed onto "George's" windshield. The family is further dissociated from the headline announcing unification when Udo immediately turns on the Trabi's windshield wipers to dispose of the newspaper.

Throughout *That Was the Wild East* the changes brought with unification are not, however, limited to matters of locale. The Struutzes and their car are not always treated with esteem as they were in *Go Trabi Go*. In the first film, the Struutzes were at least viewed compassionately by most of the characters they encountered. "George" is presented as an appealing vehicle that attracts the attention and fond admiration of just about everyone who sees the vehicle. The curiosity the car invites in *Go Trabi Go* is always good-humored and the cause of great merriment. But by the sequel, the status of "George" and the East Germans is noticeably diminished: the Struutzes are periodically scorned, and their car, dilapidated after their holiday, is ridiculed. The Trabant no longer rouses the curiosity or fond indulgence of capitalists from the west. The Saxons are referred to as "blockheads" and the car as "a pile of shit."

In *Go Trabi Go,* "George" was Udo's lifelong companion—at least their "partnership" extended as long as Udo's actual marriage to Rita. In the first film, Udo treats "George" better than his own offspring, certainly lavishing more attention upon the vehicle than upon his daughter. Udo is praised in the first film for the care he devotes to "George"; he clearly cherishes the automobile, tending to it even before himself. One morning Udo is shown washing the car before he washes his own face, both tasks performed with the same materials. Throughout *Go Trabi Go* driving a Trabi is related to good character. Udo's experience of driving this vehicle has seemingly imbued him with virtuous qualities such as loyalty, modesty, humility, patience, and a sense of humor: the "old-fashioned," admirable values of the GDR. The Trabi is equated with the nuclear family and even manages to strengthen the family unit when it is temporarily ruptured by adversity. At one point the car's wheels are stolen leaving Udo distraught. Jacqueline and her father argue, and the teenager runs away from her parents, partly because Udo is more concerned about the car than about her. When she finally returns, she brings with her a peace offering of new tires for the Trabant; the gesture, whose only justification seems to be its reinforcement of family values, restores harmony to the Struutzes.

In *Go Trabi Go,* the Trabant is presented as a vehicle that rouses such interest and curiosity that West Germans will pay to see it, to sit in it, or to drive it. Italian beauties are similarly intrigued by the vehicle, which they seem to find irresistible. The Trabi is also a source of delight for the truck driver who transports the Struutzes, together with "George," to Italy. Evidently he knows enough Trabant riddles to amuse himself for the entire duration of the journey across Europe.

These responses aside, the Trabant is included in every significant and many superfluous scenes in *Go Trabi Go.* Even when there are instances of gratuitous nudity, such as when young women remove their clothes to sunbathe, they do so immediately beside the Trabi, presumably so that there will be something for everyone in the audience to observe.

Go Trabi Go was able to utilize the Trabant as a symbol of what was quaintly outmoded, yet cherished in the GDR. During the first film we are, for example, reminded that Trabants were highly sought-after in the GDR; they were the source of tremendous pride, and demand for the vehicle far outweighed supply—Udo refers to the many years he had to wait for his automobile. As Korngiebel and Link explain in their study of images used to represent the "before and after" of unified Germany, the car was already established as a collective symbol that emphasized splits between the Federal Republic and the former GDR by 1990 (48) when *Go Trabi Go* was produced and released. *Go Trabi Go* evidently depends upon and capitalizes on this symbolism.

In the first Trabi film, Udo's car, like his accent and clothing, is a conspicuous, immediately recognizable index of difference between east and west. Yet in *That Was the Wild East* the vehicle's symbolic function has shifted. Even in *Go Trabi Go,* the Struutzes are the only family in the neighborhood to have kept their Trabi. Already all the other neighbors drive new, imported cars. Rita even makes passing reference to grandfather Struutz having a new car. By the sequel, at least initially, to drive a Trabi is no longer a source of pride but possibly of embarrassment, a sign of complacency and lack of ambition. In *That Was the Wild East* it is the recollection of the backwardness of the Trabant, as a symbol of the GDR, that is shunned. And it is this unwelcome association that facilitates the vehicle's expulsion from the film.

The Trabi assumes a much more ambivalent role in the sequel than in the first film. It functions partly as a symbol of East Germany and partly as an object of derision. As well as evoking the backwardness of the GDR, the Trabant also comes to represent the eastern states when it is subject to the menace of neo-Nazism.[2] This menace is made especially clear in one scene set in Dresden, an early 1990s center of East German neo-Nazism, when a group of right-wing thugs threatens to destroy the family car and finally succeeds in pushing it off a bridge. The bridge looks like the Augustbrücke, a structure built in the seventeenth century that itself was damaged by the Nazis: toward the end of World War II, members of the SS tried to destroy the bridge. This scene on the famous bridge evokes the threat Nazism has posed to Germany in the present and in the past: just as the Nazis sought to destroy a part of German heritage—the bridge—the neo-Nazis target a part of East Germany's heritage—the Trabant. When the Trabi is pushed off the bridge and crashes onto the deck of a scrap-metal barge that happens to be passing by, the car is literally removed from the diegesis. It is a mangled wreck indistinguishable from junk.

The vehicle had already sustained considerable damage during the family's trip through Italy and had undergone a major transformation. By the time the Trabant returns to Germany in the sequel, its fenders, doors, hood, and bumper have been replaced by brightly colored spare parts. Gone is its monochrome pastel exterior. Now the car is rainbow-colored and customized. The Trabant has been westernized and turned into a convertible. The transformation is identified as western through the introduction of Charlie's American car, which is also brightly colored and a convertible. In effect, the Trabi is removed from the narrative so that it can be remodeled and restored to its original condition, that is, divested of western influences. The restoration of the car and the removal of all signs of its

---

2. From January through 23 November 1992, 1,912 acts of violence motivated by right-wing radicalism were committed in the Federal Republic (compared to 1,483 in 1991). Sixteen people were killed and 442 people injured. The overwhelming majority of attacks by the radical right were acts of hostility against foreigners ("Chronik der Gewalt").

westernization coincide with the restoration of eastern values and the family unit at the end of the film.

The car's resurrection carries with it mixed connotations. On the one hand, the Trabi's belated restoration is marred by an association with non-western "primitivism," which in the context of the film may take on racist dimensions. An African-German bearing the children's-book name of Bongo is the figure responsible for "George's" resurgence at the end of *That Was the Wild East.* Bongo is a bicycle repair man, a trade that apparently qualifies him to refurbish a Trabant to its original condition. Remarkably, Bongo makes necessary mechanical repairs and also provides "George" with new fenders, doors, trunk, roof, and hubcaps, all in a uniform baby blue. Diana, Jacqueline's girlfriend, squeals with delight when she views the results of her neighbor's handiwork. She exclaims: "Bongo, you are a real medicine man!" aligning Africans with western notions of superstition and tribal culture. The racist inflection is then accentuated as Bongo "spontaneously" begins to dance.

On the other hand, the racial stereotype presented in this scene carries with it positive connotations. The film succeeds in making some alliance between the former GDR and all industrial backwardness (tribalism or cottage industry) through including the figure of Bongo. His restoration of the East German icon, the Trabant, suggests that cultures such as those of Africa and the old East Germany rely on magic and the favor of the gods, that is, the rewards of virtue.

However childishly racist the figure of Bongo may be, his presence nevertheless counteracts the threat posed by the neo-Nazis earlier in the film. *That Was the Wild East* introduces skinheads as a threat to what is traditionally East German. They are identified as unpatriotic—they are responsible for vandalizing the Trabant—and they are susceptible to western fads: they find Charlie's "unification condoms" (which are western insofar as they are banana-flavored and decorated like Germany's flag) especially appealing.

Bongo, by contrast, appreciates the ways of the east rather than what is ephemeral and western. He has the skills and the know-how to refurbish the twenty-year-old Trabant. When he kindheartedly repairs the vehicle, he facilitates the reunion of the family. He is aligned with Udo insofar as he values eastern goods, and he works outdoors in the sunshine like the craftspeople at Red Cap. Bongo counteracts the presence of the neo-Nazis in several ways: he is a good-humored figure who is integrated into the Dresden neighborhood and has a sense of community spirit and civic duty—he volunteers to repair the Trabant, and no payment exchanges hands. By extension, his integration into the community can be read as an index of the tolerance of "real" East Germans, as opposed to the neo-

Nazis, who have no place in the community—they wander the streets aimlessly—and desecrate things East German that the Struutzes and Bongo value.

Whatever pride "George" may have generated in "his" owner in the first film, Udo seems to abandon the image of loyal Trabant driver with relative ease in the sequel. One scene in particular in *That Was the Wild East* appears to rationalize and invite critical reflection upon Udo's image change, and it does so acutely and with utmost economy. The scene, which takes place outside the Institute for Creative Management in Dresden, highlights Udo's transformation from loyal Trabi driver to western-style businessman. There it seems as if the Trabant's symbolic value is reassessed. Standing before the institute with Charlie, Udo comments to the West German, "Maybe we [East Germans] are a discontinued model, old fashioned, passé . . . just like a Trabi." Further reflection on the status of *Ossis* is invited when Udo observes two posters advertising the institute. The two posters that flank the entry to the institute promise, "You arrive as an Ossi, you leave as a boss." The first poster depicts a Trabi driver standing next to his vehicle like an obedient schoolchild. He is clothed drably, complete with dilapidated cloth hat, paunchy stomach, and stunned expression. The impression he generates is decidedly provincial, ineffectual, and dull. The East German and his vehicle are placed directly in front of a very high brick wall, representative of the closed society of which he was part and a general lack of prospects and opportunity. He has none of the dynamism or the assurance of his compatriot from the west, who is featured on the adjoining poster.

Details swiftly distinguish the men in the two posters. The easterner, for instance, carries an old-fashioned cloth shopping bag. His purchases are carried in one small bag alone. This is a reminder of the lack of consumer opportunity in the former GDR, and it prompts fleeting recollection of the time-consuming nature of waiting and queuing for goods in perpetual short supply. But, in a more positive light, the easterner is also presented as a family figure and provider who attends to the mundane activities of shopping for the household, the sort of (female) activity that is beneath the boss in the neighboring poster.

The figure in the second poster carries no shopping bag but rather a briefcase: he is prepared for business. Not without a degree of schadenfreude, the westerner is shown with a magazine tucked casually under his arm. This accessory acts as a reminder of the widespread censorship that prohibited the distribution of western publications in the GDR. Perhaps more important, the magazine carries with it connotations of the pursuit of types of leisure activities and consumer opportunities that were not available in the east.

Further differences distinguish the men. Whereas the easterner's orientation is to the family, the West German is depicted as unattached and self-centered. He is defined by his role as a consumer as much as by the material goods that surround him. The westerner is defined through what he has (or consumes); the easterner is defined by what he is—a provider who is committed to his family.

Without any degree of ambiguity, this second image is of the figure appointed boss, the "new man" that the institute promises it will make of its students "in just three hours." Here the boss beams confidently, perhaps with a degree of narcissistic self-satisfaction, as he stands next to a Mercedes, itself a symbol of achievement. The discreetly stylish, expensive business suit he wears further underscores his affluence. Resplendent in his own newly acquired 1,000 DM suit, Udo has already undergone part of the image transformation associated with being successful, western, and the boss. He has abandoned his casual East German clothes and has relinquished his Trabi. When Udo steps out of the Institute for Creative Management having undergone its course, his transformation is made even more conspicuous. He has another vocabulary and bandies around market economy jargon. Apparently, once Udo has undergone this transformation, he has little apparent reason to notice the absence of his Trabi. When he needs to get somewhere, Udo simply slips into the passenger's seat of Charlie's bright red convertible.

Not only does the scene outside the institute appear to provide Udo with the initiative to westernize himself and rationalize the disposal of the Trabi. This scene, with its focus on the posters, also provides opportunity to distinguish between East and West Germans. The immediate impression that is generated is that the East German is inferior to his West German neighbor. As Martin Ahrends explains, by the early 1990s, comparisons between East and West Germans often resulted in feelings of shame for Ossis: "One has to make up for and catch up to what the West has accomplished in the previous years. In the sober light shining into one's little nook, one is ashamed to face the West. One drives a shabby jalopy, walks around in simple clothes, eats gray bread and artificial honey. That did not use to be so important, but now it is shameful, now that there is no pride left in sacrifice, no dignity in poverty" (44). This is the sort of humiliation that one expects comparison between the two posters to generate: one expects that the comparison is made at the comic expense of the East German Trabi driver. But ultimately it is the definition of the East German that is lauded and emerges as the positive element in the equation.

What the institute's promotional slogan and images suggest is that, although it is possible to transform an easterner into a westerner, West Germans are less flexible and do not have the option of a dual identity.

The implication is that West Germans (the bosses) are superficial: the institute can, after all, turn its students into successful westerners in just three hours. Western-ness is reduced to little more than appearance, or perhaps it is even a type of masquerade: it is a costume anyone can wear, and its accessory is the ostentatious display of wealth. (This impression is also fostered elsewhere in the film. When Udo dons a tuxedo and gate-crashes a banking convention, guests at the convention simply presume he is a high-powered and influential entrepreneur. In a later scene Udo's successful negotiation with an American millionaire is associated with his acquisition of another new item of attire, a pair of cowboy boots.)

Whereas Udo undergoes a transformation and is westernized in *That Was the Wild East,* importantly the film provides him with the opportunity to revert to being an easterner (the reversal also extends to "George" when the car is fully restored to its original condition). Although Udo *is* recognized as the boss by the end of the film, and he *has* become a successful entrepreneur, by preference he reverts to eastern ways, priorities, and values. This happens when Udo recovers a distinctively eastern item of clothing, his floppy cloth hat, at the end of the film. (The hat was blown away at the same moment as Udo's Trabi was disposed of, with both landing on the barge.) When he once again sports the hat, Udo reidentifies himself, by choice, as an Ossi. Udo's resurgent eastern identity relates to the poster depicting the Ossi outside the Institute for Creative Management: in that picture the floppy cloth hat is one of the East German's most conspicuous accessories. Although Udo has learned the ways of the west and has the option to "be" western in the Trabi sequel, for him the option is meaningless. He prefers what is defined as eastern—prioritizing family life, fulfilling the role of provider for the family, prudence, and modesty—over the western tendencies of egotism, consumerism, and ostentation. Although the easterner is presented as flexible enough to assume a western identity in *That Was the Wild East,* the self-centered westerner has no choice about his identity: he has lost touch with traits and values that are attributed to easterners and does not share the easterner's adaptability. When Udo resumes his position as head of the family and returns to the driver's seat of his restored Trabi, his judgment is based on the moral superiority of eastern values. His preference discredits the western image of affluence, ambition, and prestige originally pictured in the poster, which sought to promote western creativity and "development."

Udo can have the best of both worlds. Even though he is presented as a parochial figure who has only been outside of East Germany once, he takes to jet-setting with surprising ease. Udo does not hesitate to board a plane in Dresden to fly direct to New York. Moreover, once he is in New York, he readily accepts being chauffeur-driven in a limousine after he has

driven a Trabant for most of his life. Curiously, a fear of flying is attributed to Udo's urbane West German companion, Charlie. His phobia is all
the more incongruous when one recalls that Charlie sings about his extensive world travel in one scene. Initially his phobia restricts him from
accompanying Udo on the flight to New York. Charlie's affiliation with
America is nevertheless the strongest, and he is the one with business
sense. He is the big brother to Udo, whom he seeks to motivate and
inspire. He knows of concepts such as "life-style," foreign to East Germany at the time of unification. The West German can quote Janis Joplin,
and not only does he drive an American convertible around East Germany, but he displays a compulsion to sing in English every time he is
behind its wheel. Despite his fear of flying, Charlie enjoys a degree of
mobility, and as the worldly-wise West German, his is the magnanimous
task of passing on his knowledge to Udo. The initiation into the ways of
the west is ritualistically enacted, once Udo assumes the position of mas-
tery in Charlie's Cadillac: Udo finally gets behind the wheel of the car, and
despite his ignorance of English (established on several occasions throughout the film), he also spontaneously starts singing in this foreign language.
His sense of triumph is as exuberant as it is embarrassing.

CHAPTER 10

The "Trabi Comedies," Part 2

Go Trabi . . . Gone

Made during dramatically different periods in the history of unification, *Go Trabi Go I* and *II* utilize a range of collective symbols whose predominance shifted from the period of the Wende to the early 1990s. The repertoire of popular unification images from which these two films drew was constantly being remixed and matched, often resulting in paradoxical images, relations, and impressions (Korngiebel and Link 51). There are numerous grounds for the revision of those images, grounds that encompass political, social, industrial, and economic factors, some of which I would like to investigate here. The impact of economic changes in the east and the consequences those changes had upon industry cannot be ignored when one is discussing unification films such as the Trabi comedies.

Jo-Hannes Bauer notes that *Go Trabi Go* came "out of the time between the Wall opening and the currency union" (34). This was the period before formal negotiations over unification had been instigated, before East Germans became victims of what is referred to as the "adjustment crisis" of unification (Kreille 83–84). An East German psychologist has described this period as one in which fellow citizens experienced

> a wonderful liberation from fear. . . . Everything that had been painfully suppressed could be carefully brought to light/unfolded and formulated: activity, courage, spontaneity, hope, excitement, optimism, critical ability, openness, [and] honesty. . . . long-forgotten yearnings and wishes, thwarted possibilities were again actualized. (Maaz, *Das gestürzte Volk* 29)

Go Trabi Go is predicated on the good fortune of East Germans who could, for the first time, enjoy the freedom of travel. In the first Trabi comedy, Udo and his family also have their first innocent experience of dealing in western currency. Access to a new currency leads to their adventure, the major part of which is to indulge in the luxuries and commodities of capitalism. Throughout the film western money is linked to exotic locations, prosperity, sensual indulgence, and good fortune. In this sense, *Go Trabi Go* embraces the prospect of economic union, which in turn precipitated unification. Whereas *Go Trabi Go* has its protagonists revel in the material *gains* that were demanded and eagerly anticipated during the period of the Wende, the second Trabi comedy deals with *losses* considered to be a consequence of unification (loss of work places, of family harmony, of Heimat, of housing, of cultural heritage, of sense of community, etc.).

Currency union brought disaster to the east, at least in the short term. "The collapse of East Germany's economy occurred almost overnight" (Kreille 72), and the situation only worsened in the year that followed. By the end of 1990, it was clear that East Germans "were in for a full-blown drawn out depression" (McArdle 31). The boom that had been taking place in *West* Germany (referred to as the unification dividend) in 1990 led to stagnation by the end of 1991. Meanwhile in the east the "only real question was how long it would take for the economy of the new *Länder* to reach bottom" (McArdle 29). Moreover, throughout 1991, the year in which *That Was the Wild East* was in production, the patience of West Germans facing the cost of unification was tested. After having been promised that they would not have to suffer tax increases to pay for unification, West German taxes were increased on 1 July 1991. Interest rates were also increased, as were social security contributions. These economic measures were thought to "drain the already depleted reservoir of goodwill and compassion that the West Germans . . . traditionally felt towards their eastern counterparts" (Stares 3).

It was in this socioeconomic climate that *That Was the Wild East* was produced and released. The optimism and idealism of *Go Trabi Go* would hardly have been compatible with the "crisis adjustment" that was taking place in the new federal states. The second film emerges from a period when it was clear that living in united Germany was not necessarily a romantic prospect. To Hans-Joachim Maaz, this was a period when, having already witnessed the collapse of socialism, East Germans experienced the shattering of another great illusion, that of a life of flourishing prosperity (*Das gestürzte Volk* 97). This was for many a time of bitter disillusionment, of intimidation and disappointment (33). Maaz describes the mood that prevailed in the east throughout 1991 (and for many continued into the year that followed). "After the election in December of 1990, the promise that no one would be worse off turned out to be humbug. For just about everyone [in the east] things were, on the whole, worse, and the psychic consequences of renewed humiliation, illness . . . uncertainty, and anxiety were not to be overlooked" (117). Psychological devastation was without doubt widespread. Many in the east were disorientated and without a clear sense of purpose and meaning if not in a state of crisis. Maaz claims that this crisis manifested itself in "fear of freedom, of independence and of change" (*Der Gefühlsstau* 162).

One can see that *That Was the Wild East* emerged not only from a drastically altered economic climate but from a period motivated by another political and economic agenda, the *Aufschwung* (upturn or upward swing). Once the decrepit infrastructure of the east had been dismantled, the Aufschwung that was predicted for the eastern states became a national priority. The Aufschwung Ost program of economic recovery was launched in March 1991, a year that saw 140 billion DM of public money transferred to the new states (this sum was about equivalent to two-thirds of East Germany's GNP). By 1994, the federal government had transferred 500 billion DM to the eastern states. This upturn is alluded to very early in *That Was the Wild East*. After the Struutzes witness the demolition of their house, a foreman approaches them and berates Udo for having gone on holiday, claiming, perhaps too earnestly, "We need everybody, all [our] strength, for the Aufschwung."

In the midst of its comic indulgence and caprice, *That Was the Wild East* addresses a set of concerns and politically topical developments that arose as a result of the Unification Treaty. Michael Kreille asserts that one "of the most controversial issues" that surrounded negotiations of the treaty "involved ownership rights on property expropriated and nationalised between 1945 and 1949 in the Soviet Occupation Zone and later in the GDR" (62). Following the implementation of the treaty, more than one million claims for the restitution of property in the former GDR were made (McArdle Kelleher 30). The Trabi sequel picks up on precisely this controversial issue, as do other unification comedies I discussed in chapter 8. In *That Was the Wild East,* Udo stands to inherit part of the GDR heritage, and his claim is dependent upon his making Red Cap an economically viable venture through which employment can be secured. Accordingly, the economic domain the Struutzes inhabit in this film is infinitely more intricate and challenging than the tourists' world they explore in *Go Trabi Go*.

That Was the Wild East is more historically specific than *Go Trabi Go* in referring to the social and economic hardships and challenges East Germans faced in the first year of unification. It uses a modified set of symbols and motifs to convey the conflicts, the demands and the adjustments of the period. Korngiebel and Link comment on images that have been popularly summoned to represent different stages of German unification (31–53), and their research is especially valuable for a historical reading of

That Was the Wild East. They maintain that "the opening and the dis-mantling of the Wall resulted in the definitive upheaval of the symbolic order of the whole postwar epoch" (45). This was most pronounced in the eastern states, where the infusion of western money was accompanied by the importation of symbols as well as goods from the west (49). The two Trabi films attest to this process and the upheavals that unification brought with it.

Outmoded Automobiles

According to Korngiebel and Link, the economic and political significance of the Aufschwung was popularly imaged either as "aircraft (aeroplanes, rockets, and missiles) or (paradoxically) as automobile travel" (35). Once fears about the velocity of unification abated, it was the modern (often German) automobile that was popularly imaged as a freedom machine, associated with the democratization of the east. As I remarked in chapter 9, the American convertible, the limousine, and the aeroplane are among the vehicles that superseded the Trabant in *That Was the Wild East.* These vehicles were more reassuring in invoking the economic recovery and upturn anxiously awaited in the east.

In spite of the Trabi's disappearance in *That Was the Wild East,* the car's symbolic value has shifted and broadened in this film. Reminders about the backwardness of the GDR, which the Trabant in part prompted, were not especially amusing or welcomed when the second Trabi film went into production (director Peter Timm had already shifted to the subgenre variant of the Manta film). By the early 1990s the Trabant was already an emblem that marked the failure and extinction of East German industry. With the collapse of GDR industry the Trabi became an outmoded commodity. No one needed further reminders of the problems and lies of "real, existing socialism," of which industry was an inextricable part. With levels of productivity higher than in other eastern bloc countries, industry had once been a source of tremendous national pride in the former GDR. As noted in chapter 1, those achievements were discredited in the early 1990s, and what once generated pride became a source of shame. "The eternal successes, the production increases, and the quotas [that were] exceeded proved to be falsified statistics, [the result of] inefficiency, sloppiness, mismanagement, a living from vital resources, and above all from the merciless exploitation and destruction of the natural environment" (Maaz, *Der Gefühlsstau* 161).

The pungent fumes emitted by Trabants made them conspicuous everyday reminders of the GDR's systematic pollution of the environment (awareness of environmental damage being acute among the broad population in West Germany). Other more prosaic factors strengthened the negative connotations attributed to the Trabant. The vehicle's conspicuous absence for most of the second Trabi film is less surprising if one recalls that after currency union, East Germans abandoned their Trabants by the million. Once they had access to deutsche marks, East Germans boycotted most former GDR products with a vengeance, exacerbating economic ills in "their" half of Germany, at least in the early 1990s. The deterioration was perhaps most drastic in the automobile industry. The last Trabant was produced in April 1991, by which time the devastation of East German industry was all but complete. Relative to population, during the 1991–92 period, Germans in the eastern states set worldwide records in purchasing imported cars. "After the liquidation of their own automobile industry, the new *Länder* imported 2.2 million cars from all over the world" (Bittorf 54). And as they acquired their new imported cars, they paid for them in jobs. Each time an imported car was brought in the eastern states in the early 1990s, two local jobs were lost. Escalating unemployment meant that severance pay was often spent on buying the new family car. The gusto with which East Germans purchased imported cars actually hastened the deindustrialization of whole regions of the newly unified states (Bittorf 56).

Recognizing the traumas East German industry faced as a consequence of unification, it was probably inevitable that the Trabi's symbolic function was modified once the euphoria over unification abated. Because the Trabant came to carry with it associations of inferiority and privation, evoking the economic and industrial failures of the GDR, *That Was the Wild East* is a film that looks elsewhere for distinctive, less vexed motifs to capture the uniqueness of the ex-GDR. The motifs it utilizes are more archaic and largely devoid of associations with twentieth-century industrialization. The symbolic function attributed to the Trabi in the first film is broadened in the sequel to include the garden gnomes, the steam train, and Red Cap. The positing of these objects as uniquely East German allows the sequel to privilege tradition over modernization and heritage over change, an emphasis provided in Heimat films from the period of western reconstruction. Entities like the garden gnomes, cottage industry, and the antiquated locomotive come to symbolize "East-German-ness," and in doing so they redefine the Trabant, setting the scene for its revival at the close of the film.

Clearly "George's" symbolic functions are more diverse in *That Was the Wild East*. Apart from carrying the negative connotations of obsolescence, "George" continues to be associated with old-fashioned values, in particular the sanctity of the family: the vehicle is a safeguard for family unity and harmony, an association established in the first Trabi film. The absence of the car jeopardizes the old-fashioned values it embodies (family togetherness and harmony, monogamous marriage, the innocence and chastity of youth, community awareness). In effect, the disposal of the Trabi in the sequel precipitates the disintegration of the family unit. Jacqueline realizes this when more than halfway into the film she remarks when "'George' crashed, so did the family." Discord and misunderstanding prevail, mostly after the Trabant and family members are separated. Udo harbors suspicions that his wife has been unfaithful to him, and Rita argues with Jacqueline whom she suspects has become promiscuous. Later, when Jacqueline locates "George" and sets about restoring the vehicle, she does so to bring the family back together as she did before finding new tires to replace the stolen ones. Only when the vehicle is resurrected in the final scene of the film can the family be reunited. Even though the Trabi disappears from *That Was the Wild East* because of its industrial and economic affiliation with the ex-GDR, its reappearance at the end of the film marks an assertion of family values and "small is better" practices over rationalist economics and "big business."

Metropolis, Suburb, Rural Paradise

Apart from its definition through various artifacts and vehicles, "authentic East-German-ness" also becomes a geographical question in *That Was the Wild East*. The film itself is marked by a gradual eastward movement, with Charlie rationalizing his journey with the claim that the future is in the east. His belief echoes that of Kühn who, earlier in the film, asserts that "the path to the future leads east."

That Was the Wild East's portrait of unified Germany and its designation of "authenticity" also depends upon the establishment of an opposition between the regions of Landwitz and Bitterfeld. Following the pattern common to western-based, -funded, -directed, and -produced unification comedies, Landwitz is classified as a type of preindustrial paradise, the essential and genuine East Germany, which is threatened with extinction. The town-country opposition is a distinguishing feature and major structural characteristic of Heimatfilme, in which the town and especially the large city are almost invariably presented in a negative light (Trimborn 42; Höfig 386). In the case of *That Was the Wild East,* the unfavorable contrasts that are drawn between Landwitz and Bitterfeld serve several functions. The comparison helps to justify the Struutzes' decision to sever their ties with Bitterfeld. Misgivings about unification can also be invited once Landwitz is introduced as the Eden threatened with contamination by the west. Landwitz is represented as authentically East German, in contradistinction to the despoiled ruins of Bitterfeld. Landwitz is com-

plete with verdant pastures and rolling meadows, with ancient villas grac-
ing picturesque hillsides, with half-timbered, late medieval dwellings, with
lakes and spectacular mountains. The region has an abundance of natural
beauty and rare wildlife (the Sächsiche Schweiz National Park near Dresden provides many of the location shots for the Landwitz surrounds).

That Was the Wild East can present Landwitz as a type of Eden, or as
an anti–big business paradise, because it identifies the region as one
untouched by mechanization, mass-produced goods, and a commercialized leisure industry. Such signs of modernization have no place in this
Heimat. Its natural beauty aside, it is the antiquated mode of production
employed in Landwitz that facilitates the region's classification as paradise. Mechanization, mass-produced goods, and a commercialized
leisure industry are, however, presented as phenomena that have reached
areas around Landwitz. These big business by-products of capitalism are
presented as concomitants of Dresden and of Bitterfeld. In accordance
with the Heimat film schema, rural custom and tradition must be protected against the threats posed by such manifestations of "progress" and
modernization.

Bitterfeld is similarly associated with commercialized leisure and the
distribution of mass-produced goods. In an early scene in the film, for
instance, a pair is briefly shown amusing themselves as they record the
demolition of the Struutzes' home on a video camera. Elsewhere, Jacqueline comments on the proliferation of furniture warehouses in the Bitterfeld district. And the region is, of course, destined to be transformed into
a golf course. By contrast, the leisure activities Landwitz offers are not
specifically profit-oriented or commercialized. These environs are, for
example, provided with an outdoor swimming pool, and the leisure activities pursued in the region include rock-climbing, hiking, bird-watching,
and countryside picnics.

Dresden's association with the mass-produced carries with it over-
tones of locker-room humor. Charlie, for instance, tries to sell his supply
of condoms by accosting passersby with jokes about penis sizes and the
demands for his goods. The supply is without a doubt substantial (he has
5,000)—especially if one recalls that in the days of the GDR, condoms
were not readily available. Customarily, postal orders were placed for condoms at a limited number of distribution outlets, and clients' orders were
sent to them through the mail, so Charlie's direct-marketing approach is
definitely an innovation.

That Was the Wild East establishes a hierarchy among the locations it
presents with the country town of Landwitz being treated most favorably
and the suburb of Bitterfeld being dismissed as uninhabitable. Bitterfeld's
business district is desolate, its industrial section is no longer operational,

and the residential part of the town has been leveled. The American millionaire and property developer William Buck (also called Bill Buck in double reference to his wealth and representation of American capital) is ultimately held responsible for the demolition of the town. Complying with the conventions of the Heimat genre, America embodies the "foreign" (Höfig 386; Trimborn 42) and the "absolute in misanthropy." It is the demanding, unjust environment par excellence (Trimborn 42) here also. Udo encounters the United States firsthand in *That Was the Wild East:* he flies to New York for one day in an effort to contact William Buck. Udo is overwhelmed by the city with its bustling traffic, towering skyscrapers, and strange and hostile inhabitants. A security guard forcefully evicts him from the millionaire's high-rise business complex, and Udo must scale the building's exterior like a window cleaner in an effort to gain entry to the building and access to Buck. Just as he has acquired Bitterfeld, Buck is in the process of taking over Dresden when he is first introduced. He fills the comic stereotype of the abusive and ruthless business executive: his assistants cringe, accustomed to his verbal assaults. At one point he blusters: "Dresden—is that East Germany or West Germany? I don't give a shit. Buy the whole fucking town." Buck's venture suggests that Dresden may await a fate similar to Bitterfeld. As a synecdoche for the United States, New York emerges not only as foreign and hostile, but also based on a system of exploitation and class difference,[1] furthering the country-city antagonism common to the Heimat genre.

Although the suburbs of Bitterfeld are presented as beyond all hope and either decrepit or in ruins, Dresden is identified, in part, as a cultivated region worthy of preservation. If Landwitz is the Eden of the east, a paradise that unification threatens to despoil, Dresden comes to represent the elite cultural heritage of the east. To a degree, Dresden is loosely associated with Landwitz through the earthenware produced at Red Cap. The choice of the porcelain gnomes as a symbol of East German-ness in this context is quite fitting. The garden gnomes are made in the vicinity of the city, making the figurines a chunky variant of Dresden china and part of the east's cultural tradition. Whereas Dresden is represented as the domain of culture, Landwitz is also linked by association to culture and tradition through its production of ceramic goods from one generation to the next. Outsiders like Fricke and Kühn present a threat to the survival of that tradition.

That Was the Wild East manages to associate Dresden with the cul-

---

1. Whereas Buck is monolingual and has no option other than to conduct his business dealings in English, the cleaner who is engaged to wash the floor in Buck's headquarters can act as a mediator between Buck and Udo: she speaks both Russian and English and can clarify their business transaction.

tural heritage of the east by fixating upon the city's majestic opera house. In one scene the exterior of the opera house is highlighted through a simple strategy: Charlie and Udo do not drive directly past the building, but drive around in circles several times in front of the structure to ensure it is kept in frame. Later in the film we are virtually taken on a tour of the building and are also shown architectural details of the concert hall. The foyer of the opera house becomes the location for a lavish banquet Udo and Charlie attend as uninvited guests.

The attention granted by *That Was the Wild East* to the Dresden opera house is not incidental. The building is a particularly apt example of the endurance of the eastern cultural heritage and is used in the film to highlight the importance of preserving that heritage. The Dresden opera house is one of the city's most famous monuments. It was designed by Gottfried Semper in 1838 and completed in 1841, but had to be reconstructed by his son, Manfred, in 1871 after it was damaged by fire. Wagner premiered a number of his operas there. Then the structure, known as the Semperoper, was reduced to ruins in 1945 when it was bombed like the rest of Dresden. The current opera house was painstakingly restored to its original splendor over the decades and was reopened again exactly forty years after Dresden was bombed.

Semper was a prominent figure in German and European architecture and was viewed as an innovator who introduced a particularly humanist style of architecture, inspired by Italian Renaissance design, to Germany. In this sense his work may be an appropriate emblem of East German culture. Thus, the prominence the opera house is granted in many scenes in *That Was the Wild East* takes on greater significance in the light of the history of the building and its architect. In addition, the city's synagogue, which Semper also designed, is shown dominating part of the city skyline in the film. The construction of the Dresden synagogue coincided with the outbreak of cholera in the city. Many drew a direct link between the two events and viewed Semper—clearly someone linked to calamities—as inadvertently responsible for the spread of the disease.

However, the attention drawn to this architect's buildings in various scenes of *That Was the Wild East* acts primarily as a reminder of the cultural heritage and history of the east. The opera house becomes an emblem of the city itself, rebuilt from the ruins of World War II (before it was bombed, the architectural beauty of Dresden was such that it was sometimes known as "Florence on the Elbe"). The passing visual reference to Semper's synagogue is a momentary reminder of the antifascist foundations on which the GDR was supposedly founded and through which it differentiated itself from the Federal Republic. Like other synagogues, this one also serves as a reminder of the survival of Jewish people and Jewish culture. The repeated display of the Semperoper connects eastern cultural heritage with a tradition of humanism that was attributed to Semper's architectural style. The opera house too can be read as a symbol of the resilience of (East German) culture, which, despite historical calamity, can rise from the ruins to reassert itself. The suggestion here may be that, just as Dresden, its opera house, and its Jewish culture endured Nazism, defeat in World War II, and occupation by the victors, the cultural heritage of the east may once again survive unification and conquest by the west. Even though it is threatened, eastern culture (or at least its architectural emblem) is presented as eternal and irrepressible.

The attention *That Was the Wild East* devotes to the opera house and the cultural heritage of which it is part also allows distinctions to be drawn between "legitimate" and enduring high culture and "illegitimate" low culture of the east. The sex industry and high culture exist side by side in Dresden, which thus embodies the cultivated and the crude. The city is presented as the one location in the film that exploits ribald aspects of the entertainment market. Dresden is host to the Pigalle Bar, a club/brothel featuring erotic dancers. Surprisingly, the "debased" forms of entertainment provided at the Pigalle Bar are related to the old communist regime rather than western capital. When Jacqueline first approaches the bar, she observes that the building was previously the headquarters for the local branch of the SED. A red light illuminates the facade of the building, and when Jacqueline draws attention to its hue, a comparison between the current and the former workers in the building is invited.

Further links are suggested between communism, corruption, and the activities in the brothel when Jacqueline is shown working there. While her girlfriend dances for customers, a scantily clad Jacqueline waits on their tables and acts as hostess. Kühn's three assistants are among the customers at the bar, and Jacqueline overhears them discuss their investment in the brothel, financed by funds they have embezzled from the Red Cap pension fund. Once the group notices Jacqueline, they presume she is a prostitute and collectively proposition her. Yet Jacqueline succeeds in humiliating the men, whom at one stage she encourages to disrobe in anticipation of sexual favors. In their state of undress they are subsequently ejected from the nightclub, and their vulnerability is publicly displayed. When they cluster together outside the bar in broad daylight, a tilt shot highlights the men's feet. Each sports identical red socks, one presumes as a residual sign of their loyalty to the deposed regime. They appear as compromised by their socks as by their undress and are ridiculed by a group of passing neo-Nazis. The uniform footwear of the men in turn links them to the neo-Nazis who are also uniformly dressed.

This brief encounter between neo-Nazis and former communists allows the film to collapse extreme ends of the political spectrum, so that both groups are connected through their costume, demeanor, and impulses. The communists are lascivious; the neo-Nazis think they can use 5,000 condoms. Both groups are dim-witted: none of their members is capable of autonomous or individual action. Moreover, their respective activities are criminal and unpatriotic insofar as they violate what is defined as essentially East German: the neo-Nazis are vandals who are responsible for "George's" destruction and disappearance, whereas Kühn's assistants have defrauded Red Cap, the institution upon which all of Landwitz is supposedly dependent.

Landwitz knows nothing of the sex industry or of neo-Nazis associated with Dresden. The country village further distinguishes itself from the city and Bitterfeld through its modes of production. The suburb and the city are identified as industrial domains where mass-produced goods circulate (the scrap-metal barge, the furniture warehouses, and the factories suggest the industrialization of Bitterfeld and Dresden). By contrast Landwitz is graced by preindustrial modes of manufacture and labor. The country-city, progress-tradition oppositions common to Heimat films of another epoch resurface again here. In *That Was the Wild East,* when Udo Struutz becomes a businessman, he enters into cottage industry rather than into mass manufacture. This is emphasized toward the end of the film when the viewer is virtually taken on another guided tour, this time of Red Cap. This scene allows for the gnome-production process to be demonstrated at length. Manual labor is highlighted, together with the near absence of mechanization and of the technology of mass production. The gnomes are shown being fired in a kiln that is manually stoked. The clay figures are not ushered through stages of production on a conveyor belt, but rather carried by workers from one phase to the next. Workers are involved in the production and are shown hand-painting the gnomes. The gnomes are hand-packed into wooden crates and transported off in an ancient pickup truck. Women coworkers saunter through the sunny, open-air production area, where drudgery and strenuous exertion have no place. The overall impression of the Red Cap complex is of a collective staffed by gratified volunteers rather than workers involved in the numbing routine of manufacturing hundreds of thousands of identical products. The depiction of the business is a populist fantasy.

Fairy Tales and Steam Trains

In a fashion redolent of the Heimat film of the postwar west, *That Was the Wild East* champions rural heritage, customs, and life-style while presenting modernization and progress—the proposed autobahn and futuristic skyscrapers—as a threat. As I have suggested earlier in this chapter, the designation of tradition, custom, and heritage in *That Was the Wild East* involves the amalgamation of motifs and a slippage of symbols. With the Trabi shoved out of the sequel, the garden gnomes produced at Red Cap come to symbolize the cute and cuddly obsolescence of the GDR and eastern heritage worthy of preserving. They carry with them reassuring connotations of childlike innocence. The gnomes invite comparison between the respective economic strengths of the two Germanies, with the east being "dwarfed" by the economic "giant" of the Federal Republic and its domineering allies.

Gnomes are linked to the earth, and with their night-lights they fulfill the role of guardian of the homeland, making them an appropriate mascot for the east as it faces the menaces associated with unification and modernization. By extension, Udo assumes the role of guardian of the region, too; the gnomes resemble him. The impression of sleepiness and slowness of life in the GDR also extends to the figuring of the gnomes produced at Red Cap. Each of the gnomes is clad in a nightshirt, a nightcap, slippers, and dressing gown. Apart from conveying old-fashionedness and the sleepiness of the GDR, the gnomes' accessories—their night-lights—act as reminders of what was formerly a closed society—one that was "kept in the dark."

It is not uncommon for the imagery of gnomes, dwarfs, and figures from fairy or folktales to be deployed by those who have devised parables of life in the GDR. Similar images from fairy tales, from childhood, and of slumber abound in descriptions that filmmakers, psychologists, politicians, and historians have provided of existence in the ex-GDR. Fairy-tale analogies are prevalent most notably in those films set in the east that seek to dramatize the processes of unification. In *Ostkreuz,* an almost unbearably tawdry neorealist account of survival in the collapsing east, Michael Klier has constructed such a drama. One critic has drawn attention to *Ostkreuz*'s fairy-tale-like qualities and narrative closure, which sees two waifs comfort one another in the urban wilderness as they share in a symbolic wedding feast (Gansera 43). Helke Misselwitz's *Little Angel* works even more self-consciously with fairy-tale motifs. *Miraculi* and *The Country behind the Rainbow,* films that deal with the heritage and demise of the GDR, similarly draw on the fantastic elements and figures of folklore. *Miraculi,* for example, has at its center a figure named Sebastian who undergoes a series of quasi-mystical transformations.

Fairy-tale scenarios have also been metaphorically deployed by a whole series of East German writers intent on characterizing the GDR, its achievements, its shortcomings, and its eventual collapse. Dieter Hochmuth uses the folktale analogy when he examines the situation of former GDR filmmakers in 1990, comparing them with the children featured in various fairy tales or *Märchen*—offspring whose impoverished parents send them out into the woods to perish ("Tausend und zwei" 17).

This emphasis is pertinent if one considers the function of the fairy tale in the ex-GDR. Initially, German fairy tales were not considered suitable for publication in the east because their fantastic, mystical, and uncanny elements made them ideologically objectionable. In the late 1940s, Grimms' tales were considered a "potential threat to the self proclaimed 'rationalist' *Kulturpolitik*" of the GDR (Bathrick 169). This attitude was revised in the early 1950s when it was realized that the stories could be

> sanitized . . . along the lines of domesticated proletarian good behaviour, much the same way the Grimms themselves had rewritten and reworked the original versions to conform to the norms of bourgeois morality some 140 years before. In both cases, the effect was to deradicalize the tales by bowdlerizing the elements of the fantastic, the uncanny, the grotesque, and the obscene. (168)

Even though particular tales (e.g., "Hansel and Gretel") were viewed as irredeemable, in others socialist sensibility led to the elimination of religious activities (prayers and baptisms), and daughters of kings were transformed into peasants throughout. By 1952, fairy tales "were seen as important documents of class struggle," suffering, and liberation from feudal order (Bathrick 168). Members of East Germany's avant-garde in turn "looked to folklore traditions and paradigms of myth as a means to critique the status quo" (175).

Apart from folktale analogies, the GDR has been regularly described as being asleep and/or arrested in development that has not advanced past childhood. Commonly, emphasis has been placed upon the infantile subservience of GDR citizens to the state. Few would dispute Maaz's contention that in the GDR "its repressive educational system, the authoritarian structure of every aspect of society, an intimidating state security apparatus, and a banal yet effective system of rewards and punishments" ensured conformity, childlike dependence, and psychic disorders. "The existential, psychological and moral forms of control" the state imposed upon its subjects, together with the quasi-religious glorification of the power of the state, sanctioned infantilism throughout GDR society (*Der Gefühlsstau* 15, 29). Like the writer-cum-politician Stefan Heym, Maaz tellingly refers to the period of the Wende as a time when one "walked upright" (*Das gestürtzte Volk* 29). West German author Peter Schneider deploys similar analogies in his critical account of life in the GDR. In *The*

German Comedy: Scenes of Life after the Wall, Schneider focuses upon the backwardness and "sleepiness" of the country in a chapter titled "Some People Can Even Sleep through an Earthquake" (66). Christa Wolf also used the metaphor of the GDR as a nation asleep in a protest speech she delivered at Berlin-Alexanderplatz on 4 November 1989. Martin Ahrends compares living in the GDR with sleeping in an "enchanted castle," transfixed as if under a magic spell. He alludes to a society that lived the life of a dilettante, likening existence in the GDR with that of the child who lives in the "Not-Yet": "The freedom of the East is the freedom not to have to grow up entirely, to be allowed to keep one foot in the unself-consciousness of childhood" (42). Like Maaz in *Das gestürtzte Volk* (96), Ahrends views the opening of the GDR borders to the rest of the world as a rude and disappointing awakening. He describes how, after having awaited the prince's arrival in Sleeping Beauty's castle, "some unauthorized person has turned on the light and started making nasty remarks about the slum in which one has been living" (42).

Devoid of the lyricism of Ahrends's writing, *That Was the Wild East* also draws upon this imagery, in particular imbuing East Germans with a childlike innocence, presenting them as figures who inhabited a child's coddled world. This impression is advanced not just through the gnomes but through the Red Cap/*Rotkäppchen* estate itself. In the German context, Red Cap is the name by which the folktale figure Little Red Riding Hood is known. Red Cap is also the brand name of a popular East German sparkling wine. It is locally produced and one of the few East German products still in demand after the GDR collapsed.

Throughout *That Was the Wild East,* the Red Riding Hood enterprise is presented as an essentially East German establishment. It carries with it a sense of tradition like the age-old tale. Not unlike the figure after which it is named, Udo's business epitomizes a wholesome innocence, virtue, and vulnerability. The wolfish antagonists in this scenario are West German big business interests and their foreign allies. Fricker, the bureaucrat with whom Udo must deal and who refers to the east as being "primitive," is one such villainous figure. The most duplicitous character in this tale is, however, Kühn. He is the predator in disguise who poses a mortal threat to Udo and to the survival of Red Cap. Kühn embodies wickedness, corruption, and evil. He also attempts to lure Rita into his den.

Both *That Was the Wild East* and the first Trabi film draw on the iconography of unification, relying upon certain objects or figures such as Little Red Riding Hood and the gnomes to signify cultural difference and what is distinctively East German. One other such image used in the title sequences of both films is the steam-powered locomotive. The "unity train" assumed a central place in the period of history from which the

Trabi comedies emerged. The metaphor of unification as a train was one adopted by many political figureheads late in 1989 and through the following year. Oskar La Fontaine and Willy Brandt imaged unification in this way, as did members of the Christian Democrats, whom they opposed. The unity train was a central motif and strategic element in Chancellor Kohl's election campaign in 1990 (Hofmann 68). It was a political vehicle for the Christian Democrat Party, which sought to capitalize upon the desire for swift unification, widespread in the east.[2] In the video clip the West German government produced to celebrate Unification Day (3 October 1990), a modern, high-speed train is a conspicuous leitmotif (Hofmann 68).

Since the railway train was such a predominant theme, it is no wonder that the title sequence of *Go Trabi Go* opens with a variation of that symbol. The very first image we see is a train rattling down a set of railway tracks. This locomotive is not, however, the sleek, ultramodern, intercity express that speeds between capitals. Rather it is an old-fashioned steam engine that becomes a distinctive emblem of the GDR. The locomotive is first shown against an industrial backdrop of factories, their chimney stacks smoking. For continuity or good value, the steam train is also included in the scene that immediately follows, except there it is shown traveling in the *opposite* direction to the previous scene, but still against a bustling backdrop. The impression generated is one of quaintly obsolescent yet functioning industry—of old-fashioned trade and inefficient productivity. We are invited to view the train as a motif for the cozy industrial retardation of the east, as opposed to the technological advancement of the west. In these scenes the locomotive is divorced from the political symbolism of a "train racing to its final destination"—unification (Hofmann 68). Instead it represents routine inefficiency, a lack of purpose or destination; the train tows no carriages, and carries no cargo or passengers. Lacking direction, the locomotive just bustles back and forth like a child's toy train set (the association of GDR products and child's play is further established in *Go Trabi Go*, when "George" is referred to as a toy). Here the connotations are much more of the 1900s rather than the present day. In Korngiebel and Link's terms, the train serves multiple functions as a collective symbol. It may, as they argue, have acted as a reassuring symbol within unification discourses, allowing for fears about the velocity of unification to be allayed by invoking related imagery of timetables, sidings, stations, and platforms. Such images provide the impression that

---

2. This impulse prompted punning reference to *Deutschland eilig Vaterland* (Germany—the Fatherland-in-a-hurry) as contrasted to the more sombre *Deutschland einig Vaterland* (Germany united Fatherland).

unification could be regulated and controlled. Alternatively, the authors assert that in inviting association with the turn of the century, the train is a mode of transport that evokes the collective, socialism, and impending industrialization (47).

The utilization of railway motifs is slightly more elaborate in *That Was the Wild East*. This imagery in particular strengthens the hierarchy established among the film's various locations, and a vague affinity is established between the movement of the Struutz family and the locomotive. When the Struutzes reenter Bitterfeld in the sequel, they pass railway tracks and a railway crossing. Tumbleweed is blown across the tracks, adding to the desolation of the scene. Udo provides verbal confirmation of the situation: "No smog. No trains. It's as if the place has been abandoned." Here the iconography of the western genre, signaled also through the film's title and theme song, initially overrides unification symbolism. Insofar as the scene invokes unification, it is perhaps as a dim reminder of the mass exodus the GDR suffered throughout 1989 and 1990, an exodus that accelerated economic and monetary union. The "unification train" has long left this decrepit and forsaken station that stands as a ruin, like the rest of Bitterfeld. The departure of the train echoes in the theme song that simulates the syncopated rhythm of train wheels clanking along train tracks. The Struutzes are quick to follow and do not hesitate to leave the town.

Even though its title sequence evokes the structural dichotomies of the western, *That Was the Wild East* does not present East Germany as a frontier to be conquered or cultivated as is done by *No More Mr. Nice Guy*'s utilization of western iconography. The second Trabi film rather presents "unified" East Germany (i.e., Bitterfeld) as a ghost town. *That Was the Wild East* manages to identify unification not as a civilizing force, but rather as one associated with collapse, decay, desertion, destruction, and wastelands. Factories are idle, businesses have closed, neighborhoods are deserted, railways no longer function, and homes are razed to the ground. Moreover, unification seems to pose an unspoken threat to fertility: Rita's pregnancy announced at the end of *Go Trabi Go* does not extend into the sequel. Even the sheep that grazed on the outskirts of Bitterfeld in the first film seem to have left town by the sequel.

With the opening scenes of *That Was the Wild East* drawing attention to Bitterfeld's deserted railway and the absence of the steam train, the locomotive's reappearance in Landwitz further into the film is all the more remarkable. Significantly, the train makes its appearance just as the Struutzes approach the outskirts of the village. Rita draws Udo's attention to a feature of the location, and when they approach a level crossing, they are obliged to stop their car to allow the steam train adequate time to be observed and to pass from one side of the frame to the other. The steam train and the signpost announcing entry into the town are shown within the one frame. In effect, the steam train seems to *follow* the Struutzes when they migrate from Bitterfeld to Landwitz (and from one film to the other). With its nineteenth-century associations, its slowness, its dependence upon fossil fuel, and the physical toil necessary to stoke its ovens, the locomotive allows for the introduction of Landwitz as "authentic" GDR. The village is depicted as a quaintly antiquated region that has evaded modernization, a type of paradise that may face extinction or a Heimat for the 1990s. Moreover, the relocation of the steam train seems to suggest prosperity for the region of Landwitz: in contrast to the engine that bustles around in the opening scenes of *Go Trabi Go,* the train that enters Landwitz tows carriages. It is an immaculately maintained passenger train.

"We are one people." (easterner)
"So are we." (westerner)

That Was the Wild East raises a series of contentious issues and contradictions that can neither be contained nor adequately resolved within the film's narrative framework. With its narrative excess and intensified contradiction, unification is presented in a derogatory light. Efforts to harmonize and regulate the conflicts within *That Was the Wild East* become more strained and cumbersome as the film progresses. Other unification comedies, like *Rising to the Bait, No More Mr. Nice Guy,* and *Burning Life,* do not shy away from presenting social and economic conflicts that are attributed to the process of unification, nor do they refrain from presenting caustic and savagely critical portraits of national traits. In contrast to *That Was the Wild East,* however, *Rising to the Bait* and *No More Mr. Nice Guy* move deliberately and determinedly toward a euphoric closure where community and integration are celebrated.

In *That Was the Wild East,* unification is characterized as a force that threatens most forms of relations—marital, vocational, environmental, and communal. The Bitterfeld of the first film was characterized by a developed sense of community. There the town was shown to be industrialized and polluted, but also cozily suburban. Familiarity among neighbors is conveyed when they are shown together out of doors, leisurely washing their cars and casually exchanging wisecracks with one another. The neighbors are loosely grouped together as they wave the Struutzes good-bye when the family sets off on its holiday. It is the community of *Go Trabi Go* that has been extinguished in the Bitterfeld to which the Struutzes return in *That Was the Wild East.* In that film, unification means privatization; consequently, the Struutzes' neighbors, like the sheep, have simply disappeared.

Surplus conflict is especially conspicuous in the case of the family reunion that forces *That Was the Wild East* to closure. After all, it was their experience of the west, in particular of Italy, that fortified the Struutzes as a family, whereas their return to unified Germany results in discord and fragmentation. Considering the ruptures that unification and capitalist enterprise have brought to the Struutzes, the final image of the abruptly reconstituted family is somewhat more disconcerting than reassuring. The estrangement they have endured overrides the last idyllic scene where they drive off together into the countryside. During what is virtually their only other encounter in the film, Mama Struutz has accused her daughter of being an "anarchist slut" (she finds her in bed with a young man), while Jacqueline has identified her mother as a "capitalist whore" (she has altered her appearance and dresses expensively like a successful western businesswoman). Afterward these prophecies seem to come true: it is implied that Rita commits adultery with the mayor of Landwitz, and Jacqueline finds employment working as a hostess in a sex bar. Udo Struutz's transformation is of a less carnal nature: his development is from "qualified GDR citizen" to jet-setting entrepreneur who negotiates with West German bankers by quoting Goethe.

That Was the Wild East lacks the romantic interest of unification comedies like *Adamski* and *Love at First Sight*. The range of the cultural, economic, and moral dilemmas the film mobilizes leaves it no time for such trivia. The film portrays the former GDR as a site of rampant exploitation, corruption, and bigotry—its territory colonized by aggressive and ruthlessly self-serving West Germans. Its towns and cities are in the process of being taken over by American capital. In accord with Heimat conventions, throughout the film, strategies to develop and modernize the east are shown to be patently abusive of the environment and of local heritage. Its perpetrators are motivated by nothing other than unbridled avarice: from the standpoint of the residents of Landwitz, Kühn "comes from the west, wants the business, and treats us like idiots."

That Was the Wild East is highly critical of the whole issue of development and of the corruption that was associated with the privatization of East German industry. Even though the operation is unnamed, Treuhand is clearly the major target of disparagement. The company is inextricably linked with the term *Abwicklung*. In *That Was the Wild East* the Zentrale fur Abwicklung—Dresden is supposed to represent Treuhand. Udo deals with this office in an effort to secure his ownership of Red Cap. *That Was the Wild East* clearly presents Treuhand in a highly critical light, but the critique presented is not so daring as it may initially appear. For what the film simply affirms are the suspicions that Treuhand's unpopular dealings have prompted. However, once that affirmation is complete, responsibility for the colonization, exploitation, and ruin of the eastern states is deflected away from West Germany to the United States.

In *That Was the Wild East,* it is not West German capital that instigates the modernization and development of what used to be the Democratic Republic, but rather a single individual, the American millionaire William Buck. A billboard bearing his name announces the development of the east early in the film. When the Struutzes set out to travel to Dresden, they crash their Trabi into the billboard, knocking it over—surely an act of defiance. In one of the film's otherwise rare instances of consistency, Buck is also the financial force behind the modernization of Landwitz. Again we see his name, aptly representative of American capital, on a billboard accompanying futuristic illustrations of skyscraper architecture planned for the idyllic region. As the embodiment of big business, Buck is exploitative, tyrannical, and capricious. He is an impatient figure who is susceptible to fads (for example, he subscribes to a pop-psychology formula for success). Like most negatively portrayed city-dwellers that populated the old genre, Buck is ignorant of the eternal values of Heimat. He knows nothing of the tradition and heritage associated with Heimat, such as the cottage industry of Red Cap or Udo's garden gnomes. Buck is unfamiliar with the folklore of gnomes and mistakes the figurines to be stress-relieving executive toys. His impulses are acquisitive and destructive, whereas Udo's are to salvage tradition and parochial heritage. If Udo's emblem, the garden gnome, links him to earth and hearth (themselves integral to Heimat), Buck's emblem, the cellular telephone, emphasizes states foreign to Heimat like itinerancy, transientness, and omnipresence.

Mitigating the film's critique of the colonization of the former GDR, in *That Was the Wild East* the United States rather than the Federal Republic is presented as the economic power determining the course of unification. Conveniently, a non-German is held responsible for despoiling the former GDR. Because American capital is associated with the changes unification brings and the modernization of the east, Germans are divested of responsibility. They are capable of recognizing and valuing the east as Heimat and may pride themselves on its preservation. Even the West German, Kühn, eventually comes to appreciate what the east as Heimat has to offer. By the end of the film he is sensitive to the unspoiled natural beauty of the country: he makes the transition from listening to recordings of exotic birdcalls to spotting birds in the wild. He also experiences the invigorating effect of working on the land. Heimat awareness is identified as exclusively German, at least in unification films that issue from the old states of the Federal Republic; it is something intrinsic to virtuous East Germans and something less sensitive West Germans can acquire. Even Charlie is placed against a backdrop fitting to a Heimat film by the end of *That Was the Wild East:* in an otherwise painfully protracted long take, he is shown driving along in front of a spectacular outcrop of mountains in Sachsen National Park. These mountains would be well placed in a Heimatfilm from the 1950s, a matter already suggested in a related scene toward the end of the film that sees Udo and Rita also high in the mountain range, calling to one another from the mountain tops, a standard Heimat finale (Konz 91). In this scene, the natural beauty of the wilderness is amply displayed in broad panorama, as Rita makes allusions to another universally recognizable myth of origins, paradise, and primitivism when she likens "her" Udo to Tarzan.

That Was the Wild East's Germany may be unified, but it is decidedly lacking in harmony. Relations between many East and West Germans are fraught with indignation and hostility throughout the film, its portraits of East and West Germans being equally harsh. The film is populated by a diverse range of characters including marauding and imbecilic neo-Nazis, dim-witted obsequious East Germans, and supercilious and unscrupulous West Germans. Charlie, the flamboyant would-be entrepreneur from the west, is a comic embodiment of the enterprise and initiative that capitalism supposedly engenders: he displays agility in his attempts to save Red Cap and its oversupply of gnomes. When he tries to convince a banker that the gnomes could be economically viable, he suggests, "We'll give the stuff a completely different finish—I say, chrome." His proposal is comical but also reflective of his superficiality in that he thinks in terms of veneers. More important, his maneuvers ensure that Udo is introduced to the most powerful figures in international financing during the banquet scene at the Dresden Opera. In the same scene, Udo's timidity and obsequiousness are effectively highlighted through his comically circumspect appraisal of the banquet offerings as much as through his lower-class selection (he settles for a frankfurter rather than lobster or caviar).

Further parodies of East German servility are provided through the characterization of Mayor Kühn's red-socked assistants. Out of condition and slovenly dressed in sweat-stained, synthetic work clothes, the assistants are incapable of showing initiative or reason. In one scene, they all willingly jump, fully clothed, into a lake when they misunderstand Kühn's instructions. They present a threat to Udo in that they seek to take sexual advantage of his daughter, just as Kühn attempts to seduce Udo's wife. Certain parallels are established between the West German Kühn and his East German sidekicks. They are all dishonest and unscrupulous, but Kühn is more manipulative and exploitative than the others. Ultimately all of these characters are thwarted by their own stupidity. By the close of the film they are defeated by Udo and the integrity he has displayed in salvaging Red Cap.

Throughout the film, Udo is distinguished from Kühn and his assistants not only because he is a righteous figure, but also because he is fortune's favorite (just as he is in *Go Trabi Go*). Udo does not seek power, authority, or wealth, but nevertheless he is a leader (it causes him embarrassment that the workers at Red Cap insist on calling him "boss"). He ultimately manages to defeat his enemies and secure his inheritance of Red Cap not by design or calculated scheming, but rather despite himself. In this sense Udo functions like a true Heimat film hero. As Höfig explains, protagonists in Heimatfilme rarely display business initiative. Whatever "they do is defined in their relation[s] to family and inheritance. They don't deal as such, they allow things to happen" (Höfig 360). *That Was the Wild East* follows this schema: rivalry over the proprietorship of Red Cap is averted by a chance event. Udo meets the proposal deadline for securing employment and making Red Cap an economically viable venture whereas his adversary, Kühn, does not. Kühn, an urbane figure, manages to get lost in the woodlands surrounding Landwitz, and thus he misses the appointment that determines ownership of Red Cap.

Neither Udo nor his compatriots are spared the scorn of West Germans in *That Was the Wild East,* which distinguishes this film from the first Trabant comedy. Referring to the Red Cap enterprise "expropriated from that bunch of socialist party numbskulls," Udo's uncle declares in his will: "I only remember Udo as a really boring youngster, but perhaps he has amounted to something since then. Let him deal with those Saxon blockheads." Kühn further berates East Germans when he delivers a harsh tirade to Rita toward the end of the film: "Grumble, grumble, grumble. That's all you can do. Afraid of this and afraid of that. No capacity for enthusiasm, no sense of discovery. If it were up to you everything would be like before; cars that look like a pile of shit, three-hour queues for a stupid banana and pride in being isolated."

Even what was thought to be "best in the GDR: its inefficient comfort and slowness" (de Bruyn 63), does not escape censure in *That Was the Wild East.* Identified by the motto "Small but Great," the business that the family inherits is the picture of obsolescence. That the Struutzes honor this vestige of the GDR is perhaps the film's cruelest irony. As a cottage industry, the Red Cap produces antiquated and useless goods that are unappealing, that have no value, and for which there is neither a local market nor ongoing demand. Ultimately the family struggles to salvage what is worthless: their resistance to the western takeover of their homeland is reduced to a commitment to kitsch. Eastern culture, as embodied in the gnomes, is quaint, outmoded, and parochial, and tied to the fancies of childhood. Their associations are with infantilism and retardation.

That Was the Wild East presents a critical and at times damning portrait of united Germany. Unification is presented as an exploitative operation ultimately benefiting American economic imperialism and marred by political corruption and greed. Relations between East and West Germans are portrayed as strained and duplicitous, and the film suggests that life in unified Germany jeopardizes family unity. *That Was the Wild East* pictures the GDR as DEFA country, worth no more than the spiraling value of its real estate.

The sovereignty of the Struutzes is no more secure at the end of this reunification comedy than at the beginning, even though they have stubbornly preserved a meaningless fragment of GDR trade and tradition. In the process of doing so, they have relinquished their house in Bitterfeld and are homeless. When Udo and Rita first arrive in Landwitz, they sleep in a tent. Udo has no accommodation after that night and is nomadic for the rest of the film. Rita sleeps in a bungalow that seems to belong to Kühn, so that in effect, unification has made Rita a guest of the West German, even though she is in her own country. At the end of the film, when the family is reunited, they drive off through the countryside, their destination unspecified. For several minutes the landscape features—glorious imagery of rugged mountain ranges and picturesque meadows—suggesting that although the Struutzes are homeless, they have found their Heimat.

The music that accompanies the film's credit sequence nevertheless signals disaster for Udo and perhaps also for his family. In conclusion, Udo delivers a rap-music commentary in a heavy Saxon accent that acts as a kind of epilogue. The rap rhymes are awkwardly contrived. In tone the lyrics convey an impression of resignation, dejection, and misfortune. Udo's claim—"money is the only thing that is missing. No one told me that" (*Geld ist alles was fehlt. Niemand hat mir das erzählt*)—is clearly a reference to the consequences of unification in the east. His portrait of life under unification is one of doom: he refers to "something stirring in the house" and rent increases so excessive that he will have to shift. Apart from references to his wife presenting him with camel-hair blankets—exotic consumer goods (at least in German it rhymes)—Udo announces in the rap finale that his business faces closure: he awaits Red Cap's Abwicklung the next day. The rap lyrics counteract the closure of the film's narrative, which depicts the reconstituted Struutz family as they merrily drive off into an idyllic sunny eastern landscape. By contrast, the final tune identifies the family, or at least Udo, as disenfranchised, apprehensive about being homeless, and facing the loss of the business he struggled to save for the duration of the film. The musical epilogue constitutes a pos-tunification update in which Udo is a passive victim of unfortunate cir-cumstances. The acquisitions and achievements of the East German are dismissed; what remains is a comic, yet dispirited admission of defeat.

Despite this pessimistic musical epilogue, *That Was the Wild East* does recognize that German-German relations not only are possible, but may be mutually beneficial. The rapport established between Charlie and Udo throughout *That Was the Wild East* is one of the film's most positive aspects. As I have already remarked, most other 1990s unification films do not allow for strong bonds of friendship and reciprocity to be established between East and West Germans. The second Trabi comedy is exceptional in this sense. In contrast to other West Germans featured in unification films, Charlie assumes the role of accomplice to Udo rather than acting as his adversary. He is perhaps less threatening than other stereotypical West Germans in this cycle of films in that he is nomadic and displays no inter-est in settling in or colonizing the east. Moreover, he treats Udo with respect, unlike condescending West Germans such as Fricker. In contrast to Kühn and numerous other West Germans in unification comedies, Charlie sees a positive side to unification: he seems to welcome the chance it provides for him to encounter East Germans. He even promotes unification at an intimate level through the condoms he brings to the east: their appeal depends upon two unmistakable unification icons—bananas and the West German flag. He doesn't grumble about the east being "like the wild west," like the West German sheriff in *No More Mr. Nice Guy.* For Charlie, the east is not wild enough. He accepts unification as such a natural thing, he even begins *singing,* in English, about it at the end of the film. Having bid farewell to Udo, Charlie sets out on his trip further east.

In contrast to Wessis in other films, Charlie is devoid of cynicism and capable of recognizing eastern virtue: he realizes that Udo has an inherent goodness together with special qualities that he himself does not possess. Charlie acts as witness to Udo's initiation into the ways of the west—being chauffeur-driven around New York, gambling in a casino, completing a course in business management, securing his legal ownership of Red Cap with the trustees—and in the final scene of the film, Udo consolidates the bond between Charlie and himself. When Charlie and the Struutzes' paths cross for the last time, Udo offers his West German friend the ultimate honor: he assures Charlie that if need be, there is always a spare place for him in the family Trabi. This display of loyalty and trust between East and West Germans is such a rarity in unification comedies that it turns *That Was the Wild East* into a something of an anomaly in its genre.

CHAPTER 11

Directions in East German Filmmaking after DEFA:
The Tango Player, Quiet Country, Nikolaikirche, Little Angel, To the Horizon and Beyond

In previous chapters, I focused largely on unification films funded, produced, and directed by individuals established in the old states of the Federal Republic (Peter Timm, Detlef Buck, Günther Rohrback, Margarethe von Trotta, Vadim Glowna). I noted that in the early 1990s a number of West German filmmakers addressed unification within the broad generic framework of comedy. This was not, however, the case in the eastern states: few former DEFA directors were immediately drawn to unification as a topic for their fiction films;[1] they were also less inclined to treat unification as a laughing matter.

Ex-DEFA filmmakers had other priorities and vantage points then. At least in the first few years of the new decade, many preferred to look back to examine what the GDR *was:* they embarked upon a process of critical reassessment. Some thought it imperative to reevaluate the past, precisely because objective, critical reflection on life in the GDR had been impossible under the old regime. As Marc Silberman rationalized in his survey of eastern documentaries in the early 1990s, "the process of remembering was employed as a defense against the speed of actual events" ("Post-Wall Documentaries" 28).

---

1. This of course was not the case for documentary filmmakers: the collapse of the Berlin Wall and unification were events documentary filmmakers did not hesitate to address in their films. The popularity of these topics led to the recognition of a new documentary subgenre known as the "Wall film" (see chap. 6).

The last feature films planned at DEFA and financed by the defunct state engaged in this process of critical reckoning, assessing the legacy of socialism and/or its collapse. Interestingly enough, the task was initially allocated to DEFA's most outspoken and credible Nachwuchs, Jörg Foth (*Last from the Da Daer*), Herwig Kipping (*The Country behind the Rainbow*), Helke Misselwitz (*Herzsprung*), and Peter Welz (*Banal Days*). More established filmmakers, like Roland Gräf (*The Tango Player*), Heiner Carow (*Missing*), and Egon Günther (*Stein*), also concerned themselves with the project of remembering the GDR at the start of the 1990s. Frank Beyer's *Der Verdacht* (*Suspicion, 1991*), Andreas Kleinert's *Lost Landscape,* and Horst Seemann's *Zwischen Pankow und Zehlendorf* (*Between Pankow and Zehlendorf,* 1991) shared this priority: these films critically examine life in the GDR, in particular generational conflict. Like most of the films listed above, these features investigate the adverse impact Party values and initiatives had on the everyday lives of individuals and families. Other films such as *Jana and Jan* present detailed portraits of the disillusionment and frustration youth faced within the bureaucratized, institutional framework of the GDR. The early 1990s provided filmmakers from the ex-GDR with their first real opportunity to reckon with the past and the impact the old regime had upon individuals and institutions. The critiques presented in many of those films were informed with a candor that the Party would never have tolerated.

Reappraisals of the political history of the GDR seemed to predominate in East German films of the early 1990s (even if production of other features, in particular children's films, prospered). Like Frank Beyer, Heiner Carow, and Peter Welz, Roland Gräf engaged in this process of critical reckoning and retrospection with his film *The Tango Player.* Throughout this film he provides a scathing account of crucial events and turning points in the political history of the GDR. *The Tango Player* succeeds in ridiculing the surveillance network of the GDR and the injustices of its legal system: the activities and representatives of the Stasi and the judiciary emerge as insidious, capricious, and unrelentingly oppressive. Gräf's film provides disturbing insight into the ways in which the Stasi insinuated itself into individuals' lives, fostering their transition from passive conformism to complicity with the dictatorship.

The tango player at the center of Gräf's film is Dr. Hans-Peter Dallow (Michael Gwisdek) a part-time pianist and historian. The film opens with Dallow's release from prison: the events leading up to his incarceration are gradually revealed through flashbacks. Dallow's downfall is traced to a completely fortuitous and absurd string of events. He is mistakenly identified as a political agitator one night when he fills in for a pianist at a nightclub. Dallow is subsequently jailed for twenty-one months for pro-

Fig. 11. *The Tango Player* **(1991). Film still reproduced with permission from Progress Film Verleih.**

viding musical accompaniment to a tango with supposedly provocative lyrics. The chance event also leads him to lose his position at Leipzig University—in part because of his newly acquired criminal record but also because of his general reluctance to cooperate with the Stasi.

Dallow's firsthand experience of the hypocrisy of state officials and their arbitrary dealings leaves him a broken and profoundly traumatized man. His dejection and sense of powerlessness are exacerbated when the previously banned tango song he once played receives official approval and is performed in the local cabaret. Dallow's indignation is palpable: the judge who sentenced him to jail is part of the receptive audience. The bitter irony of his situation becomes even more apparent when, on the very day that Warsaw Pact troops invade Czechoslovakia, Dallow is once again offered his old position at the university. The political tables have turned: a shift in the balance of power has led to the elimination of Dallow's rival within the university. Agreeing to resume his position at the university is an act of complete political complicity on Dallow's part: it signals his willingness to cooperate with the Stasi and inform on his colleagues. His acceptance also carries with it profound political implications: it marks his tacit agreement over the 1968 invasion and occupation of Czechoslovakia. Dallow acquiesces to the machinations of the state when he signs his employment contract. His handwriting nevertheless becomes a disturbing hysterical symptom: his signature is no longer recognizable as his own, and his jagged script is illegible. His complicity comes at the cost of whatever personal integrity he had.

The Tango Player does not exonerate individuals who conformed to the totalitarian regime by simply claiming that the state's agencies of coercion left no option. Gräf's film presents a more intricate study of compliance: it not only accentuates the state's capacity to undermine the resolve and resilience of its subjects, but also makes correlations among individual subservience, opportunism, and authoritarian rule. Nor does *The Tango Player* subscribe to stereotypical depictions of SED villains as seen in western productions like *Rising to the Bait, Apple Trees,* and *The Promise.* In those films reprehensible Party members and apolitical, principled protagonists are readily identifiable and clearly polarized.

Things are not so clear-cut in Gräf's film or in other eastern productions, such as *Farewell to Agnes.* In that film, which also stars Michael Gwisdek, Heiner, a seemingly ineffectual, if not pathetic character, is victimized and held captive by a violent former Stasi agent, Stephan. Distinctions between fugitive and victim are, however, dramatically effaced. Heiner's own capacity for cunning surveillance and dissimulation matches that of his antagonist. The gloomy claustrophobic interior of Heiner's apartment with its mazelike corridors, the frequent use of tightly framed shots, and the repeated framing of Heiner and Stephan in doorways, hallways, and windows contribute to the oppressive and menacing mood of the film. Elaborate long takes are included tracing Stephan's movement through the apartment as he prowls around like a caged beast.

Farewell to Agnes resists neatly moralistic solutions and homilies, as does *The Tango Player.* The latter film is made all the more disturbing because its protagonist is neither corrupt nor malevolent, but rather could be anyone at all—a "person . . . without special qualities" ("Ich will keinen Prototyp"). Part of *The Tango Player*'s resonance rests in the burgeoning suspicion that Dallow's story of defeat and complicity is no less exceptional than the ordeals experienced by countless others living in the GDR.

Not only did many ex-DEFA directors turn to unification as subject matter for their fiction films somewhat later than directors in the old states of the Federal Republic, many emerging East German filmmakers tended to

Fig. 12.   *Farewell to Agnes* (1993). Film still reproduced with permission of DEFA-Stiftung.

prioritize other historical events in their early 1990s features.[2] Usually the focus is on the Wende rather than the decade that brought unification.

Often events leading up to 1989 are highlighted in eastern productions: the opening of the Berlin Wall provides a point of closure for their films rather than a point of departure.[3] This is the culminating point in early 1990s films such as *Quiet Country, Der Strass* (1991), *Stein, Jana and Jan, Nikolaikirche* (1995), and *Sonnenallee. Miraculi* also shares this focus, even though it alludes to the disappearance of the GDR in parable form. *Quiet Country* is probably the most cynical film of the group from the early 1990s. Its director, Andreas Dresen, who came from a background in Schwerin theater, has rationalized that in this and other films he wanted "to show how the everyday looked in the country," to consider the problems people had communicating with one another under the old regime and how they adapted to shortages by improvising, making something out of inadequate material (DEFA NOVA, 307).

---

2. Helke Misselwitz's tragic love story *Herzsprung* is a rare and notable exception to this tendency.

3. Von Trotta's film *The Promise* also closes with a freeze-frame image at the Berlin Wall when its borders were first opened.

Made after his beguiling comedy of manners *As Quickly as Possible to Istanbul* (Dresen's graduation short for the Konrad Wolf film school), *Still Country* is set in the provinces of Brandenburg/Berlin in autumn of 1989. It deals with a theater group preparing to launch an ill-timed season of *Waiting for Godot*. The predicament of the actors and their production of the Beckett play could be seen as a general critique of the endemic passivity, conformism, and monotony of life in the GDR, more specifically that of the GDR during the Wende. Whereas some thought the GDR could be redeemed during this period and demanded political reform, the solution for others was to join the mass exodus to the Federal Republic. The theater troupe reflects these dilemmas: some of its actors are drawn to the west while those who remain engage in debate about the importance of open discussion and protest. Ultimately their deliberations are as inconsequential as the act of waiting that absorbs the protagonists in the Beckett play. Commitment to change is not especially convincing among the theater troupe and is in any case too late: the east is on the brink of collapse but the theater community is so isolated that its cohorts don't appear to fully realize the consequences of the political developments occurring around them. They just placidly watch scenes of mass protest on television. The group seems strangely removed from the events it observes, a matter emphasized by the director of the troupe when he asks whether they need a more powerful television antenna to capture events.

Indeed, the circumspect deliberations of various individuals in the theater troupe make them seem all the more stolid and ineffectual. After much deliberation, some decide to take the theater bus and travel to the west, but once they are seated in the bus and prepared to leave, the vehicle's engine troubles leave the group stranded. Similarly, the theater production is doomed. It cannot hope to compete with real events; one can only suspect that the immediacy and novelty of the west is more attractive. After their dress rehearsal of *Waiting for Godot,* what is left of the troupe resigns itself to revert to classical costume drama.

Quiet Country is probably the most somber and restrained reflection on the Wende to emerge from the eastern states at the start of the 1990s. It is clear that the film is determined to avoid mythologizing and glorifying the Autumn Revolution by focusing on an aloof, provincial community, removed from the spectacle of the Wende and the media event of unification. *Quiet Country* may be justified in privileging the everyday over monumental events of 1989. Investing in an objective vision of those only tangentially affected by the Wende, the film's chorus of apathetic, stolid, and largely ineffectual characters leaves a lasting impression of lethargy and indifference. This perspective clearly counters television images of swarms of euphoric East Germans spilling over the border between east and west—telegenic scenes broadcast across the world consolidating popular memories of unification.

Frank Beyer's *Nikolaikirche,* released three and a half years after *Quiet Country,* is devoid of the cynicism and sardonic humor of Dresen's production as much as the scathing irony of *The Tango Player.* Even though it focuses on the Wende, *Nikolaikirche* details more heroic, memorable events that led to the implosion of the GDR. Beyer's film succeeds in recapturing the volatility and momentum of the Wende.

Nikolaikirche tells an intricate story of intrigue, resistance, and conspiracy in the last years of the GDR. It re-creates the Monday night peace gatherings in the Nikolai church in Leipzig and the mass protests that precipitated the downfall of the Honecker regime. Beyer recollects the way the church provided a sanctuary for those disillusioned with the state and aspects of life in the GDR. Drawing on actual historical events, the church is presented as a vital forum out of which various oppositional groups emerged. For example, *Nikolaikirche* attends to the environmental and democratic reform groups that clustered there. It also depicts strategies of the state and the Stasi to intimidate, incarcerate, and silence any oppositional voices. The film recounts modest yet heroic acts of political incendiarism and highlights the personal cost of protest (conscription, civil service in isolated and distant provinces, imprisonment, expulsion from the work force, confinement in psychiatric wards). It charts opposition to the widespread environmental pollution of the GDR and the North Sea condoned by the SED.

The film presents the family as a site of political conflict and dissension. *Nikolaikirche* revolves around three generations of a Leipzig family, the Bachers, increasingly troubled by irreconcilable political allegiances. Frau Bacher, mother of Sasha and Astrid, is identified as something of an unquestioning conformist to the regime. Differences in value systems and political engagement splinter the family, alienating siblings from one another and Frau Bacher from her offspring. Relations between Astrid and her brother are irreparably damaged when Astrid becomes increasingly involved in the protest movement.

When Sasha accepts the dubious task of spying on his immediate family, his own personal and political integrity is compromised. He and his mother are shattered by revelations about her youth, in particular her incriminating premarital love affair with and pregnancy by a West German. When mother and son discover the coercive measures used to dispose of her former lover, the deception of a lifetime is uncovered. Like *The Tango Player, Nikolaikirche* examines the ways in which political imperatives of the state are internalized, naturalized, and used to egotistical ends. Characters' lives are marred by decades of deception and mistrust

Fig. 13. *Nikolaikirche* **(1995). Film still reproduced with permission of Progress Film Verleih.**

throughout this film: corruption is presented as an endemic feature of intimate relations and political life.

Nikolaikirche has as its grand climax the spectacular protest march that took place in Leipzig on 30 October 1989: attended by 300,000 East Germans, similar protests were conducted in other East German cities. In the light of the Beijing massacre where tanks were used to dispel crowds and the People's Police were instructed to shoot protesters, gatherings like the Leipzig protests were rightly viewed as heroic. Participants faced the very real risk that the SED would use the "China solution" to disperse the crowds and protesters—a likelihood explicitly referred to in the final scenes of *Nikolaikirche.*

The film recollects and glorifies the activities of those involved in the protest movements of 1989, recalling the tension and vexation that surrounded their activities. *Nikolaikirche* certainly provides a fitting tribute to and reminder of the idealism and heroism of those involved in outlawed demonstrations against a totalitarian government. Beyer's film evokes incredibly moving scenes when "the People" took to the streets in objection to the SED government and denounced its leadership as corrupt and nefarious. *Nikolaikirche* recollects the historic events of 1989 that led to the Autumn Revolution, a development since eclipsed by the turmoil and imperatives of unification.

Little Angel

Helke Misselwitz's second unification love story *Little Angel* is among a group of eastern productions that shifted the focus from the critical assessment of the *Wende* and the collapse of the GDR to present-day life in the new federal states. Together with other eastern productions such as *Adamski, Nikolaikirche, The Tango Player, Farewell to Agnes,* and, to a lesser extent *Burning Life, Little Angel* disavows the western equation of East Germany with the rural idyll, a perspective taken by the films discussed in chapters 8, 9, and 10.

Helke Misselwitz's films probably enjoyed greatest exposure late in the 1980s when she worked at the DEFA Studio for Documentary Films. She still remains one of the most famous female filmmakers from the ex-GDR. As one of the last generation of directors to have been trained at DEFA, she is most well-known for her first feature-length film *Winter Ade* (1988), a documentary widely praised for its immediacy and freshness of vision. Her film attracted wide critical and public acclaim as a candid and surprisingly revealing survey of women's lives in the GDR: *Winter Ade* attested to the diversity of women's lived experiences in the east while avoiding Party rhetoric.

When Misselwitz turned to fiction, her focus was still on the intimate lives and stories of GDR women. Set in the east, *Herzsprung* and *Little Angel* present damning critiques of the human costs of unification. Both films are located in small communities, the first in the rural East German village of Herzsprung, the second in an eastern suburb on the outskirts of Berlin. In the first film, the east is identified as a hapless region blighted by unemployment, xenophobia, and right-wing violence. The second love story presents a no more flattering picture of life in the modern-day east. Although there is less overt political violence in *Little Angel,* the film still presents what is by now is a familiar portrait of alienation, isolation, and despair in unified Germany.

Most of *Little Angel* takes place in and around a single tenement block that overlooks the local S-Bahn railway station in Ostkreuz.[4] Mis-

---

4. The DEFA warehouse where film prints were stored was also located in this immediate neighborhood. The suburb looks even more desolate and bleak in Michael Klier's early unification film, simply titled *Ostkreuz.*

selwitz's background in documentary filmmaking is evidenced in numerous scenes, such as the long shots of commuters spilling off the train during rush hour and otherwise uneventful night scenes of train carriages accelerating away from Ostkreuz station.

Susanne Lothar plays the role of Ramona, the little angel of the film's title. She is quickly identified as a lonely and vulnerable woman in her thirties who appears to have lived a life devoid of love and tenderness. The emotional impoverishment of her childhood has carried through into her adult life. Her young, attractive sister Lucy is the sole figure in Ramona's life with whom she experiences any ongoing intimacy. In the retreat of her modest apartment, Ramona's only companion is a pampered pet bird.

All this changes forever after Ramona's chance encounter with a Polish man, Andrzej, who sells black-market cigarettes at Ostkreuz railway station each weekend. He impetuously and literally sweeps Ramona off her feet during their first encounter. When police blitz the railway station looking for black marketeers, Andrzej grabs Ramona as she passes by and locks her in an embrace to avoid detection. A friendship soon develops between the pair, and increasingly Ramona looks forward to each of Andrzej's visits. He in turn is sensitive to this delicate figure. When she greets him at the railway station early one evening, attired in an unflattering raincoat, Andrzej displays his naive romanticism, endearing himself to Ramona by commenting on how pretty she looks in her raincoat, just "like a flower wrapped in cellophane." Andrzej and Ramona soon fall in love, and they establish a de facto relationship with Andrzej spending his weekends at Ramona's and returning to Poland to work during the week.

The film's elliptical narrative structure serves the love story and location equally well. As Andrzej and Ramona's relationship flourishes, so too their immediate environment takes on a newfound radiance. Seasonal changes are registered in the skies and foliage surrounding Ramona's apartment, and by winter even the bleak and previously uninviting railway station assumes a luminosity, covered in a blanket of snow. Winter also brings tranquillity to Ramona, who is shown in an advanced state of pregnancy. Andrzej showers her with gifts in delighted anticipation over their baby's arrival, and the pair seems set to re-create a scene of blissful nativity.

Any likelihood of the deserving couple's sustained contentment is, however, quickly dispelled. Disaster strikes in Andrzej's absence when Ramona goes into labor, is hospitalized, and loses the baby at birth. The moment of catharsis comes when, after an attempted suicide, Ramona returns home to find that, in her absence, her much loved pet bird has also died. She collapses with the tiny creature in her hands, overwhelmed by despair. Later, in a scene of almost unbearable pathos, Andrzej strives to comfort Ramona, oblivious to their baby's death. Ramona is devastated and perceives the loss of her infant as a mortal threat to her relationship with Andrzej.

Showing signs of acute psychological disturbance, Ramona takes desperate measures to compensate for the loss of her baby. One day she follows her impulses and steals another woman's baby from its stroller. When Andrzej returns from Poland for his weekly visit, he is delighted to accept the "new" baby as his own and reveals his plans to stay permanently with Ramona. Momentarily her universe is harmonious and beatific. But Andrzej soon realizes that the baby has been abducted when the police launch their search for Ramona. In a quintessentially melodramatic moment Andrzej recognizes Ramona's identity-kit portrait on the television news: he abruptly turns the television off to protect Ramona from the disclosure, remarking that the tears in his eyes come "from happiness." The police soon descend on Ostkreuz in full force with helicopters and search dogs. They track Ramona down to her apartment and take custody of the baby she has abducted. In the final scene, Andrzej watches helplessly as Ramona is arrested.

Misselwitz's Germany is a callous, godforsaken place, populated with distraught families and misfits. In the harshest light, the microcosm of the tenement block might be identified as a halfway house for delinquent, dysfunctional, and disabled individuals. After all, the only figure living there who does not appear to have a major psychological disorder or affliction is Andrzej, and he is officially an unwelcomed foreigner.

Like many other eastern films that address unification, *Little Angel* presents Germany as a place completely lacking in community spirit. Ramona's neighbors appear indifferent to her, and they display no involvement with or concern for one another. Neighbors live isolated lives, and even when there is occasion for celebration such as when a de facto couple living in the tenement marries, neither Ramona nor others living in the apartment block participate in the festivities: Ramona watches the drunken wedding procession from the isolation of her apartment.

However limited Ramona's encounters with her neighbors, they are nevertheless profound. Although she does not engage in any meaningful exchange with them, she is privy to intimate details of their lives that she surreptitiously observes from the quiet of her own abode. We are often shown her point of view of the other apartments facing onto a shared courtyard. She is witness to banal domestic activities of various neighbors along with rare moments of tenderness. More common are domestic disputes and bouts of drunken excess. The scenes of escalating domestic violence Ramona observes are made all the more distressing as they evoke the neglect and abuse of her own childhood. Her distress intensifies along with her neighbors' despair: in a bout of drunken hysteria, one of Ramona's neighbors suffers a hallucination and kills the family's pet rabbit by throwing it several stories out of an apartment window. When Ramona realizes what has happened, she is so traumatized that she has a seizure.

Of all the characters in the film, Ramona displays the strongest affinity with Maria, a young child who lives in the apartment block opposite Ramona's. Although it is never overtly specified, Ramona, her sister, and Maria are all of an age to be children of the GDR. Now in what appears to be her mid-thirties, Ramona would have been born when the Wall was built, whereas Maria appears old enough to have been born just before the Wall fell. All seem scarred by the indelible and damned legacy of the old regime. Unification offers little compensation or amelioration for these generations of women and children. None seems to have been able to adjust to unification. Ramona's life is remarkably sedentary: unification has not provided her with any obvious, newfound freedom, even though the boundaries that segregated the GDR and the west are long dismantled.

Visual echoes of gesture, costume, and demeanor strengthen the affiliation between Ramona and Maria, making parallels between these characters unmistakable. Even in the very first scene a rapport is established between the pair: Maria's mother kicks her de facto husband out of their apartment. Ramona watches Maria as she runs into the courtyard after Pappa Klaus and then falls to the ground grasping his ankles. When she stands up again the child's face is smudged with dirt, and Ramona seems to respond on the child's behalf by rushing to the basin to immerse her face in water. Elsewhere various gestures present the characters as mirror images of one another: they are shown grooming and parting their hair in similar styles; Maria tends to the carpet fringe in Ramona's apartment just as Ramona obsesses over this domestic detail on other occasions. They also share a common history: just as Maria cares for her baby sister, Ramona acknowledges that she too brought up her younger sister, Lucy. Different men fathered Lucy and Ramona, and it is also suggested that Maria and her baby sister do not have the same father. Moreover, at the start of the film, Ramona responds to the name Maria: in the scene when she first encounters Andrzej at the train station and he calls out to (Mother) Maria summoning her protection, Ramona is adamant that he has uttered her *own* name.

Ramona watches as the traumas of her own childhood are replayed across the courtyard in the neighboring apartment. Maria becomes Ramona's surrogate, and it is through her that Ramona appears to recollect the deeply traumatic incidents of her own childhood that have left her a debilitated adult. In one scene, the parallels between the young Maria and Ramona become more distressing when it is suggested that Maria (hence by extension Ramona) has been subject to sexual abuse. Maria is shown from the neighboring apartment window dressed in a slip, a minia-ture version of the undergarment Ramona wears when she relaxes at home. When Maria notices her drunken stepfather enter the room and she lifts her slip to reveal her naked torso, the gesture appears habitual on her part. Even though Maria's stepfather covers her up again before he kneels down to embrace her, the suggestion is made that Maria has learned to expose herself to adult men, and perhaps the response has been encour-aged by other men in her mother's life. By association, the inclusion of this scene and others suggests Ramona's personal familiarity with sexual abuse. A history of incest is already implied at an earlier point in the film: Ramona is not shocked by, and nor does she resist, the sexual advances of her sister's boyfriend: she obediently complies to his sexual demands as if this were a hideous duty to which she was already inured. She hints at her own sexual debasement when she reflects upon her childhood to derive reassurance from the realization that "being a woman is so much nicer than being a child." Drunken abuse, domestic violence, and childhood neglect are presented as commonplace, extending from one generation to the next throughout this film.

Bound by shared experiences, Maria and Ramona display a psychic affinity that rarely depends on verbal communication: they exchange glances of mutual recognition and awareness, each compassionate toward the other's predicament. After Ramona loses her baby during childbirth, Maria instinctively provides her with the compensation of her own baby sister whom she leaves in Ramona's care. She seems to realize that the infant actually deserves a better mother than she has, and that Ramona would be an ideal parent for her young sister. After Ramona is obliged to return the baby to its real mother, the tragedy of her own position and Maria's is compounded. Ramona compensates for her loss by doting over a life-size baby doll, which she clothes, cuddles, and takes shopping. Maria's deprivation is of another order: she has no dolls of her own to play with and no opportunity for childlike games. Rather she unquestioningly accepts the responsibility of caring for her baby sister. Ideally, Maria's and Ramona's roles should be reversed: Ramona's doll should belong to Maria, just as the baby she tends should be in Ramona's permanent care.[5]

Ramona and Maria also seem similar in conspiratorial intent. Not only does Maria make Ramona's life tolerable again by bringing her a sur-rogate baby, she attempts to sustain this domestic arrangement. Perhaps in protest over her own abysmal domestic situation, Maria conspires to

---

5. I am grateful to Claere Perkins who drew my attention to this inversion.

preserve the domestic ideal of rightful mother with deserving baby by setting fire to the interior of her own apartment. No explanation is provided for her pyromania, which could well be an attempt to kill herself and dispose of her negligent and perpetually distraught mother. Ramona appears aware of Maria's actions, but is loath to accept the consequences. She desperately draws the drapes in her apartment to block out the light from the burning tenement. Maria survives the fire, inviting further comparison between herself and Ramona, who reveals that not only is she unable to tolerate heat, but that she awakes in feverish panic during the night.

It is largely because of the predominance given to the relationships among Ramona, Maria, and Ramona's sister that the male gaze is infrequently cast throughout *Little Angel.* Even in the numerous scenes that feature Andrzej in Ramona's apartment, he does not predominate over her or her space, nor is our vision of Ramona filtered through him. He is only occasionally granted an autonomous frame independent of Ramona. The first night that Andrzej sleeps at Ramona's apartment, a quaint equity is established between the pair as they conduct a conversation from different rooms. The camera dutifully dollies back and forth between Ramona sitting upright in bed and Andrzej sitting in the living room. Here the camera movement emphasizes the strained formality that distances them from one another, but it also provides humorous comment on the decorum to which they hesitantly comply.

The equity between Ramona and Andrzej is noticeable even before their love affair is consummated. In their early dalliances at Ostkreuz railway station, the pair shares symmetrically ordered frames. In these scenes, Andrzej's presence is regularly marked by Ramona's point of view, a matter that makes her apprehension at the railway station at the end of the film all the more devastating. During her arrest in the final scene, her exalted gaze at the gawking crowd of onlookers reveals the extent of her dementia. As the police usher her into a waiting van, and a reinforced metal door slams shut in Ramona's face, the obliteration of her image and vision assume a disturbing and malevolent finality.

On the rare occasion that the male gaze is deployed in the film it signals a brutal and potential threat to Ramona. Its application makes her utterly vulnerable. In this sense the film succeeds in denaturalizing the male gaze, attributing suspicion and menace to it. For instance, in the dance hall scene, the direct gaze of Lucy's boyfriend is answered by his view of Ramona: this sequence of shots leads to her immediate violation in the following tawdry scene outside the dance hall.

The male gaze is equally threatening elsewhere, most strikingly during the abduction scene staged later on a train. Ramona is shown in a train as she parks a stroller containing her baby doll next to another baby car-

Fig. 14. *Little Angel* (1996). Film still reproduced with permission of DEFA-Stiftung.

riage in which an infant sleeps. Oblivious to Ramona's presence, the baby's mother gossips idly with another passenger. As Ramona's attention is captured by both strollers, her image is mediated through the point of view of another passenger; a young man with a shaven head and a steely, fixed gaze. His gaze is almost predatory in its intensity, and it is indeed threatening: he witnesses Ramona abduct the baby and watches her furtive escape from the train carriage. We see from his perspective as Ramona runs along the platform pushing the abducted baby in its carriage. His surveillance of the scene and Ramona presumably allows him to provide an identity-kit portrait of her, and hence it is his gaze that is directly associated with her capture. In this instance the male gaze is identified as remorseless and punitive.

Somewhat later when the police track Ramona down and forcefully enter her apartment, we are made acutely aware of their menacing presence. A low angle shot accentuates their heavy-duty boots as they traipse across Ramona's pristine wedding veil lying on the floor. The police slam down their evidence, a life-size baby doll, next to Ramona as she huddles on the floor. Ramona is denied even the pathetic solace the baby doll once provided. She cannot even imagine an exchange of looks as the baby doll's eyes are firmly closed for the first and final time. As the two face one another on the floor, Ramona appears even more fragile and defenseless than the doll she once coddled.

The following shot is unlike any other in the film: the chief of police hovers over Ramona, who has hedged her way into the corner of the room where she quivers like a small trapped animal. For a moment he towers over her, and we see him glance down at her. His gaze makes her all the more vulnerable as she cringes in response. Her exposure compromises her further in that, although she tries, she cannot cover her nakedness with her hands, whereas he is fully and formally dressed, with overcoat and hat. The shot opens with the policeman dominating space as he looks at Ramona's crumpled, naked body. The conspicuous scar that marks her abdomen intensifies the pathos of her situation, reminding us of the baby she has so recently lost. In this scene the policeman's gaze immobilizes and enfeebles Ramona. Pitying her vulnerability, and perhaps in shame, he can only look away. A gesture of consolation follows. The film turns full circle when Ramona sinks to the floor and grabs the ankles of the police chief: the gesture echoes an early scene in which Maria falls to the feet of Pappa Klaus in an attempt to prevent him from deserting the family. By association, Ramona's atavistic gesture marks the resurgence of the abject terror of her childhood and her complete psychological disintegration.

With its waifs, outcasts, and scenes of intense personal tragedy, *Little Angel* is reminiscent of folktales or *Märchen,* like those recorded by the brothers Grimm early in the nineteenth century. But the film also captures rapturous moments common to folktales. Babies are taken from the hands of neglectful parents and bestowed upon more deserving and loving guardians. The worthy and the poor find home and hearth; paupers become princes; heartrending losses are magically replenished; misery and wretchedness are briefly transformed into splendor. Once engrossed in this fairy-tale world, we are assured that although the suffering of the innocents is intense, it is also transitory. *Little Angel* draws on such expectations and inversions.

However tragic and ineluctable *Little Angel*'s outcome, the film abounds in exquisite scenes of blissful fulfillment and enchantment: when Ramona initially encounters Andrzej and he sweeps her off her feet, she admits it is the first time she has been kissed in her life. Redolent of momentous encounters in fairy tales, it is the kiss that heralds a new life for Ramona. She has found her Prince Charming, as Lucy comments when she first meets Andrzej. Strengthening the fairy-tale allusions, in the same scene Ramona wears silver-colored shoes that glisten in the light like glass slippers. Throughout the film Ramona undergoes a transformation reminiscent of Cinderella: once a plain, insecure, and lonely woman, she becomes an assured and sensual beauty. Her transformation is initiated when Andrzej provides her with a beautiful velvet dress and takes her dancing for the first time in her life: Ramona exclaims that she wishes the night and the dancing would go on forever. Together with the picnic that takes place in the park toward the end of the film, this is one of the film's most enchanting scenes.

In its serenity and splendor, the picnic scene stands in contrast to the first supper Ramona and Andrzej share. Then Ramona fretted over the menial task of brewing tea and offered her guest a precisely ordered, modest array of refreshments. The picnic in the park is far more sensual and indulgent, a veritable feast that draws on archetypal imagery from fairy tales. The scene functions as a symbolic wedding with Ramona and Andrzej assuming the roles of bride and groom at a wedding breakfast. Ramona is delighted by the gift Andrzej brings with him from Poland: an ornate headdress decorated with pearls and other jewels. Initially, when she assumes the headdress and cradles the baby in her arms, she evokes the images of the Madonna she and Andrzej admire earlier in the film. When Ramona wears the headdress for the first time, it effects another transformation as well: she becomes both a princess, dressed in a royal blue velvet gown and resplendent in her crown, as well as a bride swathed in tulle. The two figures coalesce, and the symbolic wedding is complete once a photographer passes by and records the festivities. This iridescent image of the wedding feast functions equally well as the "happily ever after" of the Märchen.

Frank Zipes has reminded us that whatever magical elements they may contain, across the centuries Märchen tell tales of great sorrow and hardship: "No matter what has become of the fairy tale, its main impulse was at first revolutionary and progressive, not escapist, as has too often been suggested. The realm of the fairy tale contains a symbolic reflection of real socio-political issues and conflicts" (*Breaking the Magic Spell* 36). With greater measure of tragedy and wretchedness than most other unification films of the period, *Little Angel*'s social critique parallels that of the archaic form of narration. Misselwitz's film is complete with the "real socio-political conflicts and issues" that plague life in unified Germany.

Little Angel's portrait of life in the new Germany acts in part to affirm impressions registered in a wide variety of unification films. In striking accord with films discussed in part 2 of this book, Misselwitz's film explores the motifs of criminality and theft while depicting the sorts of family configurations common to other unification films. Right at the start of *Little Angel* Andrzej's black-market activities are curtailed by forceful police intervention. Further suspicion about his criminal involvement is invited when he is shown to be an accurate marksman who carries and wields a pistol for protection. Similarly, Lucy is involved in theft and black-marketing: she steals lipsticks from the cosmetics factory where she and Ramona work. Lucy also initiates Ramona into petty crime. After indulging in fantasies about Ramona and Andrzej marrying, the two sisters visit a bridal boutique where Lucy helps Ramona shoplift a wedding gown and veil. The motifs of theft, criminality, and disrupted families coalesce in an uncanny manner in *Little Angel*. Already identified as the product of a broken and dysfunctional family herself, Ramona believes that the only way to reconstitute the family unit and to maintain her union with Andrzej is to literally *steal* a baby. Ramona is driven to crime to safeguard the only happiness and intimacy she has known.

Little Angel shares with a variety of other unification films suspicions about law enforcement in the new Germany (equally evident in *No More Mr. Nice Guy, Life Is a Construction Site,* and *Burning Life*). This too is established early in the film when Ramona first encounters Andrzej at the railway station amid a police blitz. In contrast to the police, who intimidate passengers and indiscriminately search passersby, Andrzej is identified as a harmless, affectionate figure: he simply kisses an unsuspecting commuter, making her swoon.

In each instance when the police visit Ostkreuz, their blitz seems misdirected: they concentrate on minor, victimless offenses—policing mutually beneficial transactions between Poles and Germans—rather than dealing with violent crime. For instance, the police are conspicuous in their absence in another scene at the railway station when Ramona is attacked by two men who attempt to rape her. Later in the film, police responses to Ramona's distraught actions seem exaggerated. When the police descend en masse at the local railway station, accompanied by a pack of search dogs, one suspects that the scale of their commando-style operation is designed to track down a murderer, a terrorist, or at least a violent criminal. The force they mobilize seems excessive, once we realize that Ramona is their target. The extremity of their operation is highlighted as a police helicopter descends on Ramona's apartment. As the helicopter hovers outside her apartment window, and a rush of breeze billows the curtains, Ramona takes innocent and sensual delight in the draft of wind as she spreads her arms in a gleeful pirouette. She is oblivious to the police intrusion and their foreboding presence.

In a comparable vein to her earlier unification film, *Herzsprung,* in *Little Angel* Misselwitz also suggests that racism is rampant in unified Germany. As Andrzej observes after he and Ramona fall in love, "No one spoke to me in this country like you." She shows him a warmth he has never experienced with any other German. Moreover, Andrzej is identified as figure against whom characters automatically and unthinkingly discriminate. In the local *Kneipe* (bar), Ramona's drunken neighbors engage in crude innuendo, suggesting that the Polish-German relationship is purely carnal.

In the space of at least a year, Andrzej does not befriend or make the acquaintance of any Germans apart from Ramona. The only gesture of solidarity any other German shows him comes from Ramona's wheelchair-bound neighbor at the scene of her arrest. Amid the crowd of onlookers, the disabled man conceals Andrzej's pistol, saving him from police detection and scrutiny. Frustration leads Andrzej to unexpectedly assault the man after the police drive off with Ramona. Disgusted by Ramona's fate and his own powerlessness, Andrzej tips over the man's wheelchair. With a newfound cynicism "made in Germany," Andrzej walks away from the man, whom he leaves stranded like a beetle on its back. Andrzej's initiation into a callous social hierarchy, which sees the brutalization of the frail and underprivileged, is complete.

Points of divergence distinguish *Little Angel* and other eastern productions that depict life in unified Germany from the fiction films I discussed in detail in chapters 8, 9, and 10. For example, West Germans are not featured as narrative agents or crucial antagonists in eastern unification films, like they are in *Rising to the Bait, The German Chainsaw Massacre, God Bless, Comrades, That Was the Wild East, The Promise,* and *No More Mr. Nice Guy.* In East German unification films, the isolation of Ossis from Wessis is just about complete. The east emerges as a more closed community in eastern unification films: West Germans have no real place or purpose in *Little Angel, Farewell to Agnes, Herzsprung,* or *Nikolaikirche.* They are not drawn to the east as they are in *No More Mr. Nice Guy, That Was the Wild East,* and *Rising to the Bait.* The eastern production *To the Horizon and Beyond* does manage to present a significant rapport between East and West Germans, but in this film German-German relations are only established under duress and prove to be fatal. As East German fugitives, Katja and Henning do develop a bond of mutual respect and admiration with Beate, a West German judge. But their relationship is only consolidated after she has been kidnapped, held hostage, humiliated, ridiculed, tortured, bound, gagged, pistol-whipped, and threatened with certain death if she attempts to escape her kidnappers. In any case, the east-west relationship that ensues is short-lived and doomed, as Henning and Katja are pursued by a squadron of commando police: when they are captured, Beate watches helplessly as the pair of East Germans commit joint suicide.

Eastern productions adopt a much harsher view of life in the work force under unification, in contrast to features made by westerners. For example, early in *Little Angel,* during an exchange at the railway station, Ramona and Andrzej gauge their weeks in terms of levels of productivity—she estimating how many lipsticks she has manufactured at the cosmetics factory, he in relation to the number of automobiles he has repaired. For her, employment at the factory is menial and tedious. She spends her workdays stationed at a conveyor belt, absentmindedly surveying mass-produced lipsticks. Like many protagonists in unification films from the east, Ramona is involved in the manufacture of goods for which she herself has virtually no use. Nor does Andrzej appear to derive any benefits from his employment in Poland: although he repairs cars, he has no automobile and must rely on public transport. Similarly, in *Adamski,* the protagonist's life is not improved in any tangible or material way as a result of his employment in a large, city department store. He cannot afford to purchase the video camera he is compelled to use to record Lilli's clandestine activities.

On the whole, in eastern films such as these, labor is fragmented, depersonalized, and mechanized, or else characters fail to find employment, meaningful or otherwise. Henning is an unemployed coal miner with no vocational prospects in *To the Horizon and Beyond.* His partner, Katja, resorts to crime to survive in unified Germany. The situation is equally grim for protagonists in *Paths in the Night (Wege in die Nacht,* 1999). Walter, an East German in his fifties, is chronically unemployed and must rely on the wage his partner, Sylvia, earns working as a waitress in a fashionable upscale restaurant. His daylight hours are idle and without purpose.

When characters in these films are employed, the workplace is usually hostile, hence Ramona's isolation from the other coworkers at the lipstick factory and the derisive attitude that the secretary, boss, and coworkers display toward Adamski in the film of the same name. Employment in unification films from the east does not provide characters with gratification, incentive, or fulfillment. In *Burning Life* Anna aspires to become a cabaret performer, but she cannot secure any venues or bookings. She only manages to perform to an attentive audience when she holds them at gunpoint and launches into a song-and-dance routine during a bank robbery. In *Herzsprung* Johanna's employment is also menial: initially she works in a poultry factory whereas her husband is a recently laid-off slaughterhouse worker. Unification films made by East Germans are more inclined to focus on blue-collar workers with limited employment possibilities, distinguishing them from western unification films' characters with more prestigious qualifications such as Konrad the physicist (*The Promise*), Zenon the archaeologist (*Love at First Sight*), or Udo the Goethe expert and business manager (*That Was the Wild East*).

Employment in eastern unification films is alienated, compared to the vocational possibilities presented to East Germans in unification films from the west. Western productions tend to highlight the entrepreneurial opportunities that unification offers and to focus on the windfalls characters enjoy. Udo earns a small fortune when he launches the Trabi peep show in *Go Trabi Go;* he wins a pile of money at the casino in *That Was the Wild East;* Buddy wins a thousand deutsche marks in a talent quest and Vera follows suit in *Life Is a Construction Site;* Most fills his pockets with money when he plays poker machines in *No More Mr. Nice Guy;* Lene and Heinz inherit an orchard in *Apple Trees.* The entrepreneurial ventures characters embark upon are usually lucrative and novel. By the end of *No More Mr. Nice Guy,* Most finds himself occupied in a beer garden, where he dispenses beer like a publican to country locals. Ada's whole goods business diversifies in *Rising to the Bait,* and Udo's management of Red Cap saves the community in *That Was the Wild East.*

Whereas unification films from the west emphasize the prosperity that unification affords East Germans, in east films unification is more regularly associated with privation. East Germans emerge as losers rather than beneficiaries in the new Germany. For example, unification is presented as a health hazard in *To the Horizon and Beyond.* There Henning develops an unspecified form of cancer, one may presume from the radiation emitted by the huge electricity towers that have been built in the immediate vicinity of the family homestead after unification. Even more dramatically, unification proves to be a mortal threat for East Germans in various eastern productions. Living in united Germany drives easterners to suicide in *Little Angel, Herzsprung, Paths in the Night,* and *To the Horizon and Beyond.* East German characters commit murder in *Die Vergebung (Forgiveness,* 1994), and in *Farewell to Agnes* Heiner becomes a budding serial murderer. Characters lose jobs (*Forgiveness, Herzsprung, Paths in the Night*), social standing, orientation, and a sense of belonging (*Burning Life, Lost Landscape, Adamski, Farewell to Agnes, Miraculi, Quiet Country, Herzsprung, Paths in the Night, To the Horizon and Beyond*), loved ones (*Burning Life, Jana and Jan, Farewell to Agnes, Forgiveness, Lost Landscape, Paths in the Night*), sanity (*Little Angel, Farewell to Agnes, Paths in the Night, Stein*), and freedom (*Jana and Jan, Little Angel, Nikolaikirche, Miraculi*). Almost invariably East Germans are misfits or social outcasts in these films; they are ostracized from the communities in which they live, or they are deranged. These are the consequences East Germans characters face with unification.

The East as the Antithesis of Heimat

Other differences distinguish east and west unification films. In eastern productions like *Little Angel, Adamski, Farewell to Agnes, Farssmann or by Foot to the Dead End,* and, to a degree, *Burning Life,* the focus is on the afflictions of unification on urban life.[6] In contrast to western productions released during the first half of the 1990s, these films do not subscribe to stereotypical portraits of East Germans as rural dwellers. Nor do eastern productions reclaim the former GDR as a lost paradise, as Heimat, a point of pristine, mythical origin. Protagonists in east films are less likely to be aligned with or gravitate toward the countryside. Rarely do they experience the east as a rural idyll. In *Forgiveness* an extended East German family is reunited to celebrate a wedding in the countryside. The celebrations are, however, less than idyllic and result in the brutal murder of one of the youngest guests. In *Little Angel* none of the characters experiences country life. Most of Ramona's experiences of the outdoors take place in environments that are "man-made" and associated with commercialized leisure: early in the film she and Andrzej take a breathtaking ride on a Ferris wheel at a fairground. Elsewhere she is thrilled to go dancing on a river barge. When she and Andrzej first become friends, any expedition to the world outside her apartment is made with the protective covering of several plastic raincoats. Ramona's horizons are literally limited. And as Ralf Schenk has remarked, her apartment remains both a haven and a prison ("Excursion" 84). The only time she is seen in a quasi-natural setting is during the picnic in the park and even then, the setting is tame and urban.

Similarly, the protagonists in *Adamski* have no connection with the countryside. Adamski lives in a cramped apartment in the middle of Berlin, and Lilli has the street smarts of a city dweller. This urban emphasis is common to other eastern films, which address the disintegration of the GDR and unification. For instance, *Farewell to Agnes* is located in modern-day Berlin, mainly within one apartment overlooking a long-established and crowded graveyard. *Last from the Da Daer* sees its protagonists in various industrial sites, in a Berlin underground railway station, a jail, and garbage dump. High-density apartment blocks mark the horizons in one scene, identified as "paradise." *Nikolaikirche* is located for the larger part in the urban center of Leipzig. Retro scenarios that address comic aspects of everyday life under the watchful eye of the old GDR

---

6. At the same time, this perspective is also adopted by the western production *Life Is a Construction Site.* Becker's film is set predominantly in the decrepit working-class region of the Berlin suburb of Kreuzberg; it is probably one of the most successful and popular unification comedies/romantic comedies to be made in the latter half of the 1990s.

Fig. 15. *Adamski* (1993). Film still reproduced with permission of DEFA-Stiftung.

regime, such as *Sonnenallee* and *Helden wie wir* (*Heroes Like Us,* 1999), have an urban, high-density setting.

The affinity with nature commonly attributed to East Germans in unification features from the west does not surface in eastern productions discussed throughout this chapter. Whereas East German protagonists in western films such as *Rising to the Bait* and *That Was the Wild East* may marvel at the beauty of their natural habitat and commit themselves to the preservation of Heimat, those priorities and pastimes do not extend to easterners in eastern productions. East Germans' supposed pastoral affiliation is satirized in *To the Horizon and Beyond,* directed by former DEFA filmmaker Peter Kahane. Even though the male protagonist of that film, Henning Stahnke, has rural origins, he does not gravitate toward the sort of unspoiled countryside that constitutes Heimat in West German films. His nostalgia is not for any preindustrialized rural idyll but for what was the locus of GDR primary industry—the open-cut brown coal mines where he once worked. Nor does his mother especially appreciate the supposed pristine charms of rural life, even though she still lives in the provinces in the family homestead. When we are first introduced to her she is neither part of a bucolic scene and nor does she display any particular empathy for nature. When she practices her considerable skills as a sharpshooter on the farm, she is aided by her trusted dog, Rolfi, who joins in the sport by releasing clay pigeons from an automated dispenser. Markswoman and dog engage in target practice with great gusto and impressive coordination, suggesting greater commitment to hunting than to environmental conservation. Although Mother Stahnke has a fondness for animals, in particular the pet rabbits she breeds and whose photos she keeps in a family album, pragmatism prevails over sentimentality. In one scene she sacrifices her favorite pet rabbit Ilse who is ceremoniously served up as part of a ghoulish family roast dinner. Moreover, Mother Stahnke and her trusted dog succeed in parodying the sort of hospitality and tolerance commonly attributed to rural dwellers in Heimat films of another era. She takes potshots at those who approach the homestead. Rolfi also displays aggression toward strangers whom he is known to hold captive, sometimes for several weeks at a time.

Even though the title *To the Horizon and Beyond* may suggest the sweeping vistas of a Heimatfilm and a heightened sensitivity for Heimat, the rapport East Germans supposedly have with nature is negated elsewhere in the film. Henning's lover Katja displays a complete lack of survival skills and familiarity with the countryside when she seeks refuge outside of the city: she fails to find adequate sustenance in the forest. When she seeks nourishment from wild herbage, the vegetation she selects proves to be inedible, and she can only spit it out in bitter disgust. She has no insight into the fruits the forest may provide. Hunger eventually drives her to threaten a convenience store clerk from whom she steals a partially eaten sandwich.

In another scene, the sort of Heimat imagery I have identified as a feature of western unification films is inverted: Katja is shown in an extreme high angle shot reclining in a meadow, content as she slumbers in the sun. Any sense of serenity and harmony is, however, effectively banished by the shot that follows. The romantic idyll is despoiled when the camera is repositioned to reveal the massive electricity towers that dominate the meadow where Katja seeks repose.

In a specific sense eastern- and western-backed productions[7] addressing life in the new Germany present irreconcilable visions of the eastern states. Throughout the 1990s, almost without exception, eastern productions that address the consequences of unification do not subscribe to the western formulation of the east as Heimat. The conception of the former GDR as Heimat has virtually no currency in east unification features of the 1990s. This is a western formulation and vantage point that East Ger-

---

7. For reasons of access and availability, series and films produced exclusively for television are not taken into consideration.

man filmmakers have eschewed as irrelevant. The country-city opposition emphasized in Heimat films, together with the negative connotations associated with the city and industrialization that resurface in the western unification films discussed earlier, are inconsequential in eastern productions. Similarly, the polarization of tradition and progress, evident in West German Heimat films of the 1950s and in 1990s generic variants, has no place in eastern productions examined throughout this chapter.

One of the greatest incongruities that differentiates east and west visions of the ex-GDR and unification relates to the depiction of the eastern landscape. Rather than presenting the east as a preindustrialized paradise, a number of East German films that critically assess the impact of unification in the east depict the region as a deindustrialized wasteland. This vision is most clearly evident in late 1990s eastern productions such as *To the Horizon and Beyond* and *Paths in the Night.* The east emerges as the antithesis of Heimat.

The deindustrialization of the east results in chronic unemployment, hardship, and despair for protagonists in these films. This emphasis may not be all that surprising considering the impact privatization of industry had in the east, which was evident even before the time these films went into production. "Apart from a few individual cases, [the] privatization [of industry in the east] was complete by 1995" (*Fischer Chronik* 1281). From 1991 to 1997, more than two-thirds of all positions in industry (excluding construction) were lost in the eastern states (*Fischer Chronik* 1283). Brown coal was the major primary source through which electricity could be generated in the GDR, and mining was a central component of GDR industry. Because this form of generating power led to environmental pollution on a vast scale, many coal mines and plants now lay dormant in the east, and miners are among the long-term unemployed: less environmentally hazardous means of generating power have been introduced. In each of the films under discussion here, the implementation of new power policies in the east is obliquely criticized. Deindustrialization and the unemployment that accompanied it are registered through on-location shooting at abandoned coal mines and defunct power plants. *Paths in the Night* opens and closes with scenes of derelict furnaces at a deserted power plant. The settings are equally desolate, nevertheless it is to these locations that protagonists return in moments of utter despair and crisis.

For the larger part of the film, *To the Horizon and Beyond* is shot on location in and around deserted open-cut coal mines. Henning returns to this surreal terrain with his hostage, Beate, and on numerous occasions the pair survey the mine surface, which looks like a barren moonscape. Enormous cranes and mining machinery are scattered across the colliery, which itself extends to the horizon, testimony to the activity and scale of the

Fig. 16.   *To the Horizon and Beyond* (1999). Film still reproduced with permission of Progress Film Verleih.

Fig. 17.   *Paths in the Night* (1999). Film still reproduced with permission of Ö Filmproduktion.

industry in the ex-GDR. Lakes have formed in the craters left from exca-
vation, and the industrial debris that litters the site evokes distant planets
as much as a scene of aborted space travel. The ex-GDR is pictured as a
compelling yet alien world—another planet from which signs of life have
been extinguished. Eerie de-industrialized landscapes and city centers are
marked as *fremd* (foreign, strange) in these films; as *unheimlich,* simultaneously unhomely (in the literal sense) and uncanny. In these films various
landscapes and city vistas become the inverse of Heimat and the comfort
and familiarity associated with it. Characters in *Paths in the Night* draw
attention to the east as the antithesis of Heimat. When Walter and Sylvia
drive through the newly redeveloped and fully modernized shopping
precinct located in the center of the old East Berlin, they comment on the
strangeness of the cityscape: "It is uncanny [*unheimlich*] the way it looks
now. It's like the hereafter." Both agree: "Yes, we are entering the king-
dom of the dead."

Late 1990s East German features like these, and others considered by
some to display objectionable degrees of nostalgia for life in the old GDR,
avoid associating the east with Heimat. *Paths in the Night* and *To the Horizon and Beyond,* like *Sonnenallee* and *Heroes Like Us,* avoid the sorts of
narrative conflicts, settings, and character constellations that can be traced
back to Heimat films from the period of western reconstruction. *Sonnenallee* and *Heroes Like Us*—both adaptations of novels by East German
author Thomas Brüssig—focus on the tribulations, anxieties, and aspirations of East German teenagers living in urban East Berlin. Enamored of
popular youth culture, rock 'n' roll, and experimentation with drugs as
much as the opposite sex, the teenagers in *Sonnenallee* strive to maintain a
facade of urban sophistication and modernity. Their priorities and aspirations are divorced from the romanticized vision of rural heritage, customs,
and tradition manifested in western depictions of the east. The vantage
points adopted by East German filmmakers depicting life in the new Germany and the GDR resist reconciliation with western perspectives.
Whereas western films prioritize the preservation of Heimat, in eastern
productions, there is very little left to salvage. The eastern border zone featured in *Sonnenallee* turns into a decrepit ghost town by the end of the film,
long deserted by its inhabitants.

Although the western equation of East Germany and Heimat has virtually
no currency in eastern unification films, this is not to say that this vantage
point is without its appeal to eastern audiences. In its most idyllic embodiment (premodern, anti-industrial, pristine environment), the east
becomes the "before" of the capitalist west, its point of imaginary origin in
unification films from the west. In these features the GDR becomes the
childhood for Germany as a whole. Barton Byg has rationalized:

Fig. 18. *Paths in the Night* (1999). Film still reproduced with permission of Ö Filmproduktion.

Fig. 19. *Sonnenallee* (1999). Film still reproduced with permission of Delphi Filmverleih.

Because the GDR has no continuing history and because its past is potentially connected to an image of Germans as victims rather than as Nazis or collaborators, it can represent an innocent childhood to post-unification "adult" Germans. As such, the representation of the GDR as "other" (an Other within the self) is parallel to the otherness encoded in romanticized images of women, people of colour, gays and lesbians, and all "others" who are seen as separate from the dominant culture. ("Parameters" 71)

Although this formulation of the GDR as the west's terminus a quo is one to which unification films from the east do not subscribe, it is still a fabrication capable of appealing to Germans in both the new and old federal states. For East German audiences, these films' depiction of the former GDR might be viewed as a highly nostalgic idealization of what easterners have left behind. Corporate capitalism and the market economy are shown to jeopardize the idealism and innocence attributed to easterners. Quite obviously the depiction of East Germans triumphing and prospering in the face of unification's challenges would be potentially satisfying for audiences in the east. Moreover, the portrait of the east as premodern paradise, evident in a range of western unification films, is clearly capable of cajoling eastern viewers, with the ex-GDR posited as the embodiment of all the west has lost. For West Germans, on the other hand, the depiction of east as Heimat, as rural idyll, involves nostalgic reflection on their own origins, with the east being narcissistically defined as a primordial version of the west. Many of these films depict callow easterners undergoing an initiation into the ways of the west, something in which western audiences can take comic, if not condescending delight. Furthermore, as Barton Byg suggests, positing the ex-GDR as Germany's childhood implicitly exorcises Germany's past by banishing the specter of Nazism. The GDR's insertion into the chain of social and political evolution of the Federal Republic further distances the Federal Republic from Nazi Germany, providing an imaginary point of origin detached from and insulated against fascism. However, the depiction of the ex-GDR in unification films from the east does not indulge in the comforting assurances of such an alibi.

Conclusion: Unification
Siegergeschichten

Throughout this book I have addressed the impact of unification on filmmaking in the former GDR and representations of unification in German film. I considered the ways in which unification may have contributed to the erasure of aspects of GDR history and the disavowal of the culture and values associated with the deposed regime. I argued that the incorporation of the ex-GDR into the west entailed the denigration and subordination of eastern culture, traditions, and experiences, which were dismissed as foreign to the Federal Republic and lacking relevance to life in the new Germany.

Attending to the cultural consequences of unification I focused specifically on unification Filmpolitik, examining one branch of local industry, the previously nationalized film studios, DEFA. I treated the studios as an emblem of the GDR, judging that they both encountered similar obstacles, challenges, and crises during and immediately after unification. Treating DEFA as representative of the GDR allowed me to consider issues related to the cultural heritage of the GDR as well as the ideological and political forces that shaped the country's film culture.

In examining events surrounding the Abwicklung of DEFA, I maintained that the western takeover of the studios had devastating cultural implications for the filmmaking community in the former GDR as well as for East German film culture. Unification has led to a drastically diminished public sphere for East German filmmakers: "possibilities for public articulation of experience" (Kluge 211) were constricted when their film industry was dismantled and the cultural capital of the east was transferred into western hands. As I explained in chapter 5, the decimation of eastern screen culture was furthered when West German public broadcasters assumed control of East Television at the end of 1992. Since unification East German filmmakers have been obliged to fathom the intricacies of a long-established western subsidy system and negotiate within a precarious marketplace that could barely accommodate films produced in the old states of the Federal Republic.

Filmmakers from the former GDR now find themselves in the position where, although they are freed from political censure, they are no longer assured an audience for their films as they were under the old regime. Rarely are their films accessible to a broad cinema public throughout the whole of the Federal Republic. Almost without exception, the eastern unification films discussed in chapter 11 were destined for box-office disaster. Structural issues related to the nature of these productions and the market have virtually ensured that, whatever their relevance or merit, eastern productions like *Little Angel, The Tango Player, Lost Landscape, Jana and Jan,* and *Nikolaikirche* did not generate substantial or even meager profit in cinemas. They are low-budget productions; when they are circulated it is through small distribution companies; their producers are often struggling for survival; they are distributed with meager print runs and minimal or nonexisting promotional budgets; and they are often television coproductions, or a significant percentage of their budgets is provided by public television.

For instance, *Quiet Country* and *Little Angel* each had minimal budgets of 1.5 million DM (less than 1 million dollars). Initially Misselwitz planned on a budget of 2.5 million DM for her feature, but 1 million were withdrawn when she went into production; she persevered despite diminished funds as she did not want to delay the project's completion (Schenk, "Excursion" 85). Usually the entire production budget for an eastern film was only a fraction of the advertising budget for a modest-scale feature from the United States. Like Misselwitz's film, the majority of eastern unification films are heavily dependent on public television broadcasters for funding and exposure. Because *Little Angel* and *Nikolaikirche* were television coproductions, their theatrical release was severely limited. Large distributors tend to display an aversion to films such as these, seeing them as destined for the small screen rather than the large.

Like the majority of East German films that have addressed unification, Helke Misselwitz's films have only attracted small audiences during limited screenings in tiny repertoire cinemas such as the Börse in Berlin, or in eastern cinemas in city centers. In the first two years after its release, *Little Angel* was viewed by less than 4,500 paying spectators ("Black Box Office" April/May 1998, 7). Otherwise films like these reach specialized audiences when they tour the festival circuit. Some like *Sonnenallee* find it difficult to benefit from even this avenue of exposure: it is thought that their culturally and historically specific references to the ex-GDR would baffle non-German audiences.

In the context of 1990s east productions that take the ex-GDR as their point of diegetic reference, *Sonnenallee* is nevertheless an exceptional feature. With a budget in excess of 7 million DM and close to 250 prints in circulation at the start of 2000, *Sonnenallee* is, to date, the most profitable eastern production to have been released since Germany was unified. Leander Haussmann's comedy, however, assumes a different historical vantage point—that of the GDR in the 1970s—distinguishing itself from the unification films discussed throughout this book. In any case, none of the eastern productions I examined in chapter 11 had such large budgets at their disposal, nor did they benefit from broad national media coverage and press exposure. Moreover, many contemporaneous eastern features, like *Paths in the Night,* are darker and more somber in tone.

In contrast to unification films from the west, such as *Life Is a Construction Site* or *No More Mr. Nice Guy* (and *Sonnenallee*[1]), the eastern films discussed in chapter 11 were never really screened in modern, well-equipped cinemas in the west for any duration for large western audiences. No matter whether these films were appealing or uninteresting for the overwhelming majority of spectators (West Germans), they were not especially accessible for that audience.

None of the east films addressed in chapter 11 benefited from the production configurations that characterized the most successful of western unification films. Their producers were eastern-based with none of the powerful connections of the old league of western producers like Günther Rohrbach or Bernd Eichinger. Their directors were not German "brand names" like Sonke Wörtman, Helmut Dietl, or Doris Dörrie, nor did they include major stars like Katja Riemann (Germany's answer to Meg Ryan), Til Schweiger, or Götz Georg, immediately recognizable to viewers in the western states. Often eastern films struggled to be distributed at all, and even if they were fortunate enough to secure distribution, their theatrical exhibition extended to a couple of continuous days. Limited theatrical release in turn meant that eastern features usually disappeared before word-of-mouth recommendations spread. In most cases (like for *Quiet Country*), the maximum theatrical release in any given cinema was four continuous days. Moreover, these films were also inclined to be marginalized by television programmers and allocated the least favorable of broadcasting slots—*Quiet Country* was programmed for one Sunday night at 11:00 P.M. on ARD (DEFA NOVA 296). Initially *Little Angel* seemed like it would be treated more kindly by ZDF, but the broadcaster hesitated and postponed showing the film, which was originally planned for broadcast in an attractive summertime slot in 1996 (Schenk, "Excursion" 85).

Without exception, unification films from the east were circulated

---

1. *Sonnenallee* is distributed by the West Berlin firm Delphi, and is a Boje Buck production in co-production with the eastern-oriented company Ö-Film.

with copy runs so meager it was impossible for them to profit. For instance, *Quiet Country* was fortunate to go into distribution with five copies. Throughout 1996 *Little Angel* was distributed with only one print in circulation. By contrast, *Independence Day* opened with 885 copies in German cinemas in the same year. After two and a half weeks, 5,734,486 tickets had been sold for the blockbuster.

However divergent eastern representations of life in united Germany may be, those impressions have only been granted extremely limited exposure. The same cannot be said about slick comedies of the sexes from the west, like Helmut Dietl's *Rossini—Or the Deadly Question of Who Sleeps with Whom* (1997), Sonke Wörtmann's *A Most Desirable Man,* and *The Super-Wife* or the animated film *Kleines Arschlock* (*Little Arse-hole,* 1997).

Box-office returns on unification films from the east are so paltry that even Margarethe von Trotta's *The Promise* managed to sell more tickets than just about *all* prominent eastern unification films combined. Yet with 203,860 viewers ("Jahresübersicht 1996" 11) and a considerably larger budget than most eastern unification films, *The Promise* was hardly a major box-office success. Its returns do not compare to the Trabi comedies and *No More Mr. Nice Guy.* Box-office returns for eastern productions are embarrassingly low by comparison: *The Land behind the Rainbow* did especially poorly, attracting 2,000 paying customers ("Black Box Office" Oct. 1992, 6). The east-west coproduction *Rising to the Bait,* identified as "one of the most successful reunification comedies" (Hughes and Brady 287), drew only 11,301 viewers ("Black Box Office" Oct. 1992, 6), and that was with forty prints in circulation ("Haie"). *Nikolaikirche* was seen by a disappointing 3,167 paying customers ("Jahresübersicht" 11–12); *Cosimas Lexicon* drew 3,633 ("Black Box Office" July 1992), and *Verfehlung* did not do all that much better—8,208 ("Black Box Office" Oct. 1992, 6). *Quiet Country* was seen by around 10,000 spectators in the first three months of its release (DEFA NOVA 296). *Forgiveness* was never commercially released. *Burning Life* is probably one of the most successful eastern unification films to date, having drawn 40,686 cinema viewers ("Black Box Office 1995"), still a modest figure that precludes anything approximating a profit. With its casting of popular East German stars, such as Wolfgang Strumph, lead actor in the Trabi films, and Corinna Harfouch, *To the Horizon and Beyond* seemed to present great box-office potential in 1999. Nevertheless the film only drew a modest attendance figure of 72,000 spectators during its first year of release, considerably less than anticipated. These returns were even more disappointing considering its cast and production pedigree.

It is very much the vicissitudes and long-standing structure of the western market that limit the exposure and circulation of eastern films: no matter what degree of veracity these films' vision of the east may display, they have little currency throughout the whole of the Federal Republic. Eastern views of unification are deprecated within the new marketplace they are expected to compete in. As Thomas Brüssig observes as part of a general discussion of eastern unification films: East Germany's demographics are not large enough to initiate an examination of the GDR that will succeed ("Nachdenken über Thomas B." 46–47).

Just as production details and critical and public reception distinguish eastern unification films from western-funded productions like the Trabi comedies and *No More Mr. Nice Guy,* east and west unification films foster some irreconcilable impressions of life in the new federal states. I have argued that western features reclaim the east as Heimat—part rural idyll and part preindustrial paradise. Western unification films draw on this distinctively German generic legacy through their common approaches to the treatment of the landscape, characterization, motifs, narrative motivation, conflict, and closure. These films place emphasis upon antiquated agrarian modes of production: venturing into cottage industry and dealing in primary produce are consistently presented as solutions to the economic ills of the east in these films. Like the Heimat-filme of the postwar period, many unification features revel in wholesome forms of residual culture and customs. As I discussed in chapter 7, Heimat heritage is also evident in the recurrent motifs of inheritance and bequeathed private property in these films—motifs that allow for related issues like heritage, sudden reversals of fortune, fate, and nostalgia about the past to be raised.

The western unification films I examine embrace the Heimat ethos in other ways as well: most commonly they display a yearning for integration into a stable, harmonious community or, as is ultimately the case in *Rising to the Bait* and *No More Mr. Nice Guy,* they celebrate the foundation or rediscovery of that community. However critical these films may be of unification, they express no doubts about the positive values of Heimat. They reiterate the utopian constitution of familial and communal relations. The restoration and preservation of Heimat is something to which virtuous characters in these films are devoted. It is even a cause to which West German capitalists and less than virtuous profiteers can be converted.

Through championing Heimat, unification comedies revert to a tried and tested "social and psychic balm" (Fehrenbach 151). In this instance, Heimat is evoked to mitigate apprehension about life in the new Germany and to distract attention from the discord and upheavals unification brought to the east. Heimat becomes a unifying force that presents the possibility of reconciling differences and dualities while providing some imaginary sense of unity (of origins, heritage, ideals, values, priorities) in western unification films. In integrating the individual and the community and "inviting audiences to imagine some form of collective unity or identity" (Walsh 6) these films invest in the national imaginary. They are cultural forms that are involved in an ideological operation: "the constitution of national identity through the promotion of certain meanings and the subordination of other meanings and social groups within the nation state" (7).

In one sense it is certainly understandable that films that address events, experiences, and historical developments specific to Germany in the early 1990s would draw upon or allude to what is probably the oldest and most resilient of German film genres. Again, Heimat becomes representative of what can "be salvaged from the . . . ruins" (Appelgate, qtd. in Fehrenbach 151) of a deposed regime, as it was presumably in the late 1940s and 1950s. The popularity of Heimatfilme in the 1950s has been attributed to their potential to "address German audiences as potential consumers." In contrast to Hollywood films of the period, which "never addressed German audiences as Germans," Heimat films could do exactly that and refer to their "national past, present, or future" (Fehrenbach 163).

Like their 1950s counterparts, unification films were designed to capitalize on the domestic market, in contrast to the international flavor of various Euro-films like *Voyager, The Innocent,* or *The French Woman.* Unlike the unification films I analyze, these Euro-films were international coproductions with much larger budgets and involving internationally recognizable stars. They were distributed internationally and promoted as art house productions made by famous directors. Unlike unification films, many Euro-films have literary pedigrees. They also found international, commercial video release, which the unification comedies did not. The restoration of Heimat may seem appropriate within western unification films: at its peak the genre's commercial potential was considerable, even if its appeal was domestic and restricted to Germany and Austria.

As I suggested at the end of chapter 6, the generic links between Heimatfilme and western-backed unification comedies of the 1990s may carry with them distressing ideological and historic implications. This reappropriation of Heimat and its glorification in various films about German unification have implications that are consistent with the cultural politics of unification itself, outlined in part 1 of this book. As Walter Benjamin maintained when he reflected upon the institutionalization of history and dominant representations of the past, it is the victor's privilege to write and shape history (258). In this sense, the yearning for and rediscovery of Heimat evidenced in various western unification films can be seen as yet one more instance of the East German cultural heritage being supplanted by that of the west—for eastern unification films do not define the east as

Heimat, nor do these films recycle iconography or sentiments common to the earlier genre. Productions like *Farewell to Agnes, Burning Life, To the Horizon and Beyond, Sonnenallee, Little Angel,* and *Adamski* do not subscribe to Heimat mythology by suggesting that East Germans have an inherent affinity with nature. Nor do protagonists in these films display any compulsion to champion rural culture and residual customs associated with it. As I remarked in chapters 6 and 10, characters in eastern productions eschew these priorities and values. They derive no succor from the pastoral idyll: as urban dwellers, their lives in the new Germany are characterized by isolation, alienation, and loss—of loved ones, sanity, social standing, freedom, and in many cases their own lives. The depiction of the east in many eastern productions is the antithesis of Heimat. Eastern environs are more *fremd* (strange, alien) than *heimlich* (familiar, homely, cozy) in *Paths in the Night, Jana and Jan, Farewell to Agnes, Herzsprung, Lost Landscape, Burning Life,* and *To the Horizon and Beyond.* Rather than presenting the east as the unscathed and reassuring rural paradise of Heimat, on occasion eastern unification films depict the new federal states as a deindustrialized wasteland where labor is alienating and community is in an advanced state of disintegration. Granted the disparities in eastern and western visions of unification, the western productions discussed in detail in chapters 7 to 10 are particularly revealing cultural artifacts that form part of the Siegergeschichte of German unification.

Colonial attitudes also surface at the level of characterization in a number of these films. Unification comedies often draw affiliations between East Germans, Africans, and supposedly "primitive" cultures that are viewed as depending on the favors of the gods. Sometimes characters display a particular affinity with primitive mysticism and charms (like Ada in *Rising to the Bait*) or with folklore. In *That Was the Wild East* Udo's talisman is the garden gnome, a figure who is guardian of the earth and of homeland. The business he inherits is named after the folktale "Little Red Riding Hood." On occasion, African-Germans are identified as exemplary civic-minded easterners, like Bongo in *That Was the Wild East.* In this sense, associating East Germans with blacks is a further instance of a colonizing ethos that can be seen to characterize the cultural politics of unification. "Primitivism" is also attributed to the political and social order of the ex-GDR in these films. For instance, even though the GDR was an industrialized, communist state, in western-backed unification films the east is historically repositioned and represented as a "primitive communist" society, almost bordering on feudalism (in *Apple Trees,* Sinke behaves like the lord of the manor in his community; Kipp and Most defer to the lady of the manor who directs them to the farmer's cottage/serf's abode in *No More Mr. Nice Guy;* and the entire community of Landwitz is dependent upon the ancient cottage industry of ceramics in *That Was the Wild East*).

In western unification films, the fiction of Heimat sweetens this portrayal of the east; it ultimately allows for the reconciliation of cultural difference. Reviving Heimat, or inviting nostalgia about it, in some measure tempers the criticisms these films make about unification. Unification, for instance, is regularly presented as marred by corruption, greed, and attempts to exploit virtuous East Germans in the course of these films. Criminality and theft are presented as unification's by-products, and theft is often one of the first lessons protagonists learn. Because Heimat is invariably associated with the east in these films, unification (the west) is presented as something that threatens to despoil Heimat. The old country-city, tradition-modernization oppositions that thrive in the Heimat genre prevail. But the resolution of the west's corruption does not lie in the virtue of the east but in the purity of Heimat.

That various unification films from the west locate Heimat in the east can be viewed as one of unification's most bitter ironies, at least for East Germans who have witnessed the disintegration of the GDR. Stuart Hall's reflections in "Culture, Community, Nation" come to mind here. Even though his observations about dislocated cultures and fractured communities were not directed specifically to the east, they are of some relevance, as it would seem that since unification the Federal Republic's new citizens

> are obliged to inhabit at least two identities, to speak at least two cultural languages, to negotiate and 'translate' between them. . . . They [or perhaps more accurately their offspring] are the products of cultural hybridicity. . . . These 'hybrids' retain strong links to and identifications with the traditions and places of their 'origin.' But they are without illusion of any actual 'return' to the past. Either they will never . . . return or the places to which they return will have been transformed out of all recognition by the remorseless process of modernisation. In that sense, there is no going 'home' again. (262)

In part 2 of this book, I noted that despite their divergent portraits of the east, unification films from both the east and west present a generally consistent portrait of German-German relations. Mostly, these films suggest that those relations do not exist. No alarm is displayed about this situation, which is accepted as perfectly normal. Some unification films go as far as to redefine the heritage and identity of characters so that any likelihood of intimate or meaningful relations between East and West Germans can be avoided. This is a further irony that emerges from this cycle of

1990s films. What these films ultimately effect is a segregation of East and West Germans.

None of the films I have examined declares emphatically that east and west perspectives on unification are contradictory or incongruous. The second Trabi comedy does, however, come close to suggesting as much, even if only as part of a musical interlude. This takes place in one of the most frivolous moments toward the end of the film when Charlie breaks into song as he drives alone, and carefree, through the East German countryside. Undeterred by his limited vocal range and inclination to sing off-key, Charlie persists: he delivers not only lyrics but also his own vocal rendition of the song's (non-diegetic) guitar refrain. Ostensibly his song is a reflection on German-German relations and the liaison the West German has had with Udo, an East German. But the lyrics also serve as a commentary on unification. When Charlie intones, "You know/ What my freedom means to me / Heh! Heh! Heh! / Look what you do to me / Heh! Heh! Heh! / Look what you' done," he conveys a degree of apprehension about his encounter with Udo and other East Germans. In a painfully protracted long take Charlie just keeps on singing. He voices suspicion that east and west views of unification are, after all, irreconcilable when he wails, "But we don't agree / Just exactly what it's all supposed to mean." In any case, Udo would never know what Charlie suspects—after one final chance encounter, the East and West German bid farewell to one another and drive off deeper into the countryside—in opposite directions.

Bibliography

Translations for articles listed in German are my own. Pagination is not always listed for short articles and newspaper reports because the references I have located in German archives do not usually provide this information.

"Abschied von gestern." *Der Tagesspiegel* 9 Jan. 1992.

Ahrends, M. "The Great Waiting, or the Freedom of the East: An Obituary for Life in Sleeping Beauty's Castle." *New German Critique* 52 (1991): 41–49.

Albertz, H. "Vom Sessel aus—Ohne Fernsehen wäre es anders gelaufen." *Medium* 4 (1990): 33.

Alexandrow, E. "Anmerkungen zur Filmförderung in Berlin-Brandenburg." *Filmproduktion, Filmförderung, Filmfinanzierung.* Ed. J. Berg and K. Hickethier. Berlin: Sigma, 1994. 43–45.

"Ansichten zu Kunst und Politik. Die Hoffnung stirbt nicht, weil das Eigentliche bleibt. [Gespräch mit Helke Misselwitz]." *Sächsische Zeitung* 24 Jan. 1993.

Arnold, F. *"Apfelbäume." Epd Film* 8 (1992).

———. *"Wir können auch anders." Epd Film* 4 (1993): 40.

"Auch das West-Kino schnappt sich in der DDR." *Frankfurter Rundschau* 20 June 1990.

"Aufgeben oder weitermachen? Neue Produzenten nach zwei Jahren." *Film und Fernsehen* 2 (1994): 32–39.

"Aus Gesprächen der Herausgeber mit Armin Mueller-Stahl." *Filmland DDR: Ein Reader zu Geschichte, Funktion und Wirkung der DEFA.* Ed. H. Blunk. Cologne: Verlag Wissenschaft und Politik, 1990. 59–70.

Baer, V. "Der grösste Zuspruch galt Deutsch-deutschen Themen—Die 34. Internationale Dokumentarfilmwoche Leipzig—Ihre Zukunft gilt als gesichert." *Der Tagesspiegel* 8 Dec. 1991: xii.

———. "Doch keine *Unendliche Geschichte:* Arbeitsbeginn beim Filmboard Berlin-Brandenburg." *Film Dienst* 47.18 (1994): 12–13.

Bathrick, D. *The Powers of Speech: The Politics of Culture in the GDR.* Lincoln: University of Nebraska Press, 1995.

Battenberg, A., and J. Herdin. "Heimatfilm in der DDR. Annäherung an eine

Fragestellung." *Der deutsche Heimatfilm. Bildwelten und Weltbilder. Bilder, Texte, Analysen zu 70 Jahren deutscher Filmgeschichte.* Tübingen: Ludwig-Uhland-Institut für Empirische Kulturwissenschaft der Universität Tübingen, 1989. 149–50.

Bauer, J. *"Go Trabi Go." Epd Film* 3 (1991): 34.

Baum, A., and D. Kuhlbrodt. "Die Poesie des Stempelbuchs." *Die Tageszeitung* [Ausgabe Ost] 25 Mar. 1991.

Becher, U. "Notizen aus der Provinz. Kleinbürgertum und Spießigkeit in Widerspiegelungen des DDR-Alltags—Kritik oder erwünschtes Ideal?" *Der DEFA-Spielfilm in den 80er Jahren—Chancen für die 90er?* Beiträge zur Film und Fernsehwissenschaft, vol. 44. Ed. P. Hoff and D. Wiedermann. Berlin: Vistas Verlag, 1992. 192–209.

Becker, J. "Endstation Bülowbogen? Warum der Filmregisseur Heiner Carow jetzt Fernseserien macht." *Der Tagesspiegel* 2 Nov. 1993: viii.

"Begrenzte Freude." *Der Tagesspiegel* 16 June 1991: xii.

Benjamin, W. "Theses on the Philosophy of History." *Illuminations.* Trans. Harry Zohn. New York: Harcourt, Brace and World, 1968. 255–66.

Berg J., and K. Hickethier, eds. *Filmproduktion, Filmförderung, Filmfinanzierung.* Berlin: Sigma, 1994.

Bericht des Politbüros an die 11. Tagung des Zentralkomitees der SED, 15.–18. Dezember 1965. Berlin (DDR): Dietz Verlag, 1965. 56–63.

"Berlinale—Abschluß mit Komödie *Der Brocken.* Lob und Interesse für deutschen Beitrag." *Volksstimme Magdeburg* 25 Feb. 1992.

Bernhard, S. "Riese Babelsberg? Schlöndorffs 100 Tage-Bilanz: schon Einiges erreicht und jede Menge Optimismus." *Film Echo/Film/Woche* 51–52 (1992).

Beyer, F. "Die Spur des Stalinismus—Opfer und Täter." *Epd Film* 1 (1990): 2–3.

Bis zum Horizont und Weiter. Press information. Berlin: Progress Film Verleih, 1999.

Bisky, L., and K. Wiedermann. *Der Spielfilm—Rezeption und Wirkung.* Berlin: Henschelverlag Kunst und Gesellschaft, 1985.

Bitterman K., ed. *It's a Zoni. Zehn Jahre Wiedervereinigung. Die Ossis als Belastung und Belästigung.* Berlin: Edition Tiamat, 1999.

Bittorf, W. "Das Glitzern in der Wüste." *Der Spiegel* 39 (1993): 42–58.

"Black Box Office—Deutsche Filme im Kino." *Black Box* 69 (1992): 6.

"Black Box Office—Deutsche Filme im Kino." *Black Box* 84 (1994): 12.

"Black Box Office—Deutsche Filme im Kino." *Black Box* 91 (1995): 5.

"Black Box Office." *Black Box* 113 (April/May 1998): 6–7.

Blaney, M. "Franco-German Group Plans DEFA Studio Euro-Complex." *Screen International* 832 (1991): 1.

———. "Screen Box Office." *Screen International* 839 (1992): 12.

———. "Treuhand Set to OK Franco-German DEFA Plan." *Screen International* 834 (1991): 2.

Bleicher, J. K. "Übernahme. Zur Integration des 'Deutschen Fernsehfunks' in die Programme der oeffentlich-rechtlichen Anstalten." *Mauer-Show. Das Ende der DDR, die deutsche Einheit und die Medien.* Ed. R. Bohn and K. Hickethier. Berlin: Sigma, 1992. 127–38.

Blokker, A. "Berlinale 1958—Ein Korrespondentenbericht von damals." *Medium* 4 (1990): 29–30.

Blunk, H. "Zur Rezeption von 'Gegenwartsspielfilmen' der DEFA im Westen Deutschlands." *Filmland DDR: Ein Reader zu Geschichte, Funktion und Wirkung der DEFA.* Ed. H. Blunk and D. Jungnickel. Cologne: Verlag Wissenschaft und Politik, 1990. 107–18.

Blunk, H., and D. Jungnickel, eds. *Filmland DDR: Ein Reader zu Geschichte, Funktion und Wirkung der DEFA.* Cologne: Verlag Wissenschaft und Politik, 1990.

Böhme, M. "Wo steht heute die Filmförderung?" *Filmproduktion, Filmförderung, Filmfinanzierung.* Ed. J. Berg and K. Hickethier. Berlin: Sigma, 1994. 17–33.

Böhmer, A. "6. Spielfilmfestival der DDR: Wirklichkeit, wie sie ist. Kinobesuch 1990 sank im Vergleich zum Vorjahr um 40 Prozent." *Sächsisches Tageblatt* 1 June 1990.

Bohn, R., and K. Hickethier, eds. *Mauer-Show: Das Ende der DDR, die deutsche Einheit und die Medien.* Berlin: Sigma, 1992.

Bohrer, K. H. "Why We Are Not a Nation—And Why We Should Become One." *New German Critique* 52 (1991): 72–83.

Borgelt, Hans. "Filmförderung—Pflicht oder Gnade?" *Film in Berlin 5 Jahre Berliner Filmförderung.* Ed. H. Ortkemper. Berlin: Colloquium, 1983. 33–49.

Borschers, A. "Wiedervereinigung und Neonazism: Von der Zionskirche bis Hoyerswerda." *Un-Heil über Deutschland FremdhaB und Neofaschismus nach der Wiedervereinigung.* Ed. R. Schmidt-Holtz. Hamburg: Stern, 1993. 120–35.

"Brandenburg geht eigene Weg." *Der Tagesspiegel* 1 Sept. 1991.

Brenner, W. "Eine Firma für die Ewigkeit." *Tip Film Jahrbuch: Daten, Berichte, Kritiken* 7. Berlin: Stemmler, 1992. 280–85.

Bretschneider, J. "VEB Kunst—aus der Traum." *Babelsberg ein Filmstudio 1912–1992.* Ed. W. Jacobsen. Berlin: Stiftung Deutsche Kinemathek. 1992. 289–314.

Brockmann, S. "Introduction: The Reunification Debate." *New German Critique* 52 (1991): 3–30.

Broder, H. M. "Aufruhr unter Bummelanten." *Der Spiegel* 40 (1999): 158–62.

Brömsel, S., and R. Biehl. "Die Spielfilm der DEFA 1946 bis 1993." *Das zweite Leben der Filmstadt Babelsberg 1946–1992.* Ed. R. Schenk. Berlin: Filmmuseum Potsdam und Henschel, 1994. 356–541.

Bulgakowa, O. "Richtung Osten und dann immer geradeaus." *Tip* 7 (1993): 28–29.

"Bundesminister kommt zu Film-Gespräch." *Sächsische Zeitung* 25 Oct. 1991.

"Bundesstart für *Miraculi.*" *Sächsische Zeitung* 18 Feb. 1992.

Bunge, B. "Ein Jesus der Schwarzfahrer [*Miraculi*]." *Junge Welt* 18 Feb. 1992.

Byg, B. "Generational Conflict and Historical Continuity in GDR Film." *Framing the Past: The Historiography of German Cinema and Television.* Ed. B. A. Murray and C. J. Wickham. Carbondale: Southern Illinois University, 1992. 197–219.

———. "Parameters for Institutional and Thematic Integration of Filmmakers from the Former GDR." *What Remains? East German Culture and the Postwar Public.* Ed. Marc Silberman. AICGS Research Report 5. 64–74.

———. "Two Approaches to GDR History and DEFA Films." *Studies in GDR*

Culture and Society 10. Ed. Margy Gerber et al. Lanham, MD: University Press of America, 1991. 85–103.

Bylow, C. "Killer und Käuze im wilde Osten: High Noon auf deutschen Straßen." *Elle* Apr. 1993: 55–56.

Chapters of Life in Germany, 1900–1993. Berlin: Deutsches Historisches Museum, 1993.

"Chronik der Gewalt: Fremdenhass forderte 1992 schon 16 Tote." *Berliner Morgenpost* 24 Nov. 1992.

Clover, C. *Men, Women and Chainsaws: Gender in the Modern Horror Film.* London: BFI, 1992.

"*Coming Out:* Interview mit dem Regisseur." Press information. Berlin: Progress Film Verleih.

Dahn, D. "East German Identity." <http://www.sunderland.ac.uk/~us0cma /europe/dahn.html> 31 Jan. 2000.

Dalichow, B. "Das letzte Kapitel 1989 bis 1993." *Das zweite Leben der Filmstadt Babelsberg 1946–1992.* Ed. R. Schenk. Berlin: Film Museum Potsdam und Henschel, 1994. 328–55.

———. "DEFA—Letztes Kapitel." *Film und Fernsehen* 6.1 (1993–1994): 4–11.

———. "Die jüngste Regiegeneration der DEFA—Aufbruch oder Abgesang?" *Der DEFA-Film Erbe oder Episode?* Augenblick 14. Marburg: Schüren, 1993. 70–89.

———. "Von den Mühen der Großartigkeit. Das Babelsberger Filmstudio nach der Wende." *Fischer Film Almanach 1994.* Ed. H. Schäfer and W. Schobert. Frankfurt am Main: Fischer, 1994. 436–42.

———. "Wettlauf der Zwerge: Zur Situation des deutschen Films in Ost und West." *Film und Fernsehen* 8–9 (1991): 18–23.

Dannowski, H. W. "Der Traum von weitem Raum: Bundesdeutsche Filme 89/90." *Epd Film* 6 (1989–90): 2–5.

Davies, N. "Avoiding the Euro-Pudding." *Screen International* 829 (1991): 9.

de Bruyn, G. "On the German Cultural Nation." *New German Critique* 52 (1991): 60–66.

"DEFA ade!" *Film und Fernsehen* 2 (1992): 33–35.

DEFA NOVA–nach wie vor? Versuch einer Spurensicherung. Berlin: Freunde der Deutschen Kinemathek e. V., Heft 82, Dec. 1993.

"'Dein Lebens-Budget voll ausschöpfen' Regisseur Vadim Glowna mit *Der Brocken* im Berlinale-Wettbewerb." *Junge Welt* 21 Feb. 1992.

Delius, C. F. "The West Is Getting Wilder—Intellectuals and the German Question: The Claims Are Being Staked Out." *When the Wall Came Down: Reactions to German Unification.* Ed. H. James and M. Stone. New York: Routledge, 1994. 71–76.

"Den Kinos geht es glänzend." *Frankfurter Rundschau* 18 Nov. 1993.

"Ein 'deutsch-deutsches Märchen'." *Leipziger Zeitung* 3 June 1992.

"Deutsche in Ost und West beklagen mangelndes Verständnis." *Der Tagesspiegel* 1 Oct. 1994.

"Dick und Doof vom platten Lande." *Der Spiegel* 18 (1993): 212–14.

Dierick, A. P. "'Schreckbild Land.' 'Heimat' as Topos in Contemporary German

Literature." *Der Begriff "Heimat" in der deutschen Gegenwartsliteratur.* Ed. H. W. Seliger. Munich: Iudicium-Verlag, 1987. 150–72.

Dockhorn, K. "Bahlke mit 'St' und Udo Lindenberg." *Filmecho/Filmwoche* 3 (23 Jan. 1999): 45.

Donner, W. "Nackgehakt—Was Frauen lieben: Deutsche Erfolgsfilme." *Frankfurter Allgemeine Zeitung* 30 Dec. 1993.

———. "Polemische Thesen zur Filmförderung." *Filmproduktion, Filmförderung, Filmfinanzierung.* Ed. J. Berg and K. Hickethier. Berlin: Stigma, 1994. 35–45.

Dornberg. J. "Still Divided—Germany Ten Years after the Fall of the Wall." <http://www.germanlife.com/Archives/1999/9910_01.html> 31 Jan. 2000.

Ebel, C. "Das harte Brot der Cineasten." *Rheinischer Merkur* 26 Apr. 1991.

Ehrich, U. "Mankurten. Wird das Gedächtnis der DDR ausgelöscht?" *Medium* 4 (1990): 47–48.

Elsaesser, T. "Der deutsche Film—ein Opfer der Geschichte?" *Neue Züricher Zeitung* [Internationale Ausgabe] 29–30 Apr. 1995: 53–54.

———. *The New German Cinema: A History.* London: Macmillan/BFI, 1989.

Elsaesser, T., and M. Wedel. "Defining DEFA's Historical Imaginary: The Films of Konrad Wolf." Conference paper. The Cinema of Eastern Germany: The View from North America. University of Massachusetts, Amherst, 2–3 October 1997.

Endlich, L. *Neue Land. Ganz einfache Geschichten.* Berlin: Transit, 1999.

Enzensberger, H. M. "Rigmarole." *When the Wall Came Down: Reactions to German Unification.* Ed. H. James and M. Stone. New York: Routledge, 1992. 83–85.

"Erfolg—das meint Publikum, Kasse, Silberne und Goldene Bären, Löwen, Palmen [Gespräch mit Klaus Keil]." *Film und Fernsehen* 1 (1995): 5–10.

Fehrenbach, H. *Cinema in Democratizing Germany: Reconstructing National Identity after Hitler.* Chapel Hill: University of North Carolina, 1995.

Feinstein, J. I. The Triumph of the Ordinary: Depictions of Daily Life in the East German Cinema, 1956–1966. Diss. Stanford University, 1995.

"FFA Fördert." *Film Dienst* 10 (1990): 42.

"Filmboard Berlin-Brandenburg: Fördermodalitäten." *Black Box* 84 (1994): 4–8.

"Ein Filmland wird 'abgewickelt': Gespräch mit den DEFA-Film-Schaffenden Roland Gräf, Michael Gwisdek und Thomas Knauf." *Film Dienst* 45.22 (1992): 4–8.

"Filmpreis im Streit—Erklärung der Auswahlkommission." *Frankfurter Allgemeiner Zeitung* 5 June 1994.

Findesein, H. V. "Exodus—Überlegungen zu drei Jahrzehnten Fluchtberichterstattung." *Medium* 4 (1990): 30–33.

Fischer Film Almanach 1993 Filme Festivals Tendenzen. Frankfurt am Main: Fischer, 1993.

Die Fischer Chronik Deutschland 1949–1999. Ereignisse Personen Daten. Frankfurt am Main: Fischer, 1999.

Foth, J. 1989. "Forever Young." *Filmland DDR Ein Reader zu Geschichte, Funktion und Wirkung der DEFA.* Ed. H. Blunk and D. Jungnickel. Cologne: Verlag Wissenschaft und Politik, 1990. 95–105.

――――. Letter to Lutz Haucke. 14 Feb. 1993.

――――. Personal interview. Berlin, 18 Oct. 1993.

Freyermuth, G. S. *Der Übernehmer—Volker Schlöndorff in Babelsberg.* Berlin: Christoph Links Verlag, 1993.

Frickel, T. "Verwertungsgesellschaften: Nur Peanuts für den Dokumentarfilm." *Black Box* 84 (1994): 10–11.

Fuchs, M. "Auf welchem Weg befindet sich Berlin? Unklares und Widersprüchliches in der Kulturpolitik." *Film Dienst* 45.10 (1992): 12–13.

Gansera, R. "*Ostkreuz.*" *Epd Film* 3 (1992): 43.

"Geh über die Dörfer!" *Der Spiegel* 40 (1984): 253–55.

Gehler, F. "*Schtonk.*" *Film und Fernsehen* 2 (1992): 79.

Gemeinsame Presserklärung der Treuhandanstalt und der Companie General des Eaux. 1992.

Gemünden, G. "Between Karl May and Karl Marx: The DEFA Indianerfilme (1965–1983)." Conference paper. The Cinema of Eastern Germany: The View from North America. University of Massachusetts, Amherst, 2–3 October 1997.

Gersch, W. "Film in der DDR Die Verlorene Alternative." *Geschichte des deutschen Films.* Ed. W. Jacobsen, A. Kaes, and H. H. Prinzler. Stuttgart: Metzler, 1993. 323–64.

"Gespräch mit Helma Sanders-Brahms: Unsere Geschichte müssen jetzt erzählt werden." *Film und Fernsehen* 8–9 (1991): 24–28.

"Gespräch mit Rolf Giesen: Des Kaisers neue Kleider." *Film und Fernsehen* 5 (1990): 2–6.

Giesen, R. "Des Kaisers neue Kleider." *Film und Fernsehen* 5:4.

――――. "Troja Babelsberg." *Babelsberg ein Filmstudio 1912–1992.* Ed. W. Jacobsen. Berlin: Stiftung Deutsche Kinemathek, 1992. 317–30.

――――. "Viel Kopf, kein Bauch." *Der Tagesspiegel* 19 Sept. 1991.

"Ein glatter Gegenwartsfilm. Pressekonferenz zum *Tangospieler.*" *Die Tageszeitung* 20 Feb. 1991.

Goodwin, P. "After Unification." *When the Wall Came Down: Broadcasting in Germany.* Ed. G. Nowell-Smith and T. Wollen. London: BFI, 1991. 48–55.

Goulding, D. J., ed. *Post New Wave Cinema in the Soviet Union and Eastern Europe.* Bloomington: Indiana University Press, 1989.

Grass, G. "What Am I Talking For? Is Anybody Still Listening?" *New German Critique* 52:66–72.

Greverus, I. M. "The 'Heimat' Problem." *Der Begriff "Heimat" in der deutschen Gegenwartsliteratur.* Ed. H. W. Seliger. Munich: Iudicium-Verlag, 1987. 9–28.

Hagedorn, C. "Steckt die DEFA in einer Sackgasse? Treuhand hat Vermarktungsrechte an Schweize Bank verkauft." *Berliner Zeitung* 30 Oct. 1991.

"Haie vor Rügen. Vadim Glowna und sein Film *Der Brocken.*" *Thüringer Allgemeine* 26 June 1992.

Hall, S. "Culture, Community, Nation." *Cultural Studies* 7.3 (1993): 349–63.

Hamacher, R. R. "Und wenn sie nicht gestorben sind. . . . Die DEFA vor ungewisser Zukunft und eine Utopie." *Film Dienst* 43.24 (1990): 14–15.

Hanke, H. "Das 'deutsche Fernsehen'—doch kein Null-Medium? Fernsehgesellschaft und kulturelle Chance." *Medien der Ex-GDR in der Wende.* Beiträge zur Film und Fernsehwissenschaft, vol. 40. Berlin: Vistas, 1991. 7–23.

Hartung, K. "Die Baustelle der Wiedervereinigung." *Die Zeit* 1 Oct. 1993: 3.

Häselbarth, R. "Mit Porno und Popcorn. Oder: Wie weiter mit dem Kino?" *Thüringische Landeszeitung* 18 June 1990.

Haucke, L. "Das Theatre der Clowns. Jörg Foths Versuche mit dem Liedtheater der DDR." *Der DEFA-Spielfilm in den 80er Jahren—Chancen für die 90er?* Beiträge zur Film und Fernsehwissenschaft, vol. 44. Ed. P. Hoff and D. Wiedermann. Berlin: Vistas, 1992. 107–19.

Hennings, D. "Im Lauf der Zeit—Die Entwicklung der Kinolandschaft in den neuen Ländern." *Film und Fernsehen* 4 (1993): 4–7.

Herdin, J. "Kulturpolitik und Filmschaffen in der DDR—Ein Überblick von 1945 bis heute." *Der deutsche Heimatfilm. Bildwelten und Weltbilder. Bilder, Texte, Analysen zu 70 Jahren deutscher Filmgeschichte.* Ludwig-Uhland-Institut für Empirische Kulturwissenschaft der Universität Tübingen, 1989. 150–56.

Hermann, W. *Gottfried Semper: In Search of Architecture.* Cambridge: MIT Press, 1984.

Heyne, U. "Der See, der über Nacht verschwindet [*Miraculi*]." *Neues Deutschland* 19 Nov. 1992.

Hickethier, K. "Babelsberg in Aufwind: Auf dem Wege zur 'Medienstadt'." *Epd Film* 2 (1997): 7.

———. "DEFA-Verkauf Versprechung." *Epd Film* 7 (1992): 46.

———. "Hie Berlin—hie Brandenburg: Die Film und die Folgen eines gemeinsamen Bundeslandes." *Der Tagesspiegel* 23 Feb. 1992: x.

———. "Neue deutsche Filme auf der Berlinale." *Epd Film* 5 (1991): 5–7.

———. "Statt DEFA 'Media City Babelsberg'?" *Epd Film* 10 (1991): 8–9.

———. "Das Zerschlagen der Einrichtung. Der Weg vom Staatsfernsehen der DDR zum Rundfunkföderalismus in den neuen Bundesländer." *Mauer-Show. Das Ende der DDR, die deutsche Einheit und die Medien.* Ed. R. Bohn and K. Hickethier. Berlin: Sigma, 1992. 71–93.

Hilmer, R., and R. Müller-Hilmer. "Die Stimmung stimmt für Kohl." 30 Sept. 1994: 13–15.

———. "Es wächst zusammen." *Die Zeit* 1 Oct. 1993: 17–21.

Hindermith, B. "Der DEFA Spielfilm und seine Kritik Probleme und Tendenzen." *Filmland DDR Ein Reader zu Geschichte, Funktion und Wirkung der DEFA.* Ed. H. Blunk and D. Jungnickel. Cologne: Verlag Wissenschaft und Politik, 1990. 27–57.

Hochmuth, D., ed. *DEFA Nova—Nach wie vor? Versuch einer Spurensicherung.* Berlin: Freunde der Kinemathek, 1994.

———. "Ostdeutscher Protestantismus. In Farber, aber keinesfalls ganz entspannt im Bunt und Jetzt [*Adamski*]." *Die Tageszeitung* 2 June 1994.

———. "Tausend Töpfe." *Die Tageszeitung* 25 Oct. 1990.

———. "Tausend und zwei Töpfe: Filmföderung für Regisseure aus der sogennanten ehemaligen DDR." *Die Tageszeitung* 15 Nov. 1990: 17.

Hoff, P. "Armenbegräbnis für eine teure Verblichene. Geschichtsbild und Point of View von Fernsehrückblicken und Videokassetten (Ost/West) zum 'Jahr der deutschen Einheit' 1990." *Mauer-Show: Das Ende der DDR, die deutsche Einheit und die Medien.* Ed. R. Bohn, K. Hickethier, and E. Müller. Berlin: Sigma, 1992. 175–88.

———. "'Continuity and Change': Television in the GDR from Autumn 1989 to Summer 1990." *After the Wall: Broadcasting in Germany.* Ed. G. Nowell-Smith and T. Wollen. London: BFI, 1991.

———. "Der kurze Augenblick bei sich selbst: Zur Deutung der Massendemonstrationen in der DDR." *Medium* 4 (1990): 38–40.

———. "Die schlimmste mögliche Wendung, die eine Komödie nehmen kann, ist die in die Geschichte." *Der DEFA-Spielfilm in den 80er Jahren—Chancen für die 90er?* Beiträge zur Film und Fernsehwissenschaft, vol. 44. Ed. P. Hoff and D. Wiedermann. Berlin: Vistas Verlag, 1992. 87–105.

Hoff, P., and D. Wiedermann, eds. *Der DEFA-Spielfilm in den 80er Jahren—Chancen für die 90er?* Beiträge zur Film und Fernsehwissenschaft, vol. 44. Berlin: Vistas Verlag, 1992.

Hoffmeyer, U. "Commercial Broadcasting in United Germany." *After the Wall: Broadcasting in Germany.* Ed. G. Nowell-Smith and T. Wollen. London: BFI, 1991. 40–47.

Höfig, W. *Der deutsche Heimatfilm 1947–1960.* Stuttgart: Ferdinand Enke Verlag, 1973.

Hofmann, M. "The Unity Train." *After the Wall: Broadcasting in Germany.* Ed. G. Nowell-Smith and T. Wollen. London: BFI, 1991. 56–68.

Holighaus, A. "Killer wider willen [*Wir können auch anders*]." *Tip* 4 (1993): 21.

"Hollywood enteilt Statistik der deutschen Filmverleiher." *Frankfurter Allgemeine Zeitung* 1 July 1991.

Honecker, E. *Bericht des Polibueros an die 11. Tagung des Zentralkomitees der SED, 15.–18. Dezember 1965.* Berlin (DDR): Dietz Verlag, 1966. 56–63.

Hübner, W. "Lebt der deutsche Film in einem Geisterhaus?" *Berliner Morgenpost* 23 Dec. 1993.

Hughes, H., and M. Brady. "German Film after the *Wende.*" *The New Germany: Social, Political and Cultural Challenges of Unification.* Ed. D. Lewis and J. R. P. McKenzie. Exeter: University of Exeter Press, 1995. 276–96.

Huyssen, A. "After the Wall: The Failure of German Intellectuals." *New German Critique* 52 (1991): 109–43.

"*Ich war ein glücklicher Mensch,* Festival Blätter Nr. 8." Berlin: 21. Internationales Forum des jungen Films, 1991.

"Ich will keinen Prototyp zeigen. Gespräch mit Roland Gräf." *Junge Welt* 17 Feb. 1991.

"Ist die DEFA noch zu retten? (2)." DEFA Betriebsratsversammlung. *Filmspiegel* 23 (1990): 34–35.

Jacobsen, W., ed. *Geschichte des deutschen Films.* Stuttgart: Metzler, 1993.

"Jahresubersicht 1996." *Black Box* 103 (Feb. 1997): 11–12.

James, H., and M. Stone, eds. *When the Wall Came Down: Reactions to German Unification.* London: Routledge, 1992.

"Jammer statt Glamour." *Der Spiegel* 34 (1994): 154–59.

John, H. "Karikierte Westler sind so. Am letzten Tag im Wettbewerb: *Der Brocken* (Deutschland)." *Märkische Allgemeine* 25 Feb. 1992.

Johnston, S. "A Star is Born: Fassbinder and the New German Cinema." *New German Critique* 24–25 (1981–82): 57–72.

Journal für Deutschland Informationen aus der Politik. Presse und Informationsamt der Bundesregierung, ed., vol. 2, 1993.

Junghänel, F. "Kino wird bunter und teuerer. Westliche Verleiher bestimmen, was läuft." *Ostsee Zeitung* 17 July 1990.

Kaschuba, W. "Bildwelten als Weltbilder." *Der deutsche Heimatfilm. Bilder, Texte, Analysen zu 70 Jahren deutscher Filmgeschichte.* Tübingen: Ludwig-Uhland-Institut für Empirische Kulturwissenschaft der Universität Tübingen, 1989. 7–13.

Kersten, H. "Durchaus Perspektiven für Babelsberg. Fertige Produktionen und künftige Filmprojekte der DEFA." *Frankfurter Rundschau* 13 Aug. 1991.

———. "Pessimismus ist nicht mehr gefragt. Fertige Produktionen und künftige Projekte der DEFA." *Der Tagesspiegel* 16 Aug. 1991.

———. *So viele Träume. DEFA-Film-Kritiken aus drei Jahrzehnten.* Ed. C. Drawer. Berlin: Vistas, 1996.

———. "Von Allen bis Zanussi—Berlinale-Filme und andere Importe in DDR-Kinos." *Der Tagesspiegel* 1 Mar. 1987.

———. "Von der Berlinale nach Jahresfrist in die DDR-Kinos—Deutsch-deutsche Gemeinsamkeit im Filmangebot." *Der Tagesspiegel* 1 Mar. 1987.

———. "Winter ade, Sommer o weh! Kongreß der Film—und Fernsehschaffenden der DDR." *Frankfurter Rundschau* 28 Feb. 1990.

Kilb, A. "Die Halbstarken—Eine Passage durch neue deutsche Filme in diesem Herbst." *Die Zeit* 22 Nov. 1991: 66.

"Das Kino darf nicht sterben." *Black Box* 9 (1985): 4–7.

"Kino mit Popcorn und Eis ist bald möglich." *Märkische Oder Zeitung* 26 June 1990.

Klingsporn, J. *Filmstatistisches Taschenbuch 1991.* Spitzenorganisation der Filmwirtschaft E.V. 1991.

———. *Filmstatistisches Taschenbuch 1992.* Spitzenorganisation der Filmwirtschaft E.V. 1992.

———. "Zur Lage der deutschen Kinowirtschaft." *Media Perspektiven* 12 (1991): 794–805.

Kluge, A. "On Film and the Public Sphere." *New German Critique* 24–25 (1981–82): 206–20.

Klunker, H. "Sunny politisch Sorgen herzungewisse: Zur deutsch-deutschen Rezeption des DEFA-Films *Solo Sunny.*" *Jahrbuch Film Berichte/Kritiken/Daten 80/81.* Ed. H. G. Pflaum. Munich: Carl Hanser Verlag, 1980. 135–52.

Knauf, T. "Zoo-Palast oder Brief über den ungeliebten DEFA-Film." *Film und Fernsehen—Aproros DEFA* (N.d): 50–52.

Knight, J. *Women and the New German Cinema.* London: Verso, 1992.

Koch, K. "The German Economy: Decline or Stability." *The New Germany:*

Social, Political and Cultural Challenges of Unification. Ed. D. Lewis and J. R. P. McKenzie. Exeter: University of Exeter Press, 1995. 127–47.

Koebner, T. "Kein Grund für 'helle Aufregung': Bundesfilmpreis 1994 in Berlin verliehen." *Film Dienst* 47.13 (1994): 12–13.

Köhler, M. "Abschied vom Autorenfilm? Diskussion über Deutsche Filme und Filmförderung." *Film Dienst* 47.3 (1994): 9–11.

———. "Fernsehen im Kino: Neue Deutsche Filme beim Filmfest München." *Film Dienst* 47.16 (1994): 38–40.

———. "Filmmetropole mit Zukunft? Die Film und Medienstadt München." *Film Dienst* 43.10 (1990): 10–13.

———. *"Herzsprung." Filmecho/Filmwoche* 20 (1993).

———. "Nach dem Zufallsprinzip: Deutsche Filme auf der 'Berlinale'." *Film Dienst* 46.6 (1993): 14–15.

———. "Opas Kino lebt! Deutsche Vereinigungskomödien." *Film Dienst* 45.8 (1992): 10–11.

———. "Sozial—oder Intensivstation? Deutsche Filme auf der 'Berlinale'. " *Film Dienst* 45.6 (1992): 15–17.

Koll, H. P. *"Adamski." Film Dienst* 47.9 (1994): 28.

———. "Deutsche Kinofilm: Letzte Ausfahrt? Anmerkung zu einer bedenkliche Situation." *Film Dienst* 43.14 (1990): 8–10.

———. "Go, Kino, Go!? Anmerkungen zum deutschen Filmpreis." *Film Dienst* 44.13 (1991): 8.

———. "Marktgerecht produzieren!? Stellungnahmen zum neuen FFG." *Film Dienst* 44.18 (1991): 11.

———. "Ruhe vor dem Sturm—Zum Kinogeschäft am Jahresende 1990." *Film Dienst* 44.2 (1991): 8–9.

———. "Tag der Rechnung. Rückblick auf das Kinojahr 1991." *Film Dienst* 45.2 (1991): 7.

Konz, K. "Wo der Hirsch überm Sofa röhrt . . ." *Der deutsche Heimatfilm. Bildwelten und Weltbilder. Bilder, Texte, Analysen zu 70 Jahren deutscher Filmgeschichte.* Ludwig-Uhland-Institut für Empirische Kulturwissenschaft der Universität Tübingen. 89–94.

Korngiebel, K., and J. Link. "Von einstürzenden Mauern, europäischen Zügen und deutschen Autos. Die Wiedervereinigung in Bildern und Sprachbildern der Medien." *Mauer-Show: Das Ende der DDR, die deutsche Einheit und die Medien.* Ed. R. Bohn, K. Hickethier, and E. Müller. Berlin: Sigma, 1992. 31–69.

Körte, P. "DDR ade." *Frankfurter Rundschau* 20 Nov. 1992.

Kracauer, S. *From Caligari to Hitler. A Psychological History of the German Film.* Princeton: Princeton University Press, 1971.

Krauts! Ed. B. Buford. London: Granta 42, 1992.

Kreille, M. "The Political Economy of the New Germany." *The New Germany and the New Europe.* Ed. P. B. Stares. Washington, DC: Brookings Institute, 1992. 55–92.

Kreitling, H. "Vom Auf und Ab in einem Berliner Kaufhaus: Die gelungene Komödie *Adamski." Der Tagesspiegel* 19 May 1994.

Kruttschnitt, C. "Der Osten leuchtet [*Der Brocken*]." *Stern* 23 Apr. 1992.

———. "Opas Enkel startet durch [*Wir können auch anders*]." *Stern* 15 March 1993: 240–41.

Kürten, J. "Tutti Frutti statt Truffaut. Die Kinoszene in den neuen Ländern." *Medium* 3 (1991): 11.

Lacher-Remy, G. "VEKino: PROGRESSives Filmsehen in Berlin, Hauptstadt der DDR." *Medium* (1985) 10: 24–34.

Lemke, U. "Das kalte Herz—eine makabre Filmstory. DEFA Film-Kopien kommen zur Abwäsche nach Prag." *Sächsische Zeitung* 21 June 1991.

Lenssen, C. "Film der siebziger Jahre Die Machte der Gefühle." *Geschichte des deutschen Films.* Ed. W. Jacobsen, A. Kaes, and H. H. Prinzler. Stuttgart: Metzler, 1993. 249–84.

Leonhard, S. D. "Testing the Borders: East German Film between Individualism and Social Commitment." *Post New Wave Cinema in the Soviet Union and Eastern Europe.* Ed. D. J. Goulding. Bloomington: Indiana University Press, 1989. 51–101.

Lewis, D. "The GDR *Wende* and Legacy." *The New Germany: Social, Political and Cultural Challenges of Unification.* Ed. D. Lewis and J. R. P. McKenzie. Exeter: University of Exeter Press, 1995. 52–73.

———. "The German Language: From Revolt to Division." *The New Germany: Social, Political and Cultural Challenges of Unification.* Ed. D. Lewis and J. R. P. McKenzie. Exeter: University of Exeter Press, 1995. 297–320.

Licht, S. "Schöne Welt, Du gingst in Fransen." *Außerhalb von mittendrin Literatur / Film.* Berlin: Neue Gesellschaft für bildende Kunst, 1991. 106–10.

Lubowski, B. "Vom Herzsprung in Herzsprung." *Berliner Morgenpost* 19 Nov. 1992.

Lux, S. "*Adamski.*" *Film Dienst.* N.d.

———. "*Der Tangospieler.*" *Film Dienst* 5 (1991).

———. "*Wir können auch anders.*" *Film Dienst.* (1993): 28.

Maaz, J. *Das gestürzte Volk. Die ungückliche Einheit.* Berlin: Argon, 1991.

———. *Der Gefühlsstau Ein Psychogram der DDR.* Berlin: Argon, 1992.

Maennling, H. "Kostenlose Bereicherung: Mehr als 20 Stunden Film, Video, Fernsehen aus Ost und West." *Märkische Volkstimme* 21 June 1990.

Marcuse, P. "The East German Requiem." *When the Wall Came Down: Reactions to German Unification.* Ed. H. James and M. Stone. London: Routledge, 1992. 202–4.

Markovits, M. "Germany: Power and the Left." *When the Wall Came Down: Reactions to German Unification.* Ed. H. James and M. Stone. London: Routledge, 1992. 209–17.

Maron, M. "Writers and the People." *New German Critique* 52 (1991): 36–41.

———. "Zonophobia." *Krauts.* Ed. B. Buford. London: Granta, 1992. 117–24.

Martenstein, H. "Abgeschminkte Hoffnung." *Der Tagesspiegel* 11 Jan. 1994.

———. "Genies ohne Geheimnis: Höhen und Tiefen des deutschen Spielfilms, besichtigt bei den Hofer Filmtagen." *Der Tagesspiegel* 3 Nov. 1993: 17.

———. "Narrenjagd durch die mystische Prärie [*Wir können auch anders*]." *Der Tagesspiegel* 18 Feb. 1993.

Martiny, A. "Die bundesdeutsche Filmförderung—Aus politischer Sicht." *Jahrbuch Film 83/84 Berichte / Kritiken / Daten.* Ed. H. G. Pflaum. Munich: Carl Hanser Verlag, 1983. 30–34.

Matussek, M. "Keine Opfer, keine Täter." *Der Spiegel* 10 (1999): 120–42.

Mayer, A. "Die Bundesdeutsche Kinokrise." *Media Perspektiven* 11 (1985): 791–803.

McArdle Kelleher, C. "The New Germany: An Overview." *The New Germany and the New Europe.* Ed. P. B. Stares. Washington, DC: Brookings Institute, 1992. 11–54.

"Medienpolitischer Überblick Fruhjahr '90." *Medium* 3 (1990).

"Mehr Geld für weniger Filme." *Black Box* 52 (1990): 1.

Meier, A. "Das neue Deutschland will andere Clowns *Letztes aus der Da Daer* ein Film von Jörg Foth." *Die Tageszeitung* 11 Nov. 1990.

Merkel, A. "Wir brauchen Menschen, die uns Mut machen." *Journal Information aus der Politik für Deutschland* Oct.–Nov. 1993: 23.

Mihan, A. "Der Wettlauf um die Visionen über eien Medienstadt." *Märkischer Allgemeine* 8 Dec. 1992.

Mitscherlich, A., and M. Mitscherlich. *The Inability to Mourn.* Trans. B. R. Placzek. New York: Grove, 1975.

Mommert, W. "Vom *Untertan* bis zum *Coming Out:* Bleibendes oder Unerhebliches?—Rückblick auf 40 Jahre DDR-Filme." *Thüringe Tageblatt* 27 Nov. 1990.

Müller, E. "Dokumente der Distanz: Identitätsbestimmungen in Dokumentarfilmen über die DDR November 1989 bis zur Vereinigung." *Mauer-Show: Das Ende der DDR, die deutsche Einheit und die Medien.* Ed. R. Bohn, K. Hickethier, and E. Müller. Berlin: Sigma, 1992. 139–55.

Müller, M. "Zur Zukunft des Kinos: Abschied in Aussicht." *Sonntag* 1 May 1990.

Murray, B. A., and C. J. Wickham, eds. *Framing the Past: The Historiography of German Cinema and Television.* Carbondale: Southern Illinois University, 1992.

"Nachdenken über Thomas B." *Tip* 21 (1999): 46–48.

"Nahe der Katastrophe liegt: Gespräch mit Helmut Dzuiba." *Junge Welt* 27 May 1992.

Naughton, L. "Dealing with DEFA: The Euro-Chainsaw Massacre." *Metro* 91 (1992): 34–37.

———. "*Germany Pale Mother:* Screen Memories of Nazism." *Continuum* 5.2 (1992): 141–58.

———. "*Heimat:* Backs to the Past." *Film News* 15.6 (1985): 13–14.

———. "Party Poopers: The Forbidden Films." *Film News* Sept. (1993): 11–12.

———. "Recovering the Unmastered Past: Nazism in Film." *History on/and/in Film.* Ed. Brian Shoesmith and Tom O'Regan. Third History and Film Conference. Murdoch University: Perth, 1987. 121–30.

Neale, S., and F. Krutnik. *Popular Film and Television Comedy.* New York: Routledge, 1990.

Neckermann, G. 1991. *Filmwirtschaft und Filmförderung: Strukturveränderung—Daten.* Berlin: Vistas, 1991.

Neumann, H. J. "Berlinale 92: Festivalitis." *Zitty* 4 (1992): 44.

——. "Im jahr der naiven Helden: Ein Ruckblick auf das Filmjahr 1991." *Zitty* 1 (1992): 54–55.

Nicholls, A. J. "Germany." *European Fascism.* Ed. S. J. Woolf. London: Weidenfeld and Nicholson, 1968.

Nichols, B., ed. *Movies and Methods.* Berkeley: University of California Press, 1976.

Nowell-Smith, G., and T. Wollen, eds. *After the Wall: Broadcasting in Germany.* London: BFI, 1991.

"Ob mein Film einmal Premiere haben wird, weiß ich noch nicht. Interview mit Roland Gräf." *Neues Deutschland* 7 July 1990.

Oehmsen, S. "Zum Schießen [*Wir können auch anders*]." *Tempo* Apr. 1993.

Oehrle, W. "Kleinbürgers Traumfabrik." *Der deutsche Heimatfilm. Bildwelten und Weltbilder. Bilder, Texte, Analysen zu 70 Jahren deutscher Filmgeschichte.* Ludwig-Uhland-Institut für Empirische Kulturwissenschaft der Universität Tübingen, 1989. 80–89.

"Ohne eine Art von Wahnsinn könnte man es nicht durchstehen—neue Produzenten—nach einem Jahr. Gespräch mit Katrin Schlösser, Lew Hohmann, Joachim Tschirner und Erika Richter." *Film und Fernsehen* 6.1 (1992–93): 4–11.

Ortkemper, H. "Erfolg—Versuch einer Begriffsbestimmung." *Film in Berlin. 5 Jahre Berliner Filmförderung.* Berlin: Colloquium, 1983. 68–75.

Pawlikowski, P. "Home Movies." *Stills* 14 (1984): 5–6.

Paul, W. *Laughing, Screaming: Modern Hollywood Horror and Comedy.* New York: Columbia University Press, 1994.

Peitz, C. "Eigentlich bin ich Trompeter: *Adamski* und *Alles auf Anfang:* Zwei neue deutsche Filmkomödien aus Berlin." *Die Zeit* 3 June 1994.

Petrie, D., ed. *Screening Europe: Image and Identity in Contemporary European Cinema.* London: BFI, 1992.

Pflaum, H. G. "Geschäftsschädigungen—Anmerkungen zur inländlischen Produktion." *Jahrbuch Film 83/84 Berichte / Kritiken / Daten.* Ed. H. G. Plaum. Munich: Carl Hanser Verlag, 1983. 35–44.

——. "Im Osten (ka)lauert der Westen: Detlef Bucks Komödie *Wir können auch anders. . . .* " *Süddeutsche Zeitung* 6 Apr. 1993.

——. "Kampf um den Kuchen." *Süddeutsche Zeitung* 19 May 1992.

——. "Konzentrierte Aktionen—Materialien zu einem Fall." *Jahrbuch Film 83/84 Berichte / Kritiken / Daten.* Munich: Carl Hanser Verlag, 1983. 21–29.

——. "Same Procedure as Every Year." *Frankfurter Allgemeine Zeitung* 17 Jan. 1994.

Philipsen, D. *We Were the People: Voices from East Germany's Revolutionary Autumn of 1989.* Durham: Duke University Press, 1993.

"Plötzlich und unerwartet: Besuch vom Intendanten am Set." *Black Box* 84 (1994): 1–4.

Prantl, H. "Gott sei bei uns—Drei Jahre deutsche Einheit: Ach, wie war es ehedem im alten Deutschland so bequem." *Süddeutsche Zeitung* 1 Oct. 1993: 15.

Radevagen, T. T. "Die DEFA zwischen dem Verschwinden der DDR und einem möglichen neuen Anfang Von November 1989 bis Sommer 1991." *Mauer-Show: Das Ende der DDR, die deutsche Einheit und die Medien.* Ed. R. Bohn, K. Hickethier, and E. Müller. Berlin: Sigma, 1992. 189–200.

Reif, C. "Die Provinz schlägt zurück. Über die Tugenden des Ländlers und Detlev Bucks neuen Heimatfilm *Wir können auch anders.*" *Film und Fernsehen* 2 (1993): 28–29.

Renke, K. "Vom Sterben aller Hoffnung." *Neues Deutschland* 19 Nov. 1992.

Rentschler, E. "American Friends and the New German Cinema: Patterns of Reception." *New German Critique* 23–24 (1981–82): 7–35.

———. *The Ministry of Illusion: Nazi Cinema and Its Afterlife.* Cambridge: Harvard University Press, 1996.

———. *West German Film in the Course of Time.* Bedford Hills, NY: Redgrave, 1984.

"Rettet dieses Kulturgut! Aus der Erklärung der Filmschaffenden der neuen Bundesländer." *Märkische Allgemeine* 19 June 1992.

Richter, R. "Zur Rekonstruktion der 'Verbotsfilme'." Press conference. 5 Feb. 1990. Akademie der Künste (Berlin/DDR).

Rigby, K. "Germoney and the 'Change'." *Arena Magazine* Feb.–Mar. 1993: 25–26.

Rohrbach, G. "David gegen Goliath—Die Konkurrenzfähigkeit des deutschen Films stärken." *Epd Film* 9 (1990): 16–21.

Römer, R. "Dein Lebens-Budget voll ausschöpfen." *Junge Welt* 21 Feb. 1992.

Roth, W. "Die letzte Generation der DEFA." *Epd Film* 6 (1994): 10.

———. "Mehr Geld für weniger Filme." *Epd Filme* 12 (1991): 17.

———. "Programmänderung Leipzig 1989." *Epd Film* 1 (1990): 3–4.

Rust, R. "Die DEFA auf 'Motivsuche': 6 Spielfilmfestival der DDR in Ost-Berlin." *Film Dienst* 43.13 (1990): 14–15.

Sanders-Brahms, H. "Unsere Geschichten müssen jetzt erzählt werden." *Film und Fernsehen* 8–9 (1991): 24–28.

Sandford, J. "The German Media." *The New Germany: Social, Political and Cultural Challenges of Unification.* Ed. D. Lewis and J. R. P. McKenzie. Exeter: University of Exeter Press, 1995. 199–219.

Schäfer, H., and W. Shobert, eds. *Fischer Film Almanach 1993.* Frankfurt am Main: Fischer Taschenbuch, 1993.

Schamus, J. "To the Rear of the Back End: The Economics of Independent Cinema." *Contemporary Hollywood Cinema.* Ed. S. Neale and M. Smith. London: Routledge, 1998. 91–105.

"Schäuble-Gespräch bei DEFA ohne Treuhand-Beauftragen. Peter Schiwy zog anderswo Bilanz seine Arbeit." *Berliner Zeitung* 31 Oct. 1991.

Schares, G. E., and K. L. Miller. "Germany: Is Reunified Failing?" *Business Week* 15 Nov. 1993: 22–26.

Schenk, R. "Excursion." *Epd Film* 5/6 (1996): 84.

———, ed. *Das zweite Leben der Filmstadt Babelsberg 1946–92.* Berlin: Filmmuseum Potsdam und Henschel Verlag, 1994.

———. "Gruss Gott, Agnes und Genossen—Einige neue deutsche Spielfilme auf der Berlinale '94." *Film und Fernsehen* 2 (1994): 22–25.

———. "*Miraculi.*" *Film und Fernsehen* 5 (1992): 66–67.

———. "Schattenboxer und Kinderspiele. Über einige neue deutsche Spielfilme während und im Umfeld der Berlinale." *Film und Fernsehen* 2 (1993): 23–27.

Schieber, E. "Anfang vom Ende oder Kontinuität des Argwohns 1980 bis 1989." *Das zweite Leben der Filmstadt Babelsberg 1946–92.* Ed. R. Schenk. Berlin: Filmmuseum Potsdam und Henschel Verlag, 1994. 265–327.

Schlöndorff, V. "Die Vision oder wem gehört Babelsberg? DEFA und kein Ende: Offene Anwort Schlöndorffs auf einen Brief Günther Reichs." *Berliner Zeitung* 21 Nov. 1992.

Schmidt, E. ". . . Und allen Beteiligten das grösste Vergnügen an der Arbeit." *Ausserhalb von Mittendrin Literatur / Film.* Berlin: Neue Gesellschaft für bildende Kunst, 1991. 91–94.

Schmidt, G. "Die fünfziger Jahre. Heide und Silberwald." *Der deutsche Heimatfilm. Bildwelten und Weltbilder. Bilder, Texte, Analysen zu 70 Jahren deutscher Filmgeschichte.* Ludwig-Uhland-Institut für Empirische Kulturwissenschaft der Universität Tübingen, 1989. 69–74.

Schmitt-Gläser, A. "Die Dieben und der Detektiv—Jan Beckers gelungene deutsche Filmkomödie *Adamski.*" *Frankfurter Rundschau* 4 June 1994.

Schneider, E. *The G.D.R.: The History, Politics, Economy and Society of East Germany.* New York: Hurst, 1978.

Schneider, M. "Fathers and Sons Retrospectively: The Damaged Relationship Between Two Generations." *New German Critique* 31 (1984): 3–51.

Schneider, N. "Weinnachten in Troja—zur Filmförderung in Deutschland." *Medium* 4 (1991): 15–19, 22–23.

Schneider, P. *The German Comedy: Scenes of Life after the Wall.* London: I. B. Tauris, 1992.

Schoefer, C. "The Attack on Christa Wolf." *When the Wall Came Down: Reactions to German Unification.* Ed. H. James and M. Stone. London: Routledge, 1992. 205–8.

Schönemann, S. "Stoffentwicklung im DEFA-Studio für Spielfilme." *Filmland DDR Ein Reader zu Geschichte, Funktion und Wirkung der DEFA.* Ed. H. Blunk and D. Jungnickel. Cologne: Verlag Wissenschaft und Politik, 1990. 71–81.

"Schritt nach Western? Aus Dokumenten zu Goya." *Babelsberg ein Filmstudio 1912–1992.* Ed. W. Jacobsen. Berlin: Stiftung der Deutsche Kinemathek, 1994. 315–16.

Schülke, C. "Himmelsmacht hinter den Bergen. *Der Brocken:* Eine deutsch-deutsche Filmsatire von Vadim Glowna." *Frankfurter Allgemeine* 23 May 1992.

Seeßlen, G., and F. Jung. "Das Kino der Autoren ist tot. Glauben wir an ein neues?" *Epd Film* 9 (1997): 18.

Semiotexte. Special German issue, vol. 2 (1982).

Senfeld, S. "Pick, Pick, Pick. Ein Kinomärchen." *Sonntag* 12 Aug. 1990.

Short, K. M., ed. *Western Broadcasting over the Iron Curtain.* New York: St. Martin's, 1986.

Silberman, M. "Post-Wall Documentaries. . . ."

Sonnenallee. Press information. Berlin: Delphi Filmverleih, 1999.

Sontag, S. "Fascinating Fascism." *Movies and Methods.* Ed. B. Nichols. Berkeley: University of California Press, 1976. 31–43.

"Spurensicherung: Gespräch mit Ralf Schenk." *Film und Fernsehen* 6.1 (1993–94): 12–15.

Stares, P. B., ed. *The New Germany and the New Europe.* Washington, DC: Brookings Institute, 1992.

Stiehler, H. J. "'ELF 99'—vor der Wende für die Zukunft konzipiert." *Medien der Ex-DDR in der Wende.* Berlin: Vistas, 1991. 114–32.

"Die Stunde der 'Big Players.' Die Filmförderung alten und neuen Typs." *Epd Film* 7 (1997): 12.

"*Der Tangospieler.*" *Der Morgen* 28 Feb. 1991.

Teschner, U. ". . . die haben unseren Sozialismus nicht verstanden." *Filmland DDR Ein Reader zu Geschichte, Funktion und Wirkung der DEFA.* Ed. H. Blunk and D. Jungnickel. Cologne: Verlag Wissenschaft und Politik, 1990. 9–25.

Tip Film Jahrbuch Daten, Berichte, Kritiken. No. 7. Berlin: Stemmler, 1991.

Tok, D. D. "Ein 'deutsch-deutsches Märchen'. Auskünfte von Regisseur Vadim Glowna und Produzent Harald Reichebner über *Der Brocken.*" *Leipziger Volkszeitung* 3 May 1992.

Trimborn, J. *Der deutsche Heimatfilm der fünfziger Jahre. Motive, Symbole und Handlungsmuster.* Cologne: Teiresias Verlag, 1998.

Umard, R. "*Go Trabi Go.*" *Tip Filmjahrbuch Nr. 7—Daten, Berichte, Kritiken.* Berlin: Stemmler, 1991. 40.

"Die Vision oder wem gehört Babelsberg. DEFA und kein Ende: Offene Antwort Schlöndorffs auf einen Brief Günther Reichs." *Berliner Zeitung* 21 Nov. 1992.

Voester, C. E. "Nachdenken über Europa." *Epd Film* 8 (1989): 9.

Voigt, J. "Eigendwie Niemandsland." *Epd Film* 3 (1990): 14–15.

"Volker Schlöndorff über den Stand der Dinge in den Babelsberger Filmstudios." *Berliner Morgenpost* 3 Dec. 1992.

"Volle Fahrt voraus!" *Journal für Deutschland Information aus der Politik.* Presse und Informationsamt der Bundesregierung, ed. Oct.–Nov. 1994: 5.

von Kortzfleisch, S. "Der Alptraum wirkt nach: Staat, Kirche und Medien lassen unschuldige Opfer des SED-Regimes noch immer auf die Rehabilitierung warten." *Medium* 4 (1990): 34–37.

Voss, M. "Rot wie Blut, schwarz wie . . . *Herzsprung*—ein Film von Helke Misselwitz." *Berliner Zeitung* 20 Nov. 1992.

Walsh, M. "National Cinema, National Imaginary." *Film History* 8 (1996): 5–17.

Warneken, B. J. "'Aufrechter Gang' Metamorphosen einer Parole des DDR-Umbruchs." *Mauer-Show: Das Ende der DDR, die deutsche Einheit und die Medien.* Ed. R. Bohn, K. Hickethier, and E. Müller. Berlin: Sigma, 1992. 17–30.

"Was stinkt hier?" *Neue Zeit* 17 Nov. 1992.

Weber, R. "Filmlandschaft Thüringen—Entwurf einer Ortbeschreibung." *Film und Fernsehen* 4 (1993): 8–11.

Weis, J. O. "Soweit die Trabis tragen. Eine Reise durch die triste Kulturlandschaft Ostdeutschlands." *Stuttgarter Zeitung* 13 Dec. 1991.

Welsh, H. A., A. Pickel, and D. Rosenberg. "East and West German Identities: United and Divided." *After Unity: Reconfiguring German Identities.* Ed. K. R. Jarausch. Providence, RI, and Oxford: Berghahn. 103–36.

"Wen ein Wessi ein Haus auf Rügen haben will. . . . [*Der Brocken*]." *Märkische Allgemeine* 25 Apr. 1992.

Wenner, D. "Unruhe im Biotop: Wie Berlin-Brandenburgs neues Filmförderungsmodell in der Szene aufgenommen wird." *Frankfurter Rundschau* 24 Oct. 1994.

"Wessis über Ossis—Drei Beispiele." *Film und Fernsehen* 2 (1992): 41–42.

Wettig, G. "German Democratic Republic Censorship and West German Broadcasting." *Western Broadcasting over the Iron Curtain.* Ed. K. R. M. Short. New York: St. Martin's Press, 1986. 204–22.

Wetzel, I. K. "Harte DM: Wie tief wird der Griff in den Geldbeutel. Guckt das Kino in die Röhre?" *Sächsische Zeitung* 25 June 1990.

Wetzel, K. "Böse Deutsche? Rechte Gewalt im Spiegel neuer deutscher Filme." *Film und Fernsehen* 3 (1994): 4–11.

———. "Das Imperium schlagt zurück." *Tageszeitung* 9 Dec. 1983.

———. "New German Cinema: Economics without Miracle." *Semiotext* iv.2 (1982): 220–29.

———. "Über einige deutsche Filme der Berlinale." *Epd Film* 5 (1990): 3–4.

———. "Was geht noch?" *Medium* 4 (1990): 11–14.

———. "Das wirtschaftliche Schicksal berlingeförderter Filmproduktion im Inland und Ausland." *Film in Berlin 5 Jahre Berliner Filmförderung.* Ed. H. Ortkemper. Berlin: Colloquium, 1983. 50–67.

"Wie geht es weiter mit Babelsberg? Fragen zur DEFA, zur Film Förderung, zum Filmstock." *Film und Fernsehen* 4 (1992): 10–13.

Wiedemann, D. "Der DEFA-Spielfilm im Kontext gesellschaftlicher Kommunikations-prozesse in den achtziger Jahren." *Der DEFA-Spielfilm in den 80er Jahren—Chancen für die 90er?* Beiträge zur Film und Fernsehwissenschaft, vol. 44. Ed. P. Hoff and D. Wiedermann. Berlin: Vistas Verlag, 1992. 67–86.

———. "Fluchtpunkt DEFA-Filme? Zur Funktion von DEFA-Spielfilmen bei der Identitätsfindung Jugendlicher in der ehemaliden DDR." *Weiterbildung und Medien* 4 (1991): 49–51.

———. "Kino als Dienstleistung: Untersuchung zu einer medialen Werbestrategie." *Film und Fernsehen* 5 (1990): 7–8.

———. "Wird das Kino hundert Jahre alt? Überlegungen zur Zukunft eines Mediums." *Film und Fernsehen* 4 (1990): 2–6.

———. "Wo bleiben die Kinobesucher? Daten und Hypothesen zum Kinobesuch in der neuen deutschen Republik." *Medien der Ex-DDR in der Wende.* Berlin: Vistas, 1991. 81–99.

"Der Will zum Überleben? Fragen nach der Zukunft des DEFA-Systems." *Film Dienst* 44.17 (1991): 9.

Wilzcek, B. "Was wird aus der Ufa?" *Der deutsche Heimatfilm. Bildwelten und Weltbilder. Bilder, Texte, Analysen zu 70 Jahren deutscher Filmgeschichte.* Ludwig-Uhland-Institut für Empirische Kulturwissenschaft der Universität Tübingen, 1989. 74–80.

"Wir sind ein Volk." *Journal für Deutschland. Informationen aus der Politik.* (Okt.–Nov. 1994): 17.

Wolf, D. "Das Ende einer Institution . . . und Profession? Anmerkungen zur DEFA-Dramaturgie." *Film Dienst* 44.11 (1991): 16–17.

Wördehoff, B. "Journalistische Sternschnuppen: Das Medienereignis Revolution hat auch Brüche gesamtdeutscher Identität deutlich gemacht." *Medium* 4 (1990): 38–40.

"Wunderbares Spielzeug." *Der Spiegel* 18 May 1992.

Zahlmann, S. "Erinnerungskultur und Spielfilme in der DDR vergessen?" *Epd Film* 5/6 (1997): 72–75.

Zipes, J. *Breaking the Magic Spell: Radical Theories of Folk and Fairy Tales.* New York: Routledge, 1992

"Zweierlei Maß." *Black Box* 63 (1992): 1.

Index

Adamski, 9, 76, 94, 141, 146, 165, 170, 200,
    226, 227, 241
Adlon, Percy, 170
Ahrends, Martin, 180, 196
Aktuelle Kamera, 83
Alarm in the Circus, 27
All That Jazz, 41
Apple Trees, 94, 96–97, 126, 130, 141, 154,
    170, 171, 172, 207, 226, 241
As Quickly as Possible to Istanbul, 170, 211

Bagdad Cafe, 170
Ballhaus, Michael, 36
Banal Days, 62, 68, 207
Battenberg, Annette, 137
Bauer, Jo-Hannes, 183
Bearing Another's Burden, 41
Becker, Wolfgang, 227
Beckett, Samuel, 211
Beethoven—Days in a Life, 34
Beethoven, Ludwig van, 18
Benjamin, Walter, 240
Berlin Alexanderplatz, 69
Berlin around the Corner, 27, 33, 34
Berlin Bahnhof Friedrichstraße, 99
Berlin—Prenzlaver Berg, 99
Berlin Romance, A, 27
Berlin—Schönhauser Corner, 27
Bernt, Hans-Joachim, 51
Bertelsmann, 53, 56, 58, 59
Betrothed, The, 39
Between Pankow and Zehlendorf, 207
Beyer, Frank, 35, 40, 65
Bicycle, The, 39
Biermann, Wolf, 35

Bisky, Lothar, 74
Black Box, The, 99, 101
Black Forest Girl, 133
Bleicher, Joan, 88
Blue Angel, The, 23
Blunk, Harry, 25, 62
Boeser, Knut, 141
Bohrer, Karl Heinz, xii
Born in 1945, 33, 34, 35, 99
Böttcher, Jürgen, 99, 100
Brady, Martin, 142
Brander, Uwe, 134
Brandt, Willy, viii, 197
Bretschneider, Jürgen, 34, 39, 40
Brüssig, Thomas, 232, 239
Buck, Detlef, 155, 157, 160, 206
Büld, Wolfgang, 167
Bulgakowa, Oksana, 70
Burning Life, 69, 94, 95, 141, 146, 154, 198,
    223, 225, 226, 227, 238, 241
Byg, Barton, 4, 232, 234

Carné, Marcel, 23
Carow, Heiner, 27, 35, 38, 61, 65, 67, 72,
    207
Children, Cadres, Commanders, 99
Cosimos Lexicon, 67, 69, 238
Countdown, 101
Country behind the Rainbow, The, 29n, 63,
    194, 207, 238
Crocodile Dundee, 42

Dalichow, Bärbel, 40, 44, 47, 57, 60, 67, 69,
    70
Delius, Friedrich Christian, xii

de Maizières, Lothar, 17
De Niro, Robert, 141
Deppe, Hans, 132
Der Strass, 210
Dietl, Helmut, 64, 237, 238
Dirty Dancing, 42
Divided Sky, The, 137
Doctor, The, 40
Dörrie, Doris, 166, 237
Dresen, Andreas, 210
Dzuiba, Helmut, 40

E.T., 42
Eastern Landscape, 62, 99
Eckert, Tilbert, 100
Eichinger, Bernd, 237
Elsaesser, Thomas, 63
Excalibur, 41

Fan Fan La Tulipe, 28
Fank, Arnold, 150
Farewell to Agnes, 9, 207, 224, 226, 227, 241
Farssmann or by Foot to the Dead End, 67, 69, 227
Fassbinder, Rainer Werner, 36, 99, 134
Fehrenbach, Heide, 133
Fiend, The, 55
Fleischmann, Peter, 51–52, 134
Flitterabend, 79
Forgiveness, 226, 227, 238
Foth, Jörg, 36, 37–38, 61, 207
French Woman, The, 55, 240
Froelich, Carl, 131

Ganghofer, Ludwig, 133
Garbo, Greta, 23
GDR Without [a] Title, 99
Gehler, Fred, 69
German Chainsaw Massacre, The, 224
German Spoken [Here], 167, 168–69, 170
Germany, Germany, 99
Gersch, Wolfgang, 34–35, 40, 42
Glowna, Vadim, 141, 142, 206
God Bless Comrades, 224
Goethe, Johann Wolfgang von, 97
Go Trabi Go, 94, 97–98, 129, 135, 141, 146, 155, 165–73, 175, 176, 183, 184, 198, 199, 226
Gräf, Roland, 65, 66, 207

Green Is the Heather, 133
Grube-Deister, Elsa, 141
Gute Zeiten, schlechte Zeiten, 58
Gwisdeck, Michael, 43, 69, 207

Hall, Stuart, 242
Hanke, Helmut, 80, 82
Harfouch, Corina, 238
Härtling, Peter, 67
Hauff, Reinhard, 134
Haussmann, Leander, 65n, 237
Heavenly Bodies—Aerobic Non-Stop, 42
Heiduczek, Werner, 67
Heise, Thomas, 62
Heroes Like Us, 19, 228, 232
Herzsprung, 171, 207, 210n, 223, 224, 226, 241
Heym, Stefan, 195
Hickethier, Knut, 43, 58, 85, 89
Hitchcock, Alfred, 23
Hitler, Adolf, 55
Hochmuth, Dieter, 194
Hoff, Peter, 14, 16, 83
Höfig, Willi, 129, 137, 146, 158, 159, 203
Home Alone in New York, 76
Honecker, Erich, 20, 26, 38, 81, 85, 87,148
Honecker, Margot, 38
House of Spirits, 64
Howard, Karin, 54
Hughes, Helen, 142
Hunting Scenes from Lower Bavaria, 134

I Am the Rabbit, 27, 33, 34
In a Beautiful Meadow, 99
Independence Day, 238
Innocent, The, 55, 240
In the Splendour of This Happiness, 99
Iron Age, 62
Island of the Swans, 39
I Was a Happy Person, 99, 100

Jadup and Boel, 31, 33
Jakob the Liar, 26
Jana and Jan, 68, 170, 207, 210, 226, 236, 241
Johanna d'Arc of Mongolia, 101
Junghänel, Frank, 69

Kahane, Peter, 228
Karniggels, 155

Katzelmacher, 134
Kersten, Heinz, 63, 66
Kessel Buntes, 83
Key, The, 34
Kipping, Herwig, 207
Kirch, Leo, 54, 58, 59
Klein, Gerhard, 27
Kleinert, Andreas, 207
Klier, Michael, 194
Klingsporn, Johannes, 75
Kloos, Rheinhard, 170
Kluge, Alexander, 71
Knauf, Thomas, 61, 70
Knockin' on Heaven's Door, 64
Kohl, Helmut, viii, 135, 197
Köhler, Margret, 146
Kohlhasse, Wolfgang, 27, 34
Korngiebel, Wilfred, 16, 17, 176, 185–86, 197
Kracauer, Siegfried, 150
Krause, Horst, 161
Kröl, Joachim, 161
Krücke, 67
Kürten, Joachim, 75, 76

La Fontaine, Oskar, 197
Last from the Da Daer, 61, 93, 207, 227
Last Year of the Titanic, The, 99
Leander, Zarah, 131
Legend of Paul and Paula, The, 29, 33, 34, 38, 63, 71
Leone, Sergio, 160
Leonhard, Sigrun, 4, 34
Lewis, Derek, 96
Licht, Sibylle, 29, 70
Life Is a Construction Site, 110, 114, 171, 223, 226, 227n, 237
Lindenhotel, 99
Link, Jürgen, 16, 17, 176, 185–86, 197
Little Angel, 9, 172, 194, 236, 237, 238, 241
Little Arse-hole, 65, 238
Little Piece of Germany, A, 99
Locked Up Time, 63, 101
Lollabrigida, Gina, 28
Loriot, 169
Lost Landscape, 68, 207, 226, 236, 241
Lothar, Susanne, 215
Love at First Sight, 200, 226
Lux, Stephan, 63

Maaz, Hans-Joachim, 184, 185, 195, 196
Mäde, Dieter, 41
Malina, 166
Männerpension, 64
Man O Man, 79
Manta-Manta, 167
Manta—the Film, 167, 169
Mark Brandenburg Research, 39
Mark of Stones, The, 35, 71
Maron, Monika, xii
Martenstein, Harald, 160
May, Karl, 133
McArdle Kelleher, Catherine, xi
Me and Him, 166
Men, 42
Mikesch, Elfi, 36
Miraculi, 66, 94, 95, 141, 194, 210, 226
Misselwitz, Helke, 102, 194, 207, 216, 222, 223, 236
Missing, 32n, 67, 207
Moonstruck, 42
Most Desirable Man, A, 64, 65, 238
Mühlfenzl, Rudolf, 78
Müller, Robby, 36
Müller-Stahl, Armin, 38
Murderers among Us, 71

Naked Man on the Sports Field, The, 34
Name of the Rose, The, 42
Nekes, Werner, 32n, 64
New Sorrows of Young W, The, 31, 32
New Year's Eve Punch, 28
Night Spirits, 94–95
Nikolaikirche, 210, 224, 226, 227, 236, 238
No More Mr. Nice Guy, 94, 96, 126, 129–30, 135, 139–40, 154, 155, 165, 170, 198, 205, 223, 226, 237, 238, 239, 241
Not Farewell—Just a Parting, 100
Nowell-Smith, Geoffrey, 83
Now We Will Travel Overseas, 99

Oedipussy, 167, 169
Oehrle, Wolfgang, 129
Olle Henry, 35
Once Is Never Once, 137
Once Upon a Time in the West, 160
One-Way Ticket, 101
Ophüls, Marcel, 101n
Ostkreuz, 94, 95, 170, 171
Ottinger, Ulrike, 64, 101

Otto the Outer Fresian, 167
Out of Africa, 41

Pappa ante Portas, 64
Paths in the Night, 225, 226, 230, 232, 237, 241
Pflaum, Hans Günther, 46, 53, 63, 133, 165
Pink Floyd, 100
Platoon, 42
Polizeiruf 110, 83
Pretty Woman, 173
Prince—Sign o' the Times, 42
Prisma, 83
Promise, The, 141, 207, 210, 224, 226, 238

Quiet Country, 170, 171, 172, 210–12, 226, 236, 237, 238

Rabenhalt, Arthur Maria, 129
Radevagen, Thomas Til, 67, 77
Rambo III, 168
Reitz, Edgar, 134
Rentschler, Eric, 5
Richter, Erika, 23n
Richter, Rolf, 23, 33
Riefenstahl, Leni, 150
Riemann, Katja, 237
Rising to the Bait, 67, 93, 94, 126, 129, 130, 136, 139–55, 164, 165, 171, 199, 207, 224, 226, 238, 239, 241
Ritschel, Hans, 141
Rohrbach, Günther, 50, 169, 206
Rohweder, Detlef, 60
Rosler-Kleint, Alfred, 86
Rossini—Or the Deadly Question of Who Sleeps with Whom, 64, 238
Roth, Wilhelm, 43, 63
Russians Are Coming, The, 31, 33
Rusty Pictures, 99
Ryan, Meg, 237

Sabine Wulff, 39
Sanders-Brahms, Helma, 54, 64, 96, 97
Sandford, John, 84
Schenk, Ralf, 227
Schirmer, Herbert, 48
Schlesinger, John, 55
Schlöndorff, Volker, 50, 51–52, 55, 58, 60, 96, 134, 166

Schneider, Peter, 195–96
Schroeter, Werner, 166
Schtonk!, 64
Schweiger, Til, 237
Seemann, Horst, 40, 207
Semblance of Duty, 40
Semper, Gottfried, 191
Seven Freckles, 39
Silberman, Marc, 206
Simplicissimus, 35
Sojourn, The, 40
Solinger Rudi, 94
Solo Sunny, 32, 38, 39, 41, 63, 71
Sonnenallee, 19, 64, 210, 228, 232, 236–37, 241
Sons of Great Bear, The, 28
Sontag, Susan, 150
Springer, Axel, 54, 59
Star Trek, 42
Stau—jetzt geht's los, 76
Stein, 141, 170, 207, 210, 226
Stumph, Wolfgang, 167
Subservient, The, 71
Sudden Wealth of the Poor People of Kombach, The, 134
Summer Day Doesn't Bring Love, A, 28
Super-Wife, The, 64, 238
Surety for a Year, 39
Suspicion, 204

Tango Player, The, 63, 66–67, 69, 207–9, 236
That Was the Wild East, 93, 94, 97, 126, 129–30, 135, 136, 139, 143, 155–64, 167, 169, 172, 173–82, 184–94, 224, 226, 241, 242
Timm, Peter, 166, 167, 186, 206
To the Horizon and Beyond, 94, 172, 224, 225, 226, 228–29, 230, 232, 241
Towering Inferno, 41
Trabi Goes to Hollywood, 167
Treuhand, 6, 7, 46–47, 49, 50, 51, 52–53, 54, 57, 60, 200
Treut, Monika, 36
Trimborn, Jürgen, 127, 129, 158
Tutti Frutti, 79
Two Brothers, Two Worlds, 99

Ulbricht, Walter, 148
Until Death Do Us Part, 39

von Trotta, Margarethe, 206, 210n
Voyager, 166, 240

Waigel, Theo, 21
Waiting for Godot, 211
Wall, The, 99
Wall Street, 168
Wedel, Michael, 63
Weiß, Ulrich, 35
Weizsäcker, Richard, 148
Welz, Peter, 207
Wenders, Wim, 36, 57
Werner Beinhart, 64
Wettig, Gerhard, 81
Where the Train Halts Briefly, 28

Whoever Lies Twice, 76, 165, 170
Wiedemann, Dieter, 42, 74, 81, 82
Wilder, Billy, 23
Winter Ade, 63
Wittstock! Wittstock!, 101
Wolf, Christa, 196
Wolf, Konrad, 35, 38–39, 59, 211
Wollen, Tania, 83
Wörtman, Sonke, 237, 238

Your Unknown Brother, 31, 35, 39

Zacher, Rolf, 141
Ziegler, Regina, 51
Zipes, Frank, 222

Social History, Popular Culture, and Politics in Germany
Geoff Eley, Series Editor

(continued from pg. ii)

Catholicism, Political Culture, and the Countryside: A Social History of the Nazi Party in South Germany, Oded Heilbronner

A User's Guide to German Cultural Studies, Scott Denham, Irene Kacandes, and Jonathan Petropoulos, editors

A Greener Vision of Home: Cultural Politics and Environmental Reform in the German Heimatschutz *Movement, 1904–1918,* William H. Rollins

West Germany under Construction: Politics, Society, and Culture in Germany in the Adenauer Era, Robert G. Moeller, editor

How German Is She? Postwar West German Reconstruction and the Consuming Woman, Erica Carter

Feminine Frequencies: Gender, German Radio, and the Public Sphere, 1923–1945, Kate Lacey

Exclusive Revolutionaries: Liberal Politics, Social Experience, and National Identity in the Austrian Empire, 1848–1914, Pieter M. Judson

Jews, Germans, Memory: Reconstruction of Jewish Life in Germany, Y. Michal Bodemann, editor

Paradoxes of Peace: German Peace Movements since 1945, Alice Holmes Cooper

Society, Culture, and the State in Germany, 1870–1930, Geoff Eley, editor

Technological Democracy: Bureaucracy and Citizenry in the German Energy Debate, Carol J. Hager

The Origins of the Authoritarian Welfare State in Prussia: Conservatives, Bureaucracy, and the Social Question, 1815–70, Hermann Beck

The People Speak! Anti-Semitism and Emancipation in Nineteenth-Century Bavaria, James F. Harris

From Bundesrepublik *to* Deutschland: *German Politics after Unification,* Michael G. Huelshoff, Andrei S. Markovits, and Simon Reich, editors

The Stigma of Names: Antisemitism in German Daily Life, 1812–1933, Dietz Bering

Reshaping the German Right: Radical Nationalism and Political Change after Bismarck, Geoff Eley